The Avant-Garde and the Popular in Modern China

The Avant-Garde and the Popular in Modern China

TIAN HAN AND THE INTERSECTION OF PERFORMANCE AND POLITICS

Liang Luo 羅靚

THE UNIVERSITY OF MICHIGAN
ANN ARBOR

Published in the United States of America by
The University of Michigan Press
Manufactured in the United States of America
♾ Printed on acid-free paper

2017 2016 2015 2014 4 3 2 1

A CIP catalog record for this book is available from the British Library.

ISBN 978-0-472-07217-0 (cloth : alk. paper)
ISBN 978-0-472-05217-2 (paper : alk. paper)
ISBN 978-0-472-12034-5 (e-book)

To the Loving Memory of My Father, Luo Fuxu 羅富旭 *(1947–2006)*
For My Family in Chongqing, Lexington, and Täby

Acknowledgments

I have incurred so many debts writing this book. It gives me great pleasure to have an opportunity to express my gratitude here. I thank Professors Leo Ou-fan Lee, David Der-wei Wang, Wilt L. Idema, and Andrew Gordon for helping me lay the foundation for this book in my dissertation and continuing to offer inspiration to this day. I am truly grateful for their unwavering support. David Der-wei Wang, Wilt L. Idema, and Pär Cassel read the manuscript and offered valuable feedback in the past few years. Xiaomei Chen and three anonymous readers read the manuscript throughout the review process and provided crucial guidance. My editor at the University of Michigan Press, LeAnn Fields, her assistant, Alexa Ducsay, and the project manager for my book at the press, Marcia LaBrenz, have all been most helpful and a pleasure to work with.

I am truly grateful to the following colleagues and friends who read earlier iterations of parts of the manuscript and offered feedback: Russell Berman, Miranda Brown, Theodore Fiedler, Carolyn Fitzgerald, Jennifer Goodlander, Denise Ho, Gordon Hogg, Masamichi (Marro) Inoue, Andrew Kimbrough, Haiyan Lee, Valerie Levan, Joseph O'Neil, Christine de Pee, Suzanne Pucci, David Rolston, Douglas Slaymaker, Akiko Takenaka, Ban Wang, Matthew Wells, Yiching Wu, and Hui Faye Xiao.

I have drawn strength and inspiration from the many wonderful scholars and friends who became part of my professional life in Mainland China and the United States over the years, and I must also thank the many individuals in Japan, Sweden, Germany, the Netherlands, Hong Kong, and Taiwan whose generosity has helped to make my research and lecture trips both fruitful and enjoyable. Although this list is necessarily incomplete, I thank, in particular, Cristina Alcalde, Jennifer Altehenger, Ashida Hajime, Mingzhen Bao, Weihong Bao, Srimati Basu, Theodore Bestor, Kate Black, Susan Bordo, George Bornstein, Anna Brzyski, Duncan Campbell, Dongshin Chang, Ch'a T'ae-gŭn, Anarchichi Chen, Jianhua Chen, Liana Chen, Ya-chen Chen, Chen Yongguo, Likkwan Cheung, Robert Chi, Eileen Cheng-yin Chow, Rey Chow, Joscha Chung, Claire Conceison, Verena Coney, Jacqueline Couti, Annika Culver,

Kirk A. Denton, Xinyu Dong, Dong Limin, Liliana Drucker, Fredrik Fällman, Geraldine Fiss, Christopher Forth, Fujii Shōzō, Qian Gao, Mary Gluck, Beth Goldstein, Joshua Goldstein, Laurence Goldstein, Frederik Green, Anup Grewal, Guo Yingde, Lorri Hagman, William Hammell, Han Kuo-Huang, Satoru Hashimoto, Man He, Shana Herron, Qin Higley, Kazuko Hioki, Carma Hinton, Maeda Hisaka, Michel Hockx, Hu Jiangfeng, Alexa Huang, Nicole Huang, Chang-tai Hung, Theodore Huters, Kim Su-yŏn, Kotari Ichirō, Inata Naomi, Gerald Janecek, Jian Yi, Hui Jiang, Wei Jiang, Jiang Yuanlun, Marja Kaikkonen, Thomas Kampen, Kathi Kern, Shigehisha Kuriyama, Lai Xia, Charles Laughlin, Yuk Ying Lee, James Lee, Minggang Li, Li Runxia, Waiyee Li, Li Zhengrong, Zhiying Li, Yi-chieh Lin, Chiung-yun Liu, Liu Hongtao, Liu Xiangyu, Liu Yong, Sheldon Lu, Luo Gang, Christopher Lupke, Ma Hailiang, Kenny Kwok-Kwan Ng, Lien-Hang Nguyen, Maruyama Noboru, Andrew Maske, Huajing Maske, Jason McGrath, Meng Dengying, Jiayan Mi, Barbara Mittler, Ōki Yasushi, Stephen Owen, Shaw-Yu Pan, Pu Bo, Jeff Richey, Steve Riep, Cynthia Ruder, Joanna Rutter, Leon Sachs, Saji Toshihiko, Tze-lan D. Sang, Rosemary Schindler (Xin Li), Shi Zhecun, Shu-mei Shih, Darryl Sterk, G. Andrew Stuckey, André Stufkens, Ronald Suleski, Keiko Tanaka, Xiaobing Tang, Tao Dongfeng, Karen Thornber, Tian Benxiang, Tian Dawei, Tian Qinxin, Tian Shen (Tian Hainan), Xiaofei Tian, Karen Tice, Hitomi Tonomura, Caitlin Joan Torres, Jing Tsu, Tu Weiming, Nicolai Volland, Anna Voskresensky, Rudolf Wagner, Cecilia Wang, Wang Dan, Eugene Wang, Wang Furen, Wang Guimei, Wang Xiangyuan, Wang Yichuan, Yugen Wang, Wang Zheng, Kristen Wanner, Jeff Wasserstrom, Vivien Yan Wei, Jeanmarie Rouhier-Willoughby, Linda Worley, Shengqing Wu, Wu Wenguang, Lanjun Xu, Haiping Yan, Yang Lianfen, Xiaobin Yang, Catherine Yeh, Yu Sheng-kuan, Kyoim Yun, Enhua Zhang, Zhang Longxi, Zhang Wanmin, Yingjin Zhang, Xueping Zhong, Yawen Zhou, Yu Zhou, and Zhou Zhiqiang for their generous support.

I am deeply indebted to the many librarians at the following libraries, archives, and museums whose support and expertise have been crucial along the way: University of Kentucky libraries, University of Michigan libraries, Harvard-Yenching Library, Beijing Normal University libraries, Beijing University libraries, National Library of China, China Film Archive, National Museum of Modern Chinese Literature, Chongqing Library, Hong Kong Film Archive, Shanghai Library, Shanghai Municipal Archive, Diplomatic Archives of the Ministry of Foreign Affairs of Japan, Tokyo University libraries (especially the Library at the Institute of Oriental Culture), the Oriental Library in Tokyo, the National Film Center in Tokyo, the Tsubouchi Memorial Theatre Museum at Waseda University, the Yoshino Sakuzō Memorial Museum in Furukawa, National University of Singapore libraries, Stockholm University libraries, the Joris Ivens Archive in Nijmegen, the Netherlands, Stanford University libraries, Hoover Institution Library and Archives, and the Library at the Sinological Institute at Leiden University.

This book has benefited greatly from the feedback, critiques, and encouragement I have received after sharing my work in progress with many groups and individuals, some of which include members of the Sanjū nendai kenkyukai and Fujii zemi at Tokyo University, the University of Michigan's Center for Chinese Studies, Michigan China Fellows, members of the 2010 National Endowment for the Humanities summer seminar at Stanford University, members of the University of Kentucky Asian Studies Faculty Workshop, University of Kentucky Social Theory working papers series, University of Kentucky Gender and Women's Studies Research Matters series, University of Kentucky Russian and Eastern Studies working papers series, the Crane House, Berea College East Asian Studies lecture series, the Graduate Institute of National Policy and Public Affairs at National Chung Hsing University, the Graduate Institute of Anthropology at National Chi-Nan University, the Department of Taiwanese Literature at National Cheng Kung University in Taiwan, the Hall Center for the Humanities at the University of Kansas, the Division of Humanities of Hong Kong University of Science and Technology, Pants Theatre Production (Hong Kong), and the Department of Cultural and Religious Studies at the Chinese University of Hong Kong.

I thank the following institutions for their invaluable support: the Department of Chinese Language and Literature at Beijing Normal University; Department of East Asian Languages and Civilizations, the Harvard-Yenching Institute, Reischauer Institute for Japanese Studies, Asia Center and Fairbank Center for East Asian Research at Harvard University; the Center for Chinese Studies and Department of Asian Languages and Cultures at the University of Michigan; the Department of Modern and Classical Languages, College of Arts and Sciences, Office of the Vice President for Research, Center for the Enhancement of Learning and Teaching, and the Hive at the University of Kentucky; the Tian Han Foundation in Beijing; the European Foundation Joris Ivens in Nijmegen, the Netherlands; and the National Endowment for the Humanities.

During the final hectic months of manuscript preparation, I was rescued by my mother, who flew from Chongqing to Lexington to help with household chores and child care. The constant long-distance encouragement of my parents-in-law in Täby, Sweden, counted for more than they know. Last but not the least, my deepest love and gratitude go to Pär and Ingrid for being their wonderful selves and sharing the joys of life with me.

Contents

Selected List of Tian Han's Works

"Xin Jiaozi" (jingju). Serialized in the "Juqu" (Theatre) section of *Changsha ribao* (Changsha Daily News), March 14–16, 1913.

(Han'er) "Xin Taohua Shan" (yuanben). "Yuxing" (Aftertaste), supplement to *Shibao* (Shanghai Times), May 26, 1915.

"Eguo jinci zhi geming yu pinfu wenti" (The Russian Revolution and the Issue of Rich and Poor). *Shenzhou xuecong* (Divine Land Review), no. 1 (September 1917).

"Zhi Zuo Shunsheng" (Letter to Zuo Shunsheng), May 12, 1919. In *Tian Han quanji* (Complete Works of Tian Han), vol. 20. Shijiazhuang: Huashan wenyi chubanshe, 2000.

"Meiyu" (Rainy Season) (1919). In *Tian Han quanji,* vol. 11.

"Zui'e" (Evil) (1919). In *Tian Han quanji,* vol. 11.

"Mimi lian'ai yu gongkai lian'ai" (Secret Love and Open Love). *Shaonian zhongguo* (Young China), vol. 1, no. 2 (August 15, 1919).

"Disi jieji de furen yundong" (Women's Movement of the Fourth Class). *Shaonian zhongguo,* vol. 1, no. 4 (October 15, 1919).

"Shiren yu laodong wenti" (The Poet and the Issue of Labor). *Shaonian zhongguo,* vol. 1, nos. 8–9 (February–March 1920).

"Xin luoman zhuyi ji qita: Fu Huang Rikui xiong yifeng changxin" (On Neo-romanticism and Other Matters: A Long Letter to Brother Huang Rikui). *Shaonian zhongguo,* vol. 1, no. 12 (June 1920).

"Ye" (Night) (1920). In *Tian Han quanji,* vol. 11.

"Huo" (Fire) (1920). In *Tian Han quanji,* vol. 11.

"Chile 'zhiguo' zhihou de hua" (Words after Eating the "Wisdom Fruit"). *Shaonian shijie* (Young World), vol. 1, no. 8 (August 1920).

"Fan'elin yu qiangwei" (The Violin and the Rose). *Shaonian zhongguo,* vol. 2, nos. 5–6 (November–December 1920).

"Shōnen to shinjin tono mondō" (A Dialogue between the Young Man and the New

Man). *Dōhō* (Brothers), no. 4 (January 1, 1921). Reprinted in *Shinjinkai kikanshi* (Official Journals of the New Man Society). Tokyo: Hōsei Daigaku Shuppankyoku, 1969.

"'Lingguang' xuyan: Zhi Li Jiannong xiansheng de yifeng xin" (Preface to "Spiritual Light": A Letter to Mr. Li Jiannong). *Taiping yang,* (The Pacific), vol. 2, no. 9 (January 1921). In *Tian Han quanji,* vol. 16.

Lingguang (Spiritual Light). *Taiping yang,* vol. 2, no. 9 (January 1921).

"Shaonian zhongguo yu zongjiao wenti—zhi Zeng Muhan yifeng xin" (The Young China and the Issue of Religion—a letter to Zeng Muhan). *Shaonian zhongguo* (Young China), vol. 2, no. 8 (February 1921).

Shalemei. Shaonian zhongguo, vol. 2, no. 9 (March 1921). Translation of *Salome* by Oscar Wilde.

"Baimei zhiyuan de neiwai" (Inside and Outside the White Plum Garden). *Shaonian zhongguo,* vol. 2, no. 12 (June 15, 1921).

"Emo shiren botuolaier de bainian ji" (Commemorating the Centenary of the Demonic Poet Charles Baudelaire). *Shaonian zhongguo,* vol. 3, no. 3 (November–December 1921).

Qiangwei zhilu (Road of the Roses). Shanghai: Taidong tushuju, 1922.

Piyaluo zhigui (The Ghost of the Piano). *Shaonian zhongguo,* vol. 3, no. 9 (April 1922).

Kafeidian zhi yiye (A Night in a Café). *Chuangzao jikan* (Creation Quarterly), vol. 1, no. 1 (May 1922).

Wufan zhiqian (Before Lunch). *Chuangzao jikan,* vol. 1, no. 2 (August 1922).

"Huohu zhiye" (The Night a Tiger Was Captured). *Nanguo banyuekan* (Southland Bimonthly), no. 1 (January 1924).

"Dao minjian qu" (To the People). In "Nanguo tekan" (special issues of *Nanguo*), nos. 23 and 24, supplemented to *Xingshi zhoubao* (Awakened Lion Weekly), nos. 74 and 75 (March 12 and 20, 1926).

"Wo de shanghai shenghuo" (My Life in Shanghai). *Shanghai shenghuo* (Shanghai Life), inaugural issue, December 15, 1926.

"Kang Jingzhao nüshi xiaoshi" (A Brief Biography of Ms. Kang Jingzhao), *Shanghai huabao* (Shanghai Pictorial), June 6, 1927.

"Youchou furen yu jiejie—liangge butong de nüxing" (Ms. Melancholy and Sister—Two Kinds of Women), *Nanguo yuekan,* vol. 1, no. 1 (May 1, 1929).

Muxing zhiguang (film story), *Chenbao* (Shanghai), July 21–25, 1933. Published under Bu Wancang.

Shuofeng (Harsh Wind). Part 1: "Ruci Bali" ("So This Is Paris"). Originally published in *Fanbao* (Shanghai), vol. 1, no. 1 (January 1, 1927), in *Tian Han sanwenji* (Collected Essays of Tian Han). Shanghai: Jindai shudian, 1936.

"Fanpaiya de shiji" (A Century of Vampires). Originally serialized in *Yinxing* (Silver Star, or The Movie Guide), nos. 5-13 (February 1927-), reprinted in *Yinse de meng* (Silver Dream), Shanghai: Liangyou tushu yinshua gongsi, 1928, and collected in *Tian Han sanwenji,* Shanghai: Jindai shudian, 1936.

"Kaligeli boshi de sishi" (The Cabinet of Dr. Caligari). Originally serialized in *Yinxing,* nos. 5-13 (February 1927-), reprinted in *Yinse de meng,* Shanghai: Liangyou tushu yinshua gongsi, 1928, and collected in *Tian Han sanwenji,* Shanghai: Jindai shudian, 1936.

"I Stand Alone" (original title in English). Originally serialized in *Yinxing,* nos. 5-13 (February 1927-), reprinted in *Yinse de meng,* Shanghai: Liangyou tushu yinshua gongsi, 1928, and collected in *Tian Han sanwenji,* Shanghai: Jindai shudian, 1936.

Wenxue gailun (A Concise Theory of Literature) (1927). Shanghai: Zhonghua shuju, 4th edition, 1932.

"Women wei shenme yao jianshe women de juchang: AB duihua" (Why Do We Need to Build Our Own Theater? A Dialogue between A and B). *Minguo ribao* (Republican Daily), March 29, 1928.

"Xiaojuchang zhi yiye" (A Night at the Little Theater). Supplement to *Shenbao* (Shen Pao, or Shanghai News), June 14, 1928.

"Letter to Tanizaki Jun'ichirō." *Nanguo yuekan* (Southland Monthly), no. 5 (August 1928).

"Letter to Muramatsu Shōfū." In Maramatsu Shōfū, ed., *Sōjin* (Literary Man), vol. 2, no. 10 (October 1928).

"Xin guoju yundong de diyisheng" (The First Cry of the New National Theater Movement). *Liyuan gongbao* (Newsletter of the Pear Orchard, Shanghai), nos. 22–23, November 8 and 11, 1928.

"Diyici gongyan zhihou" (After the First Public Performance). *Minzhong ribao* (People's Daily, Shanghai), December 22, 1928.

"Gongyan zhiqian: Ti ziji hanjiao, ti minzhong hanjiao" (Before the Public Performance: Roar for Myself, Roar for the Masses). Supplement to *Shenbao,* June 23, 1929.

"Shanghai" (1927-1929). In *Tian Han quanji,* vol. 13. Originally serialized from October 16 to December 3, 1927 in *Yishu jie* (Artistic Circle), supplement to *Shenbao* (unfinished); then published in *Nanguo yuekan,* vol. 1, nos. 1, 3, and 4 (May-August, 1929) (complete).

"Nanguo yu guanfu" (Southland and the Government). *Nanguo zhoukan* (Southland Weekly), inaugural issue (August 1929).

"Du *Hunan niu*" (Reading *Hunan Bull*). *Nanguo zhoukan,* no. 7 (October 1929).

Mulisi zhi yishu de shehui zhuyi (Morris's Socialism of Art). Shanghai: Dongnan shudian, 1929. An introduction of William Morris's art and socialism.

Nanguo yuekan (Southland Monthly), vol.1, nos. 1–6 (May 1929–February 1930).

"Women de ziji pipan" (Our Self-Criticism). *Nanguo yuekan,* vol. 2, no. 1 (March 20, 1930).

"Carmen." *Nanguo yuekan,* vol. 2, nos. 2–3 (May–June 1930).

"Bianji houji" (Editor's Afterword). *Nanguo yuekan,* vol. 2, no. 3 (June 1930).

"Sulian dianying yishu fazhan de jiaoxun yu woguo dianying yundong de qiantu" (Lessons from the Development of Soviet Film Art and the Future of the Film Movement in Our Country). *Nanguo yuekan,* vol. 2, no. 4 (July 1930).

"Bohui'er zhige" (Song of Pawel) (1932). Lyrics by Tian Han, music by Lü Ji. In *Tian Han cizuo gequji* (Collection of Songs with Lyrics by Tian Han), edited by Sun Shen, Li Yinghai, and Xiang Yansheng. Beijing: Renmin yinyue chubanshe, 2003.

"Xiju dazhonghua he dazhonghua xiju" (The Popularization of Theater and the Popularized Theater). *Beidou* (The Plough), vol. 2, nos. 3–4 (1932).

Zimei (Sisters). In *Tian Han xiquji* (Selected Plays of Tian Han), vol. 1. Shanghai, Xiandai shuju, 1932.

Bo Hong (Tian Han). "Zhongguo jiuxi yu Mei Lanfang de zai pipan" (A Second Critique of Chinese Old Theater and Mei Lanfang) (1934). *Zhonghua ribao* (China Daily, Shanghai), October 21, 1934.

Tian Han xiquji (Selected Plays of Tian Han). Rev. ed. Shanghai: Xiandai Shuju, 1934.

"Xiju yu shehui" (Theater and Society). "Jukan" (Drama), literary supplement to *Beiping chenbao* (Beiping Morning News), January 19, 1936.

"Baofengyü zhong de Nanjing yitan yipie" (A Glimpse of Nanjing Artistic Circles amid a Wild Storm). *Xinmin bao* (New People's Daily, Nanjing), June 9, 10, 12, 14, and 29, 1936.

Huichun zhiqu (Spring Returns). Preface by Hong Shen. Shanghai: Putong shudian, 1936.

Fuhuo (Resurrection). Shanghai: Shanghai zazhi gongsi, 1936. Includes sketches by Wu Zuoren for stage design.

Tian Han sanwenji (Collected Essays of Tian Han). Shanghai: Jindai shudian, 1936.

"Review of Zhan Jingtang." *Lianhua huabao* (Lianhua Pictorial, Shanghai), vol. 9, no. 5 (July 1, 1937). Reprinted in *Tian Han quanji,* vol. 17.

Lugou qiao (Marco Polo Bridge). Chengdu: Xiemei yinshuaju, 1937.

"Abixiniya de muqin" (Mother of Abyssinia). In *Limin zhiqian* (Before Sunrise). Shanghai: Beixin shuju, 1937.

Kangzhan yu xiju (Anti-Japanese War and Drama) (1937). Changsha: Shangwu yinshuguan, 1938.

Zuihou de shengli (The Final Triumph). Hankou: Shanghai zazhi gongsi, 1938.

Shagong (Killing in the Palace) (1938). In *Tian Han quanji,* vol. 7.

"Lun zhanshi xiju de xin yu jiu" (On the New and the Old of Wartime Drama). In Tian Han, *Kangzhan yu xiju.* Chongqing: Duli chubanshe, 1939.

Jianghan yuge (Yangtze Fisherman's Song). *Kangzhan wenyi* (Anti-Japanese War Literature and Art, Chongqing), vol. 5, nos. 2–3 and 4–5 (December 1939–January 1940).

"Fu Juzan fashi" (A Reply to Abbot Juzan). *Shizi hou* (Roar of the Lion), no. 1 (December 15, 1940).

Xin ernü yingxiong zhuan (A New Legend of Lovers and Heroes). *Kangzhan wenyi,* vol. 7, no. 1 (January 1, 1941). A three-volume, fifty-two scene Peking Opera.

"Qiusheng fu" (Rhapsody on the Sounds of Autumn) (1941). In *Tian Han quanji,* vol. 4.

"Guanyu xin fojiao yundong" (On the New Buddhist Movement). *Shizi hou,* nos. 8–9 (September 15, 1941).

Muqin (Mother). *Tian Han daibiaozuo* (Representative Works of Tian Han), Shanghai: Santong shuju, 1941, vol. 1. Play based on Gorky's novel *Мать.*

"Guanyu kangzhan xiju gaijin de baogao" (Report on Anti-Japanese War Theater Reform). *Xiju chunqiu* (Theater Annals, Guilin), vol. 1, no. 6, and vol. 2, nos. 2–3 (April, July, and September 1942).

"Guanyu Wu Song yu Pan Jinlian" (On Wu Song and Pan Jinlian). *Pinglun bao* (Daily Review, Kunming), May 12, 1945.

"Zenyang zuo xigai gongzuo? Gei Zhou Yang tongzhi de shi feng xin" (How to Conduct Opera Reform? Ten Letters to Comrade Zhou Yang) (1950). In *Tian Han quanji,* vol. 17.

Jinbo ji (Story of the Golden Bowl). Beijing: Zhonghua shuju, 1951.

"Women bici faxian le shi" (We Discovered Poetry in Each Other). *Renmin ribao* (People's Daily), November 17, 1951.

Baishe zhuan (White Snake). *Juben* (Plays), August 1953.

Baishe zhuan (White Snake). Beijing: Baowentang shudian, October 1953.

Baishe zhuan (White Snake). Beijing: Zuojia chubanshe, June 1955.

Baishe zhuan (White Snake). Beijing: Baowentang shudian, 1957.

"Baishe zhuan xu" (Preface to "White Snake"). In *Baishe zhuan.* Beijing: Zuojia chubanshe, 1955.

Ah Q zhengzhuan (The True Story of Ah Q). Beijing: Yishu chubanshe, 1955. Five-act play based on Lu Xun's short story.

Guan Hanqing. Beijing: Zhongguo xiju chubanshe, 1958.

"Yingshi zhuihuai lu" (Remembrance of Filmmaking Activities). *Zhongguo dianying* (Chinese Film) and *Dianying Yishu* (Film Arts), 1958–59.

"The Composer Nieh Erh." *Zhongguo wenxue* (Chinese Literature), no. 11 (1959).

Xie Yaohuan. Juben (Plays), nos. 7–8 (1961).

"Dui dang lingdao dianying gongzuo de yixie tihui" (Thoughts on Film Work under Party Leadership). *Dianying yishu* (Film Arts), no. 3 (1961). Reprinted in *Tian Han quanji,* vol. 18.

Hongse niangzi jun (The Red Detachment of Women) (1964). In *Tian Han quanji,* vol. 9.

"1965 nian riji" (1965 Diaries) (1965). In *Tian Han quanji,* vol. 20.

"1966 nian riji duanpian" (Parts of the 1966 Diaries) (1966). In *Tian Han quanji,* vol. 20.

"1967 nian riji canpian" (Fragments of the 1967 Diaries) (1967). In *Tian Han quanji,* vol. 20.

"Zizhuan" (Autobiography) (1967). In *Tian Han quanji,* vol. 20.

"Zuo Shunsheng he *Xingshi zhoubao*" (On Zuo Shunsheng and *Awakened Lion Weekly*) (1967). In *Tian Han quanji,* vol. 20.

"1968 nian riji canpian" (Fragments of the 1968 Diaries). In *Tian Han quanji,* vol. 20.

"The White Snake: A Beijing Opera." *Chinese Literature* (Beijing), no. 10 (1979).

Yingshi zhuihuailu (Remembrances of Film Activities). Beijing: Zhongguo dianying chubanshe, 1981.

Tian Han wenji (Collected Works of Tian Han). 16 vols. Beijing: Zhongguo xiju Chubanshe, 1983.

Tian Han dianying juben xuanji (Selected Filmscripts by Tian Han). Beijing: Zhongguo dianying chubanshe, 1983.

Tian Han quanji (The Complete Works of Tian Han). 20 vols. Shijiazhuang: Huashan wenyi chubanshe, 2000.

Prologue

Questions about the intersection of the personal and the political impact almost any intellectual project, whether acknowledged or not, but in the case of a book written by a student of Chinese literature who left Mainland China more than a decade ago, the questions are especially pointed. As someone who came to the United States in pursuit of higher education in Chinese studies at the tail end of the twentieth century, I share with my generation of Chinese students who went abroad a desire to better understand our own country and the world around us. Inherent in our situatedness is a belief in the peculiar power of the distanced perspective. In other words, we try to exploit to the fullest our particular angle of vision as simultaneous outsiders and insiders.

In thinking about the relationship of my generation of Chinese emigrants to those of the early generation of Chinese students who ventured abroad during the first decades of the twentieth century, I am struck by how both generations came of age during transformational times. Those earlier students were educated both in Confucian classics and in westernized new-style schools around the time when the imperial examination system was abolished in 1905. As a Chinese person abroad in the early twenty-first century, I feel a kinship with their search for their own voices in foreign lands (*bieqiu xinsheng yu yibang*), at the moment when the idea of a modern Chinese nation-state was just forming. Going to Japan then was like coming to the United States now. Just as Japan was the powerful enemy the Chinese both hated and loved to imitate in the first half of the twentieth century, so is the United States both admired and resented today. In both cases, the foreign land is the source of new ideas in a dialectical relationship through which Chinese students then and now discover(ed) their own voices.

The generation that came of age in the immediate aftermath of the World War I in Japan experienced a peculiarly heightened sense of "Chineseness." The new subjects of the young Republic (est. 1912) were still addressed as *shinajin*, a term that originated from Sanskrit and replaced the earlier *chūgokujin* to refer to subjects of the Qing dynasty (1644–1911) in Japan. Perceived by many Chinese as derogatory after the founding of the Republic, and definitely not as flattering as the earlier term designating them as "people of the Central Kingdom," *shinajin* registered the tensions and ambiguities of being Chinese in Japan in the early twentieth century.

A hundred years later in the United States, Chinese sojourners face a different historical legacy and an equally complicated challenge. "Mainland Chinese" (*daluren*) is for the US government (and other Western governments for that matter) a legal category distinct from Hong Kong Chinese and Taiwanese. On the other hand, culturally speaking, in the eyes of many Americans, "Asians" (whether Chinese, Singaporean, Japanese, Korean, Vietnamese, etc.) are now frequently equated with "Chinese," just as a few decades ago they were likely to be equated with "Japanese"—in both cases because of the rise of perceived and real economic and cultural influence.

But the elephant in the room is still that of difference in ideology and system between (communist) China and (capitalist) America. But how real is the ideological divide? Is the elephant a mirage? After all, the People's Republic of China has been dubbed the "People's Republic of Capitalism" in a six-episode Discovery Channel documentary on the new riches and social disparities in my fast-developing home city, the inland megametropolis Chongqing.[1] "Socialism with Chinese Characteristics," as claimed by the Chinese government, has been convincingly renamed "Capitalism with Chinese Characteristics" by the MIT economist and mainlander himself, Yasheng Huang,[2] with Chinese companies increasingly buying out leading brand names such as Lenovo and Volvo. Meanwhile, US president Barack Obama is accused of "socializing" big corporations and banks in order to deal with the American economic crisis! Frequently fear grounded and reflecting deep-rooted suspicion on both sides, taken together the rhetoric nevertheless converges on an imagined hybrid: "socialist capitalism."

When Tian Han (1898–1968), an eighteen-year-old Chinese man, arrived in Tokyo in 1916, Europe was still at war and the Russian Revolution was a year away. In Tian Han's time, the rigid lines between political capitalism and socialism were still inchoate, and consequently his generation regarded these categories as flexible and malleable. I find myself reading my own experience living in the United States through the prism of Tian Han's Tokyo sojourn. When I left Chongqing via Beijing for Cambridge, Massachusetts, in 1999, I was in my early twenties, not much older than Tian Han when he left Changsha via Shanghai for Tokyo. In many ways Tian Han enjoyed more privileges than I. He had close personal connections with the first generation of revolutionaries via his maternal uncle, Yi Xiang, and was taken under the wing of Yi, then manager of Hunan student affairs in Tokyo. For my part, I was the daughter of two teachers in a small town in the relatively backward Sichuan province (the town became part of Chongqing municipality in 1998, but the change did not enter our consciousness until much later) and entered Beijing Normal University for its free tuition and monthly stipend to relieve economic hardship in my family.[3]

Tian Han's experience at Changsha First Normal School was both like and unlike my experience at Beijing Normal University in revealing ways. For one thing, Tian Han was much more politically aware than I was. Arriving in Beijing not long after 1989 and right after Deng Xiaoping's "Southern Tours" of 1992, I was part of a generation of college students educated in a relatively restrictive political environment in which economic considerations were encroaching on every aspect of society, becoming the main imperative of everyday life. My monthly stipend routinely ran out within two weeks. Determined to be financially independent, I started to take odd jobs for supplementary income—but also to earn extra pocket money for the clothes and accessories for which I was quickly developing a taste. In reality, economic concerns occupied a great deal of my time and my mind during my stay in Beijing, reflecting in microcosm the larger society's increasing preoccupation with money.

But it was also in Beijing that I first made the acquaintance of a wide circle of friends from abroad, people who expanded my mind in many directions, introducing me to Western Marxist thinkers, Chinese literary theory, and Kun and Peking operas, among many other things. Tian Han took a similar intellectual trajectory even before setting foot outside his native Changsha and into the rising world metropolis of post–World War I Tokyo. I see in him traces of my own intellectual obsessions fed by those seemingly random encounters with foreign students on the Beijing Normal University campus throughout the 1990s. It was at that time I started attending Huguang Huiguan, the legendary opera house at the center of Beijing, the guild house of Hunan, Hubei, and Guangzhou provinces. My affiliation with the Chinese Department qualified me for free tickets to emerging avant-garde theater performances, as well as many other cultural activities and festivals that took place around town. My association with former Korean political activists and now PhD students in modern Chinese thought showed me a way to engage scholarship with political concerns. It seemed that everything made sense—my sense of kinship with Tian Han, my interest in the genre of Chinese opera, my scholarly identity as a

Chinese internationalist—when I looked back at those seemingly aimless years from the vantage point of 2013, writing in the quiet fifth-floor reading room in the main library of the University of Kentucky, where I now teach as an assistant professor of Chinese literature.

With the 1911 Revolution having just passed its centennial, one feels both the remoteness and the immediacy of the past. If the 1911 Revolution and the 1919 May Fourth movement had a formative influence on Tian Han's generation, the 1989 Student Movement and the 1992 "Southern Talks" equally shaped my own, just as "9/11" and the Iraq War have shaped the generation of American undergraduates I now teach. I ask myself, how to write a book on the first half of twentieth-century Chinese culture that will speak to the historical conditions of Tian Han's generation, but also to my own half a century later? How do I communicate these experiences not only to my colleagues in the field of modern Chinese literature but to a wider reading public whose frame of reference is not the May Fourth movement of 1919 in Beijing but possibly the September 11 attack of 2001 and the election and reelection of Barack Obama as the first African American president of the Untied States in 2008 and 2012?

Moreover, writing in English, how do I best communicate with the Chinese-speaking world back home and "out there"? How do I make my writing relevant to the kind of Chinese readers who keep up with the newspaper *Nanfang zhoumo* (Southern Weekend), visit the *Tianya* or *Wuyou zhixiang* (Utopia) websites, and participate in the various Chinese microblogs in contemporary China and throughout the world? Is it even reasonable to aspire to such far-ranging relevance? Or am I repeating the eternal intellectual obsession with "going to the people" while basically enclosed in the "ivory tower"?

I have come to see myself as a kind of anthropologist of my own culture. Since "history is another country," all scholars of past cultures are anthropologists of a sort. And in observing China from the United States, China takes on the status of an "alien culture." Talal Asad reminds us of the inequality in the power of languages when reading and representing other cultures, as anthropologists typically write about a non-English-speaking population for a largely academic, English-speaking audience.[4] However, I do think the specific task of the anthropologist as a translator of cultures needs to be clarified in this case, as I am performing the double identity of both the "informant" and the "researcher," while at the same time attempting to be both "inside" and "outside" of both cultures.

Am I reading another culture? Or reading my culture as if it is another culture? Indeed, can I now call "Chinese culture" my culture? What gives me that entitlement—being born and growing up in the Mainland and as a "native speaker" of Mandarin Chinese? In fact, Mandarin Chinese is my second language, as I grew up speaking Sichuanese. So what do we mean by Chinese culture? It is indeed high time to reconsider what it means to be "Chinese," in light of attempts to redefine the meaning of *Chineseness* (or to replace the term altogether) since the early 1990s.

The concepts of "cultural China" and "the Sinophone" represent two of the major interventions of the past two decades.[5] Both are attempts to reenvision a more inclusive, less hegemonic worldview in which a concrete sense of being Chinese (multiethnic) or belonging to the "Sinitic-language-speaking" (multilingual) world can be specifically articulated and locally realized. Indeed, "the third symbolic universe" of cultural China, incorporating individuals who bring their conceptions of China to their own linguistic communities and the Sinophone world out there, has been exerting great cultural influence on our understanding of modern China in the English-speaking world.

The process of finding one's voice and place in a new country is at the same time a process of finding one's voice and place within the scholarly field, for Tian Han's generation as well as my own. Self-definition took place both in the personal realm and in the professional world. The scholarly approach I adopt in the following pages emerges from a critical tradition in whose debt and under whose influence I am keenly aware of standing. An important starting point for any scholar of twentieth-century Chinese literature is the critical debate between Czech Sinologist Jaroslav Průšek and the leading scholar of modern Chinese literature in the United States, C. T. Hsia, in the 1960s.[6] Their debate, essentially between Hsia's New Critical textual analysis and Průšek's emphasis on the social mission constitutive of Chinese literature, was fruitfully resolved, for me, by Leo Ou-fan Lee, one of the leading China scholars of his generation, under whom I studied at Harvard.[7] In his groundbreaking monograph *The Romantic Generation of Modern Chinese Writers,* Lee declared his approach to be both literary *and* historical, using literary source materials to probe historical questions.[8] Both Průšek and Lee pointed the way for my own explorations of the Chinese avant-garde and its relationship to Chinese tradition and European modernism. Průšek's essay "A Confrontation of Traditional Oriental Literature with Modern European Literature in the Context of the Chinese Literary Revolution" and Lee's *Shanghai Modern: The Flowering of a New Urban Culture in China, 1930–1945* are key texts exerting a creative influence over the present book.[9]

With no knowledge of Lee's forthcoming book but certainly under the influence of his early scholarship, I wrote my master's thesis on Shi Zhecun at Beijing Normal University in 1999, calling Shi a "conservative avant-garde" (*baoshou de xianfeng zhuyizhe*) who roamed between the feminine tradition of Chinese classical poetry and Western aestheticism.[10] It is through Shi Zhecun that I was first introduced to Tian Han, as Shi listed Tian's lecture on European romanticism at Shanghai University as one of the major influences on his creative career.[11] Inspired by the debate between Průšek and Hsia, I set out to examine the relevance of the avant-garde as a category of cultural analysis from the post–World War I moment onward in modern China, with a focus on the Chinese artist and avant-gardist Tian Han.

Introduction
The Avant-Garde and the Popular

This book reveals avant-garde performance as an important political force shaped by, and in turn shaping, popular culture in modern China. It examines the multiple relationships among avant-garde performance, national politics, and popular culture in twentieth-century China with a focus on their shared internationalist visions and cosmopolitan aspirations.[1] I undertake an examination of the aesthetics and politics of the historical Chinese avant-garde in dialogue with important scholarship in the West,[2] with a focus on one of the key representatives of the Chinese avant-garde, the artist and activist Tian Han (1898–1968). Understanding Tian Han in his time sheds light on a new generation of contemporary Chinese avant-gardists who, half a century later, are similarly engaging with both national politics and popular culture.

In her study of modernism and popular culture in nineteenth-century Paris, Mary Gluck connects the self-presentation of the modern artist and the emergence of the modernist aesthetic to the changing forms of popular culture. She finds that the modern artist, in the roles of melodramatic hero, urban flâneur, female hysteric, and tribal primitive, creates an expressive, public, and popular modernity in opposition to an increasingly repressive bourgeois culture.[3] My own research into twentieth-century Chinese culture reveals a parallel to this Parisian matrix, that is, a sustained and dynamic conversation transpiring between avant-garde experiments and popular culture. Rather than a landscape of alienated avant-gardists resisting institutional control, on the one hand, and a top-down, monolithic revolutionary culture on the other, we find in twentieth-century China a cultural milieu comparable in many ways to the "popular bohemia" of nineteenth-century Paris, where the avant-garde engaged creatively with popular forms and where both the avant-garde and the popular converged on political engagement.

Avant-Garde, Popular, and Propaganda

Avant-Garde

In the Chinese context, the term *avant-garde* (usually *xianfeng* with regard to literature and *qianwei* with regard to the arts) has often been applied rather unreflectively to refer to the post–Cultural Revolution art movements that arose in reaction to the politicization of art during the socialist era, seeking to reclaim art from politics.[4] This use, however, represents an inversion of the original meaning of the term, which denoted art as deeply entwined with political purpose and aspiration.

The Chinese term *xianfeng* can be found in the *Hanji* (Record of Han), written as early as in the second century CE, where it denotes a military leader who serves as the vanguard on the battlefield.[5] Tian Han spoke of Peking University students as the avant-garde (*xianfeng*) of the "Chinese renaissance" in a letter to a friend on May 12, 1919, possibly one of the first usages of the term in the twentieth century to designate both a military vanguard and a cultural forerunner.[6] The use of *qianwei,* however, appears much later in the history of the Chinese language. The first entry in *Hanyu dacidian* (A Grand Dictionary of the Chinese Language) points to an eighteenth-century record referring to the front guard of the imperial army during the Mongol Yuan dynasty.[7] Tian Han also used *qianwei* to refer to the cultural vanguard, this time in the context of the Japanese military threat in 1936. Tian proclaimed that the wartime propaganda effort must be based on the taste of "the avant-garde among the populace," so as to both propagandize and educate.[8] Similarly in the English language, the term *avant-garde* has been Anglicized from the French to describe the foremost part of an army, or the "vanguard," since the fifteenth century, and it only gradually acquired the meaning of artistic innovation in the first half of the twentieth century.

In this book, I realign the term *avant-garde* with its historical roots to refer to literature and art that aspired to political engagement with society throughout the twentieth-century Chinese revolutions. That is to say, I am restoring the Chinese artistic avant-garde to its alliance with the political vanguard. In doing so, I define the avant-garde not only in terms of its cultural artifacts but also in terms of the cultural matrix and the modern mediasphere out of which those artifacts were constructed. In contradistinction to the Western association of the avant-garde with work that challenges and confronts the audience, that is, that which is programmatically "difficult," the Chinese avant-garde could and did produce work that aimed to be popular and accessible. The question of when an avant-gardist ceases to be one, however, is crucial. That is, once an avant-gardist represents a new order that is in power, can he or she any longer be an avant-gardist? If his or her work is broadly popular and representative, what does it say about the avant-gardist and the society in which he or she operates?

Despite its common ground with the European avant-garde, the Chinese avant-garde must be understood in relation to the specific tradition out of which it arose. In particular, the Chinese tradition, especially as articulated in the neo-Confucianism of Zhu Xi and Wang Yangming in the twelfth and sixteenth centuries, delineated the ideal path for the "men of letters" as one of engagement beyond the cultivation of one's self, to entail "rectifying the family, governing the state, and appeasing 'all under heaven'" (*Xiu qi zhi ping*). Such a "traditional Chinese" conviction regarding the centrality of social responsibility was pervasive in the minds of modern Chinese artists and bears comparison to the Saint Simonian notion of the avant-garde as a spiritual and political vanguard in pursuit of utopian socialism at the post–French Revolution moment.

Thus, notwithstanding its rigid hierarchical and patriarchal worldview, there is an often overlooked common ground between this socially engaged Chinese intellectual tradition and the post–French Revolution tradition of avant-garde utopianism, to wit, their shared emphasis on collective responsibility and solidarity. This utopian vision, with its futuristic, prophetic power, attempted to restructure the world, not only by reshaping individual psyches but also by reorganizing collective solidarity.

The twentieth-century Chinese avant-gardists, however, depart from our conventional understandings of pioneering artists from both traditional China and in the West in that they are not only socially engaged, as prescribed by the Chinese intellectual tradition, but also artistically in dialogue with an international avant-garde, with which they share mutual aspirations for both stylistic innovation and an internationalist vision.

The concept of the avant-garde hence is meaningless outside of specific cultural contexts. The Peking Opera female impersonator Mei Lanfang exposed the artificiality of theater while performing in Moscow in 1935, and hence provided a utopian landscape for the visiting Brecht, who "finds the codes of naturalized signification in his home culture so oppressive."[9] It turns out that the realistic tradition the European avant-gardist is leaving behind is precisely the future hope of the Chinese, and the symbolic operatic tradition the May Fourth avant-gardist strives to get rid of is considered avant-gardist in the eyes of Brecht and Mei Lanfang's Russian hosts, among them the avant-gardist filmmaker Sergei Eisenstein.[10] Tian Han's generation of the Chinese avant-gardists constantly ransacked the past and the West for weapons with which to subvert the Chinese present, while Brecht's generation of Euro-American avant-gardists constantly searched Chinese traditions to celebrate their avant-gardism.

In focusing on Tian Han, I am looking at a practitioner rather than a theorist of the avant-garde: he represents in his work the idea that reality comes about through action, through performance, as in ritual (calling something into being through specific acts).[11] He is interested, as an artist, in embodying ideas in actual forms, with bodies in motion. With both political and sexual desires frustrated in the dominant social structure throughout the Chinese twentieth century, performance became the means and the end, a sensitive crystallization of the mentality and practice of a generation of young people seeking to unleash their sexual and patriotic desires. The conflation of sexuality and patriotism has to do with repression and sublimation, similar to the way aesthetics and politics provide channels for the expression of one another.[12]

My investigation reveals a positive, constructive side of the avant-garde that has rarely been dealt with seriously, as it contradicts the teleological view that links the early-twentieth-century avant-garde (especially futurism) with the rise of fascism in the West. From Renato Poggioli to Peter Bürger, cultural critics have struggled with the "failure" of the avant-garde throughout the second half of the twentieth century. In Poggioli's view, the political "failure" of the modernist avant-garde was caused by its dependence on the capitalist bourgeoisie, or, as the young Roland Barthes put it in the 1950s, it failed to destroy bourgeois art because it was itself a bourgeois enterprise.[13] Although Bürger distinguishes quite sharply between aesthetic modernism and what he terms the historical or revolutionary avant-garde, in the end he also affirms the Poggiolian idea of the "failure" of the avant-garde. For Bürger the avant-garde's productive acceptance of the energies of popular culture, and its heroic attempt to channel art into social life, to make its transformative aesthetic projects into programs for social transformation, failed because the bourgeois culture industry was able to incorporate and neutralize even its most radical gestures, that is, the avant-garde's opposition to the culture industry.[14] The Chinese avant-gardists in this study echo the spirit of Bürger's revolutionary avant-garde, while charging further toward social engagement and political action in a broadly defined socialist context. The issue of co-option, however, is an important one. Can the avant-garde maintain its artistic and political edge if it becomes part of the establishment?

Revisionist critics in the field of European avant-garde studies have started to revisit the centennial debate on the avant-garde and politics, and propose to view the avant-garde as a political force in its own right, one that may have produced, and is still able to produce, solutions to problems irresolvable within its democratic political constellation. My exploration of the early-twentieth-century Chinese avant-garde and its participation in the internationalist vision fostered by the post–World War I moment thus contributes to this centennial debate by placing it in a global context. My aim is to tap into the vital popular energy of Chinese cultural productions so often tainted by the now ossified, and ostensibly mutually exclusive, categories of "avant-garde" and "popular."

China has often been excluded from discussions of the modernist movement and the avant-garde of the period. The assumption has been that China needs to be treated as drastically different from "the West" and hence must always be analyzed as an exception, or as in a state of lack.[15] Only recently scholars in China and the United States, in particular Chen Sihe and Xiaobing Tang, have started to pay increased attention to the avant-garde in the early- to mid-twentieth-century Chinese context.[16] While they highlight the imaginative and prophetic energies of the avant-garde in this period, I take their argument one step further by contending that the popular avant-garde became the cultural force that called the Chinese nation into being in the early- and mid-twentieth-century context and reshaped it at crucial moments in history. I further argue that China served as a catalyst in the making of the international avant-garde in both the post–World War I and post–World War II worlds. The democratic energy and popular participation so vital to the moment of communist national founding and the early years of the People's Republic should not be relegated to the "dustbin of history" for fear of association with the ensuing decades of state communism.

As important as the military origin of the concept of the avant-garde is its association with utopian socialism. The French utopian socialist Saint Simon first used the term in the sense of art as social engineering. The political dimension of the avant-garde was underscored when the German philosopher Hegel referred to the avant-garde as "the first teacher of the people," and the nineteenth century witnessed novelists, such as Hugo and Balzac, and painters, such as Van

Gogh, whose commitments to social justice lent them the aura of artistic messiahs. The disaster of World War I conditioned the rebirth of artists as visionaries and prophets of the new age. The transformation of the avant-garde in the 1920s and 1930s culminated in the Spanish Civil War, a "war of artists,"[17] and led to the mid-1930s' moment of the international avant-garde—the same moment when the film song "March of the Volunteers," the future national anthem of the People's Republic, was born in China. Georg Lukács, referring to his own Hungarian context contemporary with the May Fourth period, described the emergent drive for a range of social changes, from individual liberation to the creation of a world of mutual aid and fraternity, as a "Messianic utopianism."[18]

The concept and practice of the avant-garde did not privilege a specific political persuasion such as communism, or Marxist-Leninism and Maoism, in the context of modern China. Arif Dirlik pointed out two decades ago that to grasp the ideological developments of the May Fourth period we must go beyond Marxism alone to understand the immense and sudden interest in socialism in general.[19] Both the Nationalists and the Communists were important participants in this broadly defined socialist rhetoric and practice. I would add that in this expansive context not only was anarchism as important as Bolshevism, but the democratic energies of social democracy and liberalism were also part of the matrix of influences out of which a generation of avant-garde artists and activists arose. Tian Han is of particular importance in linking people of different political and cultural persuasions across party and ideological divides. Yi Junzuo, Zuo Shunsheng, Zhou Fohai, Pan Hannian, and Zeng Xubai were representatives blurring the boundary between Nationalists and Communists who had close personal contact with Tian Han.[20] Most of them ended up in Taiwan or Hong Kong, some were sentenced to death or life in prison as "traitors," and others were purged during the Cultural Revolution (1966–76) because of their political ambiguities.[21] Cultural and political developments in Taiwan, Hong Kong, Southeast Asia, and the Chinese diaspora in the post-1949 world can be better understood in the context of this generation of socialism-inspired avant-garde activists and their close personal and intellectual ties.

The politically engaged avant-garde of the twentieth century is riddled with contradictions between the individual and the social, and the personal and the political: its practitioners were driven by impulses toward individual liberation and enlightening the populace; they were haunted by the specter of tradition and the power of localities; they were the products of semitraditional, semi-modern educations; they migrated from countryside to cities; they underwent physical and spiritual liberation and exile at home and abroad; they engaged in political ambiguities; and they experimented with gender and sexual identities.

Popular

In English, the term *popular* came to stand in for *democratic* as early as the sixteenth century. As it came to refer to cultural products "intended for and suitable to the taste of the ordinary person, the primary functions of which are entertainment and amusement,"[22] "the popular" came to be seen in the West as inherently in tension with the energies of the avant-garde, which came to be associated with art that defied conventions and expectations, that challenged and even alienated the audience in the early twentieth century.

In the Chinese context, however, as individual liberation was inseparable from the quest to "enlighten" the populace, the Chinese avant-garde attempted to go "to the people" to popularize its vision from the early twentieth century onward. The ambivalent belief that "the people" possess nobility and wisdom, while at the same time they are asleep in ignorance and superstition, tended to invite an affinity between the avant-garde and the popular.

There are many different modes of the "popular" in the context of modern China. Contemporary Chinese scholars have tried to differentiate among "mass culture" (*dazhong wenhua*), "popular culture" (*liuxing wenhua/tongsu wenhua*), "revolutionary mass culture" (*geming qunzhong wenhua*), and "mass consumer culture" (*dazhong xiaofei wenhua*).[23] It has been widely acknowledged in the field of popular cultural studies in China that there is an enormous difference between politicized mass culture (such as the cultures of Second Sino-Japanese War and the Cultural Revolution) and commercialized popular culture (those produced in the post–Cultural Revolution era of "reform and opening up").

Scholars working in the United States have approached the popular in the Chinese context rather differently from their Chinese counterparts. David Johnson outlines the system of communication and the "structure of domination" in his study of popular culture in late imperial China, while at the same time borrowing from scholarship on popular culture and popular protest in the European context to point out people's desire to be indoctrinated, as "the values and beliefs of a dominant class take on the radiance of truth in the eyes of ordinary people."[24] This is equally important for the study of modern China, as the grassroots participation of the Chinese people in massive social engineering projects throughout the twentieth century can be better understood from the perspective of this aspiration for the aura of truth.

Leo Ou-fan Lee and Andrew J. Nathan used the term *mass culture* rather differently compared both to David Johnson and to their counterparts writing in Chinese several decades later. Their frame of reference was broader than both the "structure of domination" that Johnson outlined and the mass consumer culture of the post–Cultural Revolution era, as it included the cultural transformations that took place in early-twentieth-century China. More important, their emphasis on the politics of culture and the culture of politics linked commercialized popular culture with politicized mass culture.[25]

The connection between popular culture and mass politics was further articulated in Chang-tai Hung's 1994 study *War and Popular Culture.* Hung uses "popular culture" to refer to a "popular propaganda culture," as Chinese wartime propaganda, like any propaganda, was an act of persuasion, combining feelings and facts;[26] it is a propaganda made popular, meaning the masses identified with its message to a great extent. Barbara Mittler takes the discussion of "popular propaganda" into cultural productions during the Cultural Revolution. She highlights the popular cultural roots of and people's selective subjective reception to Cultural Revolution propaganda and emphasizes the accessibility and entertainment value, that is, the pleasure factor, in such propaganda art in spite (or because) of its political message.[27]

The present study is indebted to this important scholarship on popular culture and popular propaganda. It attempts to demonstrate how the avant-garde and the popular converged in their democratizing tendencies and their mutual assault on hierarchies, both political and cultural. I investigate the popular in this book both as cultural product (commercial media and mass culture) and as political force (animating social gospel and democratic mass movements). I suggest that, despite the seeming divide between commercialized popular culture and mass political movements, the two share a deep-rooted logic of "popularization" that warrants consideration of their interrelatedness as tension-ridden but mutually shaping processes. I thus identify the populist spirit and potential to inspire or instigate political participation in distinctively avant-garde, commercialized, and propagandist projects. In the process, the conventional segregation of avant-garde art, commercial popular culture, and political propaganda is renegotiated, and traditional dividing lines are redrawn or erased.

Propaganda

In this study, the crucial term linking avant-garde performance, popular culture, and national politics is *propaganda.* In English, the word *propaganda* originated in the seventeenth-century Roman Catholic Church in the context of spreading, or "propagating," the faith, specifically in foreign lands.[28] While the term did, from the beginning, denote the promotion of a particular doctrine or practice, it was free of those negative connotations that it acquired later as it came to stand for the manipulation of an audience through distortion or misinformation.

The Chinese word *xuanchuan*, often translated as "propaganda," has a much longer history and can be found in *Sanguo zhi* (Record of the Three Kingdoms), written as early as the third century. It denotes the action of announcing a message and spreading it, specifically, as in the *Shuzhi* (Record of Shu), an imperial edict.[29] In other words, there is an implicit worldview in the meaning of the word that privileges authorized discourse—be it religious or political—and thus lends itself to latter-day politicization.

In its modern usage, the Chinese word *xuanchuan* retains its original non-pejorative connotation. The dissemination of such authorized discourse was often carried out by a performance troupe, often called *xuanchuan dui*, whose aim was the transmittal of the message from the few to the many, demonstrating that the social function of art is intrinsic to the Chinese tradition, as expressed in the doctrine of "using literature to carry the way" (*wen yi zai dao*).[30] It becomes clear that the concept of *xuanchuan*, or "propaganda," is inextricable from its cultural embeddedness. One man's propaganda is another's declaration of faith, or even his anthem of freedom.

In order to understand propaganda in the Chinese context, then, we need to free ourselves of the Western preconception of an intrinsic antinomy between art and ideology, between art and propaganda, and thus between the avant-garde and the popular. Moreover, we need to shed the inheritance of aestheticism that has tainted Western theories of the avant-garde.[31] I reveal an alternative Chinese theory of the avant-garde that challenges and interrogates works of art not solely on their intrinsic aesthetic merits but also on the grounds of their *effectiveness*. It asks of a given work of art, does it make things happen in the real world?

A Chinese Avant-Gardist

As the protagonist of this story and the nexus on which its various threads converge, Tian Han (1898–1968) embodies the paradox of the bohemian populist throughout twentieth-century China. The translator of such works as *Tristan und Isolde, Salome, Romeo and Juliet,* and *Den'en no yūutsu,* he not only wrote lyrics for some of the most popular film songs of the 1930s, but he also immortalized the popular White Snake legend in the Peking Opera *Baishe zhuan* (White Snake) in the 1950s. One of his film songs ascended to the status of the national anthem of the People's Republic after 1949. Much later two songs with his original lyrics punctuated pivotal moments in Ang Lee's 2007 film *Lust, Caution.* Since the 1950s, dozens of textual and visual re-creations based on the Peking Opera "White Snake" have been produced, with a film starring Jet Li as Monk Fa Hai released in 2011. This book demonstrates how Tian Han and his legacy of cultural production provide a path through twentieth-century transformations and contemporary manifestations of Chinese aesthetics and politics.

Ultimately, Tian Han's significance in Chinese cultural history resides in the fact that he belies any easy understanding of the avant-garde as alienated from the political and the popular. As an experimentalist who achieved canonical status in contemporary politics as lyricist of the national anthem and an avant-gardist who secured his place in popular cultural memory as author of the "White Snake" opera, Tian Han embodies the convergence of performance, politics, and popularity in modern China. Yet this maverick who powerfully influenced modern Chinese political life and popular culture has never been treated in a book-length study in the English-speaking world with the exception of a couple of unpublished dissertations.[32] This book is the first monograph in English to engage with Tian Han's art and activism throughout a half-century journey while conversing with important scholarship in English, Chinese, and Japanese.[33] It is also the first book in any language to explore how a generation of Chinese avant-gardists, in spite (or because) of their inherently political nature, came to terms with different ways of being "popular" in modern times.

As a playwright, lyricist, art educator, and activist whose life and work centered on performance, politics, and the constant urge to popularize, Tian Han connected artists and activists of varying political and cultural persuasions across ideological and factional divides in modern China. Culminating in his Peking Opera *Xie Yaohuan,* one of the first literary works to be attacked during the Cultural Revolution, Tian Han's theatrical and cinematic experiments guide us through the dynamics animating Chinese cultural productions from the 1910s to the 1960s. Recognizing the "hidden dialectic" operating among the avant-garde, technology, and mass culture, and considering the avant-garde as a political force in its own right,[34] I examine the avant-garde performance of

Tian Han's generation in the context of the popular and the political, with a particular focus on how these three cultural phenomena—performance, politics, and popularity—fertilized each other. It is my hope that this study of early- to mid-twentieth-century China will lay the groundwork for a creative rereading of the cultural dynamics and political tensions at work during the Cultural Revolution, as well as in the "postsocialist" transformations of contemporary China, which will be touched on in the epilogue.

In his endeavor to connect performance, politics, and popularity, Tian Han embodied the paradox of the avant-garde in the socialist Chinese context: the aspiration by avant-garde artists to achieve popularity presented a threat to their own avant-gardism in the formal and aesthetic sense. At the same time, it enabled them to realize avant-garde aspirations in the broad context of cultural transformation and social change.

"Creating the New Woman" and "Going to the People"

The woman, the people, and the child are the three obsessions of modern Chinese intellectuals. Throughout his life, Tian Han persistently engaged, both aesthetically and politically, with two key themes: "creating the new woman" (*chuangzao xin nüxing*) and "going to the people" (*dao minjian qu*). These lifelong obsessions are dual manifestations of a single passion to champion the oppressed: that is, in his work, as in that of other avant-gardists of his generation, "woman" is often a stand-in for or representative of "the people," insofar as the people are conceived of as marginal, voiceless, or exploited.

In pursuit of his ideal, he immortalized a series of powerful female images in print, onstage, and onscreen, and his desire to engage with social problems also made possible a conversation among gender, performance, and politics. Tian Han brings a distinctly ambivalent relationship to "woman" in his work. Woman is not simply the oppressed other. The exploited virgin and the powerful femme fatale are both central to Tian's vision of the feminine. The centrality of the female image to Tian Han's work, with its populist and socialist implications, demonstrates how a preoccupation with issues of gender, class, and social justice spanned both avant-garde and commercial projects.

The idea of the woman and the idea of the people are in turn stand-ins for the dialectic relationship between the city and the countryside.[35] Again and again, the urban avant-garde superimposed on the simultaneously liberating and disorienting cityscape an image of the alluring but dangerous femme fatale; likewise, the idealized rural landscape was the locale of the innocent virgin. According to a similar dynamic, urban intellectuals imaged the "authentic" folk of the countryside as the ultimate savior for the decadent metropolis, even while they themselves were hopelessly enchanted by, and even addicted to, the "light, heat, and power" of the modern experience of urbanity. The cultural milieus of Tokyo, Shanghai, the Chinese hinterland cities, and Beijing not only conditioned the fusion of the avant-garde, the popular, and the political, but they also constituted the actual sites on which the individual and collective dramas, whether onstage, onscreen, or in the streets and squares, were performed.

Situating the Book

Responding to a general suspicion of nationalism as operating within the frame of dry, monolithic, and institutionalized politics, I treat the avant-garde operating in the socialist context in China as a body of practices that is "essentially unprogrammatic,"[36] united by a commitment to participate in social and political transformation despite obvious geographical and cultural fragmentations. More important, I find it fruitful to rethink the avant-garde in the context of the democratic founding moment of the nation. I attempt to link the avant-garde in modern China with what Andreas Kalyvas calls "the politics of the extraordinary," which "expands the boundaries of politics so as to involve more diverse, direct, physical, and conflictual forms of political participation that call into question existing institutions and seek to change them through deliberate collective action."[37] Tian Han's generation of Chinese avant-garde artists similarly expanded the boundaries of politics and engaged in extraordinary means of collective action.

The book is structured around a series of moments in time and space that were vital to the formation and development of the avant-garde in the context of twentieth-century Chinese national culture. I focus on four crucial localities of the avant-garde: Taishō Tokyo (1912–26), Republican Shanghai (1912–37), the wartime hinterland (1937–45), and the transition to Communist Beijing (1945–). These key geographic sites correspond to key historic moments: intricate interactions between the "imperial democracy" of Taishō Tokyo and Shanghai urban modernism from the mid-1910s to the mid-1930s, the politics of anti-Japanese national salvation during the Second Sino-Japanese War (1937–45), the ensuing

Civil War between the Nationalist Party (Kuomintang, or KMT) and the Communist Party (CCP) (1945–49), and the culmination and transformation of the popularizing impulses of the avant-garde in Communist Beijing.

The avant-garde movement I examine is at the same time distinctly localized and pervasively global. The representatives of the Chinese avant-garde (crossing boundaries among the Nationalists, Communists, and the "apolitical") shared an internationalist vision in a broadly defined socialist context. Meanwhile, the leading figures of the Japanese, European, and American avant-garde traveled to China on physical or metaphorical journeys, via modern means of transportation or through literary and symbolic acts of translation. This study attempts to uncover traces of mutual influence and communication going back and forth among members of the international avant-garde.

This book joins a growing body of scholarship that examines modern Chinese cultural productions in a broader East Asian and international context,[38] with particular focus on the complex relationship among Japanese modernity, Chinese nationalism, and the post–World War I international avant-garde. I call attention to the Japanese connection to Chinese modernity and revolution from the 1910s to the 1960s, a connection that persists despite the destruction of war and the increasing antagonism between the two nations.[39] At the same time, I endeavor to contribute to scholarship that complicates the conventional view of Communist Chinese cultural production as monolithic,[40] by embedding it in a historical dialogue with both its traditional and its modernist past, as well as with a cosmopolitan and internationalist context. Such a recontextualization reveals avant-garde performance as an important political force deeply penetrating popular culture in twentieth-century China, and one that, with few exceptions, remains unexplored in the fields of modern China in particular and modernist studies in general.[41]

Outline of Chapters

Within its broadly spatial and temporal framework, the book follows Tian Han's intellectual journey, and the trajectory of his imagination provides its interior arc. In following this arc, we find that Tian's life as an individual intersects with many of the major intellectual and aesthetic currents of his time.

Chapter 1, "The Lights of Tokyo," rethinks the idea of the avant-garde and the popular in the context of the rise of neoromanticism and social democracy in the post–Russian Revolution and post-World War I world. Using Tian Han's debut play *Lingguang* ("Spiritual Light," 1920, performed at Yūrakuza, Tokyo) as a point of departure, this chapter examines the Christian, romantic, and socialist spirit that permeated the art and activism of post–World War I Tokyo through a "Christian trilogy" in Tian's early plays ("Spiritual Light"; "The Ghost of the Piano," 1922; and "Before Lunch," 1922). The preoccupation with Christian and Faustian tropes in the literature and performance of the period, however, has less to do with Christianity and romanticism as such than with the social and political imaginaries built up around their iconography, which then took on new meanings for the generation of avant-garde artists active in the May Fourth movement in Tokyo.[42] The young producers and actors of the plays became social practitioners, who actualized their radical ideals through lifestyle experimentation and social action. They constructed a new trinity of spirituality, art, and politics out of an amalgam of Christian social gospel, neo-romanticism, and social democracy, which they translated into a doctrine of "ethical activism." This new form of activism aspired to remedy not only the rational scientific tradition, which had proven itself a failure in the face of war, but also the "inhumane" materialist focus of socialism and communism.

Chapter 2, "The Night and Fire of Shanghai," follows Tian Han's personal journey from Tokyo to Shanghai, a journey that was emblematic of a whole generation of avant-garde artists and activists seeking to pursue their political and erotic aspirations in the burgeoning urban culture of the leading Asian metropolis.[43] Popular cultural forms such as Peking Opera and Hollywood film served as important mediating devices for modernist and political experiments. Tian Han's independently published play *Huohu zhiye* ("The Night a Tiger Was Captured," 1924), and his highly publicized independently produced film, *Dao minjian qu* ("V Narod," or "To the People," 1926–27), enlisted the imaginary folk and the utopian countryside on behalf of both avant-garde and socialist agendas. Hollywood renderings of the modern femme fatale—Salome and Carmen—as well as European influences, such as Duncan's modern dance, prompted Tian Han to stage *Salome* (1929) and *Carmen* (1930) in Shanghai.

Chapter 3, "Lovers and Heroes in the Wartime Hinterland," looks at Tian Han's intermedia experiments and attempts at popularization throughout the Second Sino-Japanese War. The conditions of war and the need for national mobilization called for genre transgression in opera, drama, and film, where works such as *Xin ernü yingxiong zhuan* ("A New Legend of Lovers and Heroes," 1939), *Qiusheng fu* ("Rhapsody on the Sounds of Autumn," 1941), and *Ai Jiang-*

nan ("Lament of the South," 1947) stand out as prime examples of intermedia experiments. Tian Han had long appropriated "traditional" Chinese art forms such as Peking Opera and folk storytelling with a cinematic angle,[44] and he was actively involved with the film industry throughout the war. Ideas long championed among the urban avant-garde, such as "going to the people" and the "popularization of literature and arts" (*wenyi de dazhonghua*), were finally put into practice in rural settings. The hinterland experience consolidated many of the fragmented intellectual experiments prior to wartime and anticipated the rise of Communist China after the ensuing Civil War.

Chapter 4, "The International Avant-Garde and the Chinese National Anthem," recounts the journey of a popular Shanghai film song from the wartime hinterland to the new Communist capital of Beijing. A host of international artists and activists, such as Joris Ivens and Paul Robeson, regarded the "March of the Volunteers" as the Chinese national anthem long before its ascendance to official status, as they saw in it the embodiment of the popular and democratic energies and the provisional and experimental natures of both the revolutionary avant-garde and popular nationalism. Inasmuch as it was a song written for a feature film, it was linked to technology, mass distribution, and the commercial film industry from the very beginning, and these technological and commercial factors are crucial in understanding the popularity and mobilizing power of the song. Hence the story of the making of the national anthem not only highlights the international dimensions of Communist Chinese nationalism but also foregrounds the relationship between the aesthetic avant-garde and the political vanguard—how national politics made possible the popularization of the avant-garde, and how popularity further ensured the success of the song as propaganda. The history of "March of the Volunteers" forces us to unpack the complex interactions between the international avant-garde and the new technologies of mass culture as embodied in sound film. This history overturns the conventional view of the national anthem form as an instrument of top-down political control. It demonstrates how the Chinese national anthem originated from popular culture and moved up, instead of being handed down to the populace.

Chapter 5, "A White Snake in Beijing: Re-creating Socialist Opera," investigates the seemingly paradoxical blending of the avant-garde and the traditional, the fantastic feminine and the masculine new regime in the making of the "White Snake" opera in Beijing. The staging and later publication of the Peking Opera "White Snake" in the 1950s was the culmination of decades of gestation. For Tian Han, a dialogue between the vital "raw energy" in the folk legend and his attempt to "beautify" it as a great work of art had begun as early as the mid-1920s, during the most intense period of his avant-garde cinematic experiments. Consequently, the search for a "new democratic" Peking Opera, and the pursuit of a populist, humanist, and internationalist new operatic culture,[45] not only aimed at consolidating the nascent Communist national identity but also linked the Chinese 1950s to a spectrum of utopian artists and activists in the context of the Cold War. The ostensibly conservative move of returning to Chinese tradition not only reflects the transformation of a Chinese avant-garde artist under communism but also suggests the incorporation of the cosmopolitan and internationalist past into a seemingly monolithic state art. The "White Snake" opera further invokes a dialogue between fantasy and reality, and between the artistic avant-garde and socialist realism.

The increasing marketization, privatization, and globalization of Chinese society since the 1980s has conditioned members of a new generation of the avant-garde, represented by the artist and activist Ai Wei Wei, who, while following their early-twentieth-century counterparts in their engagement with the popular and the political, are often themselves unaware of or uninterested in their indigenous genealogy. Like their predecessors, they aspire to join the ranks of their Western contemporaries rather than seeing themselves as descendants of their Chinese forerunners. Their "depoliticized politics" makes their apolitical claims inherently political, and the subversive message in their works in turn makes them both popular among large numbers of the disfranchised and desirable in an international art market.[46] Meanwhile, in spite of the unprecedented socioeconomic transformations, the resilience of "mainstream popular culture" (as manifested, e.g., in the government-engineered "red songs" and "main melody films" and their contested popularity) again reminds us of the powerful and intrinsic connections among performance, politics, and popularity in the Chinese context.[47] The epilogue of the book connects Tian Han to the cultural politics of the late 1950s through his self-representation in *Guan Hanqing* and probes the contemporary relevance of such intellectual self-representation. It further contemporizes the themes of the book and shows how the various threads connecting performance, politics, and popularity are playing out in the contemporary scene through an analysis of Ai Wei Wei.

CHAPTER ONE

The Lights of Tokyo

See the light that surrounds them! Hear how the air is ringing with music!

AUGUST STRINDBERG, *A DREAM PLAY*, 1901

> It was 4:30 in the afternoon. I went to Kanda for French lessons. Lingering rain had stopped, and the firelike setting sun with its golden light was shining on the glass windows of each household. Taking the streetcar, I passed Iidabashi. Looking outside the streetcar window, I saw a rainbow showing off its colors from an opening in the red clouds. On the way back from my lesson, a bright sun was still hanging in a perfect blue sky. When I reached the sports field at Waseda, the moonlight seemed to be already within reach and the night air surrounded me. I could hear the sound of music and singing leaking from the brightly lit hotel windows. Climbing a hill and turning back, I saw the Waseda terminal and the colorful electric lights at the Imperial Cinema. The lights shone like a string of luminescent pearls draped around the face of a beautiful woman."[1]

So ends the October 11, 1921, entry of Tian Han's Tokyo diary, in which various sources of illumination reveal a magical urban landscape whose enchantments include Western-style architecture, music drifting from unseen singers, and an invocation of archetypal feminine beauty. The sun drives away the lingering rain and reflects off the glass windows, which bear witness not only to natural light but also to the recent advent of modern architecture engineered by such renowned figures as Frank Lloyd Wright.[2] A rainbow radiates colorful light from behind the red clouds, which, to the diarist, who was immersed in Japanese folklore, may have recalled the "creators" in Japanese mythology crossing the rainbow bridge. With the help of the night air, the moonlight, less passionate than the sun but more ethereal, fosters an air of the mystical and mysterious, where music and light together produce a moment out of time.[3]

Under Tian Han's gaze, the natural elements of the scene before him quickly yield, literally and figuratively, to the man-made: the brightly lit hotel, cinema, and streetcar terminal where colorful electric light shines like "luminescent pearls" and, importantly, performance takes place onstage, onscreen, and in the streets under the limelight and streetlamp. Whatever his attachment to the poetic symbology of nature, Tian Han ultimately finds the most enchanting illumination in the modernity of everyday urban life, in the architecture, popular media, and technologies that manifested the "light, heat, and power" of the cosmopolitan experience of the time.

Using "light"—both spiritual and material—as the central trope and Tokyo as the converging locale, and focusing on the textual, contextual, and subtextual implications of Tian Han's debut play *Lingguang* (Spiritual Light), this chapter examines the interpenetration of Christianity, romanticism, feminism, and socialism as embodied in the play and its performance in Tokyo in 1920. Though a minor work in Tian's oeuvre, "Spiritual Light" is one of the first expressions of many of the key threads that run through the intellectual evolution of both Tian Han and his generation. As an emblematic work of its time, it deserves more attention than it has heretofore received from scholars in the field. Its neglect is attributable in part to the fact that its explicitly Christian theme rendered it an object of political suspicion both during the May Fourth movement and after the founding of the People's Republic. However, its power as a condensed expression of a particular moment, the zeitgeist of that place and time, is disproportionate to its length and performance history and merits close attention.

The Christian imagery of "spiritual light" emerges out of the specific cultural milieu of Tokyo at the post–World War I moment, a milieu that was uniquely conducive to the development of a wide range of highly politicized and spiritualized discourses. As we shall see, the iconography of Christianity supplied the key link for Tian Han between romanticism and socialism. The spiritual and literal lights of Tokyo produced an illuminated landscape where aesthetic, social, and political movements creatively cross-fertilized.

Tian Han in Tokyo

Having arrived in Tokyo at age eighteen from the central southern Chinese province of Hunan by way of Shanghai in 1916, Tian Han had spent more than five years in this rising Asian metropolis by the time he wrote the opening diary entry. He encountered cinema for the first time and quickly became a "cinema fan" during his first year in Tokyo. He came to appreciate the popular love stories serialized in Japanese newspapers the year after, and started to frequent Western-style theater performances in 1918.

However, the very first publication Tian produced in Tokyo was a 1917 political essay on the economic cause of the February Revolution in Russia.[4] It was a decisive shift from his creative writings in the style of Peking Opera published only a few years earlier, when he was a middle school student in Hunan.[5] Through his maternal uncle's network of professional revolutionaries, in 1919 Tian joined the Young China Association, a cosmopolitan assembly of members who variously advocated anarchism, socialism, nationalism, feminism, and Marxism. He soon befriended the Japanese student radicals at the Christianity-inspired New Man Society and joined the anarchist Cosmo Club together with Japanese socialists, Korean activists, and other Chinese student radicals.[6]

By the early 1920s, Tokyo had emerged as a world metropolis, blissfully ignorant of its pending destruction in the Great Kantō Earthquake and ensuing fire a few years later. Streetcars had been largely absorbed into the fabric of daily life in the city. Carrying well over one million passengers daily in a city of two million (the population of the Greater Tokyo area amounted to four million),[7] they remained a powerful symbol of modernity and a constant presence in Tian Han's descriptions of the city during his six-year sojourn there from 1916 to 1922.

The streetcar captivated Tian Han not only as an image of modernity but also as an image of transit and exchange, of mobility. People traveled in streetcars in Tokyo with the same fluidity with which ideas traveled in the textual and visual creations of Tian Han and his contemporaries. Tian Han's Tokyo diary not only maps the physical landscape of the city, but it also outlines the mental atlas of the young Chinese as a romantic (i.e., utopian) avant-gardist. In this particular entry and his 1921 diary in general, Tian Han recounts in detail sensational newspaper stories of love affairs, whether of celebrities or ordinary people, a sign of his obsession with the notion of "free love" and the cultural mélange of Tokyo at this time, when romanticism was coexisting with modernism. Tian also describes in detail his intimate home visits and meetings with Japanese literary luminaries, including Kuriyagawa Hakuson in Kyoto and Satō Haruo in Tokyo.[8] He was taking in the urban milieu of Japan with all its sights, sounds, smells, and sensations, but notably concentrating on the bright and luminous, the rosy and romantic: indeed, he titled his diary collection *Qiangwei zhilu* (Road of Roses), and one searches in vain in its pages for any mention of the mud, crowds, and traffic hazards that fill the writings of Nagai Kafū and Tanizaki Jun'ichirō, two of his Japanese contemporaries who were observant critics of the discontents of an emerging but soon to disappear Tokyo modernity.[9]

How to interpret this rosy picture in the context of Tian Han's political activism in Tokyo? Can Tian Han the romantic avant-gardist be reconciled with Tian Han of the political vanguard? Most previous scholarship has treated Tian Han's Tokyo sojourn within the limited context of the representative "art for art's sake" group of the time, the Creation Society (Chuangzao she).[10] But such an approach fails to do justice to the impact of Tian's activities in Japan as a leading avant-gardist and activist of his time, in particular, his political activism in relation to the Young China Association, the New Man Society, and the Cosmo Club.[11] Although Tian Han was one of the founding members of the Creation Society and was probably responsible for its refusal to join the "art for life's sake" Literary Research Association (Wenxue yanjiuhui), he occupied, intellectually and personally, a more ambiguous and fraught relationship with the society's principles than is often supposed. When Tian discovered numerous errors in the transcription of his play *Kafeidian zhi yiye* (A Night in a Café), published in the inaugural issue of *Chuangzao jikan* (Creation Quarterly),[12] he suspected Yu Dafu, one of the Creation Society's key members, who had overseen the final editing in Shanghai, of having framed him. After the publication of his 1921 Tokyo diary, the harsh criticism he received from Cheng Fangwu, another key member, further alienated him from the Creation Society. These clashes not only point to the increasingly fragile personal ties between Tian Han and other members of the Creation Society, but they also reveal Tian's anarchism, avant-gardism, and independence in reaction to an avant-garde group that was becoming increasingly established. Indeed, when all is said and done, the most important outcome of Tian Han's association with the Creation Society may have been his literary friendship with Guo Moruo, a fellow key member and compatriot residing in Fukuoka who was establishing himself as a leading avant-garde poet at the time, and who was one of the first Chinese translators of *Die Leiden des jungen Werthers* and *Faust*—works that, as we shall see, would come to play a key role in Tian Han's own intellectual evolution.[13]

Performing "Spiritual Light"

> Now they had enough love filled with new power, they knelt down to thank the bounty of God and they determined to go back to their fatherland to distribute it among those miserable lives. When Christ hearing their prayer, his head gave forth brilliant rays indicating his joy, thus we finish: "Where love is, God is."
>
> TIAN HAN, "PREFACE TO *LINGGUANG*" (1921)[14]

In October 1920, a year before the publication of his Tokyo diary, a twenty-two-year-old Tian Han staged a short play in Chinese in a prestigious theater in Tokyo to an audience reportedly made up of people from twenty-four countries, with the aid of the rather poorly written English playbill from which the above quote was taken. The play, entitled *Lingguang* (Spiritual Light), tells the story of two young Chinese lovers on a spiritual journey from the United States back to China. It appeared to be semiautobiographical, with some obvious factual tweaks: Chinese students in the United States stand in for the Chinese student in Japan, and a Christian female protagonist stands in for the non-Christian male author. However, the play did capture the spiritual and patriotic longings of a not insignificant number of diasporic Chinese students, of which Tian Han was one, in the years following World War I. More important, it became one of the very first Chinese "spoken dramas" (*huaju,* as distinct from *xiqu,* "traditional Chinese theatre") to also depict Chinese characters at a time when most Western-style performances confined themselves to Western characters and subjects.[15] The emergence of this "modern" form went hand in hand with the experimental nature of its content: bringing a Christian-based social gospel to China at the post–World War I moment.

The "brief encounter" among spirituality, performance, and politics through the romantic love story between two patriotic youths in Tian Han's one-act play represents a pivotal opening up of linguistic, cultural, and political possibilities for cultural production in modern China as mediated through Taishō Tokyo. Others have observed that twentieth-century Chinese literature diluted the religiosity of Christianity in favor of its literary and symbolic value, such that it retained the secular utility and emotional appeal of Christianity while channeling its energies to political ends.[16] I would add that the emphasis on social and political salvation reinstituted a deep spiritual—if not strictly or conventionally Christian—dimension into political and social practices in modern China through the mediation of modern Japan. In Taishō Tokyo, a special blend of Christian romanticism and Christian socialism joined forces with an international socialist trend to form a special configuration of a social democratic modernity charged with political activism. Tian Han's cultural practices emphasized this convergence, expressed a cosmopolitan imagination of universal love and mutual aid, and advocated both a nationalist sentiment and an internationalist spirit.

Written by a young Chinese man soon to be classified in Japanese secret police records as a "radical" (*kagekiha*), an "anarchist communist" (*museifu kyōsanshugisha*), and a "socialist" (*shakaishugisha*),[17] "Spiritual Light" foregrounds the conflict between free love and arranged marriage, one of the central preoccupations of the May Fourth generation of modern Chinese intellectuals.[18] More important, it forges and preserves many of the now forgotten linkages among avant-garde performance, national politics, and spiritual salvation in the context of early-twentieth-century East Asia.

The play opens with the sound of a church bell tolling in the background while the female protagonist plays piano and sings her prayers in her American-style dormitory room.[19] She wears a white dress in a style that "combines the best of the Chinese and the West" (*zhongxi hebi*).[20] A suitor visits her and reports that her lover is returning to China to marry the fiancée arranged for him by his family. The female student converses with her suitor in a combination of Chinese and colloquial English phrases.[21] After dismissing him, she turns to Goethe's *Faust* for consolation, whereupon a play opens within the play, a dream sequence, in which Mephistopheles materializes onstage to guide the protagonist to a cliff where she witnesses the suffering of her countrymen in a devastating drought, as well as her lover's reunification with his fiancée. The last scene of the play takes the viewer back to the same dormitory room, where the girl awakens from her dream to find her real lover, who has come to inform her that his fiancée has found her own lover, freeing all of them from the constraints of arranged marriage. With the guidance of her dream and the support of her lover, the female protagonist develops from a sentimentalist to an engaging social activist. The story ends with the two protagonists bidding farewell to the United States and returning to China. The male lover dedicates himself to curing the physical weakness of his countrymen through medical science, while the female protagonist is determined to use her playwriting to cure them spiritually, to save the souls and regenerate the spirit of the Chinese people.

A Female Faust

Tian Han had originally named what became "Spiritual Light" *Nü fushide* (The Female Faust), for the female protagonist who reads Goethe's *Faust* and dreams of Mephistopheles in the play. The removal of any direct reference in the title does not dilute the Faustian theme deeply embedded in the play. "The Heavenly Light" (*das Himmelslicht)* is a concept and image that frequently appeared in multiple registers in Goethe's celebrated play, in which the title character, Faust, like Tian Han's protagonist, is on a quest in search of the true essence of a "bright-hued life."

The opening church bell in "Spiritual Light" signals the atmosphere of the play as distinctly foreign, exotic, and Christian, and at the same time resonates with the traditional use of bells in Chinese and Japanese culture to summon spirits, banish demons, and create a sacred space and time. It is possible that the members of Tian Han's international audience (drawn from "twenty-four countries") were already familiar with Goethe and would "catch" the allusion to church bells in Western religious traditions. Given the interest in Goethe's *Faust* in intellectual circles in both Japan and China at the time, the church bell in Tian's Chinese play could be counted on to resound with a deeper spiritual meaning.[22] In Goethe's text, church bells work like the Proustian *moment bienheureux* or the Freudian "trigger" to recall Faust from his suicidal thoughts and plunge him into deeper memories of his childhood, heralding his spiritual rebirth with an epiphanic moment that marks one of the high points of European romanticism.[23] The musicality of the church bell and the spiritual and romantic atmosphere it evokes in "Spiritual Light" connect the Faustian trope to early-twentieth-century developments in feminism and socialism in which a female Faust with a socialist spirit undertakes a quest for self and social salvation, as can be seen to different degrees in Henrik Ibsen's Nora, August Strindberg's Agnes, and Tian Han's Meili.[24]

In the dream scene of Tian Han's "female Faust" story, a lovesick Meili, whose name is a Chinese transliteration of Mary, reads and rereads the following four lines in *Faust* for consolation.

> 唉！天空中若果有精靈，
> 在這天地之間主宰，
> 請從那金色的霞彩中下臨，
> 引我到新鮮的絢爛的生命里去來！

O gibt es Geister in der Luft,
Die zwischen Erd' und Himmel herrschend weben,
So steiget nieder aus dem goldnen Duft
Und führt mich weg, zu neuem, buntem Leben!
[Oh, should there be spirits roaming through the air
Which rule between the earth and heaven,
Let them leave their golden haze and come to me,
Let them escort me to a new and bright-hued life!][25]

Tian Han used the Chinese translation rendered from the German original by his friend Guo Moruo, who was under the influence of Spinoza, Whitman, and Tagore, as well as Goethe, at the time, and whose first collection of poetry, *Nüshen* ("The Goddess"), would be published less than a year later. In Guo's poetry, the symbolic imagery of the goddess is used to ignite the "light of intelligence" (*zhiguang*) among those "lovely young brothers and sisters" (*ke'ai de qingnian de xiongdi zimei*) in a similar fashion to the female Faust Meili's use of art to lift the spirit of young Chinese in Tian's "Spiritual Light."[26]

In order to attain such a "bright-hued life," Meili follows Mephistopheles as he roams through the night air. Wearing the Virgin's blue mantle and standing with Mephistopheles on a cliff between the "land of misery" (*qiliang zhijing*) and the "capital of happiness" (*huanle zhidu*),[27] Meili, the female Faust, acquires the vantage point of an elevated spectator. However, she has to keep silent and has no power to intervene; otherwise, the devil will push her off the cliff for breaking their contract.

Thus Meili becomes a silent witness to the suffering below the cliff until one of the refugees recognizes her and addresses her directly. The sudden breaking of the interior fourth wall between the tragic drama below the cliff and the female spectator above is suggestive: Meili cannot remain disengaged, like Mephistopheles, on the elevated cliff, beyond good and evil, transcending beauty and death. Her fundamental attachment to her countrymen and, most important in this case, to her lover eventually prompts a suicidal act—jumping off the cliff into the "river of tears" (*tichuan/leichuan*).[28] The conversion from detached observer to fusion with her fellow countrymen through such a violent act suggests the triumph of collective solidarity over individualist self-preservation; on the other hand, it attests to the haunting power of sentimentality, as Meili's disillusionment with personal love is indeed the motivation for devoting herself to the collective.

In guiding her to observe the suffering of her countrymen, Mephistopheles serves as an enlightening agent in Meili's coming of age as a socially engaged female subject. Just as the serpent in the Garden of Eden led Adam and Eve to the fruit of wisdom,[29] so the devil leads Goethe's Faust onto a path that leads to his enlightenment. However, Tian Han's Meili is at the same time a subversion of Goethe's Faust. While Faust's spiritual progression requires the sacrifice of the virgin girl Gretchen, Meili embodies Faust and Gretchen in one. As Gretchen, she clashes with the world by asserting her noblest human qualities: pure concentration and commitment of the self in the name of love. As a female Faust, she reconciles the power relationship between genders and radically revises the Faustian story by transfiguring the victim into the heroine. This socialist heroine created in Tokyo already foreshadows Tian's reinvention of socialist feminist subjects in Beijing.[30]

Like Goethe's Faust, Meili and her lover, Defen, contemplate the relative merits of medicine and literature as means of social salvation. Just as Lu Xun turns away from medicine to literature a few years later,[31] Defen, Meili's lover and a medical student in "Spiritual Light," sees Meili's art as soul-saving.

> For those young people who hunger for love, only you can save them. You study literature, and you are a born artist. They need your mesmerizing, stimulating, uplifting, and caressing work of art, as we need a bright warm sun in the dark cold midnight.[32]

What emerges in the male lover's vision is the image of a female Faust turned female messiah. Defen in effect places a halo around the head of Meili, who becomes a source of light, heat, and power—key symbols in both Christianity and modernity. Tian Han emphasizes the female Faust's romantic agency in productive and reproductive power. More important, her medium of salvation is her art. The object of transmission in this female reproductivity is none other than love, the only remedy for a mostly male audience craving authentic love as a positive value against the oppressive institution of arranged marriage.

It is Meili, then, who announces that she prefers a "romantic" life and is reluctant to embark on what will be their shared "history" of married life. Distinguishing "romance" (*baishi*), as embodied in works such as Homer's *Iliad* and *Odyssey*, from "history" (*lishi*), as embodied in historical accounts such as Grote's *History of Greece*, she argues that *romance*, stories told by an unauthorized everyman, partakes of a higher truth. Hence *Three Kingdoms, Water*

Margin, Dream of the Red Chamber, and *Sea of Regret* reflect a richer reality than is recorded in *Twenty-Four Histories.*[33] Meili's repudiation of married life on the grounds that it is contaminated by institutional sanction merges anarchism with feminism. She further insists on discovering humanity and agency in the mystified and much-maligned image of women as either virgin or femme fatale. Swedish feminist Ellen Key served as a strong inspiration here, as Tian Han was under the spell of her theories, via Japanese translations, attacking the institution of marriage without the foundation of love.[34]

The character of Meili owes a debt to other strong female characters who were foregrounded in the zeitgeist of the time, via, among other texts, Henrik Ibsen's *Et dukkehjem* ("A Doll's House," 1789) and August Strindberg's *Ett drömspel* ("A Dream Play," 1901), both of which were produced onstage during Tian Han's sojourn in Tokyo. It is likely that Tian Han either saw or read these precedent texts. In any case, the trope of lodging discontent with the status quo in a female protagonist was "in the air" that Tian breathed in Tokyo at that time.

The Nora trope, in particular, as popularized by *A Doll's House* during Taishō Japan and May Fourth China, provided a strong impetus for the regendering of Faust. The final clash between Nora and her husband Torvald that prompts Nora's leaving home influenced the last scene of "Spiritual Light."[35] However, Meili and her lover Defen extend Ibsen's focus from individual to social development.

Strindberg further supplied a specific model for the making of a "female Faust" in the image of Agnes, "the daughter of Gods," in his *A Dream Play.*[36] The daughter of Gods was sent down from heaven to investigate the human condition, but the quest is also sending her "into the solitude and wilderness" to recover her self. Here self-development goes hand in hand with social development. Agnes's encounter with the happy settlement Fagervik, "Se vad det lyser av dem! Hör hur det klingar över vattnet,"[37] likely provided inspiration for Tian Han's two corresponding imaginary places, *huanle zhidu* (the capital of happiness, or Fagervik) and *qiliang zhijing* (the land of misery, or Skamsund), in the dream of his Chinese female Faust. Through witnessing the suffering of the coal heavers in Fagervik, Agnes in *A Dream Play* comes to understand the socialist and realist implications of their presence, the understanding that without the working people there would be no paradise, as "the light will go out" and "darkness and cold will descend upon" humanity.[38] The discovery of individual consciousness was thus at the same time a road leading to social solidarity.

Although it emerges within a cultural milieu broadly welcoming of feminist ideas, Tian Han's vision of the female Faust complicates the familiar landscape of anti-Confucian and anti-imperialist feminism considerably, as the joining of Christianity with feminism in "Spiritual Light" flies in the face of the "scientific" and rationalist feminism of the May Fourth mainstream. In an essay written a year before "Spiritual Light" was performed, entitled "Words after Eating the Wisdom Fruit," Tian Han portrays Eve as a strong-willed feminist in search of knowledge and power, rather than focusing on the misogynist implications of the Bible, thus opening up possibilities of reading Eve as the mother of Nora, Agnes, and Meili.[39] He quotes Ellen Key again, praising Eve as a symbol of all later feminist movements, and calls Nora the daughter of Eve in that essay.[40] These "daughters of Gods" created by Ibsen, Strindberg, and Tian himself embody a spiritually inflected feminism, which, in turn, connects a socialist reading of the Faust image and points to another essay entitled *Disi jieji de furen yundong* (Women's Movement of the Fourth Class),[41] in which Tian Han advocates a proletarian women's movement to right the wrongs inflicted by both gender and class discrimination, published as early as in October 1919.

A Socialist Faust

Faust was a presiding genius not only of German philosophy, written into the theories of Friedrich Nietzsche, Max Weber, Karl Marx, and Walter Benjamin, among many others, but also the philosophy of modern Western culture in general. Nietzsche regarded Goethe as "the last German for whom I feel any reverence" and went so far as to consider the man himself a historical representative of his *Übermensch* (superman) concept.[42] Marx, however, read the Faustian contract with the devil as the archetype of a modern intellectual forced to "sell himself" in order to make a difference in the world.[43] More figuratively, Faust briefly appeared in *Das Kapital* to illustrate the "Faustian conflict between the passion for accumulation, and the desire for enjoyment" in the mentality of a capitalist.[44] Faust reappears in Walter Benjamin's "Theses on the Philosophy of History" when the angel of history wishes to "pause for a moment so fair" in the style of Faust's final achievement of satisfaction and happiness.[45]

Unlike Weber and others whose Faustianism is linked to the rise of capitalism, the contemporary Marxist philosopher Marshall Berman specifically locates Faustian visions and designs in the fledgling socialism of Goethe's later years. In fact, since the late nineteenth century, scholars have attempted to articulate the fragmented but distinctively socialist spirit in Goethe's *Faust*, characterizing the first part of the poetic drama as the world of the individual and the second part the world of the social. Faust's last act of humanitarian goodness, building a happy settlement on the reclaimed land, is regarded as a step beyond the kind of individual romanticism to which he was committed in his youth.[46] Moreover, Goethe was a fervent reader of the Parisian newspaper *Le Globe*, one of the organs of the Saint Simonian movement, wherein the word *socialism* was coined just before his death in 1832.[47] The idea of the avant-garde as a spiritual and political vanguard, central to Tian Han and his generation of post–World War I activists, also first gained meaning in the context of the Saint Simonian movement.

As expressed in "Spiritual Light," Tian Han was deeply sympathetic to the radical romantic and socialist rewriting of the enlightenment ethos in *Faust*, where life was regarded as an unceasing process of self-realization culminating in social transformation.[48] And indeed, in the context of post–World War I Tokyo, Tian himself experienced a Faustian split between the contemplative life of self-realization and the life of self-sacrificial action on behalf of the commonweal. As a provincial Chinese in Japan during a time of rapid westernization and expansive imperialism, Tian personally experienced the multiple cultural disparities between "the West" and Japan, and between Tokyo and Changsha. A "latecomer" abroad, and at the same time ahead of the mainstream in his "backward" home country, he experienced an anguished inner division—a simultaneous distance from and devotion to his own country and a vision of a new moral order within China, as well as a new role for China on the world stage. Early-twentieth-century China, like Goethe's Germany and nineteenth-century Russia, produced what would later come to be called "third world intellectuals,"[49] individuals such as Tian Han, who thought beyond the nation and considered themselves actors and activists in the worldwide struggle to improve conditions for the underprivileged and the downtrodden.[50]

The Faustian trope thus connects spirituality and romanticism to socialism both in Goethe's time and in twentieth-century China. Tian Han was only one among a number of young Chinese intellectuals who poured their spiritual, artistic, and political passions into revamping the Faustian trope. Tian Han discussed the spiritual and socialist implications of Goethe's romanticism with Guo Moruo and Zong Baihua in their letter collection *Sanye ji* (*Kleeblatt*), an instant bestseller in the style of *Werther*, published in Shanghai in 1920 while Tian and Guo resided in Japan.[51] Zong, the young editor of the *Xuedeng* literary supplement of the Shanghai newspaper *Shishi xinbao*, who introduced Tian and Guo to each other at the time, would go on to study philosophy in Germany.[52]

Thus, in the Chinese context, spiritual and political engagement with the collective was intrinsic to the romantic pursuit of the modern intellectual. It has been argued that it was Karl Marx who anointed modern intellectuals as missionaries of the secular modern. The enlightened modern intellectual, while claiming emancipation from religious belief, turns out to be a true believer in his or her own role as savior of the world.[53] Faust embodied such a complex of aspirations endemic to modern intellectuals, their avant-gardism, and their popularizing energies. They came to understand that in order to achieve the greatest social and political mobilization, they needed to engage in a dialogue with as wide a public as possible and at the same time touch the most intimate and personal sensibilities of that audience. But the very social conditions that inspired their radicalism, such as the pervasive gender, class, and racial disparities among peoples and nations, served to frustrate its implementation. They came to learn that subversive ideas must manifest themselves through the media of the market in order to generate social change.

Tokyo at the Post–World War I Moment

What we see in "Spiritual Light," and in Tian Han's Tokyo sojourn in general, is the four-way intersection of European, American, Japanese, and Chinese ideas and practices. A contemporary reader may wonder how the United States emerged as the source of spiritual salvation for the young Chinese in the play, and what role Japan played as the ground for the meeting of East and West. What was the meaning of the Russian Revolution and its aftermath for this generation of international vanguard? Most important for our purposes, what did the young Chinese men and women bring from their own traditions to contribute to this cultural mélange? These questions bring the May Fourth movement into dialogue with the Post–World War I world to reveal important connections between the Chinese movement and contemporary projects of the interwar international avant-garde.

The emerging metropolises of the post–Russian Revolution and post–World War I world nurtured and witnessed the coming of age of a new generation of artists and activists drawn to the artistic and political centers of the world in their late teens and early twenties. Situating themselves in the urban centers where rice riots and potato revolts were seen from Tokyo to Amsterdam, where returned veterans of subaltern origin were facing discrimination in their own countries due to racial and class biases, and where the gap between the rich and the poor was constantly widening, a new generation of artists and intellectuals congregated and engaged in study and activism. Tian Han sojourned in Tokyo and Shanghai. Joris Ivens experienced the explosive changes in everyday life and artistic experiments in Amsterdam and Berlin, while the African American singer-actor Paul Robeson was active in New York City and London.

Often traveling from "minor" to "major" metropolis, from "belated" to "advanced" modernity, these emerging artists and activists engaged in writing, translation, performing, publishing, communal living, and political organizing. It was a transformative moment—variously a spiritual maelstrom; a moment of anarchism, socialism, and internationalism; and a new epoch in search of a new vision for a new moral world.[54]

Tokyo became a site for the growth of this interwar international avant-garde largely owing to the fact that World War I presented Japan with an opportunity to strengthen its imperialist presence in the economic, military, and cultural spheres in Asia. Japanese industry boomed with the opening up of the Asian market. Emerging as a cosmopolitan Asia Pacific urban center in the years following the war, Tokyo was not only the political capital of imperial Japan but also a cultural hub for Japanese, Chinese, Korean, and Taiwanese artists and activists.[55]

The old merchant quarter of central and eastern Edo-Tokyo (the city changed its name from Edo to Tokyo after the Meiji Restoration of 1868), dating from the preindustrial era, had fostered customs and cultural values known as the *shitamachi,* denoting not simply a place-name but also a way of life infused with the "Edo spirit." The Edokko, or "son of Edo," embodies this *shitamachi* lifestyle as that of "someone roaming the 'floating world' of theaters, pleasure quarters, and markets as depicted in Japanese woodblock prints known as *ukiyo-e,* literally 'picture of the floating world.'"[56]

Emerging from World War I, Tokyo gathered artistic and political exiles, students, missionaries, and businessmen into a city deeply saturated in the popular cultural traditions of premodern China and Japan.[57] The lingering Edo spirit still permeated the everyday life of modern Tokyo and was proven conducive to the bohemianism and experimentalism of Tian Han's generation. The city became a meeting place for a wide range of competing intellectual and popular trends: Hollywood melodrama, German romanticism and expressionism, Christianity and American-style social gospel, feminism, socialism, anarchism, social democracy, and Marxism. It was in this environment that Tian Han staged his play "Spiritual Light."

While nationalism elsewhere led to cultural insularity and conservatism, it worked quite differently in Japan, where the rise of empire abroad reverberated at home as a spirit of openness. The numerous parades and demonstrations that took place in the Tokyo parks and streets in support of the imperialist projects abroad gave new legitimacy to public gatherings in general and fostered a belief in "the voice of the people" in the ensuing democratic political process at home.[58] Tian Han was likely aware of one such gathering in support of universal suffrage in February 1918 in Ueno Park, site of the 1914 Taishō Exposition. Not unlike the 2010 Shanghai Exposition, the Tokyo exposition about a hundred year's earlier similarly aimed to showcase a new era of prosperity embodied in grand architectural styles, industrial and financial developments, and other symbols of modernity. Consequently, Ueno Park was transformed into the largest public space for political and other gatherings in the city. In 1920, a few months before Tian Han staged "Spiritual Light," Japan's first May Day celebration took place with passionate protesters calling for the liberation of the working class.[59]

These democratic political processes and labor movements were part of an interconnected Post–World War I world, where anticolonial nationalism went hand in hand with pro-imperialist sentiment and anarchist cosmopolitanism. United States president Woodrow Wilson's "Fourteen Points" address before Congress in January 1918 inspired nationalist self-determination movements in East Asia, the Middle East, and North Africa.[60] The "Wilsonian moment" spread from the United States to former colonies and semicolonies worldwide, one example of which was the role of the Korean diaspora in Tokyo in mobilizing for Korean independence from Japan. A major Shanghai daily reproduced the full text of Wilson's address in the same month, January 1918, hailing his ideas as "a beacon of *light* for the world's peoples."[61]

In 1920, Tian Han joined the Tokyo Cosmo Club (Cosmo for "cosmopolitanism"), organized by the Japanese socialist Sakai Toshihiko, Tokyo Imperial University Christian student leader Miyazaki Ryūsuke, and Korean activist Kwŏn Hŏi-guk.[62] The club was dedicated to "their search for liberation and freedom from the nation—which was now seen as the origin of war and suppression."[63] In November 1920, within a month of the first performance of "Spiritual Light," Tian Han attended the first general assembly of the Cosmo Club in Kanda Teikoku Gakushi Kaikan, a venue reserved under the name of the leading Christian reformer, Yoshino Sakuzō. Tian met leftist playwright Akita Ujaku among the twenty-seven attendees, seven of whom were under close police surveillance. A few months before he started the diary quoted at the beginning of this chapter, Tian Han had emerged as one of the three representatives of the fifty-four Chinese present at the June 1921 general assembly of the club in the Kanda YMCA Hall.[64]

The manifesto of the Cosmo Club aimed at "freeing human beings from national hatred and racial prejudice to enjoy proper lives of mutual aid."[65] The rules of the club were printed in five languages—Japanese, Chinese, Esperanto, Korean, and English. The appearance of Esperanto in the mix of English and three leading East Asian languages is significant as an indicator of the activists' universalist, transnational aspirations.

The perhaps unintended mobilizing power of Wilson's Fourteen Points and the institutional reach of the YMCA World Service guaranteed a strong American influence in East Asia. Tian Han wrote an essay in the spring of 1919 commemorating Walt Whitman's centennial, in which he compared Whitman to Wilson and praised both for advocating a new spirit of "Americanism," a term that denoted for Tian and his contemporaries a vanguard spirit and a democratic ideal.[66] Writing in Tokyo to his good friend Zuo Shunsheng only days after the May Fourth student demonstration and possibly influenced by the American-educated Hu Shi, Tian spoke of Peking University students as the avant-garde (*xianfeng*) of the "Chinese renaissance." He urged his Chinese contemporaries to follow the lead of the students and "get in tune" with the vanguards of the world.[67] Tian Han's friends, Huang Zhongsu and Kang Baiqing, went to the United States to study by way of the port city Yokohama, meeting with Tian in Tokyo before their departure only weeks before he started to write "Spiritual Light" with its American setting. The fact that Tian Han located his utopian longings in the United States must be read as an expression of the particular perception among the Chinese avant-garde of the United States as a symbolic marker for progressive democracy during the post–World War I "Wilsonian moment."

Japan simultaneously served as a bridge to connect the young Chinese with the new idealized America and fostered its own cosmopolitan and progressive milieu conducive to avant-gardism. At the same time, the heightened militaristic educational practice in imperial Japan made the Chinese sojourners aware that such a system only produces "national people" (*kokumin*, *guomin*) and nationalist ambition, rather than "world people" (*tenmin*, *tianmin*) and world consciousness.[68] Embracing the liberal democratic and Christian socialist trends in Tokyo, Tian Han criticized the Japanese militarists and warned against the development of a parallel militaristic "China chauvinist" (*dazhonghua zhuyizhe*).[69] The cogency of Tian Han's warning against imperialist expansion in 1919 would unfortunately be borne out in Japan's continuous military expansion in the interwar period.[70]

Tian Han would go on to struggle with the problem of how to advocate nationalism while avoiding the pitfall of cultural imperialism into which he had seen Japan fall. Tian belonged to a generation of artists and thinkers who were first and foremost internationalists. He saw his own activism as sponsored and authorized both by the traditional Chinese vision of the individual, and especially the artist, as bound within a network of social responsibilities, and by the Saint Simonian brand of avant-gardism that envisioned artists as a spiritual and political vanguard in pursuit of utopian socialism in the wake of the Russian Revolution.[71]

The Christian Context

We have seen in the previous section that Tian Han invoked a secularized version of Christianity to link romanticism, feminism, and socialism in his Tokyo theater experiment. Tokyo provided the context for Tian Han's introduction to Christianity, partly under the auspices of the YMCA, which promulgated a "social gospel" as part of its efforts to promote education, technical progress, and modernization in general.[72] It was this social justice component of Christianity that most engaged Tian Han.

From its earliest dissemination in China, the Christian social gospel was perceived as aligned with socialist thought. Indeed, the first mention in Chinese print of Karl Marx and his ideas came in *Wanguo gongbao* (A Review of the Times), an English-language monthly publication edited by the American Methodist missionaries Reverend Young John Allen and Reverend Timothy Richard, in 1899. The magazine influenced Kang Youwei and Liang Qichao, among other non-Christian reformers, and the two became loosely associated with the editors in the mid-1890s. Kang's vision of a future utopian society, *datong* (great harmony), was in many ways indebted to both socialism and Christianity.[73] More significantly, *datongxue* (theory of great harmony) was the term used in *Wanguo gongbao* when Marx and *The Communist Manifesto* were first introduced to China one year after the 1898 reform led by Kang and Liang.[74] It becomes clear that the Chinese reformers and Christian missionaries influenced each other in their mutual attempts to articulate a shared vision of personal and social salvation.

Many participants in the 1911 Revolution, which overthrew the Manchu Qing dynasty, had a Christian background of some kind. Sun Yat-sen, the founder of the Tongmeng hui (Revolutionary Alliance) in 1905 and the "national father" (*guofu*) of the Republic of China, was influenced by Christianity in his teens while living in Honolulu. Sun set out to conduct his revolutionary activities in the style of social salvation carried out by the Christian church. The spiritually and socially revolutionary message of the gospel became an important theme in the lived experience of the May Fourth generation in China in spite of the predominant discourse of radical antitraditionalism and anti-imperialism.[75]

During the period of radical anti-imperialism, the influence of Christianity on Chinese intellectuals became a contentious issue. Writers such as the female Fujianese poet Bing Xin and the Taiwan-born Xu Dishan joined Tian Han in his use of Christian imagery to endow art and activism with a strong sense of spirituality. Like Tian, Bing Xin frequently used imagery of "spiritual light" in her work.[76] Xu Dishan attended the Twelfth Congress of the World Student Christian Federation as a delegate from Yenching University in Beijing.[77] The congress provoked the founding of the Anti-Christian Student Association and Anti-Religion Association, both rooted in rationalist thinking and anti-imperialism, and spurred a serious debate on "religious freedom" in Chinese intellectual circles. Xu joined the debate and published articles advocating a new worldwide religion that was to be both populist and scientific, both emotional and rational.[78] Five professors at Peking University, Zhou Zuoren, Qian Xuantong, Shen Jianshi, Shen Shiyuan, and Ma Yuzao, declared that they were not believers in any religion but still supported religious freedom and opposed the anti-Christian and antireligious movements on the grounds that intellectuals should respect and not destroy others' opinions and that religious freedom was granted in the constitution.[79] These key countervoices to the "anti-Christian movement" demonstrate the centrality of the "problem" of Christianity from competing perspectives, though later historiography in China has largely downplayed the pro-Christian voices as they do not fit easily with the prevailing ideological paradigm of scientific materialism and rationality.

"Where Love is, God is"

The concluding line in Tian Han's English playbill for the performance of "Spiritual Light," "Where Love is, God is," echoes the title of a Tolstoy story popular in Japan at the time, expressing the essence of Tolstoy's religiosity: the conviction that God resides in the practice of human virtue (or *tokugi* as translated in Japanese), the spontaneous everyday acts of kindness and compassion that individuals perform for one another.

Japan had first been introduced to Tolstoy as a religious figure through his popular tales in the early 1900s. Tolstoy's Japanese translator, Konishi Masutarō, though educated in Tokyo and Moscow in the Russian Orthodox tradition, nonetheless came to critique Orthodox Christianity together with Tolstoy through the ethical teachings of the *Dao De Jing* (*Tao Te Ching*). Konishi synthesized the theological and social aspects of the Taoist classics into a populist, even anarchist, moral philosophy that rejected the need for institutional or state organization. In Konishi's translation of Tolstoy, the term *heimin* (commoner) became inclusive of all people and denoted their dependence on one another. Such a Russian-Chinese-Japanese transcultural reconfiguration of Tolstoy in early-twentieth-century Japan spurred the invention of a particular language of "the people" and facilitated the Japanese translation of Tolstoy's thought into a people's religion that transcended not just class but Western modernity's hierarchical ordering of the world at large.[80]

Tian Han fell under the spell of this Tolstoyan religion as introduced to Japan during his Tokyo stay. He recorded his enthusiastic reading of Tolstoy's *Ispoved* (A Confession) in his Tokyo diary entries.[81] At the time, a whole range of visionary artists, including William Blake, August Strindberg, Oscar Wilde, and Gerhart Hauptmann, among others, was becoming known in Japan. Before staging his play in October 1920, Tian had already advocated the creation of "a new religion for a young China" (*Shaonian zhongguo zhi xin zongjiao*).[82] The religious commoner's voice, with its nonchurch, nonstate, nonhierarchical, supposedly universal moral qualities central to the Japanese renderings of Tolstoyan religion, ironically came to form the foundation for a provincial young man's nationalistic longings in an alien land.

Though not physically in Beijing, Tian Han belonged to the generation of students who demonstrated against the Treaty of Versailles in Tiananmen Square in Beijing on May 4, 1919, as the treaty represented an imperialist dismissal of Chinese self-determination. Tian's sympathies were firmly with the prevailing romantic mood of the May Fourth moment. His embrace of the idea of Christian salvation, however, was not quite as compatible with the movement's anti-imperialist spirit. Although Christianity had had a presence in China since the seventh century, its increasing influence since the nineteenth was tied to real and perceived threats of Western imperialism and its "gunboat diplomacy." Notwithstanding prominent converts such as Hong Xiuquan of the Taiping Rebellion and Sun Yat-sen of the 1911 Revolution, antimissionary incidents throughout the nineteenth century culminated in the Boxer Uprising and the subsequent occupation of Beijing by the Eight-Nation Alliance at the turn of the twentieth century.[83] The imperialist taint of Christianity was not an obstacle for Tian partly because of the mediation of Tolstoyism and partly because any such regressive associations were outweighed for him by its promise of a progressive, democratic vanguard spirit as expressed both in the social gospel and in post–World War I Wilsonism.

At the same time, many involved in the May Fourth movement regarded indigenous traditions as partly culpable for China's weakness vis-à-vis foreign powers. Indeed, "religion" itself was a category that came to China in the late nineteenth century as a result of imperialism and as part of modern state formation.[84] While on the one hand some cultural elites viewed Chinese tradition as a liability, others debated the virtues of refashioning Confucianism into a state religion, or of reviving Buddhism as an ethical philosophy to rival or even complement socialism, while attacking Christianity as a tool of imperialism.[85]

Tian Han arrived at a synthesis of these contesting views conditioned by his Hunanese revolutionary background as much as by the spiritual milieu of Tokyo at the time. Without ever abandoning the power of tradition and locality throughout his modernist experiments, Tian emphasized the constructive power of the Christian social gospel and its democratic implications for "the people" in the style of a Tolstoyan religion. Thus, he attempted to integrate a nativist and revolutionary sensibility with Christian iconography in a way that distinguished his vision from those of both the believer and the pure instrumentalist.

In advocating a new religion for a young China, Tian Han revamped the Tolstoyan nonstate religion and enlisted it on behalf of state building. His bold and fluid experimentation with Christian ideas and imagery reveals the dynamism of religious and spiritual thinking during the period. Tian exploited the aesthetic appeal, ethical meaning, and emotional impact of Christianity, as it offered an iconography that materialized the abstract ideas of personal and social development. There were, of course, other iconographies available to him at the time, just as Christ was only one of the many images that hung on his wall in Tokyo, beside those of Goethe, Miller, Hugo, Tolstoy, and Beethoven.[86] Christianity offered Tian a way to synthesize his romanticism and socialism. It became an emotionally and aesthetically appealing scaffold on which to construct his vision of a spiritual and ethical dimension to political practice.

The Young China Association and the Issue of Religion

In his letter to Li Jiannong, editor of *Taiping yang* (The Pacific), where "Spiritual Light" was published, Tian Han introduced his friend Zhang Difei,[87] a self-proclaimed "Wertherian" youth suffering from a suicidal complex, as the lead actor in the play. Zhang performed the part of the Chinese Mary's atheist lover, the doctor with "fragrant morality" (*defen* literally means "moral fragrance") who hopes to save the country through medicine, and who finally kneels down together with the Chinese Mary in front of an image of Jesus Christ to receive the holy light before returning to China.

The symbolic conversion of a male atheist is not without historical and cultural references in real life. Christian socialist reformers played a crucial role in bringing forth an "imperial democracy" in the years following World War I in Japan. Yoshino Sakuzō and his disciples at the Tokyo Imperial University, especially the young student radicals grouped around the Shinjinkai (New Man Society), asserted important influences in forging the spirituality of political and social activism.[88]

The New Man Society is crucial in linking Tian Han with Christian socialist currents of the time. However, rather than the heterosexual romance portrayed in "Spiritual Light," brotherly love and mutual aid—be it Christian, anarchist, or homosocial—formed crucial bonds among young male student radicals in Tokyo at the time. In practice New Man Society members advocated building a democratic and just society and working as vanguards to save "the people" (in Russian, *narod*). Indeed, *Demokurashii* (Democracy), *Senku* (Pioneer), *Dōhō* (Brothers), and *Narōdo* (Narod) were featured prominently as titles of New Man Society journals during the March 1919 and April 1922 interlude when Tian Han was closely involved with the society.[89]

However, the very Christianity that bound the New Man Society together provoked heated debate within the Young China Association (Shaonian zhongguo xuehui). The association was founded by Li Dazhao and Wang Guangqi in Beijing with branches in France, Germany, Japan, and many Chinese cities, including Chengdu and Nanjing. Its members, including the Sichuanese Zeng Muhan and Li Jieren and the Hunanese Zuo Shunsheng, Yi Junzuo, and Mao Zedong, were from a wide range of cultural and political backgrounds.[90] Tian Han was one of the few members residing in Tokyo. In the midst of the anti-Confucian polemics of the May Fourth movement, at the center of which was Li Dazhao, future cofounder of the Chinese Communist Party (CCP), the Young China Association took the lead in questioning whether Christianity could speak for China.[91] The decision to focus on the religious question originated with a recommendation from its Paris branch that persons of religious faith be barred from membership. Composed of founding members of the association such as Zeng Muhan,[92] the Paris branch enjoyed high prestige within the Young China Association, and its recommendation was presented to members through the association's official journal *Shaonian zhongguo* (Young China)'s *Falanxi hao* (Special Issue on France). Tian Han opposed the ban and, in a passionate call for freedom of religious expression, requested reconsideration on the grounds that the Chinese constitution guaranteed religious freedom and that the teachings of Jesus and the Bible merited attention even if one did not accept Jesus as the divine Son of God.[93]

It was against this backdrop that, one month later, Tian would stage "Spiritual Light" featuring a Catholic as both the protagonist and the lead actor. Another two months later, in December 1920, as a member of the Young China Association, Tian Han would write a poem in Japanese on the occasion of the New Man Society's second anniversary, calling for the Chinese "young man" (*shōnen, shaonian*) and the Japanese "new man" (*shinjin, xinren*),[94] both sons of the "new spirit," to go hand in hand "to the people" (*jinmin no naka e*) to achieve social salvation inspired by Christianity.[95]

What element of the Christian social gospel did Tian find essential or useful in his evolving social consciousness? Was it the call to love one's neighbor as oneself? The mandate to feed the hungry, clothe the poor? The idea that the meek (poor) would inherit the earth? Although these ideas were available to him from indigenous sources such as Confucianism and Buddhism, May Fourth antitraditionalism rendered them suspicious. Like many of Tian Han's writings, this Japanese poem is itself a miniature drama, inherently performative in nature. A young man and a "new man" questioning and answering each other and finally going hand in hand to the "people" is an intriguing metaphor for the friendship and spiritual connection between the Young China Association and the New Man Society.

In an open letter to Zeng Muhan, leader of the Paris branch of the Young China Association, entitled "Shaonian zhongguo yu zongjiao wenti" (The Young China Association and the Issue of Religion),[96] Tian Han openly advocated his Catholic friend Zhang Difei's membership application. Zhang, who played the male doctor in "Spiritual Light," occupied an important place in Tian's debate with other Young China Association members on the issue of religion. Calling himself not a Christian but a pantheist,[97] Tian linked great literature directly to religious beliefs, naming Goethe, Tolstoy, and others as examples of how religion engenders great writers and philosophers, very much in the style of Whitman's deism.[98]

The idea that religion was a constituent in the construction of the modern

Chinese national culture challenges many of our assumptions about both religiosity and national culture in modern China. After the "traditional" Chinese ethnic identity was rejected as antithetical to social and political progressivism, Christianity, both because of and in spite of its foreignness, offered an alternative source of ideas and icons. Under the influence of the YMCA's social gospel, Tian and other avant-gardists found in Christianity the crucial linking term between romanticism and socialism.

From "Spiritual Light" to "The Ghost of the Piano" to "Before Lunch"

The shift from spiritual to material concerns, as exemplified by the changing titles of Tian Han's Tokyo plays, from "Spiritual Light" to *Piyaluo zhigui* ("The Ghost of the Piano," 1922), to *Wufan zhiqian* ("Before Lunch," 1922), seems to suggest a gradual shift from a more idealistic visionary socialism to a more economically and politically grounded socialism. "The Ghost of the Piano" is set in Changsha in contemporary times (January 1922), the location most likely to appeal to the especially large number of Hunanese students in the audience. It concerns Zhujun,[99] "Ms. Bamboo," the eldest daughter of a capitalist, who, out of her concern for the suffering workers, decides to sell all her family's wealth and join the working class. The parents—representing authority figures carrying the values of the past and the status quo—are tellingly absent in this play, leaving three sisters to act as independent-minded individuals. The female Faust of "Spiritual Light" here takes on three incarnations as "Ms. Bamboo," the politically conscious elder sister, "Ms. Orchid," the least "conscious" middle one, and "Ms. Plum," the naive but compassionate youngest.[100] Here Tian Han subverts these symbols' traditional gendered usage of describing male intellectual qualities, and uses them instead to capture the spirit of his female characters.

The ultraromantic impulse to transgress class barriers and the trope of using three sisters as representatives of different political orientations would become lasting features of Tian Han's dramatic style. More important, the play marks a radical turn from the Christian-inspired social salvation in "Spiritual Light." Here Meili's *aspiration* to help the downtrodden is actualized in the elder sister's complete rejection of private property, resulting in her selling their beloved piano, a material symbol of their exploitation of the female cotton factory workers, and finally joining the working class and living communally with them.

But rather than seeing the play as shifting the focus from Christianity to socialist activism, it may be more accurate to reconceive it as in fact discovering an inherent linkage between them—in a daring artistic expression of their mutual socialist obsession with "going to the people." For Tian Han, the elder sister's embrace of the female workers in "The Ghost of the Piano" is the ultimate romantic gesture of reaching out to the underprivileged gender and class. Moreover, in this gesture, key Christian teachings, such as "blessed are the poor," converge with the revolutionary edict to "go to the people." As romanticism had been intimately connected to socialism in the Chinese imagination since the French Revolution and, more urgently, since the Russian Revolution, it was close to the heart of the young activist Tian.

In such an environment, Tian Han found *Ballads of Socialism*, Edith Nesbit's poetry collection, "extremely powerful and extremely meaningful" (*jiyouli jiyouwei*). Highlighting the socialist background of the author, he emphasized that the Fabian Society in London had published the volume.[101] His portrayal of the elder sister in "The Ghost of the Piano" indeed recalled the work of another Fabian, George Bernard Shaw, whose protagonist in *An Unsocial Socialist* (1883) "tried to drop out of bourgeois society and live in the proletarian manner, [but] soon abandoned the experiment as a hopeless sham."[102] Notably, Tian's own early-twentieth-century experiment amplified the romantic elements of this scenario without engaging with the critique.

A good summation of Tian Han's Tokyo sojourn can be found in a third play, "Before Lunch," which he wrote and staged in June 1922 before leaving Tokyo for Shanghai.[103] Again using three sisters to embody three alternative attitudes toward the problems facing China at the time, Tian Han makes the elder sister a firm believer in Christianity (a la Tolstoyan nonresistance), the second sister a political activist (a factory worker who is killed during a strike), and the third a politically uninformed young girl. In the trajectory from "Spiritual Light" through "The Ghost of the Piano" to "Before Lunch," the religiosity so central to the female Faust story finally engenders radical political action in the last play. Three sisters, all female factory workers rather than three daughters of a capitalist, emerge as the protagonists of the last play. Through these three working women, Tian Han's 1919 call for "a women's movement of the fourth class" found its concrete embodiments. The death of the middle sister in the play symbolically shatters the fragile Christianity of the elder sister, who joins hands with the younger, following the steps of the martyr into political activism. Such a plot seems to suggest that Tian Han's own dalliance with Christian socialism has (already!) given way to a more secularized socialism. Had Tian Han written this play ten years later, around the time he joined the CCP in 1932, this plot may not have seemed remarkable at all, as we can conveniently read it as "propaganda," that is, as a work of art with an agenda, specifically to recommend a course of action. But given that the timing was 1922 and the location Tokyo, when Tian Han's ideological affiliation was not at all settled, these early experiments reveal the dynamic currents connecting spirituality, performance, and politics before they became established categories in the historiography of modern China.

Avant-Garde Encounters through Popular Media

In the previous section we followed Tian Han's exploration of the imagery and ideation of light into its spiritual, romantic, and socialist associations. But the passage from his diary with which we began this chapter signaled the inseparability for Tian Han of metaphoric or spiritual light and literal electric illumination, and indeed of natural and man-made illumination. And so let us imagine for a moment the peculiarly modern magic permeating Tian Han's post–World War I moment in Tokyo, the novel glamour of light and sound revealed as energy traveling through electrical transmissions, wired communication and wireless telegraph, radio, recordings, and the silver screen. We discover that, parallel to the psychic liberation of Faustian romanticism and Christian utopianism, other quite practical forms of liberation were emerging out of technology and new media. The streetcars of Toyko meant freedom of movement, the electric lights of Tokyo meant temporal freedom (the novelty of nocturnal urban street life), and telegraph and radio technology meant freedom of communication—all of which liberated a generation of avant-garde artists to imagine a borderless international community.

Hollywood Melodrama

Yet another form of liberation was propagated by the light and shadow on the silver screen in interwar Japan, namely, disruptions of the gender and class status quo. At the height of its international commercial presence during and after World War I, Hollywood imports had also helped to foster a progressive tendency in the discourse of gender and class in East Asia. Shortly after his arrival in Tokyo, Tian Han already ventured east to the sixth section of the Asakusa district, where a Hollywood melodrama, *Shoes* (1916, starring Mary MacLaren),[104] was screened, right after its American premiere.

In this film, a poor working girl is forced to support her whole family and cannot even afford a pair of much-needed work shoes. The joining of the traditionally sentimental feminine image with the issue of the laboring poor was then translated into the shockingly new medium of film. It produced magic for Tian Han. More than ten years later, when writing in Shanghai amid his independent filmmaking endeavors, Tian Han recalled nostalgically this seminal first encounter. He wrote about the large caption "Ah" issuing from the poor girl's mouth on the silent screen, each word progressively larger, while she was painfully trying to pull a nail out of her bare foot.[105]

Linguistically, Hollywood film, in particular, provided easier access to the world of fantasy and reality for Tian Han than did other media. This might also explain why it would take him one more year to catch up with newspaper serializations of popular love stories and yet another year to appreciate performances of modern drama on the Japanese stage. At the time, Japanese *benshi* performers recounted the storyline in Japanese for the benefit of the audience of silent films.[106] Given Tian Han's beginner's knowledge of written English and inadequate understanding of spoken Japanese during his first year in Tokyo,[107] watching the silent features with English subtitles supplemented with Japanese explanations (*setsumei*) was in fact easier than watching them only in English or Japanese. Tian Han claimed to have watched more than a hundred films in Tokyo. These moviegoing experiences most likely also served as pedagogical tools for the young Chinese man learning Japanese and English, as the two languages helped to make each other comprehensible. Similarly, newspapers and popular magazines, especially the widely popular autobiographical love stories such as Kume Masao's *Hotaru gusa* (Firefly Grass), serialized daily in 1917, about his love for the daughter of his famed teacher Natsume Soseki,[108] functioned as a tool for both language learning and the sentimental education of the young Chinese.

Becoming a "cinema fan" during his first year in Tokyo, the eighteen-year-old Chinese was exposed to moving images made possible by electric lights and shadows, namely, cinema, for the first time in his life. This cinematic exposure also introduced him to female sexuality, as well as the social exploration of underprivileged gender and class, if only on the silent screen. The cinematic encounter with *Shoes*, in particular, revived Tian Han's childhood memories of poverty in his native Hunan countryside. He vowed to donate half of his savings in a Japanese bank to the poor girl in the film.[109] Not until he later saw the same actress transformed into a queen in another film did he realize his comical confusion and conflation of reality and fantasy.

This initial confusion between life and art had a deep impact on the young man's coming of age both as an artist and as an activist. The film provided stimulus to and helped consolidate Tian Han's two lifelong obsessions: "creating the new woman" and "going to the people." Through the figure of the poor girl who traded her virginity for a pair of shoes, Tian Han vicariously tasted the bitter fruits of the physical sufferings of the underprivileged gender and class in a capitalist society. His impulse to donate half of his money to the beauty in the film was precisely, if unconsciously, a gesture toward realizing his double aim of restoring the "authentic" woman and the "pure" folk to their "original" state.

The fact that Tian didn't fully *perceive* real suffering in the real world around him until he encountered its reification onscreen says much about the artist he was to become. He would go on to exploit the power of art to create a more intimate human connection in art than in actual life. His own involvement in and surrender to the fictional world, the re-presented world, suggested art as the way we learn to feel. He also learned that the feelings aroused by art can lead us back to the real world in action (e.g., giving money to the poor girl for shoes).

German Expressionism with a Hollywood Twist

The popularity of Hollywood in Tokyo does not suggest a monolithic film scene. With the premiere in May 1921 of *The Cabinet of Dr. Caligari,* now considered a classic of German expressionist film, Tokyo acquired its own "moments of Caligari."[110] It has been suggested that the German film industry in the 1920s taught Hollywood how to organize and control film production within the studio, and *Caligari* was an early example of this technical rationalization. The film has all the elements of a popular Hollywood narrative, but its expressionist stage setting, costumes, and eclectic acting style has long earned it a reputation as one of the first art films in the world, making it a case study of the dialectical relation between "mass culture" and "high culture."[111]

Tian Han watched the film in the company of the visiting Guo Moruo, cocontributor to their popular letter collection *Kleeblatt,* in June 1921 in a new-style cinema, Shinseikan, located in Kanda. These two young Chinese men came to their encounter with the simultaneously avant-gardist and conventional storytelling of the *Caligari* film from a cultural background of Chinese local opera, puppet theater, and popular storytelling, where the importance of the storyteller-narrator had long been appreciated. Moreover, they were living in a Japan still permeated with the *shitamachi* spirit of Edo urban entertainment, which likewise prepared them to appreciate the importance of the narrator in the film. The parallels between German expressionism and Chinese and Japanese storytelling traditions suggest the possibility of communicating through stylized aesthetics across cultures and time.

The narrator of the German film is a college student who relates the blood-chilling serial murder case in which he became entangled. He discovers that the killer is a phantomlike somnambulist controlled by Dr. Caligari, a mad scientist. The end of the film discloses that the narrator is in fact a paranoid patient, while Dr. Caligari is in fact the head of the institution where the student is being treated. In short, the entire story is revealed as the hallucination of a mental patient.[112]

At the margins of both commercial mass culture and high modernism, *Caligari* articulates the complex interpenetration of these twin responses to the commodification of capitalism. Tian Han's generation of post–World War I artists and activists was nurtured in just such a cultural milieu: a vibrant field of cultural production at the intersection of the "high" and the "low" and between the avant-garde and the popular. Tian Han's 1921 encounter with the German expressionist *Caligari,* again a silent film with simultaneous *setsumei* by Japanese *benshi* performers, nonetheless differs in important ways from his 1916 first exposure to the Hollywood melodrama *Shoes.* If his very first cinematic exposure at age eighteen introduced him to female sexuality and feminine subjugation in a capitalist society, his encounter with *Caligari* a few years later demonstrated a more sensitive approach to the cinematic form itself. Amid his independent filmmaking endeavors in Shanghai throughout 1926 and 1927, Tian Han recalled seeing *Caligari* as one of his most memorable visual encounters in Tokyo. Quoting from reviews written by the Japanese modernist writers Tanizaki Jun'chirō and Satō Haruo, Tian Han strongly emphasized the dreamlike quality of the film.[113] Inspired by Tanizaki's film scenario *Jasei no in* (The Lust of the Serpent), created and made into a silent film under the possible influence of *Caligari,* Tian conceived a film story featuring the psychological hallucination of a male narrator and his "spring dream" involving a modern femme fatale.[114]

The Tokyo showing of *Caligari* was itself a sensational event in the history of Japanese filmmaking. Thomas Kurihara (Kurihara Kisaburo), a Japanese actor-director returned from Hollywood and a friend of Tian Han's, had just begun shooting Tanizaki's scenario *Jasei no in* when *Caligari* premiered in Tokyo.[115] *Caligari* provided Tanizaki with a timely stimulus for producing an adaptation of the White Snake legend from the Chinese folk tradition (by way of Ueda Akinari's Japanese adaptation), which Tian Han would rework as a Peking Opera piece decades later. A Japanese film scholar contemporary to Tian commented on the connection between *Jasei no in* and *Caligari:* "The grotesque film about the snake-woman haunting a man and his wife can be seen as the Japanese reproduction of the weird German cinema."[116] Although Tian Han embraced Tanizaki's and Sato's reviews focusing on the "art film" quality of *Caligari,* in reality the Japanese practice of *benshi* live narration accompanying silent films had the effect of popularizing the formal experiments of the avant-garde film and bringing it into the realm of commercial popular culture. This joining together of the avant-garde and the popular recurs, as we shall see, in Tian Han's reworking of the White Snake story onscreen and onstage in the ensuing decades.

Western Theater, Japanese Stage

The dynamic relationship between the avant-garde and the popular can be further explored through Tian Han's encounter with Western theater on the Japanese stage now illuminated with electric lighting, the first occasion of which was probably William Shakespeare's *The Merchant of Venice,* performed in Japanese by Kamiyama Sōjin and Yamakawa Uraji in Yūrakuza in June 1918.[117] The playbill also featured August Strindberg's one-act play translated as *Sacrifice* by Osanai Kaoru,[118] likely Tian's first exposure to the Swedish playwright and the strong-willed female religious subjects portrayed in his plays. Both Kamiyama and Yamakawa were members of the Modern Theater Association (Kindaigeki Kyōkai) in Tokyo at the time, and Kamiyama later enjoyed a prolific career in Hollywood from the mid-1920s to the 1950s, as he carried his Tokyo stage experiments to the United States.[119]

In the pivotal year 1918, theater became the site of linguistic and sentimental education for this young Chinese in Tokyo. Tian Han's most memorable encounter with modern Western drama was watching *Die versunkene Glocke* (The Sunken Bell) by Gerhart Hauptmann,[120] a symbolic play about a master bell maker and his struggle as an artist searching for the perfect-sounding bell. In *The Social Significance of Modern Drama,* Emma Goodman comments on the play as follows.

> "The Sunken Bell" is a fairy tale in its poetic beauty and glow of radiant color. But stripped of the legendary and symbolic, it is the life story of every seeker for truth, of the restless spirit of rebellion ever striving onward, ever reaching out toward the sun-tipped mountain, ever yearning for a new-born light.[121]

The image of a restless seeker ever striving for a newborn light recalls the image of Faust as reenacted in the 1920 performance of "Spiritual Light." Adapted in Japanese and directed by Shimamura Hōgetsu, himself a student of naturalism at Berlin University,[122] *The Sunken Bell* struck a sensitive emotional chord in Tian Han, an aspiring young artist who was searching for the magic path into the world of art and fantasy illuminated by spiritual and electric light. The motto of the play, "Open the windows, Light and God stream in,"[123] may have inspired Tian Han's early plays, including "Spiritual Light." Music played an important role in fostering the romantic, mythical, and spiritual milieus of the forest in the play. The illusive and illustrative sound of the perfect bell, an artistic ideal worth searching for at the cost of one's own life, would become a central trope in Tian Han's experiments on stage and screen in the years to come, as heard in the opening bell in "Spiritual Light" in 1920.

The Sunken Bell's ultimate attraction for Tian Han at the time, however, was the already legendary Japanese actress Matsui Sumako,[124] who played the forest spirit Rautendelein. Sumako, with her creative rendering of some of the most memorable heroines on the Japanese modern stage, including Katusha, Carmen, and most importantly Salome, not only challenged the still widespread practice of male impersonation but, in putting her femininity and sexuality on public display, made possible a concrete link between the stage persona and the real life "modern girl" (*moga* in Japanese).

As we shall see, Salome became a potent trope in Tian Han's oeuvre. And, indeed, she was the ultimate embodiment of an emerging modern female sexuality in the first decades of twentieth century, on the Tokyo stage as elsewhere.[125] Her sexually charged "Dance of the Seven Veils," offered in exchange for her object of desire, John the Baptist's head, was rendered vividly by Oscar Wilde in his notorious play and then popularized by Maud Allen in Vienna around the turn of the twentieth century. Tian Han would translate the play into the Chinese vernacular in 1920. Later, provoked by Hollywood's rendering of Wilde's *Salome* and revisiting his encounter with Sumako in Tokyo, he would put *Salome* onstage in Shanghai in 1929. Tian's staging of *Salome* and *Carmen* after being exposed to Japanese adaptations of the plays in Tokyo and watching Hol-

Matsui Sumako as the forest spirit in "The Sunken Bell" (September 6, 1918, Tokyo), in Tanaka Eizō, *Meiji Taishō Shingekishi Shiryō* (Tokyo: Engeki Shuppansha, 1964).

lywood renditions of the classics in Shanghai attests to the power of popular media in fostering avant-garde experiments.

The actress Sumako was significant to Tian Han, apart from her stage roles, as the lover of playwright and director Shimamura Hōgetsu. When Matsui Sumako committed suicide following Shimamura's death due to illness, their relationship crystallized in a real-life romantic conflation of art, love, and death reminiscent of both *The Sunken Bell* and *Salome*. For Tian Han, Matsui Sumako, the interpreter of both Hauptmann's Rautendelein and Wilde's Salome onstage and enactor of a love suicide in real life, brought the union of art and love into a higher level of ecstasy and purification through death, both on- and offstage. The "sexuality of death," the ultimate work of art in the artistic universe of Gerhart Hauptmann, Oscar Wilde, Maurice Maeterlinck, and August Strindberg, would then be introduced into the Chinese-speaking world by Tian Han and his like-minded contemporaries from the early 1920s onward.[126]

Art and Social Movements: Cross-Illuminations

Tian Han's encounter with the archetypal poor virgin in the Hollywood melodrama *Shoes*—an experience that was so emotionally powerful as to blur for him the distinction between reality and illusion—foregrounded the ethical function of art. He did not need Hollywood in particular and commercial popular media in general to teach him about poverty; his personal experience in his hometown had taught him about the suffering of the poor. Yet the physical suffering of the poor virgin on the silent screen—poverty mediated by and transmuted into artistic representation and illuminated by the electric light and shadow that is the medium of cinema—had an immediate emotional impact on the young student that the real life poverty he witnessed had not, thus engendering a renewed sense of political activism through identification with the subaltern.

Consistent with his emphasis on spiritual salvation in "Spiritual Light," Tian Han had announced his role in championing a new and fresh spiritual realm for China in a 1919 essay-poem entitled "Meiyu" (Rainy Season). Undertaking a "self-analysis in the spirit of Tolstoy," Tian paints a Faustian self-portrait that also anticipates the image of the female protagonist Meili in "Spiritual Light."

> I feel that I have strong self-confidence,
> More *romantic* elements than *realistic* ones.

> It would be extremely easy for me to turn toward evil,
> But I also have extremely strong "creative and transformative power."[127]
>
> . . . . . .
>
> Although I am not accustomed to earthly affairs, I suffered from *Fin-de-siècle* [malaise], and I experienced *Weltschmerz,* at the "dawn between the death of the old Deity and the birth of the new one," I am diligently searching! Searching! Searching for the wonderland of *Neo-Romantism* [*sic*]! [128]

Tian Han's extensive use of foreign phrases here merits close attention. He reaches out for, within one sentence, French, German, and English words, all deeply bathed in romantic self-consciousness, as if he cannot find the terms he needs in Chinese.[129] Tian's very language exhibits the spirit of internationalism and cosmopolitanism so characteristic of the interwar international avant-garde. One wonders if this particular romantic pose—as sensitive sufferer—is actually new in Chinese literature. Is there a prototype/precedent for this sort of character in China? Is he using foreign words precisely because there is no such precedent? Or is he merely exoticizing for dramatic effect? Or to borrow sophistication? As when an English speaker uses French phrases. Or to borrow gravity, as when English speakers use German?

Tian Han had been enchanted by Kume Masao's confessional love stories and regarded them as a bible for those suffering Chinese Werthers around him in Tokyo—those young Chinese students who adopted the persona of Goethe's Werther to dramatize themselves as melancholic and tragic lovers with copious tears and a suicidal complex. Tian was also under the spell of Kunikida Doppo's "poetic fever" as expressed in Doppo's personal journal, *Azamukazaru no ki* (*Buqi riji,* or "An Honest Diary").[130] Such a confessional mode of writing was influenced by the popularity of the *Confessions of Jean-Jacques Rousseau* and Tolstoyan religion in Tokyo to render writing a performative act through which an imaginary self is being constructed and contested.[131] In the end, Tian's rather positive self-analysis presents a self-consciously Faustian persona: a romantic, creative young man, endowed with transformative power, diligently searching for the world of fantasy, ecstasy, and the sublime. The obsession with "reformation" and "transformation," as manifested in the repetitive emphasis on self- and societal renewal, emerge as key motifs in this self-promotion in the guise of self-exposure, packaged in the form of a miniature play with an arresting spiritual echo.

Tian Han was not alone in seeking to link literary and social movements and in pointing out the complicated relationship between the intellectual and the people, and the avant-garde and the popular. He was, nonetheless, one of the earliest Chinese avant-gardists to venture into the connection between the arts and politics with a focus on the democratic potential in both spheres. He was a firm believer in the power of spiritual, as well as technical, enlightenment. In critiquing the oppressive nature of classicism and capitalism, his sources of inspiration ranged from Kuriyagawa Hakuson and Shirotori Seigo to Karl Marx. A prominent liberal critic and scholar of English literature at the time, whose reputation was obscured in Japan after his untimely death, Kuriyagawa came to posthumous fame in China with Lu Xun's 1924 translation of his *Kumon no shōchō* (*Kumen de xiangzheng*, "Symbols of Agony," 1921) and *Zōge no tō o dete* (*Chule xiangya zhita*, "Outside the Ivory Tower," 1920). Writing in Tokyo before the publication of both works, Tian Han drove home the same spirit of social criticism already so prominent in Kuriyagawa's popular lectures on modern literature. Tian would soon visit Kuriyagawa in Kyoto to discuss their mutual interest in stepping outside the "ivory tower" and onto the "crossroads."[132] He had also read the poet Shirotori Seigo's freshly published *Minshuteki bungei no senku* (Vanguards of Democratic Literature), which introduced Walt Whitman as a "commoner's poet" (*heimin shijin, pingmin shiren*) and used this to reflect on the conservative nature of classicism. Finally, Tian Han used Karl Marx's statement "workers are organized machines" to supply the link between classicism and capitalism, as both the poet and the laborer were subjugated to a mechanized convention under the two oppressive systems.

On the other hand, romanticism, corresponding to democracy in Tian's formula, presented "the appreciation of that which is novel and beautiful; positive and rebellious emotions; anti-formalism in grammar and rhetoric; an unbounded free spirit in poetics."[133] Tian Han considered all these democratic elements conducive to the young thinkers, writers, artists, and social activists of a "young China" represented by the Young China Association. More important, the power of romanticism could prompt bourgeois intellectuals to "betray their class interest in service of the people." However, Tian already considered the people's movement led by intellectuals to be "lukewarm, conciliatory, and incomplete" in 1920, a position that will be taken up by Trotsky and Mao in different historical contexts in the ensuing decades. Karl Marx again came to the rescue. His *Das Kapital*, "the laborers' Bible," provided a way out and introduced "the fourth class," the proletariat, as vanguards of the people and leaders of the revolution.[134] Once again a halo was placed on the heads of the secular-minded moderns in order to propagate Marxist ideology as a new spiritual light for the people. However, the Faustian split between theory and practice and the irony that not many laborers had read Marx remain thorny spots in this rosy picture.

Tian Han clarified his proposed connection between neoromanticism and social democracy, what he considered the highest stages of spiritual and social illuminations, in a letter to his onetime Tokyo classmate Huang Rikui, linking "self" with "the world."

> So-called neoromanticism is an attempt to peek into (*kuipo*) the unseen spiritual world through the material world that is seen, and to probe (*tanzhi*) the world beyond the senses through the world that can be touched by the senses . . . [while] for me [because] primitive romanticism focuses on intuition, on subjectivity, on sentiments, it is like the female sex; and [because] extreme naturalism focuses on research, on being objective, on knowledge, it is like the male sex. Neoromanticism penetrates the world of the soul through the world of the flesh, and it captures eternity in a flash of a moment. [135]

At the time of his receipt of Tian's letter, Huang Rikui had returned from Tokyo as one of the thousands of Chinese students protesting against the "twenty-one demands" and enrolled in Peking University. Under Li Dazhao and Chen Duxiu's tutelage, Huang actively participated in the May Fourth student demonstrations in 1919 and took part in the founding of the Marxist Study Group of Peking University in March 1920.[136] Although Tian Han did participate in protests in front of the Chinese consulate in Tokyo, he did not join the protesting students who left Japan for China in 1918. Neither did he join the Marxist Study Group, as Huang did, when the letter was written in 1920. At the time, he was an active member of the Young China Association whose members' political persuasions were most wide ranging. His intellectual interests encompassed Christianity, romanticism, socialism, anarchism, and Marxism—and did not allow him to settle down with any one of them. He was more concerned with synthesizing and communicating between the body and the mind, between materiality and spirituality, and between art and politics.

One can read Tian Han's characterization of what he calls "neoromanticism" on multiple levels. The imagery he presents here is rather sexually suggestive, and one could even argue misogynist. The first verb, *kuipo,* combines voyeuristic peeking with its penetrating result, and the second verb, *tanzhi*, evokes the process of knowing through physical contact. However, the object that is penetrated and touched here is not the female body; rather, it is the elusive "world of the spirit" (*ling de shijie*) and "the world beyond the senses" (*chao ganjue de shijie*). Tian Han seems to be suggesting that there exists a material path to spiritual salvation, and he is, or so he claims, creating an androgynous neoromanticism out of a gendered division of labor between romanticism and naturalism.

The illuminated physical and mental landscapes of Tokyo find a strong echo in the final line—"eternity in a flash of a moment" (*chana*, from the Sanskrit word *ksana*)—thus reinforcing the linkage between the material present that can be seen and the eternal spiritual truth that is unseen, as embodied in Buddhist teachings as well as William Blake's poetry.[137] It is notable that Blake would indeed emerge as a strong spiritual influence in Tian Han's Shanghai experiments. The androgynous figure Tian paints here further brings to mind the bodhisattva Guanyin, who can be considered as a figure representing both male and female powers of reproduction. The rejection of Confucianism and the pursuit of spiritual modernity opened the door to philosophical Buddhism.[138] The new spiritual realm Tian Han was hoping to usher in around the year 1920 further metamorphosed into a realm charged with androgynous charm simultaneously illuminated by the halos of Christianity and Buddhism, socialism and Marxism, and neoromantic and electrically lit stage and screen performances.

As we have seen, Tian Han came to embrace a social democracy deeply infused with a sense of spiritual salvation in the early 1920s. His criticisms of the anti-Christian trends in China grew out of his understanding that a romanticized form of Christian socialism offered a means of political mobilization. One could certainly argue that Tian Han was a religious instrumentalist in that he used religion as a means to promote social and political agendas. Willard Wolfe, on the other hand, cites Gustav Le Bon to argue for the religiosity of socialism itself, that it was "peculiarly well suited to the needs of nineteenth-century skeptics" who were "in need of a secular faith" following the Darwinian revolution. In Wolfe's words, socialism promised "a new, regenerated 'moral world' on earth to compensate for the loss of the heaven," thus "uniting religious and social reconstruction within a single system of belief."[139]

Conclusion

Tian Han's generation of early-twentieth-century avant-gardes fostered a new spirituality synthesizing traditional systems of belief and modern political activism. Performance became a trope in which role-playing, dialogue, movement, rehearsal, and staging took on social and political significance. Driven by a desire to communicate through words and bodily movements, to bridge the gap between idealism and action, the young artists and activists followed the Faustian search for meaning in early-twentieth-century China and Japan with an acute sense of gender and class divisions. However, in the early 1920s in Tokyo, it was not Marxism but the Faustian search for meaning and transcendence, encompassing Christianity, neoromanticism, and social democracy, that formed a new trinity of spirituality, art, and politics. The spirituality of performance and politics, and a relentless search for a new idealism, remained at the center of such early-twentieth-century avant-gardist pursuits.

Tian Han left Tokyo for Shanghai in the summer of 1922 with a pregnant Yi Shuyu, having moved together with his fiancée in December 1920 after the devastating news of his uncle's (her father's) assassination by a Hunanese warlord.[140] Only a year after Tian's return to China, the Great Kantō Earthquake would wipe away almost all physical traces of the illuminated landscape of Tokyo modernity. Kuriyagawa Hakuson, the writer with whom Tian Han discussed their mutual desire to move from "ivory tower" to "crossroads" in Kyoto in 1920, had relocated to Tokyo and died when a tsunami destroyed his cottage by the seashore of Kamakura during the earthquake.[141] Tanizaki Jun'ichirō, whose writing on film and theater had inspired Tian Han in Tokyo, survived the quake but relocated from Tokyo to West Japan for good. Tanizaki would visit Shanghai in 1926 and serve as an attentive host for Tian Han in Kyoto and Osaka during Tian's only return visit to Japan in 1927.[142] A markedly different world, one departing from the pre-earthquake, Tokyo-centered spiritual, artistic, and political experiments and leading to a major intellectual and political shift in modern East Asia, would arise from the rubble of the earthquake and ashes of the ensuing fire.

CHAPTER TWO

The Night and Fire of Shanghai

He intentionally walked toward places with few people and dim lights, and was honored by the presence of many street-walking sisters . . .

Your slim shadow,
are you for sale in the market of human flesh;
Or are you a suffering soul,
in the evil metropolis?
Ah, a suffering soul by the roadside!
no need to stand still in the darkness.
In the middle of the crossroad,
there is no sign of that bloody-red traffic light.

He sang this song to them, feeling tipsy. One of the women made fun of him with another, "crazy drunkard!" He merrily took the title and was about to jaywalk from Boyong Hospital to the side of the Great World, when a policeman suddenly flashed that bloody-red light towards Kehan. His eyes could hardly open, reminding him of his shouting out "Camera!" for a few consecutive nights on his movie set. He fantasized about replacing the traffic lights in the middle of the crossroads with carbon lights, transforming policemen into cameramen, and shooting the comings and goings of the Shanghainese as films. Wouldn't that be great?[1]

Kehan, the autobiographical male protagonist of Tian Han's novella *Shanghai,* is, like his creator, at the center of an artistic network, where frequenting the cinema, concerts, the Uchiyama Bookstore, all-night cafés, and restaurants on Si Malu is key to his identity and lifestyle as a Shanghai filmmaker.

Kehan's encounter with the group of streetwalking prostitutes occurs after he tipsily emerges from a restaurant to stroll into the darkness of the Shanghai night. "That bloody-red traffic light" appears twice in the scene, conjuring up an image of fire piercing the dark, cold night. Included in the section titled "A Night of Fantasy" in the novella, Kehan's lamentation on the "evil metropolis" is inseparable from his fascination with the slim shadows and red lights at the crossroads.

The opening quote highlights Tian Han's continuous concern with the underprivileged gender and class, the ambiguous identity of the modern artist, and the centrality of the film genre and the urban locale. The central imagery of "light" follows him from Tokyo to Shanghai, this time taking shape in the "bloody-red traffic light" and the "carbon lights" on a movie set and functions both as a realistic reference to a well-policed Shanghai and an imaginative allusion to the burgeoning film industry. The romanticized and spiritualized city Tian Han saw through rose-colored glasses in Tokyo was transformed into a more naturalistic and sordid cityscape in Shanghai. Encoded in this new imagery of light, one finds both the democratic power of the new art form of film and the oppressive control of the modern state. In this night of fantasy, the utopian and dystopian converge in Shanghai.

This chapter approaches Shanghai from the early 1920s to the late 1930s, as Tian Han did, through the filter of his Tokyo experience. It highlights Shanghai's dual role as mediating between, on the one hand, China and Japan, and, on the other, provincial China and its urban centers. The visiting Japanese found in Tian Han and Shanghai a magic formula to satisfy a dual desire: to preserve a tradition on the brink of disappearance and to capture an emerging modernity at the moment of its birth. Tian Han's brief but intense visit to Japan in 1927 at once divided and united "aesthetic" and "proletarian" writers in Tokyo. His Tokyo radicalism and Shanghai experimentation challenged the widely accepted rhetoric of radical conversion, a move from "aesthetic" school to the "proletarian" camp among Chinese intellectuals around the year 1930.

From early on in his career, Tian Han had favored the motifs of "night" and "fire" as symbolic markers in his exploration of the dialectics between self and world, art and revolution, and aesthetic and proletarian. In 1920 Tian wrote two intriguing poems in Tokyo, "Night" and "Fire," that best capture the conflicting symbolisms later materialized in Shanghai. "Night" marshals "the world of rhythm" (*xuanlü de shijie*) and "the silent sea" (*chenmo de dahai*) in the darkness to attempt an audio and visual representation of his complex range of sentiments (*qingxu*).[2] "Fire" connotes "the narrow rosy road, the ivory tower, the real, the mythical, the ephemeral, and the eternal."[3] The romantic rainbow light of Tokyo seemed to split and splinter into the complex symbolic universe of Shanghai where the melancholic met the celebratory, hatred met laughter, the sordid met the sublime, and the fire met the night. These collisions quickly threw the young artist into a state of confusion. In the mirror of the fire piercing the dark night, he could not distinguish himself from his surroundings. The ultimate remedy will have to come from the "artistic light" (*yishu de guangming*) of the "rosy fire" and the "ivory fire," which combines art with its revolutionary potential to illuminate the lingering darkness.

The epigraph to the novella *Shanghai* pointedly betrays Tian Han's alienation from Shanghai through an ironic invocation of the ideal city.

> JERUSALEM, my happy home,
> When shall I come to thee?
> When shall my sorrows have an end,
> Thy joys when shall I see?
>
> "SONG OF MARY THE MOTHER OF CHRIST"[4]

Veiled behind this reference to a sixteenth-century English hymn is Tian Han's own spiritual longing for Changsha, his ancestral home in the central southern Chinese province of Hunan, and for Tokyo, the Japanese capital and his second and spiritual home. Tian Han, like Kehan in the story, returned from Tokyo to settle in Shanghai from the early 1920s to the late 1930s. The great earthquake and ensuing fire of 1923 erased the physical traces of Tokyo modernity, but they could not eradicate the profound impact of the spiritual, artistic, and political experiments in interwar Japan. Rather than a "happy home" or a spiritual Jerusalem, Shanghai was for Tian Han a meeting place at the crossroads, always in transit and flux. It was a giant film set, one big café at night, and a cultural laboratory, where human dramas and artistic experiments were carried out amid food, wine, enchanting women, stimulating conversations, song, and dance.

The artificial and foreign qualities of the film set, the Western-style café, and the experimentalist lab vividly articulate the cultural location of Shanghai, for Tian Han at the time, as a self-contained world of cosmopolitan imagination, and as such interchangeable with Tokyo, Paris, London, and New York City. Indeed, Tian Han must have deeply felt such an interchangeability when he set his 1922 play *Kafeidian zhi yiye* (A Night in a Café) in "a certain metropolis," leaving the readers and audiences to figure out whether the story takes place in Tokyo (where the play was written), Shanghai (where it was published and later performed), Changsha (the capital of Tian Han's home province of Hunan), or any of the other metropolises that so fascinated him at the time (Paris, London, New York). In this sense, Shanghai was for him less a particularized place than it was the embodied idea of cosmopolitanism itself.

But among all these interchangeable metropolises, the one that had the most pervasive and persistent influence on Tian Han during the early years of his stay in Shanghai was unquestionably Tokyo. Although he had physically moved back to this rising Chinese metropolis soon after the publication of "A Night in the Café" in the summer of 1922, Tokyo still dominated his spiritual, artistic, and political imagination. The cultural milieu of Tokyo, as an illuminated landscape encompassing a wide range of international avant-gardism, was determinative in Tian Han's mentality and practice as a modern artist and activist in Shanghai. Indeed, Shanghai's importance for Tian Han was in large part because it provided the necessary distance (neither too close nor too far) to serve as a vantage point from which to process his Tokyo experience. It became an ideal locale in which to consolidate his cultural and political ties with Japanese intellectuals in particular and the interwar international avant-garde in general.

Shanghai Night: Connecting Japan and China

Just as Tokyo played an important cultural and geopolitical role at the post–World War I moment, Shanghai functioned as a crucial meeting ground for competing aesthetic and political forces in the late 1920s. In fact Shanghai had long served as the window into China for the Japanese situated in the Sinosphere, a China-centered regional order and sphere of influence, which, according to Joshua A. Fogel, began to crumble in the Meiji period. According to Fogel, for the last three decades of the nineteenth century, the Sinosphere remained "as a lingering recollection," and by the time of the Sino-Japanese War of 1894–95, even the memory of the Sinosphere "had been stamped out."[5]

However, in this late-nineteenth-century transition from a China-centered regional order to a Japan-centered one, intellectual and cultural changes often lagged behind institutional ones. Institutionally, Meiji Japan abolished the "unequal treaties" with the Western powers in less than three decades and embarked on modern nation building, while Qing China would not be replaced with a weak Republic until the 1910s and the unequal treaties would only be completely abolished in the 1940s.[6] In practice Sino-Japanese cultural exchanges appeared much more uneven than those institutional changes, and the power of the Sinosphere seemed to die hard.[7] Liu Jianhui (Ryū Kenki), a Chinese scholar working in Japan, claims that Shanghai facilitated a "modern" awakening for many Japanese intellectuals in the latter half of the nineteenth century and the early decades of the twentieth.[8] Liu's argument might seem paradoxical given Tokyo's power to attract intellectuals from China, Korea, and the rest of Asia and Japan's role as the first "modernized" Asian nation after the Meiji reforms of 1868. However, it hits upon a key issue in the fostering of Shanghai cosmopolitanism, especially when the 1923 earthquake and ensuing fire destroyed most of the Tokyo metropolitan area. Many Taishō intellectuals were said to be "going back to tradition" by relocating to Kansai, in the west of Japan. Tanizaki Jun'ichirō was the most representative of those intellectuals who stayed on in Kansai, discovered both the charm of tradition and an emerging modernity in Shanghai in 1926, and received a visiting Tian Han in Kyoto in 1927.

A more familiar story to students and scholars of modern China is Shanghai's status as the destination of Chinese intellectuals relocating from the Chinese countryside and provincial cities. Indeed, such provincial passages often came with coming of age stories, as in the case of Shi Cuntong of the First Normal School in Hangzhou, Zhejiang province.[9] It was in Shanghai that Shi renewed his provincial ties and developed new political alliances. Shi's brief but intense encounter with socialist activists in Tokyo caused his arrest by the Japanese police and his deportation back to Shanghai, against which Tian Han, among a few other Chinese student leaders, protested in Tokyo in December 1921.[10]

Like Shi Cuntong, Tian Han experienced his moments of modern awakening in Shanghai, first on his way to Tokyo in August 1916 and then during the summer of 1919 when he went back to visit. But this was a different modernity than that of the experimental milieu of Tokyo; Shanghai modernity, for Tian Han, was tinged with something sinister. A 1919 poem "Zui'e" (Evil), possibly written in Tokyo after his summer visit to shanghai, already portrayed Shanghai as an "evil" metropolis, where the newly opened Wing'on department store, with its imposing structure and association with materialism, became the symbol of the city. This Tokyo poem already registered Tian's love-hate relationship with Shanghai. He describes a variety of city sounds—a bird, people, electric car, horse carriage, and horn of a ship—that somehow together compose "a kind of cosmic music" (*yizhong yuzhou de yinyue*). The poem describes a heavy fog shrouding the city and concealing the many evils in the metropolis. Eventually the speaker thrusts himself into this obliterating fog, asking who will triumph, evil or self?[11] The juxtaposition of evil and self suggests the city as invasive of ego boundaries, as the speaker in the poem struggles to preserve himself amid the sensory bombardments. At the same time, the dark side of the metropolis proved dangerously attractive to Tian Han. Compared to the rosy Tokyo diary, Tian Han's writings on Shanghai reflect a deep-rooted ambivalence: the city becomes in his imagination both a utopian and dystopian landscape. This ambivalence, however, did not preclude Tian Han's love affair with the city.

After returning to China from his six-year sojourn in Tokyo, he proceeded to play host to many Japanese intellectuals visiting the city during the 1920s, as Shanghai emerged as a meeting ground for visiting Japanese and Japan-educated Chinese. Tian Han, like the city of Shanghai, embodied the alternately intimate, ambivalent, and antagonistic relationship between China and Japan from the 1920s to the 1930s. From the early 1930s onward, in particular, Tian Han the public intellectual undoubtedly felt the urgency of speaking out on behalf of the Chinese people, writing film stories and song lyrics in support of anti-Japanese national salvation with the increasing threat of Japanese military assault. On the other hand, Tian Han the private "man of letters" sustained an interest in all things Japanese, translating from and corresponding with Japanese intellectuals throughout the increasingly tension-ridden decades.

Indeed, Tian became a focal point and liaison in Sino-Japanese cultural exchanges in Shanghai. Muramatsu Shōfū brought a letter of introduction from Satō Haruo to Tian at the China Books office in early 1923.[12] According to him, Tian functioned as a crucial link in introducing him to members of the Creation Society, as well as to the Shanghai cultural scene in general.[13] Muramatsu kept up close personal communications with Tian, and the two exchanged their personal journals, *Sōjin* and *Nanguo,* until the outbreak of the Jinan Incident, when Japanese troops clashed with the Nationalist army during the Northern Expedition in 1928 and inflicted thousands of Chinese casualties. In a letter written to Muramatsu in Japanese and published by him in *Sōjin,* Tian Han refused to write for Muramatsu's journal any longer as the latter supported Japanese military intervention in Jinan. Tian severed his ties with Muramatsu after that letter.[14]

Tian Han's intellectual and personal connections to "the great aesthetic writer" Tanizaki Jun'ichirō, with whom he had close personal contact during the latter's 1926 Shanghai visit, ran much deeper than those with Muramatsu. Tanizaki's involvement with modern drama and film had interested Tian greatly during his Tokyo stay, and he wrote about witnessing the making of Tanizaki's first scenario into the film *Amateur Club* by the seashore in Kamakura.[15] Together with Ouyang Yuqian, a leading figure in opera and drama circles in Shanghai, Tian organized a grand welcoming party for Tanizaki and accompanied him every day during his 1926 visit.[16] Detailed accounts of Tian can be found in Tanizaki's two travelogues, "Shanhai kōyūki" (Shanghai Friends) and "Shanhai kenbunroku" (Records of Shanghai Travel). Tian Han's 1927 visit to Japan provided Tanizaki with an opportunity to repay his favors, this time in Kansai.[17] A photograph showing Tian Han and Tanizaki posing together in front of the ship *Nagasaki* in Kobe Harbor on June 22, 1927, provides the most vivid testimony of this intellectual connection.[18]

Tian Han wrote extensively about Tanizaki's Shanghai visit, mostly in casual essays, flaunting his own "bohemian image" and highlighting his frequenting of brothels and drinking sprees with Tanizaki. "Wo de Shanghai shenghuo" (My Life in Shanghai), written in 1926, only half a year after Tanizaki's visit, was probably his most unmediated account of this period. Mainly an account of Tian's mourning of his wife Yi Shuyu after her untimely death in January 1925, the first section, "Shanghai Rain," reflects his Wertherian sentimentality and copious tears, while the second section, "Shanghai Night," recounts his frequenting of dance halls, restaurants, and foreign prostitutes (*waiguo tangzi*) together with the visiting Tanizaki. Since Tian always looked miserable even in "happy" situations, Tanizaki jokingly described him as "a victim of melancholia" (*Melancholia huanzhe*), and commented on his nervous appearance as being more Japanese than that of a Japanese.[19] Tian finally renounces these carousing "Shanghai nights" as devoid of any real "heart to heart" connection, despite the sensuous contact of "eyes, mouths, hands, and feet."[20] Yokomitsu Ruiichi, who visited Shanghai a year later and had close contact with Tian Han, would include Sanki, the melancholic Japanese young man, as a protagonist in his novel *Shanghai*, a character representative of both Tian and Tanizaki.[21] In his own accounts and those of his Japanese contemporaries, Tian Han projected his self-representation as the bohemian, the decadent, and the melancholic onto the cultural screen of Shanghai. Yet the moral and psychic darkness of Shanghai dramatized by Tian Han and his Japanese friends is unmistakably and increasingly alluring for both parties involved.

Tanizaki Jun'ichirō meets Tian Han at Kobe Harbor (June 22, 1927, Kobe, Japan), in *Tanizaki Jun'ichirō ten* (Yokohama: Kanagawa Kindai Bungakkan, 1998).

Clearly his role as the Shanghai host to Tanizaki boosted Tian Han's artistic ego and earned him "cultural capital," but what was Tanizaki's motivation for visiting Shanghai after having "returned to tradition" in the shadow of the 1923 earthquake? Tanizaki's attitude toward China was ambivalent. On the one hand, like many other Japanese travelers, he carried a sense of cultural superiority, especially after the Japanese victories in the First Sino-Japanese War and the Russo-Japanese War and the strengthening of Japan's imperialist presence in China throughout late nineteenth and early twentieth centuries. That sense was only reinforced by the overwhelming welcome he received in Shanghai. On the other hand, as one deeply saturated in Chinese cultural tradition, Tanizaki lamented the passing of ancient traditions in his own country, noting to Tian Han, for instance, that "the custom of having all the people in a family stay up on Chinese New Year's Eve, a custom already vanishing in Japan, is still kept in your country. Even in Shanghai, a Westernized urban center, this old custom has been kept and is now one of my fondest memories."[22] It is possible to hear undertones of modernist arrogance in Tanizaki's nostalgia for vanishing Asian traditions in Japan. His genuine fondness for "quaint" old customs that his culture had already left behind in the dark, so to speak, may have been tinged with a patronizing tone.

What, then, is the significance of Shanghai as an incubator of modern sensibilities for a generation of young East Asian intellectuals? The "Westernized urban center" as mentioned by Tanizaki, with its foreign concessions, "evil" skyscrapers, and exotic prostitutes of multiple nationalities, indeed provided a distinctively modern milieu. Tanizaki's longing for Shanghai, in this sense, can be understood as a journey with double expectations: longing both for a "well-preserved" authentic past that might only persist in Kansai in fragments and for a Taishō modernity that seemingly disappeared in Tokyo after the devastating 1923 earthquake.

Remarkably, even after the Manchurian Incident of 1931 and the Japanese bombing of Shanghai in 1932, Tian Han kept publishing his translations of Tanizaki's writings, among other Japanese works, through the Shanghai office of China Books, though he did so under the protection of the penname Li Shuquan. A translation of five works by Tanizaki was published in 1934, including *Kami to hito no aida* ("Between God and Man," 1924) and a biography of Tanizaki up to 1927. This was the very first biography of Tanizaki in Chinese with a detailed *nianpu* (chronological history) attached to it.[23] It is still considered a valuable source in the study of modern Japanese literature in China today. Earlier the same year, Tian published his translation of *Den'en no yūutsu* ("Rural Melancholy," 1919) in a collection that included two translated works by Satō Haruo, with whom he had associated in Tokyo since 1921, under the same pseudonym.[24] Significantly, during the same year, 1934, Tian Han was active in the Soviet Music Group and the Denton Film Company, writing a film story that featured volunteers fighting the Japanese and composing lyrics for a song that later became the most popular anti-Japanese outcry of wartime China.

Tanizaki Jun'ichirō remembered Tian Han as his closest Chinese intellectual friend from the 1920s.[25] He recalled receiving a letter from Tian a few years after his 1927 visit to Japan, expressing his desire to stay with him in case he, like Guo Moruo, had to flee for his life to Japan due to the persecutions of the Nationalists.[26] The outbreak of full-scale war changed everything in 1937. Tanizaki lamented the unfortunate fact that Tian Han was now making anti-Japanese films in the wartime Chinese capital Chongqing. Tian Han and Guo Moruo, the two Chinese who best understood Japan's culture, had become its fiercest critics.

Tian Han's intimate connection with Japanese visitors in Shanghai was largely fostered and maintained through the Japanese-owned Uchiyama Bookstore, a crucial arena for the meeting of people and ideas across and beyond East Asia at the time. The bookstore opened in 1917 and was owned and operated by Uchiyama Kanzō.[27] One of Tian Han's essays provides a vivid snapshot of one of the gatherings hosted by the bookstore in 1929.[28] Tian met a group of Japanese and Chinese writers and journalists at the meeting, including the young Kyoto University professor Karashima Takeshi.[29] Their literary conversation was followed by a visit to Tianchan Wutai (Stage of the Heavenly Cicada), a famous Peking Opera House, where they met with Zhou Xinfang, a leading Peking Opera performer and by now Tian Han's old friend.[30] Tian first saw Zhou onstage in Shanghai in August 1916 on his way to Tokyo. Having read Tian's personal journal *Nanguo* in 1924, Zhou took the initiative to contact him in support of his independent publishing endeavor. Zhou was elected head of the theater department of Tian's Nanguo she (Southland Institute) in 1928.[31] The Chinese and Japanese young men watched Xiao Yang Yuelou, who had visited Japan a couple of years before and had a following among Japanese intellectuals, impersonating Da Ji. As "the most romantic woman" in *Fengshen bang* (Investiture of the Gods), an epic novel incorporating elements of folk legend, local custom, and imperial ritual,[32] this role, as embodied by Xiao Yang Yuelou, enchanted the honest Karashima to the extent that he whispered to Tian Han, "I am falling in love with her (him)."[33]

Tian Han's vivid account of Karashima's Shanghai visit gained new life twenty years later when Karashima's book *Chūgoku no shingeki* (The New Theater of China) was published in 1948 in Tokyo. Tian Han's autograph, a memento of Karashima's 1928 visit to Suzhou, appeared prominently on the first page of this book. In his beautiful handwriting, Tian Han wrote, "Karashima Sensei came to China and invited me to Suzhou to visit the tomb of Jin Shengtan,[34]

Tian Han's 1928 autograph as published in Karashima Takeshi, *Chūgoku no shingeki* (Tokyo: Shōheidō, 1948).

what a thoughtful man! It happened that I have one of my shabby photos with me and I presented it to Karashima sensei as a present. Tian Han in Shanghai, September 13."[35]

The circulation of autographs and photos as mementos among Chinese and Japanese intellectuals testifies not only to cultural exchange but also to intellectual self-fashioning. Karashima paid special tribute to Tian Han's autograph in a full paragraph in the introduction to his book. He briefly recounted his encounter with Tian Han in Shanghai and Tian's presentation of his autograph as a memento. He wrote sentimentally about losing many of the magazines and booklets that Tian Han mailed to him throughout the evolution of Tian's Nanguo enterprise, while thanking fate for preserving this single photo. He concluded, "It is significant to put at the forefront of this book the autograph of Mr. Tian, who not only had the deepest connection with Japanese theater circles but is also monitoring the mainstream of the Chinese new theater movement today."[36]

Like the protagonist Kehan in his novella *Shanghai,* Tian Han emerged from the textual and visual constructions of himself and his Japanese contemporaries as a key figure embodying the artistic world of Shanghai and all its contradictions, ranging from the darkness of the night to the piercing red fire. Film, as an emerging art form and artistic practice, facilitated a new way to experience and represent the world around him, similar to the way poverty on the screen was more powerful than poverty in real life in Tokyo. The Shanghai nights unfold before him as if they were situated in a movie set, as if the women and the city, the visiting Japanese and the Peking Opera performers, were all placed under limelight, being shot by a cinematographer. Kehan's ambivalence about the city, condemning its corruption while being seduced by its enchantments, reflected Tian Han's difficulty in coming to terms with Shanghai as its resident artist and activist.

Back to Japan: Between the Aesthetic and the Proletarian

To fully understand the arc of Tian Han's relationship with Japan, though, we must step back to 1927, the year of his second Japanese sojourn. Tian Han's cultural position in Japan, both self-perceived and actual, had changed between his first long-term residence (from 1916 to 1922) and his short return visit in 1927. By the time of that second visit, he was a self-conscious and self-assured artist, a maturing professional, and a cosmopolitan modernist. During his two-week visit to Japan, he was featured in newspapers such as *Asahi Shinbun* and *Yomiuri Shinbun* and was warmly welcomed at the homes of Tanizaki Jun'ichirō and Satō Haruo. His independent filmmaking endeavors were reported in detail in literary magazines as modernist experiments.[37] In interesting ways, Tian embodied the shifting power dynamics between Japan and China. The premodern status quo of Japanese cultural subordination to China had given way relatively recently to Japanese ascendancy. Now Tian's return to Japan as a cultural celebrity, "a businessman, a professor, and a producer" in Tanizaki's terms, hinted at a further renegotiation of power relations,[38] again seemed to reverse the relationship between Japanese mentors and Chinese students recently formed in modern times.

In his essay "Women de ziji pipan" (Our Self-Criticism), written in Shanghai in 1930, Tian Han quoted from a diary entry dating from his visit to Japan in June 1927.[39]

> I was dining and touring with the great Japanese aesthetic writer Tanizaki Jun'ichirō in Kyoto and Osaka: we were drinking day and night, and we stayed at Gion.[40] Surrounded by wine and women, I seemed to forget everything else. It seemed to me that Japan was still a peaceful country. However, the moment I got to Tokyo Station, I found myself shaking hands with the proletarian writers wearing worker's hats (Satomura Kinzō, Hayama Yoshiki, altogether four or five of them) on the platform. When I got to the ticket counter, Muramatsu Shōfū and Satō Haruo were already there waiting in a car. [The proletarian writer] Satomura invited me to watch them rehearsing Sinclair's *Prince Hargen* in the Tsukiji Little Theater, while Satō Haruo invited me to stay with him in his new house at Sekiguchi-machi. Having not been in contact with Japanese literary circles for quite some time, I was not at all clear about how different their opinions were, and how severe their ideological conflict was.[41]

In 1930, Tian Han realized in his "retrospective diary" that Tokyo Station, a prominent modernist landmark located at the city center, had become an ideological battlefield between the "proletarian" and the "aesthetic" writers the moment his train arrived on June 26, 1927.[42] As soon as Tian chose to go with the "aesthetic" writer Satō Haruo to stay at his new house, which was located within walking distance of Tian's former residence in Tokyo, instead of going to watch the avant-garde theater group Zen'ei za rehearsing in the Tsukiji Little

Theater,[43] he distanced himself from the intellectual Left in Japan. His affiliation with the Nationalist government in Nanjing triggered a heated debate between himself and Sasaki Takamaru, who played Prince Hargen in the Zen'ei za performance that he watched the next day.[44]

The categories of "the aesthetic" and "the proletarian," which are at the center of the passage quoted above, had become key terms of literary, artistic, and social analysis in the latter part of the 1920s worldwide. The accelerating development of heavy industry went hand in hand with the resurgence of avant-garde art in Europe and North America, in which machines and new technological advances represent the future not only of social development but also of artistic experimentation. The impact of the new Soviet Union and the newly independent nations in Asia and North Africa radically reconfigured the political and economic map of the world. Writers and artists started to form their "independent" identities as modern individuals and part of the urban petite bourgeoisie in rising world metropolises. Workers came to be recognized by urban intellectuals, and came to recognize themselves, as the "proletariat," the vanguard class most suitable to lead a modern revolution for the benefit of the exploited in a capitalist society, according to Marx's classic definition.

The association of the proletarian with low culture and the aesthetic with bourgeois decadence had, and still has, a great impact on scholarly approaches to modern Chinese cultural productions throughout the twentieth century and beyond. The relative silence in scholarship on the possible interpenetration between the aesthetic avant-garde and the revolutionary vanguard in twentieth-century Chinese culture is a testimony to the widespread tacit acceptance of the ineluctable distance between the aesthetic and the proletarian.

Although Tian Han's 1927 visit to Japan seems to have intensified the ideological divide between the aesthetic and the proletarian due to his intimate connections with leading figures within both circles, it also made possible the gathering of more than thirty prominent Japanese cultural figures of different political persuasions within a couple of days, all linked in various ways through him.[45] Tian's simultaneous dividing and unifying power in neighboring Japan, with its complex historical and contemporary ties to China, begs an explanation of his popularity in Japan despite his ambiguous aesthetic and political status in China itself. Tian's grand-scale essay entitled "Our Self-Criticism," partially quoted at the beginning of this section, provides important evidence toward such an explanation.

Tian's "Our Self-Criticism" has long served as a first-person testimony in support of the general narrative of Chinese intellectuals' conversion to Marxism, symbolically expressed in Tian's self-proclaimed emergence out of the darkness of the night and into the fire of revolution, or from the aesthetic school to the proletarian camp, around the year 1930. In other words, the dramatization of past insensitivity and current political awareness served a contemporary purpose, namely, to construct a rhetoric of conversion, making that conversion public, and supplying "historical evidence" for it. The rhetoric needed to presume a decaying past and posit a bright future in order for the conversion to be fully justified.

Tian Han's textual performance in his lengthy essay, however, betrays his pronounced purpose of "self-criticism." The essay charts the evolution of Tian's modernist experimentation in Shanghai from the publication of his personal journal *Nanguo banyuekan* (Southland Bimonthly) around late 1923 and early 1924 through his independent filmmaking and art educational endeavors in his Nanguo Dianying Jushe (Southland Institute of Film and Drama) up to the year 1930. Though entitled "Self-Criticism," it is rather an announcement of Nanguo's current position and future orientation to friends, as well as a "declaration of war" (*xuanzhan shu*) upon its enemies.[46] Reading the essay as Tian Han's self-promotion under the guise of self-criticism, and of exhibitionism under the guise of confession, complicates the narrative of political conversion and radical transformation and reveals how the symbolism of "night" and "fire" was indeed intricately interwoven throughout Tian's Shanghai experimentation.

In this grand narrative, Tian's own aestheticism becomes the object of criticism by his supposedly newly emerging proletarian sensibility, but in objectifying and dramatizing his earlier self, he in effect outlines a wide range of complex intellectual trends, including, but not limited to, his youthful experiments uniting literature, art, music, theater, and film into one powerful front (*youli de zhanxian*).[47] A deeper irony lies in the tension between the essay's pronounced intention to narrate the conversion of a petit bourgeois intellectual to Marxism and its confessional style, a narrative form originating in a wide range of cultural traditions, including Christian confessions, Buddhist *zange*, and Japanese *shishōsetsu*, and revamped as a popular genre with heavy imprints of Rousseau and Tolstoy in Japan during Tian's stay in Tokyo. As a result, Tian's "petit bourgeois" cross-genre and transmedia experiments, summarized systematically and disseminated to the reading public in this confessional narrative for the first time, position him at the center of a vibrant cosmopolitan intellectual network where constant cross-fertilization between the avant-garde and the popular can be articulated.

In the end, it is the target of the criticism, Tian himself, more than the criticism that is being promulgated. One wonders, why would both the aesthetic and the proletarian camps of writers in Japan compete to entertain Tian Han during his visit to Japan in the summer of 1927? Such a question then leads the reader back to Tian's return from Tokyo in 1922, the exuberance of the pre-earthquake Tokyo he carried with him, and his central role in connecting visiting Japanese artists to the exciting milieu of a cosmopolitan Shanghai. It becomes clear that his Tokyo engagement and Shanghai exchange with the "aesthetic" writers Shimamura Hōgetsu, Kuriyagawa Hakuson, Tanizaki Junichirō, Satō Haruo, and Muramatsu Shōfu, as well as his preoccupation with the "proletarian" movements encompassing anarchist, socialist, feminist, Marxist, and social democratic trends, rendered him a figure important to and respected by both sides in Japan. Thus it is that Tian's essay of ten thousand words, framing the author as an object of criticism in 1930, also served the purpose of establishing him as the leading figure in the intellectual exchange between China and Japan at age twenty-nine in 1927.

This doubleness of purpose doesn't necessarily mean that the narrative of Tian Han's intellectual conversion to Marxism is somehow affected or insincere. Tian had introduced *Das Kapital* as "the laborers' Bible" (probably without having read it himself) a decade earlier in Tokyo, where he upheld the proletarian "fourth class" as vanguards of the people and leaders of the revolution.[48] Most intriguingly, together with Yu Dafu, his old friend from the Creation Society (with whom he reconciled after an unpleasant dispute about the publication of "A Night in a Café" in 1922), he would meet with two Japanese proletarian writers from the *Bungei sensen* (Literary Front) group. Tian Han wrote "unite, proletariats of the world," as encouragement to his Japanese visitors in April 1927 in Shanghai, only two months before his supposedly "politically insensitive" second visit to Japan.[49]

Those two months were crucial, however, as Tian would visit Japan as a Nanjing government officer in charge of film production in June 1927. Widely perceived in Japanese leftist circles as more reactionary than the Wuhan government of the Nationalist Left, Tian's position with the Nanjing government was the major liability leading to criticism of him in 1927 and his own self-criticism in 1930. Against the background of such an ambiguous political identity, the rhetoric of conversion in 1930 not only served to erase Tian's "proletarian" past but also obscured the fact that his "aesthetic" pursuits were ongoing after his self-proclaimed radical transformation. In practice, the aesthetic and the proletarian had always been intertwined in Tian's experiments in Tokyo and would continue to assert influence throughout his Shanghai years.

Tian Han's case illustrates how the scholarly fixation on the rhetoric of conversion (i.e., from art to politics) misses the point, namely, the continual interweaving of performance and politics and the avant-garde and the popular in the intellectual climate of this period. While the political rhetoric of the time forced Tian into a rigid, "either/or" paradigm, his instinctive position, as an artist, was, as we shall see, always "both/and." Again and again in his career, he chooses to include rather than exclude and seeks to conciliate competing energies to produce hybrid forms.

Night and Fire in Independent Publishing

"The Night a Tiger Was Captured"

The writing and publishing of "Huohu zhiye" (The Night a Tiger Was Captured), one of the first modern dramas Tian Han wrote upon his return to Shanghai, legitimized his newly acquired role not only as a playwright and independent publisher but also as a concerned urban intellectual and a leading figure in the Shanghai cultural scene.[50] Exoticizing his native Hunan countryside for his Shanghai audience, and revisiting the eternal themes of love and death, Tian Han presented his Shanghai readers with an imaginary countryside that was supposedly located in his hometown. The female protagonist, Liangu, or Lotus Girl,[51] exemplified one of Tian's early attempts at "creating the new woman" after crafting the powerful three-sister imagery in Tokyo. Indeed, from "The Ghost of the Piano" to "Before Lunch," Tian Han's Tokyo plays already anticipated an imaginative portrayal of Chinese reality that would be carried further in "The Night a Tiger Was Captured."

On a superficial level, the play reads like a stereotypical May Fourth story of two young people fighting against arranged marriage as in "Spiritual Light," only the location has moved from Tokyo to the countryside of Hunan. However, Tian Han set his story among the tiger hunters living in the mountains, a setting that provided a romantic and exotic background against which the tale of the two lovers' tragic fate could be played out.[52] The symbolism of the Hunan countryside conveys a double meaning: it signals backwardness as well as innocence, and it is at once patronized and idealized, from the urban point of view. Lotus Girl, the only daughter of a rich hunter, is forced into an arranged marriage; her lover, Huang Dasha (Huang the Big Fool), climbing a hill hoping to have a last look at her house, is caught in a tiger trap set by Lotus's father. Huang comes onstage, badly wounded and soaked in blood, when the audience is expecting to see a wounded tiger. He is brought into the house and finally sees his lover again, which results in the girl being brutally whipped by her father.[53] Hearing the offstage whipping, Huang commits suicide with a hunter's knife within his reach. The realistic issue of free love versus arranged marriage, the mystic tiger mountain, and the exotic folk custom work hand in hand with Tian Han's avant-garde genre experiment in crafting his first major "spoken drama" written and performed in Shanghai. The beating, crying, and suicide onstage showcased a naked body bathed in blood, and the tiger-human connection exposed the shared fate of the tiger, the girl, and the young man as disposable bodies sacrificed by violence and power. The play centralizes a theme of metamorphosis through the tiger-human motif,[54] with mythical elements, religious retribution, and primitive power woven into Tian Han's outlandish narrative of the exotic.

However, the mythical dimension of the story coexists with strong contemporary political implications. Tian Han set his play in "real historical time," namely, "after the 1911 Revolution," but in a static postrevolution vacuum. He also created, as the location of the play, a "mountain village" close to his childhood playground, Xianguling, of the Dongxiang town of Changsha city. The story opens in the "fire room" of the Wei household, where the hunter and his family rest after dinner, receive guests, and gather around the fire to keep warm in the winter. Tian returns to his obsessions with light, heat, and fire but here in a humble, realistic stage setting that points to the raw power of nature and the primitive cruelty of an oppressive patriarchal regime in which the fire of youthful love must be sanctioned by the patriarch and unsanctioned love is relegated to the dark and cold winter night.

Indeed, Tian Han first established himself as a playwright on the Shanghai cultural scene while still studying in Tokyo with "A Night in a Café," published in 1922. As the representative piece of Tian's early focus on the intimate relationships among art, love, and student radicalism, "A Night in a Café" already opens up the intricacies of the popular avant-garde as traversing the boundary between decadence and revolution, and aesthetics and politics. The first modern Chinese usage of the term *tuifei* (decadence) was likely coined by Tian Han in the long poetic dialogue between the café waitress Bai Qiuying and the "decadent" young student Lin Zeqi in "A Night in a Café."[55] Bai describes Lin burying his sorrow in drinking at cafés as *tuifei*, a compound of two Chinese characters of similar meaning, literally "ruined and decayed."[56] In an uncanny fashion, the "decadent" young student Lin Zeqi and his long poetic monologue find their successor in the image of Huang, the lover of Lotus, in "The Night a Tiger Was Captured." The transgressive energy circulating throughout Tian Han's Shanghai endeavors finds its best embodiment in the image of "Huang the Big Fool," a hybrid of the "decadent" intellectual, the imaginary folk, and the young revolutionary.

It is worthwhile pausing over the image of the "fool."[57] Tian Han used two Chinese characters, *sha* and *dian*, to describe Huang's mental state in the eyes of Hunter Wei, who is the patriarch and ultimate authority in Lotus's world.[58] Whenever Huang's actions and words violate the boundaries set by Hunter Wei, he is deemed "insane" and is driven away by the patriarch himself. When Lotus and Huang start to discover the ugly nature of the "world of sanity," each is immediately called a fool. Thus, just as in Lu Xun's now canonized story "Diary of a Madman," the most candid and genuine words come from the mouths of the so-called madman and fool.[59]

But Tian Han's fool differs from Lu Xun's madman in his pathos. Like the young student Lin Zeqi in "A Night in a Café," Huang the Big Fool was at once a young man suffering from his lost love and a sentimental poet pouring out his sorrow through long poetic monologues.

> A child without a mother or a father, without brothers, without relatives or friends, well, it is unbearable enough in the daytime. But when the night comes, and a person must sleep all alone under the temple altar—it is so much more desolate, fearful. If I lit a fire, all I would see was my own solitary shadow; if I heard singing or crying, it would be just the sound of my own solitary voice. I finally understand that in the whole world the most fearful thing is neither wolves nor tigers, neither devils nor ghosts—it is being deserted, alone![60]

Paradoxically, Huang the Big Fool, in Tian Han's first serious attempt to reimagine his native countryside after his six-year Tokyo sojourn in the style of Yanagita Kunio's study of folk culture,[61] emerges as a narcissistic poet and a quintessential avant-garde artist whose deepest existential suffering arises from being "deserted and alone!" The spiritual and philosophical implications of the image of the loner will be echoed time and again in the writings of Tian Han and his contemporaries. Significant here is the loner's desire to break the monologue into a dialogue. The loner's pursuit of a sense of belonging demonstrates his desire to move from individual separateness toward a deeper level of spiritual and metaphorical community, to warm himself in the dark night around a collective fire fueled by love.

Lotus Girl, the female protagonist, appears passive and lost in the first half of the play, only uttering a simple "I'm coming" in answer to her father's call offstage. Her refusal to make her own wedding shoes comes to light abruptly, followed by the declaration "I don't want to live!"[62] Lotus Girl can be read as an early model of the "new woman" in the 1935 film *Xin nüxing* (New Woman) immortalized by the legendary Shanghai actress Ruan Lingyu. While Lotus rebels against family bondage, the female protagonist in the film commits suicide to protest social injustice. The 1930s new woman, however, reverses her early 1920s prototype by declaring "I want to live,"[63] announcing her spiritual awakening rather than using suicide as means of passive resistance. Indeed, concealed behind Lotus's quiet nature in the beginning of the play are signs of a rebellious spirit that emerges thereafter. When she sees her lover dying in front of her, she cries out, "Poor Brother Huang, from now on I will never leave you again," and finally declares, "No! I'll die before I let go. No one in the whole world can tear us apart!"[64]

Lotus is one of Tian Han's earliest embodiments of the new woman in Shanghai. Both the passivity of the virgin and the revolutionary potential of the femme fatale are embedded in her. But the fact that she silently endures her sufferings before Huang's dramatic stage appearance in place of a wounded tiger reminds us of how limited her resistance was and could be. After all, she indirectly causes Huang's death, or, metaphorically, her beauty and Huang's love for her bury Huang alive, long before he actually kills himself onstage. Is Lotus a Chinese incarnation of Salome, the femme fatale in Oscar Wilde's notorious play, first translated into Chinese by Tian Han?[65] Can passivity harbor transgression?

Even more dramatic than Lotus's transformation, Huang's final suicide onstage constitutes the ultimate performative and transgressive act, which also calls forth memories of Matsui Sumako's love suicide in Tokyo and foreshadows the frequent suicide scenes still to come in Tian's stories, stage plays, and films.

Suicide, the ultimate transgression in Christianity, is likewise regarded in the Confucian tradition as a selfish and unfilial act. Doubly condemned by Christianity and Confucianism, it becomes for Tian Han an act of self-determination and a declaration of individual will and autonomy. Love suicide, moreover, elevates the act of self-sacrifice to a higher level, engaging with the thanatos/eros theme already prominent in Tian's encounters with early-twentieth-century symbolic literature on the Japanese stage.

The primitive peasant, the avant-garde artist, and the May Fourth revolutionary converge in the character of Huang the Big Fool. The hybrid nature of Huang as both peasant and intellectual raises questions of representation. Like his Russian forerunner, Turgenev, whose 1877 *Virgin Soil* about Russian peasants was written from the remove of Paris, Tian Han, investing this sentimental young Hunan peasant with his notions about "the people," ran the risk of "not understanding the real situation."[66] To further complicate the issue, Tian was fully aware of the "inauthentic nature" of Turgenev's imaginary Russian peasants (*narod*), which he discussed in the long article "A Glimpse of Russian Literature" published in 1919. It is thus reasonable to speculate that while Tian Han was fully aware of the perils of misprision and wary in particular of "inauthentic" representations of the people, he consciously engages in such a representation because he may have had a consciously didactic or "consciousness-raising" goal while also having an unconscious goal of self-inscription. Moreover, the urban audience might be more effectively moved to empathize with this unrealistically depicted peasant. Hence Tian's "people" and "new woman" were inscribed with the imprints of self-writing, that is, they were modeled into stand-ins for the self-centered, sensitive, performative, and populist young romantic avant-gardists of his generation.

However self-referential the characters might have been, though, to the audience their tragic fate—Huang committing suicide onstage while Lotus is beaten offstage—must have resonated only too strongly with real life tragedies at the time. Still, Tian Han's apparent naturalism in this play actually partakes of the qualities of "magic realism." The poverty and suffering onstage appears to be more real than real life. The mythical dimension of the tiger-human connection merges with the family's plan to skin a tiger for their daughter's wedding quilt. Here the violence of killing and skinning a tiger is directly linked to the wedding quilt, a literal cover for the sexual violence directed against the innocent girl and legitimized by arranged marriage. The eroticization of violence and power and the victimization of the tiger and the girl go hand in hand. The exoticism is intensified when poor Huang falls into the tiger trap, and the "wounded tiger" commits suicide with a hunter's knife for the love of the hunter's daughter.

The William Blake of China

Almost as important as the play itself is the fact that "The Night a Tiger Was Captured" was first published in *Nanguo banyuekan* (Southland Bimonthly), the journal Tian Han inaugurated together with his wife, Yi Shuyu, in Shanghai in January 1924. This publishing venture represented an important evolutionary stage in his ongoing effort to articulate and realize his artistic and intellectual ideals. Despite having secured the prestigious position of editor at one of the leading publishing houses in Shanghai, Zhonghua shuju (China Books), Tian Han found himself in something of an artistic vacuum soon after his return to Shanghai. After dissociating himself from the Creation Society as a result of his personal clash with Cheng Fangwu,[67] Tian also witnessed the dismantling of the Young China Association due to the diverging artistic and political orientations of its members. The relatively stable income from his job at China Books enabled him to realize his dream to tend a "garden of his own" (*ziji de yuandi*).[68] The journal's inaugural issue declared that their two-person endeavor was to be modeled on the precedent of the English poet William Blake and noted that, while they could not follow Blake's "do-it-yourself" example completely, they would write, edit, and distribute the journal themselves to avoid "capitalist control."[69]

Tian Han's choice of model here was by no means without deliberation. William Blake, the English poet, painter, engraver, illustrator, and visionary mystic who hand-illustrated his series of lyric and epic poems, produced one of the most strikingly original and independent bodies of work in Western literature. Tian Han was most likely introduced to Blake's works while studying in Tokyo, where Japanese artists were going through their own "William Blake fever."[70] The unorthodox and idiosyncratic visionary motifs abundant in Blake became a configuring element of the religiosity and politics of performance in both Tokyo and Shanghai, where the "socialization of the arts" worked closely with the "artification of society."[71]

However, it is not simply Blake's fame in Japan that commended him to Tian Han. Specifically, Blake's poem "The Tyger" in his *Songs of Experience,* with its opening lines "Tyger, Tyger, burning bright / In the forests of the night: / What immortal hand or eye, / Could frame thy fearful symmetry?,"[72] likely influenced Tian Han's choice of subject matter in "The Night a Tiger Was Captured." In both cases, the tiger carries similar symbolic meaning, the contrast between "burning bright" and "forests of the night" pointing to the eternal, mysterious, and sexual connotations in the human-tiger symmetry, with symbolic implications that link Shanghai and Tokyo through Tian Han's interest in the visionary Blake and the themes of "night" and "fire."

In the Chinese original of his *Nanguo xuanyan* (Southland Manifesto) announcing William Blake as his model, Tian Han used the character *she* (society), suggesting that while it invoked a modern spirit of free association, his endeavor was still following the great tradition of artistic societies in traditional China.[73] Tian Han borrowed from an eighth-century poem in which the Southland is a symbol of romantic love where red bean, the emblem of love, grows. The South has long been imagined as both a physical and spiritual landscape endowed with amorous, poetic, and exotic associations in the Chinese literary imagination; Tian further bestowed on it explicit sexual, artistic, and revolutionary energies. Tian Han, like William Blake, was searching for an artistic utopia permeated with romantic love, sexual freedom, and avant-garde energy in his independent publishing endeavors. Tian's choice of the name *Nanguo* (Southland) recalls another *she* related to the character *nan* (south), the famous Nanshe (South Society), of which Tian Han's maternal uncle, Yi Xiang, was an active member. Tian had had intimate personal associations with Yi's generation of artists-revolutionaries since the 1910s. It is not inconceivable that he was using *Nanguo* to honor both the revolutionary and the aesthetic traditions of Nanshe, whose members were often both revolutionaries and great poets.

Indeed, from 1923 to 1924, when Tian Han was writing, printing, proofreading, and distributing "The Night a Tiger Was Captured" and other personal essays, he was also charting virgin territory in the fields of cultural production in modern China.[74] Shanghai in the early 1920s witnessed the emergence of literary societies and common interest groups competing to divide "spheres of influence." Tian Han interacted closely with his fellow members in the Young China Association and the Creation Society before he severed his ties with both in the mid- to late 1920s. Although he was a member of neither the Literature Research Group (Wenxue yanjiu hui) nor the emerging Communist Party, he maintained personal connections with members of both.

The fact that Tian Han assumed the role of independent publisher shortly after returning to his own country from Tokyo speaks to his need to define himself rather than being defined by those around him. Like Blake's Los, he needed "to create a system or be enslaved by another man's." But the endeavor was rooted in loneliness as much as independence of spirit. Like Huang the Big Fool in the play, Tian felt "deserted, alone": his independent publishing endeavor filled the spiritual vacuum created by his disassociation from the Young China Association and the Creation Society. In a performative, avant-gardist gesture endowed with an "obsession for independence" (*duli pi*),[75] he aspired to illuminate the dark Shanghai nights with the light of art.

Independent Filmmaking as a Silver Dream

"To the People"

While "The Night a Tiger Was Captured" represents Tian Han's first serious attempt to capture his imaginary "new woman" and imaginary "people" at the beginning of his Shanghai career, his independent film project *Dao minjian qu* ("V Narod," or "To the People") approaches those same issues in a simultaneously more intimate and technologically materialized fashion. Tian Han's gradually stabilized income from China Books, the newly formed cultural network of which he was the nexus, and the financial support he received from Tang Huaiqiu,[76] an aviation engineer returned from France, provided him with the opportunity to realize a long-harbored "silver dream."

Thus, at the politically critical juncture of 1926, when other leading cultural figures such as Guo Moruo and Ouyang Yuqian were leaving for the revolutionary South, Tian Han chose to take on the new role of an independent filmmaker in Shanghai. It was an ambitious role, considering both the avant-garde nature of filmmaking in the 1920s and the "independent" nature of this endeavor, that is, its lack of government or commercial sources of funding. It seems that in the midst of the emotional and artistic vacuum created by Yi Shuyu's untimely death in 1925 and the changing political affiliations of many of his friends, Tian Han escaped into film and memories of film, publishing a series of essays on his moviegoing in Tokyo and filmmaking in Shanghai. Instead of accepting an invitation to go to the South, Tian Han found consolation in like-minded intellectuals, or "fellow travelers," such as the visiting Tanizaki Jun'ichirō and the Shanghai Francophiles, such as the music critic Fu Yanchang.[77] One could argue that here Tian Han was using film as a substitute for revolution, harnessing new technology to represent a new ideology, and using media as a stand-in for utopia. The temptation of the revolutionary South was so strong, however, that Tian Han would soon lead the Southland Institute in touring the southern cities in pursuit of the amorous utopia where sex, art, and revolution could join hands.[78]

Tang Lin from the New Youth Film Company (Xin shaonian dianying gongsi) had approached Tian Han in late 1925,[79] hoping to adapt his very first play, *Fan'elin yu qiangwei* ("The Violin and the Rose"), written in 1920 in Tokyo, into a film. Although Tian declined this invitation because he considered his first play immature, this initial contact with the Chinese film industry brought back many fond memories, especially of moviegoing and the "pure cinema movement" involving Tanizaki Jun'ichirō and Satō Haruo in Tokyo. Tian Han soon decided to make a film based on his 1922 play "A Night in a Café" and a 1926 filmscript, "To the People,"[80] and he established the Southland Institute of Film and Drama in order to make this film.

"A Night in a Café," as described in chapter 1, tells the story of a young café waitress from the countryside who has run away from an arranged marriage to find her lover in "a certain metropolis" (*mou dushi*). When Tian Han wrote this play in Tokyo in 1921, he portrayed his protagonists as struggling between a "decadent" life and a more positive one, as symbolized by the physical darkness of the café and the realistic stage set epitomized by a working fireplace. The majority of the male characters, including the protagonist Lin Zeqi (modeled after Tian's friend Li Chuli, who later emerged as an avid advocate of "revolutionary literature),"[81] are weak characters suffering from "suicidal complexes." Only Lin's friend Zheng Xiangquan, who appears onstage at the very end, represents the positive power of the future and the fiery spirit of revolution. The amorous relationships between the students and the girl are whitewashed by means of the fictive relationship of brother and sister, possibly under the Christian influence of Taishō Tokyo.

Although the filmscript written in 1926 in Shanghai again opens with a café scene in which a group of college students are welcoming a Russian poet and discussing ways to reform China, it proceeds very differently from the original play. Boris Pilnyak, a "fellow traveler," as described by Leon Trotsky, was visiting Shanghai at the time and played the Russian poet in the film.[82] He was introduced to Tian Han through the Soviet-educated Jiang Guangci, later famous for his short stories featuring the formula "revolution plus love."[83] Their interactions were recorded and publicized in *Nanguo yuekan* (Southland Monthly), with pictures showing Tian, Pilnyak, and Xu Xiacun together in the country-

Boris Pilnyak and Tian Han at Nanguo she, July 10, 1926, published in *Nanguo yuekan* (1929). (Courtesy of the Shanghai Library.)

side and Pilnyak surrounded by members of Nanguo she.[84] Inspired by Pilnyak, Tian Han came to another important moment of self-realization, just as he had in 1919 in the essay-poem "Rainy Season—Who Am I?." This time in 1930, Tian wrote about his earlier self as a "fellow traveler" of the Communist revolution in an elaborate Tolstoy-style "confession," referring to both Pilnyak and himself as people who "could not fully understand revolution," who "were not proletarian artists, but only their 'fellow travelers' in the field of the arts."[85]

Pilnyak, playing himself in this film, takes on an important role in mobilizing the students by literally combining the "night" of the café with the "fire" of social salvation. He joins the students' hands with those of their mutual lover, the café waitress Meiyu (literally, "Beautiful Jade") and assures them that whoever succeeds in reforming China will win the love of the girl. Two male students set out with great enthusiasm to explore ways to save China and win the beautiful Meiyu. As it turns out, one of them is the son of a capitalist who inherits his father's factory and wins Meiyu's heart in the beginning, while the other poor student, who strives to "go to the people," loses both money and beauty. The student goes to the capitalist to borrow money to build his "new village" but is refused relentlessly. Meiyu senses the difference between the two and turns from the capitalist to the student. The story ends with the student "going to the people" (in fact, going back to Meiyu's home village) to build a utopian new village while the financially and emotionally bankrupt capitalist commits suicide by jumping off a cliff by the West Lake.[86]

The image of the utopian new village evokes the socialist Faust and his happy settlement, as well as the Japanese *atarashiki mura* (new village) movement, which was influenced by utopian socialism and popularized by Zhou Zuoren's writings in China in the late 1910s.[87] The figure of the suicidal young man jumping off a cliff not only brings back memories of the female Faust Meili jumping off the cliff in her dream in "Spiritual Light" but also connects it to the suicide trope fashioned by literary and artistic representations in Tokyo, from the much imitated young Tokyo Imperial University student who jumped into a waterfall in Natsume Soseki's novel *Kokoro* to Matsui Sumako's highly publicized love suicide.[88]

Meiyu, like Bai Qiuying, the café waitress in the original play, functions as both an object of desire and an agent of "political mobilization" for the young college students. One can even argue that it is Meiyu who *engenders* activism and guides the students back to her home village. It is she who is in charge of the fate of the two love rivals who take different paths toward "saving China." Thus "the new woman" and "the people" were one and the same "idealized object" for Tian Han and his young protagonists. At the time of Tian's first attempt at independent filmmaking, the new woman was a deliberate construct designed to kindle revolutionary fire among the young students. The young students were candidates for the making of a revolutionary hero through a painful process of self-cultivation with external stimulation from the opposite sex. The new woman would eventually lead the male protagonist (and future hero) to the people in the countryside, who would in turn provide the necessary stimulation for the future hero's strength.[89]

Tian Han discussed the intellectual context for the making of "To the People" in an essay written during the filmmaking process. He first highlighted the link between his film and the Russian Narodnik movement of the 1870s. He emphasized the yearning of Russian youths for the folk, "as if it were their first lover," and that "going to the people is like going to search for their lover."[90] For Tian Han, Russian populism was a highly romanticized movement in which art, sexuality, and revolutionary politics were mutually constructive.

This essay is only one of twelve written by Tian Han for the film magazine *Yinxing* (Silver Star), serialized in 1927.[91] These essays provide a set of rare visual

Shooting "To the People" in Chen Baoyi's Shanghai studio (1926), in *Zhongguo xihua wushinian,* edited by Zhu Boxiong (Beijing: Renmin meishu chubanshe, 1989). (Courtesy of the Shanghai Library.)

and textual materials on the making of "To the People." While the actual film has been lost and only an incomplete plot summary survives, the essay collection, together with its illustrations, reconstructs the cultural milieu of late 1920s Shanghai. Through the twelve essays and a couple of dozen photos (many of them original stills from the lost film), Tian Han presents himself as the writer and director of the film, his best friend and colleague Tang Huaiqiu as the leading actor, and Tang's wife Wu Jiaxin as the leading actress. The element of self-fashioning is very strong in that Tian Han's own publicity photo was included in the final essay. Reading the essays at the time may have felt like watching a teaser for the film. Reading them now helps the reader reconfigure the lost film through textual and visual fragments. Although the film project ultimately failed, and Tian's "silver dream" of going "to the people" did not materialize, this textual and visual evidence re-creates the light and darkness of Tian's avant-gardist experiments in Shanghai, if only through pictorial journalism.

With the film project aborted, Tian Han's privately funded Nanguo she soon found itself competing for students with an official rival, the government-funded Xihu yishu xueyuan (West Lake Art Institute) headed by the French-educated painter Lin Fengmian. Tian led his students on tour to the West Lake, in outlandish uniforms, to challenge their official rival with a display of "bohemian spirits" while trying to support themselves by means of traveling performances. And it was not only their spirits that were bohemian. The appearance of the Nanguo she group had something in common with the image of a Parisian bohemian.

> Boys all dressed in ill-fitting suits, as if borrowed from somebody else, with outlandish big blue bows; girls all in purple Qipao, with light yellow corsages. They walk in groups along the lakeshore, spring breezes kiss their long hair, and the lake water reflects their gentle smiles. . . . They look like a suicide squad marching afar, or heroic Christians ready to sacrifice themselves in order to spread the gospel to the suffering populace in the desertlike wild countryside. They shocked people around the whole of the West Lake.[92]

The nonconformist spirit of the institute had to be packaged in eccentric uniforms. The style of dress detailed in the above description is by no means insignificant. The mismatch of suits and Manchu dress (*qipao*), decorated with bows and corsages, in such bright contrasting colors as blue, purple, and yellow, remind us of avant-garde figures old and new, far and near, not least Théophile Gautier sporting a red satin waistcoat in the Paris of the 1830s and Oscar Wilde's green carnation in the London of the 1890s.[93] For the Shanghai avant-garde, their ill-fitting costumes, dramatic singing, and rowing of boats were deliberate performances for an intended audience, their official rivals at the West Lake Art Institute as well as the general public.

The reference to the "suicide squad" and "heroic Christians" revives an entire range of issues dating back to Tian Han's Tokyo sojourn, particularly the religiosity and politics of performance so characteristic of the Taishō period in Japan. For Tian Han, the notion of "going to the people" and "creating the new woman" continue to bear the religious connotation of spreading the gospel and saving the suffering populace, here the central symbolisms of "night" and "fire" again work together to highlight the power of spiritual salvation to lift the populace out of the darkness. In particular, Tian Han seems to have taken his inspiration both from the vast body of Russian literature that he so enthusiastically introduced as early as in the late 1910s and from the Japanese Christian

The Nanguo she group at the West Lake, published in *Nanguo yuekan* (1929). (Courtesy of the Shanghai Library.)

reformers, such as Yoshino Sakuzō and his New Man Society followers, who were active in Taishō Tokyo. The West Lake, with its mysterious, spiritual, and sexual associations, served as the ideal locale.[94]

Shanghai Sexuality

Both "night" and "fire" are intimately connected to the transgressive power of sexuality in the context of Shanghai. Tian Han developed his definition of the archetypal powerful and dangerous woman in relation to these central symbolisms. He was intrigued by those glamorous, "lusty, dangerous women on stage and screen," whom he categorized as "vampires," by which he meant women "who have strong self-consciousness, who value their own sensual fulfillment, or who desperately pursue sensual stimulation in their lives."[95] He created a Chinese transliteration of the English word *vampire* as *fanpaiya,* making its foreign origins explicit while at the same time trying to counterbalance the darkness associated with the word by avoiding a direct translation of its meaning. Tian Han borrowed the word from the much celebrated "vamp" tradition of Hollywood, a tradition mediated for him by the Japanese writer Tsubouchi Shōyō,[96] illustrating once again that popular media served as pedagogical tools for avant-garde experiments.

At the same time that he was writing the "vampire" essay, Tian Han came up with the idea of *Hubian chunmeng* (Lakeshore Spring Dream), a film featuring a modern femme fatale or vampire. As in the legendary White Snake story portraying the love encounter of a young scholar and a snake-turned-woman by the West Lake, this film is also set by the lakeshore. A young playwright goes to a resort by the West Lake to recover after a failed love affair. He meets a charming young woman alone in a "Red Chamber," a marker of romantic encounter in the Chinese literary tradition.[97] The woman requests his company, and the playwright willingly stays thereafter. When the woman asks to whip him for her sexual enjoyment, the playwright ultimately obeys. They enjoy each other's company in the Red Chamber night after night until one day a group of robbers shoot and seriously injure him. The story ends with the playwright waking up in a hospital bed, the whole story having turned out to be his "lakeshore spring dream." Such a plot was rather shocking and explicit for the period. The very fact that it was later produced by the leading commercial film company, which intended it to reach a wide audience in Shanghai, attested to the intimate connection between the avant-garde and the popular.[98]

Conceived by Tian Han and directed by Bu Wancang at the Mingxing (Star) Film Company only a couple of months after Tanizaki's 1926 Shanghai visit, "Lakeshore Spring Dream," unlike the abortive silver dream of "To the People," materialized with the backing of financial capital. The film incorporated sadomasochistic elements, emphasizing the lustful and dangerous nature of the powerful female image and the possessive power of the "vampire," as manifested in the Hollywood "vamp" tradition and through Tanizaki's mediation. The femme fatale shown in one of the surviving film stills, with her westernized and masculine style of dress—shirt, tie, and pants—and the playwright's naked, tied, and rather feminine body, suggest an aesthetic of feminine transgression and at the same time a reversal of the male gaze. These sexual politics and sexual aesthetics illustrate the intersection of performance, politics, and popularity in 1920s Shanghai.

In his novella *Shanghai*, mentioned at the beginning of this chapter, Tian Han presented such a seductress as vampire (this time he used the modern translation *xixuegui*, literally "blood-drinking ghost") and linked her pale face, seductive eyes, and constant search for prey to the iconography of the vampire in the Western tradition.[99] Like the virgin as embodied by the purity of the country girl in "A Night in a Café" and "To the People," the femme fatale serves an important thematic function in "Lakeshore Spring Dream." If the innocent virgin is a stand-in for the (oppressed) people (feminized in their powerlessness), the vampire, in departing radically from feminine convention, stands for revolutionary energy and its seductive power. The vampire became the embodiment of both night and fire.

The year 1927 was one of revolution and counterrevolution in modern Chinese history. The Northern Expedition, led by the Nationalist Party, unified China but ended the rivalries between regional warlords only in name. The purge of Communists from the Nationalist Party on April 12, 1927, later known as the April 12 Incident, largely eliminated the influence of the Communists in Shanghai and forced their activities underground. What gave birth to such a daring femme fatale amid the political turmoil in 1927 in China? I suggest that such female sexual transgression constituted part of the "metamorphosis" myth, forming the crucial components to make the avant-garde popular. Such metamorphoses between tiger and man and snake and woman became metaphors for the constant transformations and shifting boundaries between animal instinct and humanity, and fantasy and reality.

Yamaguchi Shin'ichi, a Japanese writer who wrote nostalgically about Tian Han's Shanghai years three decades later in provincial Japan, had been to the press preview (*shiying hui*) of "Lakeshore Spring Dream" with Tian Han, Ouyang Yuqian, and Tang Huaiqiu in 1927. According to Yamaguchi, Tian was unsatisfied with the performance of the lead actress in the film, Yang Naimei, and complained to him that she did not understand the girl in his original design for the film.[100] Tian's complaint recalls his dissatisfaction with the 1920 performance of "Spiritual Light" in Tokyo, where he similarly complained about the inadequate stage set for the dream scene in the play.[101] Tian's avant-gardist experiments were closely intertwined with popular forms of presentation, ranging from variety show to commercial cinema, in Tokyo and Shanghai. It became a tension-ridden process in which the avant-garde spirit was shaped and in some ways constrained by new technological inventions and theatrical and cinematic conventions.

Tian Han would go on to write and direct *Hushang de beiju* (Tragedy at the Lake) during the Southland Institute's first public performance at the West Lake in April 1928.[102] The play combines the sixteenth-century Kun Opera *Mudan ting* (Peony Pavilion) with a touch of love suicide sensationalized by Taishō popular culture as in the case of Matsui Sumako. Tian Han re-creates the story of a beautiful young girl named Baiwei (White Flower), who is saved from a suicide attempt in protest against an arranged marriage, only to meet her lover,

Yang Mengmei (whose given name is borrowed from the male protagonist in "Peony Pavilion"), three years later at the West Lake. Baiwei eventually commits suicide in order to protect the integrity of their love tragedy, namely, to make sure that her lover can finish writing his precious sentimental memoir in the form of a love story. Using Baiwei as his mouthpiece, Tian Han expresses his fundamental search for the *artification* of life and the perfection of art. Baiwei's final suicide represents Tian Han's relentless pursuit of the integrity of art, even at the cost of human life. However, the trope of "life imitates art" was not new for Tian Han. As early as in the winter of 1921, and not long after he finished the very first full Chinese translation of Oscar Wilde's *Salome*, Tian had shared a similar story with the leading Japanese aesthetic writer Satō Haruo while visiting him at his home in Tokyo. The story, *Buxiu zhi'ai* (Eternal Love), about a woman who commits suicide in order to preserve her perfect image in her lover's mind, was performed in Tokyo at the Chinese YMCA without a finished script.[103] This perfection of art, however, comes with the sacrifice of the female protagonist and posits a troubling devaluation of women from a critical feminist perspective.

The Politics of Performing *Salome* and *Carmen*

In his active engagement with stage performance, independent publishing, filmmaking, and independent art education in Shanghai, Tian Han suffered his share of political interference. He wrote *Sun Zhongshan zhisi* (The Death of Sun Yat-sen) in 1929 to commemorate the founding father of the Republic, who died of illness in 1925.[104] He attempted to stage the play in a public performance but was not successful due to its sensitive subject matter in the eyes of the Nationalist censors.[105] This experience only made him more determined to stage *Salome* and *Carmen*. Tian Han had rendered Oscar Wilde's notorious play in its first full Chinese translation in Tokyo in the early 1920s and rewrote Prosper Mérimée's novella *Carmen* as a "spoken drama" in the early 1930s in Shanghai.[106] Tian's staging of these female figures, symbols of "night" and "fire," and sexuality and revolution, in Shanghai during the late 1920s and early 1930s—widely recognized in Chinese cultural history as a key moment of intellectual conversion from aestheticism to politics—was itself a way to process his Tokyo experience, experiment with the art of performance, and offer political commentary in the subtext of the play.

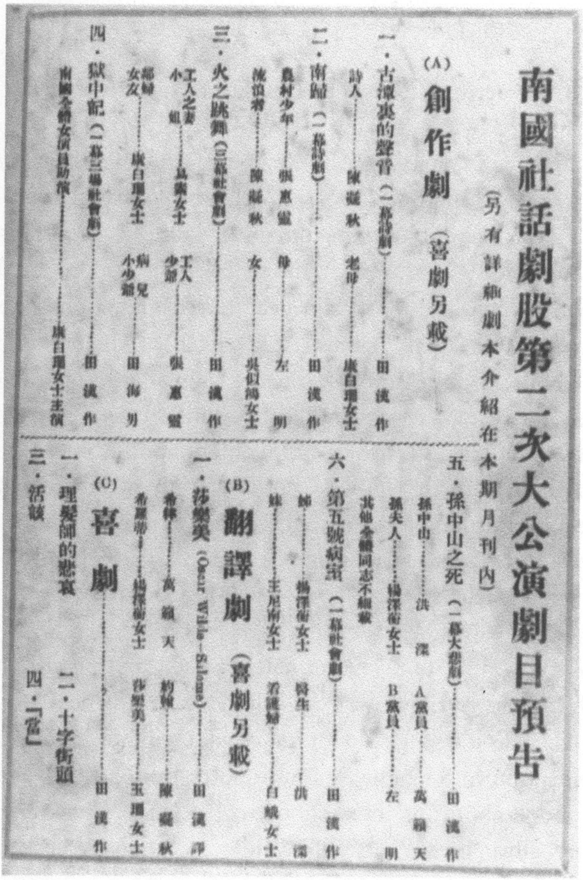

南國社話劇股第二次大公演劇目預告
(另有詳細劇本介紹在本期月刊內)

(A) 創作劇 (喜劇另載)

一・古潭裏的聲音 (一幕詩劇)……田漢作
詩人……陳凝秋　老母……康白珊女士

二・南歸 (一幕詩劇)……田漢作
農村少年……張惠靈　母……左明
流浪者……陳凝秋　女……吳似鴻女士

三・火之跳舞 (三幕社會劇)……田漢作
工人之妻 小姐……烏素女士　工人 少爺……張惠靈
鄰婦 女友……康白珊女士　病兒 小少爺……田海男

四・獄中記 (一幕三場社會劇)……田漢作
南國全體女演員助演……康白珊女士主演

五・孫中山之死 (一幕大悲劇)……田漢作
孫中山……洪深　A黨員……萬籟天
孫夫人……楊澤蘅女士　B黨員……左明
其他全體同志不細載

六・第五號病室 (一幕社會劇)……田漢作
姊……楊澤蘅女士　醫生……洪深
妹……王尼南女士　看護婦……白蛾女士

(B) 翻譯劇 (喜劇另載)

一・莎樂美 (Oscar Wilde—Salome)……田漢譯
希律……萬籟天　約翰……陳凝秋
希羅底……楊澤蘅女士　莎樂美……玉珊女士

(C) 喜劇

一・理髮師的悲哀　二・十字街頭……田漢作
三・活該　四・「色」

Advertisement for the second public performance of the Nanguo she group, published in *Nanguo yuekan* (1929). (Courtesy of the Shanghai Library.)

Tian's continuous interactions with contemporary Japanese intellectuals after his return to Shanghai highlight the robustness of the cultural connections between Taishō Tokyo and Republican Shanghai. But in practice his intimate connection to the Japanese cultural scene was achieved only through multiple mediations and displacements in popular culture and mass politics. The Hollywood mediations and Soviet contacts, as well as experiments with Peking Opera, are all examples of mediating cultural influences at work in Republican Shanghai. These mediating processes eventually made possible the staging of *Salome* and *Carmen* in the late 1920s and early 1930s, first in the little theater format, then on the grand stage for a commercial audience.

The Darkness of the Hollywood Vamp

Both the *Salome* and *Carmen* performances that Tian Han staged in Shanghai in 1929 and 1930 were triggered by his viewing of popular Hollywood renderings of the originals, *Salome* (1923, starring Alla Nazimova) and *The Loves of Carmen* (1927, starring the Mexican actress Dolores del Rio), the latter translated as *Dangfu xin* (The Heart of a Licentious Woman) in Chinese. Tian Han's first visual encounter with a Hollywood melodrama in Tokyo in 1916 initiated his lifelong obsession with Hollywood films. However, the Shanghai phase of Tian's Hollywood infatuation was equally intense. He went to watch *So This Is Paris,* directed by Ernst Lubitsch, at the Embassy Theatre right after its opening night in the United States in 1926.[107] Tian's familiarity with Lubitsch's films is evident in his comments on Lubitsch's status as a film auteur and his reference to having enjoyed the "Lubitsch Touch" (*liu wei*).[108] We can only speculate that if Tian Han had been exposed to Lubitsch's early cinematic rendition of *Carmen,* starring the Polish actress Pola Negri, during his Weimar years, he probably would have preferred it to the later Hollywood version emphasizing the character's licentiousness.

The popular Hollywood connection was intimately linked to a persistent Japanese connection. If Thomas Kurihara was the "Hollywood returnee" who inspired Tian Han when he was a young student in Tokyo, Ushihara Kiyohiko was his Hollywood connection in Shanghai.[109] Tian quotes from a borrowed copy of Ushihara's new book about his interactions with Charlie Chaplin in Hollywood in one of his "silver dream" essays.[110] While an exhaustive list of the Hollywood films Tian Han watched in Shanghai is impossible to compile, it would at least start with *Salome, The Loves of Carmen, Captain Blood, La Bohème, Modern Times, Robin Hood, Camille, The Gold Rush,* and *The Circus* and would easily number in the several dozens.[111]

More direct influences from Hollywood can be seen in Tian Han's choice of materials for his essays, plays, and filmscripts throughout his Shanghai years. For example, *Robin Hood* (United Artists, 1922, with Douglas Fairbanks) became the subject of one of the silver dream essays, and *The Phantom of the Opera* (Universal, 1925, with Lon Chaney) metamorphosed into *Yeban gesheng* ("Songs at Midnight," dir. Maxu Weibang, 1937), for which Tian Han not only set the revolutionary tone but also wrote all the lyrics for the film songs. Last but not the least, *La Bohème* (1926, with Lillian Gish as Mimi),[112] permeated the first half of Tian Han's "leftist" film story *Fengyun ernü* (Lovers in Troubled Times, 1934).[113] Tian Han's lifelong endeavor to "create the new woman" against the background of the Hollywood vamp tradition further confirms the central importance of this cinematic mediation. The popular cinematic form became a crucial channel through which to involve elites and masses alike. Through the mediation of the Hollywood screen, old stage performance was democratized and new stage performance was created. Tian Han's early embrace of the Hollywood vamp and later reaction against its darkness, as seen in his revamping of the White Snake legend in his later years, are two sides of the same coin.

The Fire of Soviet Modern Dance and Film

In addition to Hollywood film, Soviet modern dance constituted an important stimulus for the performance of *Salome* and *Carmen* in Shanghai. Tian Han's love of Russian literature and his embrace of Christian socialist thought through the Russian connection in Tokyo—including the not insignificant fact that the famed Russian ballerina Anna Pavlova had shared the stage with his production of "Spiritual Light" in 1920—paved his way to a firm Soviet connection in Shanghai. Tian became acquainted with Jiang Guangci through A Ying, himself an important playwright and cultural critic in modern China.[114] Jiang soon became an intermediary between Tian Han and the Soviet world in Shanghai. Through Jiang's introduction, Tian came into contact with the Soviet consul there. Tian was instrumental in organizing the premier of *Battleship Potemkin,* the leading Soviet avant-gardist filmmaker Eisenstein's most recent film, among a small group of Soviet residents and local artists in Shanghai in 1926.[115]

An E, also a returned student from the Soviet Union, the legendary "Red Salome" who was said to have "converted" Tian Han to communism through love, was likewise first introduced to Tian through Jiang.[116] Herself a talented poet, lyricist, and playwright, An E later wrote lyrics for some of the most popular songs in modern China, including "Yuguang qu" (Fisherman's Song) and "Maibao ge" (Newspaper-Selling Song).[117] Her secret identity as an underground Communist agent active in Shanghai, sometimes dressed like the rich wife of a high official and at other times in plain workers' clothes leading workers' movements, made her an enigmatic figure straight out of film noir. While Tian Han was drawn to the "red" An E and the two became lovers outside marriage, Jiang Guangci pursued the bohemian girl Wu Sihong of Tian's Southland

Institute, and the two became husband and wife.[118] The "marriage" of revolution and bohemianism, both symbolically and in real life, was enacted and enabled through Tian's contacts with the Soviet scene in Shanghai.

A key incident in Tian Han's contact with the Soviet cultural scene occurred when Jiang Guangci suggested that the Southland Institute host a welcoming party for the visiting Duncan Dancing Troupe from the Soviet Union,[119] which Tian did enthusiastically and successfully. The dance performance of Irma Duncan at the Olympia Theatre proved to be yet another seminal "modern" moment for Tian Han after his encounter with *The Sunken Bell* performance in Tokyo. As a disciple and an adopted child of Isadora Duncan, "the creator of modern dance," Irma Duncan embodied the avant-garde in modern dance at the time.[120] Tian's strategic emphasis on Irma's identity as a Soviet dancer and her connection through Isadora to the Moscow art scene highlighted the union of the Russian revolutionary tradition and the contemporary Soviet avant-garde. The mysterious vitality of the intersection of politics and the arts found renewed expression through Irma's dance performance in Shanghai.

This encounter not only stimulated Tian Han's creative energy but also provided a convenient rhetorical framework, namely, using politics to legitimize the aesthetic and endow art with a political edge, for the eventual realization of staging *Salome* in Shanghai. Tian praised Irma's dance as an expression of "the rebellion of the oppressed" and the spirit of the contemporary Soviet Union.[121] He made a further connection between Irma's "pure" "nontechnical" style of dance and "modern literature"; since her modern dance originated from those "unconscious movements" in our everyday lives, it embodied "symbols of suffering" and expressions of the subconscious as had already been discussed by Kuriyagawa Hakuson and Tian himself in Kyoto in 1921.[122] Tian further concluded that Irma's modern dance, with her red dress and bare feet, was like a call to arms, in which she led her followers in a fight against all evil and flew toward the land of light—and that was the "real dance for modern people" (*xiandairen de tiaowu*).[123]

The "land of light" imagery recalls the luminous Tokyo in Tian Han's diary, illuminated by Christianity, romanticism, socialism, and feminism. Tian Han wrote "A Night in a Café" in Tokyo while translating Oscar Wilde's *Salome*. Both texts were concerned with the struggle between the spirit and the flesh. Lin Zeqi, the male protagonist in Tian's play, torn between competing desires, confesses, "Spirit-flesh. Flesh-spirit. They are battling inside me. I feel so restless. My sorrow is like the fire in hell burning deep in my heart. Recently I have been tempted by death. I often feel that the God of death with his black wings stretched wide is calling me."[124] This is a direct borrowing from *Salome*, where John the Baptist states, "Art thou not afraid, daughter of Herodias? Did I not tell thee that I had heard in the palace the beating of the wings of the angel of death?"[125] Tian Han's commentary on Irma's dance highlighted the use of the female body and feminine charm to achieve an ultimate "revolutionary" goal, leading her followers to the land of light and away from the black wings of death.

Such an image of a female messiah recalls the female Faust and the role of the café waitress in Tian's earlier experiments, where romantic love and sexuality are portrayed as the ultimate weapons with which to engender political activism.[126] The feminine performance assumes a crucial role in all these persuasive acts, which attest to the importance of performance itself and the function of the powerful female image. Tian Han's renderings of *Salome* and *Carmen* a few years later bear some of the imprints of his encounter with Irma Duncan's luminous modern dance and the continuing resonance of the enlightening halos from his Tokyo experience.

Tian Han's intense encounter with the Salome trope was further intensified through an avant-garde revamping of an archetypal female image in the experimental Peking Opera *Pan Jinlian*. Tian warmly embraced Ouyang Yuqian's reinvention of Pan Jinlian (Golden Lotus), a symbol of adultery and female sexuality as canonized in such classic novels as *Shuihu zhuan* (The Water Margin) and *Jinping mei* (Plum in a Golden Vase).[127] Ouyang reconfigured Golden Lotus as "a woman longing for power and beauty," as someone with the "Salome spirit."[128] When writing a Peking Opera, *Wu Song*, in the 1940s, Tian Han commented on the reinvented Golden Lotus image as "a reincarnation of Salome."[129] Tian saw Alla Nazimova's 1923 Hollywood rendering of *Salome* around the time of the *Pan Jinlian* performance and started to realize his own conceptions of Salome and Carmen through his ideal "vampirish" actress on Shanghai stages.

This Salome complex was further manifested in Tian Han's article on contemporary Soviet cinema based on two essays written by a real life "Red Salome." Tian based his article on essays published in the first two issues of *Dianying* (Cinema),[130] whose author he identified as "Miss Sonia," a young girl who studied in the Soviet Union and had firsthand experience of Soviet cinema.[131] He borrowed Sonia's introduction of Soviet director Yakov Protazanov's *Sorok pervyy* ("Forty-First," 1927) in his essay.[132] The storyline of a fisherman's daughter turned Red Army solider, and her love-hate relationship with a White

Army officer on a deserted island, clearly enchanted Tian Han and captured his imagination. Most important, for Tian Han, the fisherman's daughter's final revelation and regaining of her "class consciousness," which culminates in her shooting the White Army officer within sight of a White Army ship approaching the deserted island, brought back the mysterious magnetism of love toward death that was planted in his consciousness as early as 1918 through Hauptmann's *The Sunken Bell.*[133] Tian Han could not help describing the Salomean moment after the shooting, when the female soldier, holding her lover's bloody head, cries, "Oh, my . . . my sweetheart . . . your beautiful eyes."[134] His commentary on this image comes from the perspective of the Salome trope as mediated through an explicit class-consciousness.

> Killing her lover and holding his head, crying, this is not something unfamiliar to those who have watched Oscar Wilde's *Salome.* However, for Salome, it is for her own sensual fulfillment, while for Maryutka, she is sacrificing her own sensual fulfillment to eliminate an enemy for the class that is trying to liberate her . . . holding their dead lovers' heads, singing praises for their lovers' bodies, and sighing about their lovers' tragic fate, the world of Salome and the world of Maryutka are far removed.[135]

This somewhat contrived class analysis, while seeming to condemn Salome, only serves to reveal the writer's obsession with her, both in the story and in real life. It is through the film story of Maryutka that Tian Han introduced to his Shanghai readers the enigmatic Soviet-educated Sonia, a pen name for Zhang Shiyuan (aka An E), the real life Red Salome who entered Tian's personal life around this time.[136]

The Ideal Actress

However, the actual performance of *Salome* on the Chinese stage would have to wait until the year 1929 when Tian Han eventually found his ideal Salome in Yu Shan, an aspiring young actress related to a high-ranking official in the Nationalist Party.[137] Pictures of Yu Shan as Salome were published in *Nanguo yuekan* (Southland Monthly) in 1929. One shows Yu Shan dancing as Salome in a seductive dress, with bare shoulder and feet, her arms stretched out in the shape of a snake, and her black hair in snakelike curls. The multivalent snake symbolism challenges Christian iconography with a heroic seductress while also gesturing toward the White Snake legend so central to Tian Han's work as a whole.

Another stage picture shows Yu Shan as Salome holding the head of John the Baptist, again with her profile in close-up, her face covered with golden powder, her eyes carefully outlined in dark eye shadow. The decision to use this photograph for publicity was not accidental. Yu Shan was chosen by Tian Han partly because her beautiful "Westernized" profile and upturned nose embodied Tian's ideal image of Salome. Here this westernized femme fatale is accompanied by the effeminate appearance of John the Baptist, performed by Chen Ningqiu,[138] which calls to mind the naked body of the weak Chinese playwright in the film still of "Lakeshore Spring Dream." Once again the Salome trope represents "masculinity besieged" by feminine transgression.[139]

In his essay "Gongyan zhiqian" (Before the Public Performance), Tian Han describes *Salome* in a politicized tone with a renewed affinity for the "red revolution." He upholds Wilde's play as a call for humanist liberation and national salvation, an eccentric interpretation not shared by many others at the time.[140] Tian Han's political rhetoric cannot hide his obsession with the deadly seductiveness of erotic love at the core of the Salome story, already engrained in his artistic sensibility in Tokyo. One might ask how the play's decadent sensibility, perceived as counterrevolutionary by many, could be construed as leftist. The answer is that for Tian Han and many of his fellow avant-gardists, Salome's aggressive female sexuality is an embodiment and displacement of radical revolutionary energy. The climate of social and political revolution granted the point of entry for the *Salome* play in 1929. For Tian Han, the play had already long preoccupied him, seeming to hold the answer to his insistent, restless search for spiritual and political liberation.

The cast for *Salome* was indeed an artistically exceptional one, with Yu Shan as Salome; Wan Laitian, with his "lion's hair and antelope's eyes," as Herodias; Jin Yan, with his melancholic expression, as the Young Syrian; and the "Poet of the World of the Spirit," Chen Ningqiu, as John the Baptist.[141] The set design and "realistic scenery" for the *Salome* performance were firsts of their kind in theater circles at the time. But the ultimate charm of the performance, according to set designer and violin accompanist Wu Zuoren, came from the "beautiful and expressive" rising star Yu Shan, whose bold and forceful performance was contagiously passionate.[142]

In fact, in 1929, the same year in which *Salome* was staged, when commenting on "art and its relationship with its times and politics," Tian Han declared, "[A]rt is the leap of soul, it leans toward idealism; while politics aims at maintaining the status quo . . . art as an indicator is more sensitive than politics, it is the vanguard of politics."[143] Tian's desire to connect avant-garde art and

Yu Shan as Salome, published in *Nanguo yuekan* (1929). (Courtesy of the Shanghai Library.)

popular politics can be seen through the transition from Nanguo she's 1929 Nanjing "little theater" performance of *Salome* to its first "grand theater" performance of *Carmen* in Shanghai in 1930.[144] Although Carmen was transformed (reformed) from "vamp" into a politicized romantic "new woman," wielding bohemian love as a magic weapon to bring about political mobilization, the play still drew criticism from all political camps. To answer such criticism, Tian Han remarked, simply, "I am neither sufficiently right nor left" (*ji bugou name zuo, ye bugou name you*).[145] Indeed, Tian Han's *Carmen,* as a "spoken drama" in performance rather than the original novella or Georges Bizet's opéra comique, must be taken seriously as a formal experiment as well as a political manifesto.

At the beginning of the third scene in this six-scene drama, Tian Han's stage instructions paint the exotic atmosphere of the interior of a Spanish inn filled with "lighthearted gypsy music."[146] When the music and dances resume, Carmen appears, "like a peacock amid everyone's claps and smiles."[147] When the music resumes again, Carmen dances the "romalis," and everyone claps in admiration.[148] Music and musical performance function in these three instances in Tian's stage instructions to stitch stories and scenes together, demonstrating the importance of music in Tian's spoken drama experiments and revealing their popularizing and political impulses. Carmen's character, in the end, emerged from these musical and dance performances as a revolutionary seductress, whose final declaration was her love of freedom and the coming of the "heaven" without a god.[149]

Conclusion

Using the central imagery of "night" and "fire," and taking Shanghai as the site of convergence, this chapter moves away from the illuminated landscape of Tokyo to the moral darkness and sexual and revolutionary energy of Shanghai. It is a move from one female archetype, the messianic female Faust of Meili, to another, the revolutionary seductress of Salome/Carmen. Tian Han's Shanghai existed in the shadow of a pre-earthquake Tokyo and finally replaced Tokyo as the cultural capital of East Asia in the late 1920s. In its darkness new forms of illumination were kindled. The night of decadence would harbor the fire of revolutionary energy.

Tian Han's experiments in independent publishing, independent filmmaking, and stage performance in a politically oppressive Shanghai illustrate that "art is the leap of the soul . . . it is the vanguard of politics." Rather than reaffirming the oft told narrative of the intellectual's conversion from aestheticism to politics, this chapter demonstrates how politics can be used to legitimize aesthetic forms, as well as the image of the femme fatale, and how transgression in ideology can be embodied in experimental art and transgressive sexuality. The double-edged symbolism of fire, real and mythical, ephemeral and eternal, captures both the sexual and the political implications of Tian Han's Shanghai experiments, at once augmenting and departing from the emphasis on spirituality in his Tokyo years. The emergence of the new woman in the form of a revolutionary seductress demonstrates how female sexual transgression became an embodiment of radical revolutionary energy in the context of Shanghai.

CHAPTER THREE

Lovers and Heroes in the Wartime Hinterland

Chivalry is the true color of heroes; gentility is the characteristic of lovers
If you think the two are different, you must be a fool talking in a dream
Romantic love is only natural instinct; heroism is humanity itself
At once the most romantic and the most heroic
Are the dragons and phoenixes among human beings

WEN KANG, *ERNÜ YINGXIONG ZHUAN*
(LEGEND OF LOVERS AND HEROES), 1872

Lovers and heroes, as embodiments of the private erotic realm and the public political realm, are coming together in the wartime Chinese hinterland as Wen Kang describes it. Literary scholar David Der-wei Wang argues that the "repressed modernity" of the 1872 novel *Legend of Lovers and Heroes* lies in Wen Kang's conscious conflation of Chinese heroism and Chinese eroticism—and in his attempt to "imagine them together in a single moral universe, not in two (or multiple) moral universes that have always existed side by side in the Chinese imagination."[1]

Tian Han's reinvention of the legend of lovers and heroes, in particular in his 1939 Peking Opera *Xin Ernü yingxiong zhuan* (A New Legend of Lovers and Heroes), achieved a similar goal, that of creating simultaneously ultrafeminine and ultramasculine, ultraromantic and ultraheroic female warriors. The figure of the modern woman takes inspiration from both "traditional" legends, such as the water goddess White Snake and the cross-dressing Mulan, and a host of Western, Japanese, and Chinese mediations of modern girl imagery.

As we have seen in the previous chapters, two enduring tropes, "creating the new woman" and "going to the people," are central to Tian Han's revolutionary vision. These tropes resurface as key concerns for wartime intellectuals. The imagined authenticity of both Chinese women and "the people," as dual allegories of a pure national spirit, joined hands during the extreme conditions of war. The need for anti-Japanese mobilization ushered in an unprecedented level of participation by women in "guerrilla drama warfare," as well as the renewed urgency of going to the people. The forced migration from the coastal, urban centers to the great hinterland (*da houfang*), due to the increasing Japanese military threat, in effect provided avenues for going to the people and materialized an enduring intellectual obsession with discovering authentic cultural roots in folk songs, storytelling, local operas, and popular entertainments.

While the hinterland was at first a temporary forced homeland under the threat of war, the *idea* of the hinterland soon took on populist and romantic meanings—closely related to the idealized countryside in the Japanese new village movement and Russian folk populism (*narodnichestvo*)—and presents an alternate utopian landscape for Tian Han and the urban intellectual avant-gardes.[2] Behind the Russian and Japanese glorification of the "folk" one finds the nineteenth-century German obsession with the *Volk* and the thought of Johann Gottfried Herder.[3] *Da houfang*, as the hinterland was described in Chinese, denotes both a sense of provincialism and a safe haven to which one can retreat and from which one can regain strength. Thus, the hinterland can be both experiential and conceptual, both real and utopian. Just as in English the word *hinterland* carries a derogatory connotation while the idea of a rural utopia is celebrated by the romantics, so in China, under wartime conditions, the idea of the hinterland was double-edged and multivalent.

The movement from coastal urban centers to the great hinterland was a journey in both space and time. The majority of cities, townships, and villages in the vast Chinese hinterland lagged far behind the cosmopolitan "film set," the all-night café, and the cultural laboratory that was Shanghai in terms of infrastructure and development. Ironically, however, for most urban intellectuals the forced migration from coastal cities to the hinterland proved to be a journey of homecoming, as a majority of them had originally come from provincial cities and rural areas before landing in Shanghai or Beijing. Many of them, including Tian Han, were able to stay in their hometowns for a period of time during the war.[4] They reconnected with the regional dialects and local cultural forms they had grown up with. Such a lived experience concretized the "folk" for the wartime intellectuals, and helped ground them in their "Chineseness." The hinterland and the Southland (Nanguo, central to Tian Han's Shanghai experimentations) are not quite interchangeable but are unquestionably connected in Tian's intellectual journeys from Shanghai on the East Coast to the southwestern interior of China. The artistic, amorous, and political meanings associated with the Southland, as discussed in chapter 2, largely apply to the wartime hinterland through the lens of Tian Han's art and activism, even though the idea of the hinterland is often connected to things traditional, conservative, and even backward.

The wartime hinterland presents several unique challenges to our usual approach to examining the condition of modernity. The shifting locality of cultural production, circulation, and consumption during the turbulent 1930s and 1940s makes it almost impossible to construct a coherent picture of wartime cultural history. The multiple cultural centers that coexisted during the war and the short-lived nature of their societies, institutions, and journals all complicate the task of elucidating wartime cultural developments.

As a result, the cultural transformations leading up to and continuing during the Second Sino-Japanese War (1937–45) have been largely understudied in modern Chinese cultural history. Rather than trying to present a comprehensive picture of the cultural dynamics of the wartime hinterland, this chapter attempts to delineate Tian Han's continued engagement with the tropes of "creating the new woman" and "going to the people" at a particular historical time and place, which served to intensify his transgressive experimentalism and the hybridity of his cultural productions.

Tian Han's role as a leading underground Communist activist in the left-leaning Yihua and Diantong film companies in the mid-1930s, and, more important, as a mastermind of "revolutionary popular songs" (many of them anti-Japanese) for the imminent war, finally landed him in a Nationalist prison in 1935. At the time, the Nationalists were still pursuing a policy of "appeasing internal turmoil before fending off external threats" (*rangwai bixian annei*), established even before the Manchurian Incident of 1931, which meant that Communists, rather than the Japanese, were their number-one enemy. Eventually, the Japanese invasion of Manchuria and the subsequent bombing of Shanghai in 1932 did push the Nationalists to engage in direct military confrontation with the Japanese. Nevertheless, Tian Han was detained until late July of 1935 and was then placed under house arrest in the Nationalist capital, Nanjing, until the outbreak of the war in July 1937.[5] The *popularity* and cultural influence of the Communist writers and filmmakers, on the other hand, made them indispensable to the Nationalists' anti-Japanese propaganda *after* the outbreak of the full-scale war. Tian Han, an expert on Japanese culture with many Japanese friends, thus became a practitioner of anti-Japanese propaganda against Japanese military expansion under the extreme conditions of war, with financial and institutional support from the Nationalists.

There were three distinctive spheres of influence competing for cultural power during the wartime period: the Japanese controlled the northeastern region, the Nationalists controlled the eastern and central-southern regions, and the Communists controlled the northwestern region. However, intellectual and cultural activities defy such divisions. The Japanese actress Yamaguchi Yoshiko, also known under her Chinese name Li Xianglan, embodies the seductive glamour of the Manchurian film industry and the colonial modernity of its hybrid Sino-Japanese bilingual cultural empire. The legendary Shanghai female writer Eileen Chang tells the story of Japanese-occupied Shanghai, while Tian Han himself represents intellectual activists in the Nationalist-controlled southern cities, as well as across the wartime hinterland. Zhao Shuli, the "model peasant writer," is considered the most pronounced voice of the Communist base in the Northeast, where the femme fatales of Shanghai modernism were metamorphosing into woman warriors in the wartime hinterland.

For many students and scholars of modern China, the first point of reference to a possible "wartime modernity" situated in the hinterland proper is the 1942 "Yan'an Talks" that Mao Zedong delivered to members of the Yan'an Forum on Literature and Arts.[6] Mao consolidated his leadership of the Communist Party through the Long March and the building of Yan'an as the Communist revolutionary base from the mid-1930s to the early 1940s.[7] It has long been taken for granted that Mao's Yan'an Talks set the direction of wartime activism and that his call to "go to the masses" and "learn from the workers, peasants, and soldiers" only then became the principal directive for wartime intellectual activists.

Situating Mao's Yan'an Talks in the genealogy of the dialectic relationship between the avant-garde and the popular from the early twentieth century onward, it becomes clear that Mao's ideas were but renewed articulations of a long-standing obsession with "going to the people" among Chinese intellectuals, of whom Tian Han was a representative case. Tian's Tokyo activism and Shanghai experimentation in both the arts and politics share a similar populist impulse with the YMCA popular education movement led by James Yen and the *geyao* (folk song) movement led by professors and students at Beijing University in the early 1920s.[8] These populist movements further developed into a double-edged political endeavor to both speak for and learn from the people under the extreme conditions of war.

The Avant-Garde and the People

The intellectual construction of "the people" in modern times has always been intimately linked to the notion of modernity and the creation of the nation-state, which can be traced back to French romantic socialism of the mid-eighteenth century, the German philosopher Johann Gottfried Herder in the late eighteenth century, and the Russian *narodnik* (going to the people) movement of the mid–nineteenth century. However, the term *the people* has radically different connotations in different languages and at different historical moments. Tian Han and his generation of transitional intellectuals in modern China often connected the notion of "the people" to the idea of "the folk," as it is used in German, where the term *Das Volk* refers to the idea of a people bound by ties of common blood. Similarly in Japanese, *jōmin*, the "eternal folk," was conceptualized by Yanagita Kunio in his study of the traditions of mountain people, and his establishment of the field of Japanese folklore studies in the early- to mid–twentieth century.[9] In modern Chinese, both the terms *nongmin* (peasant) and *nongcun* (countryside) partake of the concept of the folk, while *renmin* (the people) and *qunzhong* (the masses) are more often politically weighted terms and often exclusively class based. Yet, despite their differences, all these terms were articulated by individuals who were engaged in an interconnected global discourse about the people, were aware of and borrowed ideas from each other, and were themselves, in one way or another, the intellectual avant-gardes of their time.

Lu Xun's famous preface to his first short story collection, *Nahan* (Call to Arms),[10] includes an exchange between himself and a more radically inclined visitor in 1918 in which he introduces the now canonical "iron house" metaphor, with its image of the "caller" (the intellectual) outside the windowless iron house (China) calling (*darang*) to arouse the "lighter sleepers" (the vanguard) within—those who harbor the hope of waking their fellow sleepers. The aural dimension of "crying aloud" to spread intellectual messages and awaken the people nicely illustrates the idea of *xuanchuan* as the act of "announcing and spreading," as it would be echoed again and again throughout the twentieth century in China.

Literary scholars like Leo Ou-fan Lee and Carolyn Brown have examined the paradigm and paradox of the iron house, particularly the profound skepticism and faith in intellectual endeavors that Lu Xun intended to simultaneously perform in his account.[11] Against the predominantly romantic mood of his times, to which Tian Han also subscribed, Lu Xun was often skeptical regarding the utility of propagating intellectual ideas. At the same time, he did have faith in the importance of cultural intermediates who understood conditions both inside and outside the iron house. The iron house metaphor reveals how differently *xuanchuan* and *propaganda* resonate in their respective cultural contexts, and how easily we tend to equate propaganda with brainwashing—something that puts the intellect to sleep rather than awakening it.

The future Communist party leader Mao Zedong was under the influence of the same Japanese new village movement in Hunan around the same time as Tian Han was under its influence in Tokyo. In fact, it has been suggested that Mao's youthful proposal for a Republic of Hunan (*Hunan gongheguo*) and Hunanese independence in 1920 was built on the idea of the utopian "new village."[12] Notably, Tian Han promoted his 1927 film *Dao minjian qu* (To the People) with a full-page advertisement on a film journal, with its Russian title, *V Narod*, and English title, *To the People*, printed side by side with the Chinese one.[13] In 1927 Tian Han favored *minjian*, or *minkan* in Japanese, as best conveying the sense of a utopian cultural space wherein the authentic folk can be located.

Discussing theater and society amid the threat of war in 1936, Tian Han used the Chinese phrase *qianwei*, literally "front guard," to denote the "avant-gardists" who, though embedded in the people, can be relied on to propagate new arts and ideas to the people.

> We cannot simply use the preferences of the masses (*qunzhong*) as the criterion for the popularization (*dazhonghua*) of theater. However, we also shouldn't deviate from the populace (*dazhong*) in searching for the proper criterion. Discussing the popularization of theater without taking the populace into consideration is clearly a joke. We should try to discover the avant-garde (*qianwei*) within the populace, that is, we should use the avant-garde of the populace as our criterion.[14]

"The masses" and "the general populace" entered Tian Han's rhetoric at the time of the imminent Japanese invasion in 1936. For Tian Han, the idea of the avant-garde developed from the more cosmopolitan May Fourth *xianfeng* (vanguard), leading the cultural scene toward Westernization, to a cultural and political orientation anchored in Chinese wartime conditions.

The same year in which Tian Han wrote this piece, searching for the avant-garde within the populace, Zhao Shuli, often regarded as the leading "peasant writer" of modern China, attempted to categorize the multiple layers of relationship between peasants and their vanguards in a short piece entitled "Wenhua yu xiaohuozi" (Culture and Young Fellows) in 1936.[15] In Zhao Shuli's pre-1942 writings and cultural activities, before his later national reputation as a "faithful follower" of Mao Zedong's Yan'an Talks, we discover a lost phase in the construction of "the people" in modern Chinese intellectual history.

As a local educator in 1936, Zhao targeted his essay at the so-called young fellows of the Chinese countryside (*nong chutou de xiaohuozi*, literally, "young peasants"). However, as with Tian Han, his emphasis is on those few "young fellows" who had some education (*shangguo jitian xue*), and who could "tell the other young fellows 'what to do' when they are in trouble." Zhao further suggests that it is not enough just to give advice; one should, in fact, "stand in front of the other young fellows and shout 'follow me!'"[16] This outcry is another strong echo of Lu Xun's *Call to Arms*. In the performative aspect of both Tian Han's and Zhao Shuli's texts, we again see the embodiment of *xuanchuan* as "popular propaganda"—a means of communication that often relies on vivid physical performance to spread its message and achieve its goal. This communicative aspect of *xuanchuan* suggests a comparison with popular culture and mass media as practiced in a capitalist context, which will be discussed in the epilogue of the book to bring the story of the avant-garde and the popular to the postsocialist transformations in China.

In order to make such communication possible, Zhao Shuli focuses on those who occupy a special position among the young fellows, those who, like himself, had received some formal education. He is one of those "lighter sleepers" who knows the potential for breaking the iron house. Positioning himself inside the iron house, Zhao emphasizes the importance of the intellectual vanguard's positive function in waking up its fellow men, especially in letting them feel what the vanguard observed first, as illustrated in his journalistic activities from 1939 to 1942, before his ascendancy to national fame.

Zhao Shuli was the sole editor of a small local weekly, *Zhongguo ren* (The Chinese People), in a remote mountain village in Shanxi in 1940. While writing for this weekly, Zhao emphasized the importance of folk sayings, and he was said to bring a dictionary of the local dialect with him on every research trip. In his conscientious endeavor to expand the sensibilities of the other young fellows, Zhao translated articles about anti-Japanese fighters published in *Xinhua ribao* (New China Daily), the official Communist Party newspaper during the war, into "clapper-talks" (*kuaiban*), rhythmic monologues spoken to the accompaniment of specially made bamboo clappers, allowing news—and "propaganda"—to spread among the illiterate peasants.[17] More than ten years of propaganda work earned Zhao the position of an avant-gardist within the peasantry, particularly as a translator and educator for the benefit of other young fellows. "We should get literature," he said, "out of the attics of the leftist writers and put it on the *kangs* [warmed brick beds in northern China] of the laboring people (*laodong renmin*)." He made similar statements from the early 1930s to early 1942, before Mao Zedong's Yan'an Talks made it to his remote mountain village.[18] Zhao Shuli has attracted renewed scholarly attention in recent years, as his wartime practice remains central to the concerns of contemporary cultural politics.[19]

In *Li Youcai banhua* (Rhymes of Li Youcai), the book that made Zhao Shuli a household name in wartime China, Li Youcai is just such a model young fellow.[20] A poor man who watches other people's cows for a living, Li nonetheless possesses a sharp wit and a talent for composing satirical verses, as evidenced by this example from Jack Belden's translation in his 1949 *China Shakes the World.*

> Hooray for Yan, our village chief, who towers all above us;
> By all the years you've been our boss, it's plain to see you love us,
> Ten autumns now, the polling place has seen the folk in action:
> And each election proves once more that Yan's the big attraction.
> Yet times are getting harder now and labor we'd be saving,
> So I suggest we have your name cut on a wood engraving.
> Each voter then, instead of writing out the famous name,
> Can simply use the chop and the results will be the same.
> Then Yan, who's always first, can take the damn thing home and save it.
> For it will be a hundred years before we re-engrave it.[21]

This is what made propaganda popular. The voice of the people was channeled through the rhymes of Li Youcai, rendering the corrupt village head an object of derision or mockery. These issues raised by Zhao in the early 1940s remain close to the hearts of the many Chinese who witness official corruption in contemporary China. Zhao Shuli's early writings and cultural activities suggest that he followed his own initiative in bridging the gap between the intelligentsia and the people before the Yan'an Talks were delivered. Zhao's conscious adaptation of "the peasant language" was an outcome of his own "double identity" as peasant and intellectual rather than a response to Mao's call to "go to the people."[22]

Zhao Shuli's case not only problematizes the absolute link between Mao's Yan'an Talks and choices made by wartime intellectuals, but it also reminds one of the importance of restoring the personal in the examination of the political. Mao Zedong, the mastermind of the Yan'an Talks, and the ultimate symbol of "party control," was himself part of the May Fourth generation of modern Chinese writers. Hailing from Hunan province, the "cradle of revolution" in early Republican China, Mao, like Tian Han, belonged to the same romantic generation of intellectuals.[23] Mao and Tian searched for romance in the spirit of revolution and "made revolution" in the spirit of romance. Despite being five years Tian's senior, Mao did not go abroad to study and in fact asked Tian to buy books for him in Tokyo.[24] Contrary to a rigid understanding of the Communist Party and its leadership as constrictive and monolithic, a fruitful examination of the cultural politics of modern China calls for a more carefully calibrated approach to the linkages between the personal and the political. It requires an understanding of the intimate relationships between the Communist Party and the modern intellectual and between the intellectual and the people.

Even when recognized as a political force in its own right, the avant-gardists' ambiguous class background was something of a continuing vexation to twentieth-century Chinese politics. Mao Zedong, for example, paid special attention to "the petite bourgeoisie" (*xiao zichan jieji*), in which he included "the lower levels of the intellectuals—students, primary and secondary school teachers, lower government functionaries, office clerks, small lawyers—and the small traders," and insisted that "because of both its size and its class character, this class deserves very close attention,"[25] by which he meant that this class both serves an important function and needs to be strictly monitored.

Mao continued his dialogue with and concern about the intellectual "petite bourgeoisie" at the height of the Second Sino-Japanese War. In a series of essays published in 1939, he singled out the "vanguard role" played by China's young people since the May Fourth movement and encouraged them to "take the lead and march in the forefront of the revolutionary ranks."[26]

Mao encouraged the recruitment of large numbers of intellectuals to help the proletariat build its own culture.[27] However, suspicious of their subjective and individualist proclivities, he considered them impractical in thinking and irresolute in action and urged them to "throw themselves heart and soul into mass revolutionary struggles."[28] In his 1942 Yan'an Talks, Mao openly recognized his own intellectual "petit bourgeois" background, with the express purpose of demonstrating, in a vivid autobiographical sketch, how he had rid himself of that "contaminated" mind-set and "fundamentally changed [his] bourgeois and petit bourgeois feelings."[29]

The colloquial style and auditory appeal of the Yan'an Talks, propagated and remembered as speeches rather than written texts, demonstrated Mao's deliberate choice to perform the role of a down-to-earth leader who, though coming from the educated class, wholeheartedly embraced the anti-elitist, even anti-intellectual, stance of the working class, which was supposedly rooted in Chinese folkways and local wisdom rather than Westernized and Japanized intellectual habits.[30]

This marks Mao's radical romantic departure from the kind of philosophical doubts Leon Trotsky expressed in his assessment of "proletarian culture" in a 1923 article, "What Is Proletarian Culture, and Is It Possible?," where he considers the double-edged role of intellectuals in the struggle to construct a "proletarian culture."[31] Mao is determined to fundamentally convert intellectuals "from one class to another" while Trotsky doubts the feasibility of such a conversion.[32] What happens after a "petit bourgeois" intellectual is converted into a proletarian intellectual? Is a proletarian intellectual still a proletarian? Is he still an intellectual?

These questions of conversion and transformation are pertinent to our study of Tian Han, an avant-garde artist who, in the midst of revolution, attempts to transform himself into a popular lyricist, dramatist, journalist, and propagandist.[33] The image of an intellectual who "drops his/her pen to join the military" (*toubi congrong*) was the central image of the poet at war, as exemplified by one of Mao's favorite historical figures, the scholar-official Zeng Guofan, who founded the Hunan Army to suppress the Taiping Uprising in the mid–nineteenth century.[34]

Military identity and fascination with the military (symbolized by the military uniform and inherent in the original meaning of *avant-garde*) permeated the wartime stage and screen. For many intellectuals, the social reality of being attached to a military unit, and their semimilitary daily existence as propaganda troupes subject to military institutional control, proved to be both terrifying and fascinating. Mao Zedong and Tian Han's generation's youthful flirtations with the military around the time of the 1911 Revolution, and Tian's taking up a position in the Nanjing government and flaunting his military uniform in 1927 while teaching at Shanghai Art University, showcased the "men of letters" reconstructing and reimagining themselves as "men of action." The hinterland period finally transformed the intellectual fascination with the military into an at times exhilarating, at times terrifying daily practice. It highlighted the political edge of the avant-garde and reminded students and scholars of modern China that instead of focusing chiefly on the intrinsic aesthetic value of the work of art we also need to examine its real life effect in the Chinese context.

The outbreak of the war with Japan ushered in new means of participation in Chinese cultural history for intellectuals. It provided a radical shift from the "ivory tower" to the "crossroads." Issues such as "going to the people" (*dao minjian qu*) and the "popularization of literature and arts" (*wenyi de dazhonghua*), long debated within the urban avant-garde, were finally put into practice under rural conditions. In a way the wartime hinterland consolidated many of the fragmented intellectual experiments conducted prior to wartime and anticipated the rise of Communist China after the ensuing Civil War. However, the success of the Communist Revolution and the establishment of the People's Republic in 1949 changed some of the intellectual avant-gardists into cultural bureaucrats. How radical could the antiestablishment avant-garde remain when the establishment swallowed it? The answer may not always be negative, but this is the central question we have to keep asking ourselves when studying contemporary China.

The Nationalist and Communist revolutions in China were arguably the leading avant-garde movements of their time. They were, of course, experiments in new socioeconomic programs; perhaps more important, they were also careful and systematic efforts to use powerful visual imagery, symbols, and language to shape people's thinking. The socialist revolution launched by Mao, in particular, was a battle of words and images fought for hearts and minds. It was a battle of cultural persuasion. Wartime conditions and Chinese reality made it a strategic necessity for the Chinese Communist Party, one of the leading avant-garde forces of its time, to communicate with and mobilize the great majority of the Chinese population as the vanguard of national salvation. This desire to engineer social transformation through popularization—through images, symbols, and language—linked the avant-garde and the people and brought performance into the realm of politics.

An essentially ambivalent relationship exists between modern intellectuals and their imagined other, the people. In the rhetoric of the time, "the people" generally means the peasantry in rural areas and the proletariat in urban settings. The people and the characteristics associated with "them" (such as moral purity, industriousness, and radical conservatism in the case of the peasantry and radical progressivism in the case of the proletariat) explain the intellectuals' ambivalence toward them. On the one hand, the notion of an idealized, authentic folk invites the intellectual impulse to "go to the people" with the dual, uneasily conjoined hopes of learning from them and educating them for national regeneration. On the other hand, the revolutionary masses, more politically progressive than most urban intellectuals, force the intellectuals to face their own alienation from this more radical other.

Therein lies the dilemma for generations of Chinese intellectuals, who have aspired to assimilate themselves to what they conceive to be the purer and more radical portions of society, only to discover their own ambivalence in this aspiration. The idealization of the rural peasantry had little to do with the actual dirt and hard labor associated with the daily experience of the peasants. And yet the need to get their own hands dirty, at least metaphorically, became an urgent one for the urban intellectuals. Guerrilla drama warfare provided such an occasion for a taste of dirt and hardship for the wartime intellectuals. Propaganda at this point in Chinese history is a discourse directed at the people in the name of the people by the avant-garde, or the avant-garde turned establishment. The multilayered and interconnected discourse regarding "the people" is at the heart of wartime intellectual endeavors.

The Use of Tradition and Intermedia Experiments

The use and abuse of "tradition" (Peking Opera, folk songs and rhythms, etc.) in mobilizing "the people" and popularizing propaganda emerges as a central intellectual concern under the extreme conditions of war. It has been argued that Chinese culture relied on "the resurgence of tradition" to provide the stability of a presumably unchanging cultural core for a generation of Chinese people to cling to during a time of crisis and upheaval.[35] This is further supported by the argument that designated "traditional opera" as the ideal genre for wartime propaganda. As an art form that "comes from the masses and goes back to the masses,"[36] traditional opera earned political sanction and special status during the war. However, the traditional opera of the late 1930s and the 1940s had metamorphosed into something different from that of the 1910s.[37] Moreover, the emergence and development of film and "spoken drama" provided fertile ground for intermedia experiments and cross-genre fertilization. Hence, the traditions that served to stabilize China during its time of crisis were not frozen in time or preserved in the amber of nostalgia but were flexible, living forms that continued to evolve even while they provided a sense of continuity.

All the popular wartime genres—Peking Opera (*jingju*), folk storytelling and ballad singing (*minjian shuochang*), drum talk (*gushu*), clapper talk (*kuaiban shu*), spoken drama, sound film, and mass singing (with poetry in the form of song lyrics)—share an important quality. That is, they are all genres with a strong focus on the auditory qualities of communicating and spreading a message from the few to the many. The conditions of war and the need for national mobilization called for intermedia experiments and genre transgression in opera, drama, and film. Tian Han's cinematic sensibility and his way of appropriating "traditional" Chinese art forms such as Peking Opera and folk storytelling through a cinematic angle,[38] as well as his active involvement with the film industry throughout the war, suggest a cultural orientation that is distinctively nontraditional in its use of traditional elements.

Tian Han's long-standing interest in reforming Chinese opera found an ideal opportunity during a time of national crisis, when the search for a "national form" became a political and cultural priority.[39] Nationalism, in the form of anti-Japanese sentiments, found its best expression in a reconstructed tradition, a timely manipulation of the past and a reinvented form to which anti-Japanese sentiments could be anchored. As discussed in chapter 2, Tian Han continued to translate Tanizaki Jun'ichirō and Satō Haruo well into the mid-1930s while writing anti-Japanese lyrics and nationalist plays. Both his love and admiration for Japanese culture and his participation in anti-Japanese cultural productions were sincere: they reflect his discriminating view of the achievements of Japanese literature and Japan's imperialist culture.

Before the outbreak of a full-scale war in July 1937, Nationalist censorship of Communist activities reached a new height, as the leadership of the Nationalist Party considered the Communists a bigger threat than the Japanese. Historical plays in the form of Peking Opera and various local operas, because of their ability to disguise current affairs under layers of costume as a way to evade censorship and to both entertain and rally the majority of the populace, became one of the most popular forms of artistic and political expression.[40] The operatic form lent itself to the creation of arias and songs. In the form of lyrics for singing parts in opera, drama, and film, Tian Han's intermedia experiments during the war privileged poetry as one of the most vital genres. Finding his best poetic expression in numerous song lyrics and librettos, he gave new life to both classical Chinese and modern Western-style poetry, sometimes by deliberately fashioning his dramas, operas, and films into vehicles for the performance of his songs.[41]

Opera film (*xiqu dianying*) emerged as an important genre for Tian Han in the wartime context. Tian wrote a review of *Zhan jingtang*, an opera film directed by Fei Mu, arguably the most artistically renowned film director at the time, only days before war broke out between China and Japan in July 1937. He described the opera on which the film was based as "a moving opera with its original folkloric 'wildness.'" He further regarded the achievement of the film as "a dialogue between film art and the best of traditional Chinese performing art . . . *that the silver light gives new life to the old stage!*"[42] One cannot help but detect the parallel between Tian Han's approach to opera through film in 1937 and his appropriation of the White Snake story from a similar cinematic angle in 1927 in the film "Lakeshore Spring Dream." The cinematic impulse is a strong current running through Tian Han's aesthetic journey from his first encounter with the magic medium in 1916 in Tokyo.

Tian Han's film theory has been described as a "dream-making theory,"[43] building on Tanizaki Jun'ichirō's formulation of film as "a dream made by human beings with the help of machines."[44] For Tian, the dreamlike quality of film was endowed with a transgressive energy that had the potential to enrich the "old opera" in its presentation with the aid of modern electric lighting.

In the aforementioned review, Tian argues against the generally held view that film is realistic while "old opera" (*jiuxi*) is symbolic (Tian used the English term *stylization* in his Chinese original), perhaps recalling his enchantment with the utterly symbolic *The Cabinet of Dr. Caligari* in Tokyo in 1921. He maintains that one of the most unique characteristics of Chinese old opera is its "free stage setting" (*changmian de ziyou*), meaning that there is no limit to what old opera can present onstage.[45] For Tian this is precisely where Chinese opera meets the genre of film, in that it gains its freedom from the absence of realistic settings, while film, by its very nature, has the freedom to exploit any setting, realistic or symbolic. Tian considers film a great complement to Chinese opera in this regard. At the same time, he highlights the three-dimensional quality of Chinese opera, the fact that an audience can appreciate the performance of the actor from various angles while film is flat, and one could not achieve the same aesthetic satisfaction before the invention of three-dimensional film.[46]

However, for Tian Han the most progressive aspect of film art is its use of light, which connects his hinterland period to the lights of Tokyo and the silver light of Shanghai filmmaking. Light is also the soul of the stage. The traditional staging of Chinese opera had been literally left in the dark by new lighting techniques. The wonderful dance and performance skills of the opera actors, and the exquisite details of their elegant costumes, had never been fully illuminated. Hence Tian Han lamented that, although Chinese opera benefited from a three-dimensional stage, it had been aesthetically suffocated by its flat and rigid lighting. Tian particularly mentioned the film technique of the "close-up" (with the aid of modern lighting) and its possible contribution to highlighting opera performers' meticulous training in their facial expressions, hand gestures, and dance steps.[47] Tian's cinematic approach rejuvenated Chinese opera, and the operatic mode in turn infiltrated the genre of film, as demonstrated in his wartime experiments discussed later in this chapter.

As important as the prominence of *sight* is the persistent importance of *sound.* Tian Han's "dream making" during the war continued to highlight the auditory in visual representations and helped to generate a new wave of "popular song" in 1940s' China onstage, onscreen, and in the streets. Many of these songs were first created as "anti-Japanese" songs, including the current Chinese national anthem, the subject of chapter 4.

It suffices to mention here that during his house arrest in Nanjing, after having been released from the Nationalist prison in July 1935,[48] Tian Han actively participated in the making of *Yeban gesheng* (Songs at Midnight) by director Maxu Weibang, who is regarded by many contemporary Chinese critics as "the Hitchcock of China."[49] As well as being the lyricist of three of the most popular songs in the film—"Yeban gesheng" (Songs at Midnight), "Rexue" (Warm Blood), and "Huanghe zhilian" (Love of the Yellow River)—Tian Han was largely responsible for the final draft of the screenplay, as he cowrote the filmscript under the pseudonym Chen Yu. The film was released in February 1937 in Shanghai by the New China Film Company (Xinhua yingye gongsi). A remake of *The Phantom of the Opera,* it is regarded as "the first Chinese horror movie" by contemporary Western film critics who first saw it when it surfaced at international film festivals in recent decades.[50]

Tian Han's role in weaving together this "Chinese *Phantom of the Opera*" was largely downplayed because of his sensitive political position. He was, at best, remembered only as the lyricist of the film's songs, as was also the case with another 1937 hit, *Malu tianshi* ("Street Angel," released in July 1937 around the time of the outbreak of the Second Sino-Japanese War). The latter film featured the singer-actress Zhou Xuan and another three memorable songs of 1930s' China with lyrics by Tian Han: "Tianya genü" (Wandering Songstress),[51] "Siji ge" (Song of Four Seasons), and "Huaixiang qu" (Longing for My Hometown).

Tian Han's continuous and intimate involvement with the Shanghai film industry, even at the time of his house arrest in Nanjing, speaks to the importance of the underlying cinematic perspective in deciphering his art and activism during the war. Tian Han's role in the making of popular film songs on the basis of melodies borrowed from Chinese folklore and Western opera demonstrates the marriage of the cinematic and operatic. He composed beautiful, classical-style poems for his song lyrics (as discussed later in the chapter and in subsequent chapters), and the songs came to be known by the common man as popular love and patriotic songs. In Tian Han's reinvention of Chinese lyrical poetry amid war and national salvation, he found a way to best express his generation's erotic and patriotic desires as both sentimental lovers and aspiring heroes of the nation.

From Lovers to Volunteers

Tian Han's 1934 story and its 1935 film adaptation *Fengyun ernü* (Lovers in Troubled Times) suggest the emergence of a culturally mature expression of the anti-Japanese war in modern China. With its theme song, "Yiyongjun jinxingqu" (March of the Volunteers), rising to the status of the national anthem of the PRC after 1949, this film provides an invaluable opportunity to explore the intrinsic relationship between aesthetics and politics in wartime China. The two themes of "creating the new woman" and "going to the people" find their best manifestations in the plot, which revolves around two young intellectuals educating their young neighbor girl and then making their final decision to give up higher learning to go to the war front.

Shanghai in 1934 harbored heightened anti-Japanese sentiment. The Japanese army had invaded Manchuria and installed a puppet regime, "Manchukuo," in the northeastern provinces in 1931. The last emperor of the Qing dynasty, Puyi, who abdicated in 1911 after the Republican Revolution, was used by the Japanese as a figurehead of the state.[52] Japan soon invaded Shanghai, bombing the Zhabei district on January 29, 1932, and bringing one of the most important cultural centers of Republican China under its military shadow. The bombing destroyed many symbolic structures in Shanghai, including the Commercial Press complex and its library, cutting off the bloodline of the biggest publisher in Shanghai at the time.

By the time he came to conceive the story for "Lovers in Troubled Times" in 1934, Tian Han had undergone radical self-criticism some four years earlier. He joined the Communist Party in 1932.[53] The film and the song Tian helped to create were products of a specific left-leaning sector of the Shanghai film industry in the mid-1930s. At the same time, the film situates China within an internationalist vision, highlighting historical traces of the colonial presence of Germany and the threat of Japanese imperialism. It maps Shanghai, Qingdao, and Manchuria as three sites of contested meaning: the vertical class structure of Shanghai society is shown in the opening sequence of the film; the colonial city of Qingdao, with its Teutonic architecture and scenic beach resort, is criticized as an escapist "wonderland"; and Manchuria is constructed first as a site of national trauma, then as a possible venue for personal redemption and national salvation.

Tian Han's story, adapted for the screen by Xia Yan and directed by Xu Xingzhi, opens with a scene of flirtation between a Westernized femme fatale and two young men, an artistically inclined revolutionary and a poet. The film immediately configures its male protagonists in relation to two spatially hierarchical worlds in urban Shanghai: the world of the poor, young girl living downstairs, who is introduced with a close-up of her face as she holds a sheet of music, singing; and the world of the seductive Mrs. C, who lives in a two-story private villa facing the men's attic room.[54]

The femme fatale is introduced in an elaborate stage setting, as if in a play, as she plays the piano and sings along. Her white dress, her permanent wave, and the close-up of her eyes, with dark eye shadow and meticulously shaped eyebrows, add to her seductive power. Her perfect silhouette is projected onto a white silky curtain, which prompts the artistically inclined revolutionary to do a quick sketch and inspires the poet to compose a poem. Their joint work of art then is made into a paper airplane, which flies into the woman's open window. The young men and the femme fatale, though economically disparate, occupy a similar social status as members of the (petite) bourgeoisie—hence the similar heights of their lodgings in the vertically structured class society—while the working-class girl and her mother are positioned beneath both of them.

It was natural for Tian Han, writer, poet, and lover of music and painting, to configure his male protagonist, Xin Baihua, as "a poetic youth, who pursues literary studies, music, and painting," an almost exact copy of the characterizations of Meili, the Chinese Mary and socialist female Faust, in his Tokyo play "Spiritual Light." Xin Baihua, the handsome young poet who lives with his friend in an attic room, is not only an image of Tian's good friend, the poet Zong Baihua, but also of Tian himself and the romantic generation of modern Chinese writers as characterized by Leo Ou-fan Lee almost four decades ago.

After the death of the mother of the working-class girl Ah Feng (Little Phoenix), the poor virgin becomes a member of the young men's "artistic family." No sexual relationship in this artistic family of two young men and one young girl is depicted. However, celibacy does not mean lack of romance. On the contrary, the lack of an obvious sexual encounter could itself be an indicator of the underlying romance. Laikwan Pang, in discussing the relationship between nation and romance, highlights the intimate bond between the poet and the virgin girl in this film and traces three bases for this romantic bond: first, their shared "revolutionary" ancestry, the Northeast homeland and war front; second, their spatial affiliation, as both live in attic rooms (while the femme fatale belongs to the other world of a private villa); and, third, their mutual appreciation of the tale of the rebirth of the phoenix, a symbol of baptism by the fire of revolution. Thus, Pang reaches a conclusion similar to that of Ban Wang in discussing the film *Nie Er* in the context of desire and pleasure in revolutionary cinema,[55] that "rather than romance being sublimated by the nation, in this film the latter is only a disguise to fulfill the libidinal drive that was not permitted in this allegedly political cinema."[56]

In the "female Faust" story in Tokyo, the disguised fulfillment of the libidinal drive was manifest in the Chinese Mary's "making art" as a sublimation of "making love." For the "lovers in troubled times" in Shanghai, under the looming shadow of war, physical sacrifice and anti-Japanese activism again substitute for sexual intercourse. The sexual energy between the young men and the girl is further sublimated into educational zeal to mold the virgin girl into a modern woman. Liang Zhifu, the practical revolutionary, wants to introduce her to factory work, while Xin Baihua, the romantic poet, insists that she should go to school. With proceeds from the publication of his poems, Baihua sends her to a boarding school without informing Zhifu.[57]

When Zhifu is arrested for his radical activities and Baihua is hunted by the police, the poet finds shelter with the mysterious Mrs. C, introduced at the opening scene, who treats him like her husband, greets him with a warm kiss, and keeps him at her place overnight. The overflow of sexual energy and the mutually beneficial sexual relationship between the poet and the femme fatale releases the accumulated sexual tension surrounding the platonic relationship between the poet and the virgin.

As if mesmerized, the poet goes with the femme fatale to Qingdao,[58] a former German colony and an escapist utopia, in the same fashion as Toyō, who was enchanted by the snake woman in Tanizaki's 1921 film scenario, *Jasei no in*.[59] Meanwhile, Ah Feng, the girl under the protection of the poet, has to quit school and join a touring dance troupe to make a living. The climax, both in terms of plot and in terms of the sexual energy circulating within that plot, comes when Baihua and Mrs. C go to a variety show in which Xin Feng (New Phoenix), the virgin girl touring with the dance troupe, performs a miniature opera entitled *Tieti xia de genü* (Songstress under the Iron Hoof). The New Phoenix appears with long sleeves, a pair of shorts showing her bare legs, and a broad-brimmed hat. Her distinctively Germanic costume bears a surprising resemblance to that of the female soldiers in the film *Hongse niangzijun* (Red Detachment of Women),[60] which emerged as a locus of revolutionary iconography during the Cultural Revolution in the 1960s.[61] Young boys growing up during the Cultural Revolution and allowed access to no more than a dozen films and filmed Peking Operas, found great satisfaction gazing at the bare legs showing between the women soldiers' military shorts and long boots in this film.

This New Phoenix, the patriotic songstress, is indeed the virgin girl Baihua helped to educate. The image of a virgin under the iron hoof of the invading Japanese army, though charged with sexual energy, is used here as a warning bell to awaken the poet from the licentious life he has been living in his escapist dreamland, at least from the point of view of the revolutionaries.[62] The poet starts to feel there is a more important task waiting for him after this dramatic encounter. He gets in touch with Zhifu and through Zhifu's introduction joins the volunteer army in the Northeast. Baihua's troop happens to be in Xin Feng's village where he discovers the phoenix painting and reunites with Xin Feng, who, after meeting Baihua in Qingdao, left the dance troupe for her homeland and war front. Facing Japanese air raids with flag in hand, Baihua and Xin Feng, marching with the masses, start to sing the last stanza of Baihua's long poem "Great Wall."

Arise, you who refuse to be slaves,
With our flesh and blood let us build our new Great Wall.
The Chinese nation has come to the time of greatest danger,
Every person must join the ultimate cry:
Arise! Arise! Arise![63]

Situating the young poet, Baihua, first and foremost in his struggle between the world of the virgin girl and the world of the femme fatale, leads to an interpretation of the theme song, "Yiyongjun jinxingqu" (March of the Volunteers), as more than a simple call for patriotic devotion. "The Nationalist poet," writing his epic poem in the hopes of educating the poor girl to become a "modern woman," finds himself the prey and love slave of the femme fatale. The virgin girl stimulates the poet's anti-Japanese patriotic zeal, while the femme fatale lures him away from patriotic activities.

The displacement from a freed slave of a femme fatale to freed slaves of the national enemy is suggestive of the intrinsic connections between the personal and the political. Just as in the phoenix painting named after Guo Moruo's poem,[64] in which a phoenix throws itself into the fire to gain a new life, the young intellectuals were also transforming themselves, through a baptism by fire, from sentimentalists into revolutionaries throughout the political vicissitudes of the twentieth century.

However, the sudden and complete transformation of the poet Xin Baihua, mesmerized by a femme fatale until the very end of the film, when he not so convincingly rises up to defend a greater cause, cannot be taken as representative of a generation of modern intellectuals. The apparently seamless transition from individual desire to collective ideology did not turn out to be as smooth in real life, as Tian Han himself came to experience in the Communist era, culminating in his tragic death during the Cultural Revolution in Beijing.[65]

How to Conduct "Guerrilla Drama Warfare"?

Shortly before his death in 1936, Lu Xun had criticized Tian Han's staging of theater in Nanjing during his house arrest as "going official."[66] As a leading Communist intellectual, Tian was placed under house arrest by the Nationalists. At the same time, he would not have been able to stage big theater productions without the tacit consent of the Nanjing government. Tian's position in the Nationalist capital was indeed an ambiguous one. He continued his theatrical activities for the two-year duration of his forced stay in Nanjing, producing, among other things, a four-act play, *Lugou qiao* (Marco Polo Bridge), which was written and performed immediately after the outbreak of the full-scale war.

The significance of Tian Han's "Marco Polo Bridge" lies as much in its timely response to the national crisis as in its theatrical and formal self-referentiality. First, the Marco Polo Bridge, the location where the Japanese launched their full-scale invasion, performs the dual function of a battlefield in real life and a theatrical stage in the play. Second, within the play, the bridge becomes a contested site charged with political urgency on which a variety show for the purpose of anti-Japanese propaganda is being mounted. The actors are amateur student performers who are members of an "anti-Japanese propaganda troupe," setting up a model for the Taiwanese American director Ang Lee's cinematic reimagination of Eileen Chang's short story "Lust, Caution." In Tian's play, the students are performing for an onstage audience consisting of the neighboring masses and the Twenty-Ninth Army soldiers defending the bridge.[67] Third, the performance within the performance is a powerfully self-referential gesture, rendering the play and its action a model of guerrilla drama warfare in the style of a Brechtian *Lehrstücke,*[68] or "teaching play," in which members of the acting troupe become the collective protagonists and performance becomes the central trope of cultural and political activities, both on- and offstage. The performance makes actors into activists who, by performing their roles, come to embody those roles in real life.

In the years following the performance of "Marco Polo Bridge," Tian Han would organize nine traditional opera propaganda troupes and one drama propaganda troupe, and these would develop into thirteen troupes by 1941 and become the main practitioners of guerrilla drama warfare throughout the war.[69] Their footsteps covered many hinterland cities and townships, with Chongqing, Kunming, and Guilin as key cultural centers. In this sense, Tian's "Marco Polo Bridge" served as a pedagogic tool to convey the necessary "how-to" knowledge to future practitioners of wartime propaganda.

The play opens with a student propaganda team performing for the Chinese soldiers at the Marco Polo Bridge in June 1937, one month before Japan's full-scale invasion. One student after another stands up to deliver speeches explaining the geopolitics of the current Japanese threat to China, until a female university student (*nü daxuesheng*) approaches and kneels down in front of the soldiers, urging them to defend the Marco Polo Bridge and stop the invading

Japanese.[70] The kneeling draws a strong emotional reaction from the onstage audience, and more and more spectators stand up and tell their own stories of suffering under the Japanese invasion of Manchuria since 1931. The play itself becomes a venue for the presentation of personal stories and conflicting political opinions. A "traitor" (*hanjian*) who tries to persuade the soldiers not to defend the Marco Polo Bridge is ridiculed by the public as a "clown."[71]

The performative quality of this political gathering is further highlighted when one of the student propaganda team members takes up the role of a "traditional performing artist," with an interesting twist. He plays harmonica, a marker of cultural influence from Soviet Russia, rather than the traditional two-stringed instrument the *erhu,* while singing to the tune of an aria from *Qin Qiong fangyou* (Qin Qiong Visits His Friends) with new lyrics.[72] Tian Han's reinvention of the Qin Qiong tale established a general formula for transforming familiar Peking Opera highlights into revolutionary songs.[73] The song starts with an evocation of the legendary hero and his associations with other peasant rebels, which invites comparison with the fighters in the current war with Japan. It goes on to list the imperialist ambitions of the Japanese and ends with an urgent plea in a commanding voice.

> You audience, do not pretend to be mute and numb,
> The suffering of the Chinese nation has reached its peak.
> Quickly arm yourself and go to the war front, young or old, men or women;
> We do not want to be slaves. We want to be masters, masters of China![74]

The emphasis on aural elements to rouse the audience (both on- and offstage) through speech and song highlights the metadramatic quality of such a performance. Acting and role-playing are laid bare on the makeshift stage. The theatricality of the performance is exposed and made part of the subject matter in order to demonstrate how one can replicate such a performance. Nevertheless, the second and final lines, obviously cashing in on the popularity of "March of the Volunteers," resoundingly agitate for transforming its audience into fighters for and masters of their endangered nation.

Such a formula for transforming a familiar tale into an effective "call to arms" bears comparison with the didacticism of "Epic Theater" as described by Benjamin using Brecht's and Eisler's work as his example: "words alone can, in Eisler's formulation, bring about the transformation of the concert into a political meeting. That such a transformation does, in fact, present a high point of musical and literary technique, Brecht and Eisler have proven with their play *Die Maßnahme* (The Measures Taken)."[75] Tian Han's experimentation with songs on stage and screen shared such a Brechtian impulse. It put words to music and turned concerts into political meetings. The importance of the lyrics and the central role of the lyricist hence cannot be overemphasized in the aestheticization of politics.

A contemporary reportage style (with its realistic description) permeates the lyrics of a new-style song "Song of Seeing Off Brave Soldiers" in the play "Marco Polo Bridge." The song includes neologisms such as "anti–Japanese War" (*kangzhan*) and "freedom" (*ziyou*), and its new style is also evident in stage directions such as "the girl presents flowers with embraces and kisses" (*nü songhua baowen*). Realistic stage props, such as flowers, and modern gestures, such as kisses, are employed to intensify the emotional impact on the audience. The young lovers, performed by university students who are members of the propaganda troupe in the play, exchange their parting words in this performance within a performance.

WOMAN: (sings) My dear brother, let me present you with flowers, and bestow on you a kiss. Hundreds of thousands of freedom-loving people will back your action.

MAN: (sings) My dear sister, thank you for the fragrant flowers, and your warm kiss. We will fight until the last of us have shed our last drop of blood.[76]

Echoing the emphasis on "flesh and blood" in "March of the Volunteers," this new song again highlights bodily fluids and their dynamics as expressed in the "warm kiss" and the "last drop of blood." The lyrics convey the central imagery of human bodies kinetically interacting, as well as the transference of energy between human actions and political movements.

Hei Guniang, literally "Black Girl,"[77] who briefly appears and sings a folk song in the first scene, develops into both a flirtatious femme fatale and a folk girl of revolutionary spirit in the second. She sings love songs ending with "do not waste my moonlike eyebrows and willowlike waist" to flirt with the handsome soldier, Ma. When asked by the soldiers to sing a song for all of them, she starts with a line from Tian Han's own *Siji ge* (Song of Four Seasons), as popularized in the recently released film *Street Angel,* then concludes with a revolutionary claim: "Japanese devils (*guizi*) use their cannons to talk about peace and friendship, while our Twenty-Ninth Army fights the enemy with their big cleavers."[78]

The traveling drama troupes, together with their daring actresses, who perform the roles of woman warriors both onstage and in real life, emerge as collective protagonists in Tian Han's wartime plays. The numerous scenes of performance within Tian's wartime plays and the circulation of performers as "guerrilla troupes" in the sociopolitical world transgressed the boundary between the fictive and the real. *Zuihou de shengli* (The Final Triumph), a 1938 play calling for the final triumph over the Japanese as in "Marco Polo Bridge," portrays female students as part of a propaganda drama troupe interacting with village girls. *Song yongshi chuzheng ge* (Song of Seeing Off Brave Soldiers), first conceived in "Marco Polo Bridge," entered this play as an established song sung by the female members of the drama troupe together with local girls.[79] Thus, popular songs traveled from one text to another and reinvented themselves across different media.

"A New Legend of Lovers and Heroes" and Wartime Opera

Tian Han's role as the Jianghu laoda (Head of Heroes) leading drama troupes touring the wartime hinterland mostly took place during his "leave" from his official post at the "Third Bureau" of the political department of the Nationalist government from 1939 to 1941. During the second "united front" between the Nationalists and Communists, the two rival parties joined together again in pursuit of their mutual goal of fending off Japanese military aggression after July 7, 1937.[80] A Third Bureau, in charge of "art and communication," or wartime propaganda, was established. Most of its members were Communist intellectuals, who came together under the leadership of Zhou Enlai and Guo Moruo.[81]

The year 1939 marked an important moment in Tian Han's creative career, as well as in his wartime cultural activities. Away from his official post, Tian Han immersed himself in piles of historical materials and opera repertoires and embarked on large-scale undertakings of writing epic-length operas. In these operas, Tian Han was making a statement about his approach to "tradition" in the face of the Japanese invasion and the threat of war.[82] In an article written one year before, in 1938, articulating his view of the relationship between literary form and content, Tian argued against the general view of "opera reform" as new wine in old bottles. Instead, he suggested that the relationship between the bottle and the wine should be organic, namely, when new content is injected into the old form, the form itself is transformed.[83]

The legendary Peking Opera *Xin ernü yingxiong zhuan* (A New Legend of Lovers and Heroes), in which he created a hybrid genre by reinventing a modern legend, best exemplifies the gender and genre transgressions at work in Tian Han's wartime cultural activities.[84] He combined the popularity of the traditional "legend" genre with the charm of a cross-dressed beauty and female warrior. Thus, the opera achieved popularity through its enigmatic female characters, rendering traditional Chinese opera a fitting vehicle for anti-Japanese propaganda.

Tian's play borrowed its title from the Qing novel *Ernü yingxiong zhuan* ("Legend of Lovers and Heroes," 1872), quoted in the epigraph of this chapter, but the action of his play takes place in the Ming dynasty (1368–1644), in which setting the Japanese are conveniently characterized as the notorious "dwarf bandits" (*wokou*) violating the southeastern border of the Ming. In the new legend set in older times, combining romantic love with heroism, General Zhang Jing and his colleague Yu Dayou fight the Japanese. General Zhang's daughter, Zhang Huilan, is the female protagonist. The martial-arts-loving Huilan wants to follow her father to fight the invaders in the South (*Jiangnan*, literally, "south of the river"). In her long arias, she expresses her determination to go to the front to fight the enemy.

> My old father went south of the river
>   and severely defeated the spirit of the bandit,
> My heroic brother is also fighting enemies there.
> Although I have a powdered face, I am also a fierce fighter (*fenmian de jingang*)
> How can I just sit behind the pearl curtain
>   with a pair of furrowed brows?
> . . . . . .
> Although I am a young girl I have the heart of a hero,
>   I am as loyal and brave as a man.
>   How can I enjoy personal peace when the bandits are not destroyed?
> I am not ready to ride the phoenix or follow the dragon,
> My only wish is to jump on the horse with my sword . . .[85]

On the road to the front in search of her brother, Huilan encounters Shen Houduan, son of Shen Yan, who was purged because of his support for Zhang Jing, Huilan's father. Mistaking the cross-dressing Huilan for a young man,[86] Houduan insists on becoming "his" sworn blood brother. While Huilan and Houduan are connected through a fictive brotherhood, He Qiaogu, a girl Huilan and Houduan saved on the road, falls in love with Huilan, the handsome "young man" who saved her life. The cross-dressed Huilan has to excuse herself from Qiaogu's marriage proposal by suggesting that they become sworn brother and sister.

The sudden appearance of Big Sister Ye complicates an already complex gender relationship. Ye, a bold and beautiful "female bandit," falls in love with Huilan at first sight. Huilan, in fact, becomes the love interest of each of the three other protagonists: the young scholar Houduan, the poor girl Qiaogu, and the fierce female bandit Ye. Comparing herself with the legendary White Snake, Ye insists that even "a human-eating monster" can love dearly.[87] When confronted by Huilan about her identity as a "female pirate," Ye candidly describes herself as "a female demon on the sea who never let a corrupt officer off the hook." Huilan persuades Ye to fight her pirate husband, and she finally kills him at the critical moment and gains control of the ship. Together Huilan and Ye burn the ship's cargo to prevent the pirates from getting valuables. Ye, though severely wounded, protects Huilan and Qiaogu so they can swim toward the seashore. Her last wish is a kiss from Huilan, the "young man" she loves dearly. She dies with a smile on her face while Huilan is kissing her.[88] Big Sister Ye seems to be only the latest of the many bandit (or foreign) female warriors who fall in love with a handsome Chinese prince/warrior/scholar. This trope is perhaps best manifested in *Yangjia jiang* (Yang Family Generals) in the figure of Mu Guiying. In women-authored *tanci* ("plucking rhymes"), with all their instances of cross-dressing, the theme is not uncommon either.

What is new is the kiss. I contend that Big Sister Ye is another of Tian Han's "vamps," that is, women who value and prioritize sensual enjoyment, according to Tian's 1927 essay "A Century of Vampires."[89] Moreover, the kissing between two female fighters, the cross-dressed Huilan and the female bandit Big Sister Ye, suggests a lesbian subtext.[90] Most important, it violates conventional gender perceptions and expectations when a younger girl assumes the role of the stronger, masculine lover, while the older woman performs the role of a tragic, heroic pursuer. In Huilan's holding of the head of the dying Ye and kissing her icy lips, the "Salome trope" is reinvented via multiple role reversals and replacements: the femme fatale who desires the kiss is dying, and the female warrior who kisses her is destined to become a femme fatale.

Huilan assumes the double role of a female fighter and female demon after the death of Big Sister Ye. She describes herself (and is described by Qiaogu and others) as "a female demon who won't even blink an eye when she kills" (*sharen bu zhayan de nümowang*).[91] Act 3, scene 20 of this epic-length opera presents a bizarre reenactment of *Xixiang ji* (The Western Chamber), a romantic comedy about the sexual encounter between a young scholar, Zhang, and a beauty, Cui Yingying, compiled around the end of the thirteenth century or the beginning of the fourteenth.[92] It follows the original plot in that Huilan, acting like the beauty in the story, burns incense and mourns her father. When a male bandit climbs over the wall and describes himself as "imitating Scholar Zhang, who jumped over the wall for Yingying's beauty," Huilan tricks him into coming off the wall, whereupon she decapitates him with her sword and throws the severed head outside the wall (*zhan Wen Ba, zhitou qiangwai*).[93] Through this act, Huilan finally assumes the role of "Salome" and, indeed, goes one step further than the femme fatale in the Wilde play in that she commits the violent act herself and does so with complete emotional detachment.

The gender mismatch finds a perfect remedy in act 3, scene 28 of the opera, when Huilan's brother, Zhifang, meets Qiaogu, the girl Huilan saved on the road, and when Huilan is recognized by Houduan as female—resolving the four into two perfect heterosexual couples. The opera ends with all singing "Songs of the New Heroes" in the style of a theme song for a film, or as in Tian Han's experimental "spoken dramas," which often incorporate multiple theme songs in the performance.

While Tian Han charted new territory in this epic Peking Opera written in the Nationalist wartime capital of Chongqing during the heat of the Second Sino-Japanese War, he nonetheless made extensive use of traditional materials. Situating his new version of *Ernü yingxiong* in the genealogy of lovers and heroes in the Chinese literary tradition, one finds many ancestors of the female warrior trope going back to Tang *chuanqi* (legend) tales, such as stories about Hongxian and Nie Yinniang.[94] Tian also utilized a wide range of textual and cultural references, from the cross-dressed Mulan, the dangerous White Snake, and the death-loving Salome to a parody of *The Western Chamber*.

David Der-wei Wang, in his analysis of Wen Kang's *Legend of Lovers and Heroes*, traces the prototypes of the female protagonist He Yufeng, also known as female knight-errant Shi Sanmei, back to *huaben* tales of the seventeenth century and late Ming "scholar-beauty fiction" *Haoqiu zhuan* (after 1712), as well as a story entitled "Xianü" (Female Knight-Errant) in *Liaozhai zhiyi* ("Strange Tales from a Chinese Studio," 1679).[95] Wang treats Wen Kang's novel as "an exploration of the relationship between two ideals of secular life, romantic love (*ernü*) and heroism (*yingxiong*), and the terms under which these two ideals can be harmonized into one."[96] Tian Han's molding of Zhang Huilan and Big Sister Ye into a pair of female warriors who are at once ultrafeminine and ultramasculine, ultraromantic and ultraheroic (in Wen Kang's words) echoes Wen's attempt to understand eroticism and heroism not as belonging to two parallel moral universes but as operating in one single moral universe.

One cannot help speculating about the opera's effect on its audience when it was first performed in the Jincheng (Golden City) Grand Theater in Guilin by the Peking Opera Propaganda Team on May 20, 1939.[97] The audience could hardly miss the ubiquitous anti-Japanese theme, as well as the call to arms for men and women alike. However, what truly stood out, one suspects, were the powerful and daring female characters—especially Zhang Huilan and Big Sister Ye, one as a modern-day Mulan and a militant Cui Yingying, the other as a righteous and vampirish female pirate and a daring warrior-lover. It is tempting to suggest that these two female images were what Tian Han really meant by the title "A New Legend of [Homosexual] Lovers and Heroes."

While conceiving his new version of lovers and heroes, Tian Han further elaborated his view of the relationship between drama and opera.

> People often categorize the difference between drama and opera as the opposition between the new and the old, which is incorrect. I will not go into details of the false oppositions in the past, but we do need a new realization about the issue of the artistic new and old now. I believe that anything beneficial to the anti-Japanese war purpose is new, and anything that is not is old. So, ladies and gentlemen, please do not mistake my "sudden" shift as being from a new drama movement to an old drama movement. I am only shifting from drama to opera. On the issue of theater movement, I am still engaged in my new theater movement (*xinju yundong*).[98]

One could easily dismiss the above statement as purely propagandistic. However, in practice, this propagandistic pragmatism opened up an unprecedented cultural space for the flourishing of the arts in various forms. As Tian Han suggested, the issue was not so much about observing genre conventions as it was about responding to contemporary exigencies. Two particulars of Tian Han's formulation are worthy of critical attention. One is his sense that the opposition between the new and the old in Chinese theater is dysfunctional and counterproductive. Another is his description of himself as "engaged in my new theater movement" rather than as a dramatist per se, marking his self-identification as a cultural activist rather than a traditional "man of letters."

"Rhapsody on the Sounds of Autumn" and Wartime Spoken Drama

> One night when I was reading I heard a sound coming from the southwest. I listened in alarm and said:
>
> "Strange! At first it was a patter of drops, a rustle in the air; all at once it is hooves stampeding, breakers on a shore; it is as though huge waves were rising startled in the night, in a sudden downpour of wind and rain. When it collides with something it clatters and clangs, gold and iron ring together; and then it is as though soldiers were advancing against an enemy, running swiftly with the gag between their teeth, and you hear no voiced command, only the tramping of men and horses."
>
> I said to the boy, "What is this sound? Go out and look."
>
> The boy returned and told me:
>
> "The moon and stars gleam white and pure, the bright river is in the sky, nowhere is there any sound of man; the sound is over among the trees."
>
> "Alas, how sad!" I answered. "This is the sound of autumn, why has it come?"
>
> Ouyang Xiu, "Rhapsody on the Sounds of Autumn," 1042, quoted in Tian Han, *Qiusheng Fu* (Rhapsody on the Sounds of Autumn), 1942[99]

A "theme song" (*zhuti ge*) opens Tian Han's five-scene spoken drama *Qiusheng Fu* (Rhapsody on the Sounds of Autumn).

> . . . . . .
> Alas, this is the sound of autumn, why has it come?
> But we do not need to be sad, nor need us to feel strange and alarmed.
> Let us use our iron will to stand up amid wind and rain, waves and breakers,
> This is the era for our nation to be transformed.[100]

Despite such a heroic opening, the play nonetheless turns into a conventional love triangle featuring two rivals, as embodied by two "new women," competing for the love of the first-person male narrator, a rather blatant autobiographical depiction of Tian Han's own dilemma in 1941 in Guilin. Liaohong and Shujin serve as broad-brush versions of An E and Lin Weizhong, the two major female figures in Tian's life after his first wife, Yi Shuyu, died in 1925. An E was the Moscow-educated communist activist we encountered before, while Lin Weizhong was a Noraesque figure who had "run away" from China to Southeast Asia (Nanyang) and returned to support Tian Han's "little theater movement" with her own savings, although she was later said to have "lagged behind" in supporting his revolutionary activism.

The rivalry between the two extraordinary women is set up from the beginning of the play. Qin Shujin (based on Lin Weizhong), wife of the male protagonist Xu Ziyu, comments that the "Lijiang Boatmen's Song" she overhears "sounds like crying."[101] The song introduces the female poet Hu Liaohong (based on An E), lover of the male protagonist, as the lyricist of a certain "Jialingjiang Boatmen's Song," written in Chongqing and now popular among the wartime populace (as Tian's real life lover, the female poet An E did achieve popularity in wartime China with her songs). Both songs are modeled after the "Volga Boatmen's Song," a favorite in leftist circles worldwide and with Tian Han, the Dutch filmmaker Joris Ivens, and the African American singer-actor Raul Robeson. All were under its powerful spell, as it articulated the suffering, power, and beauty of the working class.[102]

Most significant, the "new women" of the wartime Chinese hinterland bear traces of Salome, Carmen, and the legendary female warrior He Yufeng. Both Liaohong and Shujin become hybrids of multiple modernities long existing in Tian Han's earlier literary and artistic career, from Taishō Tokyo to Republican Shanghai. Hu Liaohong is portrayed as a truly independent female intellectual, a wartime journalist and modernist poet. Qin Shujin first appears as a jealous wife who cares more about the "small family" than the "big family," then is transformed into a wartime female worker who helps refugee children together with Liaohong.

Liaohong travels by airplane from Chongqing to Guilin to meet her long-parted lover, Xu Ziyu, the autobiographical male protagonist in Tian Han's play. The moment Liaohong sees her lover, embraces replace words, and she starts to hug and kiss him passionately in her hotel room (*ta paoguoqu menglie baowen ta*).[103] As with the realistic stage descriptions detailing how the girls offer flowers and kisses to the departing soldiers in "Marco Polo Bridge," Tian Han employs open, detailed, and realistic depictions of female bodily expressions of intimacy to centralize eroticism amid wartime depression and revolutionary change.

Xu Ziyu praises Liaohong for "often losing herself, even risking her life for the sake of the mass movement (*dazhong de yundong*) in the past and urges her to maintain that spirit in the present. He claims that "whoever can keep bringing happiness to the masses is destined to bring me happiness."[104] As the male protagonist becomes the prize competed for by the two new women, it suggests a reversal of the convention of feminine beauty being used as a reward for the young men "going to the people" in Tian's Shanghai film endeavor, "To the People."

There are many important allusions to Tokyo and Shanghai in this rather unusual play written in late 1941 amid the late autumn wind and wartime depression in the hinterland city of Guilin. Wooden slippers, melancholy, and Tolstoy become unlikely markers of a seemingly long-lost avant-garde mentality embodied by the single word, *jimo* (loneliness), both the sentimentality of Lin Zeqi, the male student in "A Night in a Café," written in Tokyo, and that of the young man Huang the Big Fool in "The Night a Tiger Was Captured," written and performed in Shanghai.

"The people," however, are concretized in the wartime conditions as both the laboring boatmen on the beautiful river Lijiang in the city of Guilin and the refugee children who have to shine the shoes of the rich to make a meager living. The "Shoe-Shining Song" functions like the "Lijiang Boatmen's Song," giving voice to the working poor.

> The autumn wind rises, leaves cover the sky,
> The young girl has no cotton to cover her body.
> . . . . . .
> Look, the shoe-shining girl does not have shoes to wear,
> How pitiful is the wandering child.[105]

Hu Liaohong, the lover and leftist female poet, overhears the song, which combines three key iconographies of the underprivileged: the poor, the female, and the child. This is an important moment for Tian Han, I argue, as this song vividly recaptures his very first cinematic encounter with the Hollywood melodrama *Shoes* nearly three decades earlier in Tokyo. The childlike virgin girl, working to support her family without a pair of proper

Left to right: Hong Shen, Xiong Foxi, Tian Han, and Mao Dun, in Guilin in 1942. (Courtesy of the Shanghai Library.)

shoes, had also entered his Shanghai writings on film.[106] She returns in this wartime play as both a social commentary on wartime suffering and an expression of the universal human condition predetermined by one's gender, class, and age.

Detailed stage instructions evoke the female poet Hu Liaohong's state of mind, leading to her singing "Song of the Falling Leaves."

[A gust of autumn wind, red leaves dancing in the air.]

HU LIAOHONG: [rises and catches a leaf, speaks lightly] Ah, "Grasses and trees have no feeling, falling and floating when time comes . . ."

[She takes a small mirror from her leather purse, arranges her hair absentmindedly, and applies some lipstick. Touched by the scenery, she sings "Song of the Falling Leaves."][107]

This sentimental, utterly "modern" introductory note seems to promise a heart-wrenching love song. Although it begins with lovers pouring out their tears by the side of the "River of Longing" (Xiangsi he), with the location shifting to Lijiang in Guilin, the mood of the song is also transformed from private sentiments to public love, from personal longing to answering the call to a greater good.

Falling leaves return to their roots,
Wild grasses face their ancestors.
What originates from the masses should return to the masses.
They are waiting for me,
Those masses of children who have lost their mothers.[108]

Inspired by the singing girl who turned out to be a refugee child she had helped in the past, Liaohong journeys from Guilin to Changsha in the service of the refugee children, possibly also answering Xu Ziyu's call to "bring happiness to the masses" as it will also bring happiness to him. Her journey for the greater good, so to speak, ironically follows Xu's wife, Shujin, and Mother Xu's move to Xu's family home in the same city. Liaohong's "searching for roots" and "returning to the masses" are fittingly at the same time a journey to the ancestral home of her lover. Working for the greater good in effect facilitates the coming together of the lovers spiritually, if not physically. It even provides an opportunity for Liaohong the lover to reconcile with Shujin the wife through a heartfelt discussion when sharing the same bed at night. On Shujin's request, Liaohong sings "Night Rain in Xiaoxiang."[109]

A lonely swan from the North roams to the South,
in order to borrow its abundant sunshine
to warm her worried heart.
But the South! You bequeath her a similar sorrow.
After appreciating the autumn colors of Lijiang,
How can one stand the dark clouds at night in Xiaoxiang![110]

Here Liaohong again assumes the role of the songstress, the female singing subject. She compares herself to the lonely swan from the land of Yan and Zhao (North China) and laments that even the South, with its abundant sunshine, cannot alleviate her sorrow. In real life, Tian Han's lover, An E, was from the North and had written a collection of poems and essays entitled *Yanzhao ernü* ("Children of Yan and Zhao," or "Children of the North").[111] This sentimental lamentation of the South would be developed in Tian Han's 1947 filmscript, as discussed in the next section.

Other traces of modernity are abundant in Tian Han's portrayal of wartime intellectual life in the Chinese hinterland, a modernity expressed in the materiality of everyday life in such objects as guns, airplanes, cars, telephones, a Leica camera, and newspapers. Tian's characters also engage in distinctly modern activities such as rehearsing a play, eating in a restaurant, living in a hotel, and gossiping about Hollywood film stars. The pro-Americanism implicit in the play, as in the character of the American doctor who provides a safe haven during the anti-Japanese Nationalist struggle,[112] speaks to the intrinsic ambiguities of Tian Han's identity as a Communist propagandist during wartime. It also connects China with the worldwide antifascist movement in which the United States was an important player, a theme that will be further developed in chapter 4.[113]

The guns that bespeak modernity, however, are not without comic effects. The two love rivals, Liaohong and Shujin, forced to share a bed in an emergency situation, first sleep peacefully together and then half jokingly point a gun at each other.[114] A crucial moment involving guns comes at the end of act 4, when the two, united by their mutual devotion to fighting the Japanese, find themselves engaged in a bloody gunfight with two Japanese soldiers.[115]

ENEMY SOLDIER A: [flashes torchlight and sees Liaohong] Haha! What a beauty! (Original in Japanese)

[Liaohong shoots at the torchlight, enemy soldier falls at the gunshot]

ENEMY SOLDIER B: [Also places torch on the table and jumps at Liaohong] Ha! (Original in Japanese)

[Liaohong shoots again and misses. Her gun is kicked away by the enemy solider. The enemy soldier advances and grabs Liaohong. Liaohong ferociously pushes him away and the table lamp falls. Sound of broken glass.]

ENEMY SOLDIER B: Ha, what a fierce woman! (Original in Japanese) (He jumps at Liaohong again. Liaohong lifts a vase and hits him. The enemy solider comes right at Liaohong and tightly grabs her.)

HU LIAOHONG: (screams) Ah!

ENEMY SOLDIER B: (pulls his gun and threatens) I'll shoot you if you don't turn around! (Original in Japanese)

HU LIAOHONG: (screams) Ah! Beasts! Demons!

[The door to the kitchen suddenly opens. Shujin holds an ax and swings it at the enemy. The enemy shoots. Liaohong quickly pushes him to the side.

The gun fires and the ax swings. Only a horrible scream is heard. The torch rolls down.][116]

This is the moment of truth for the making of the "new women" at war. These dramatic encounters with guns and physical violence constitute a "baptism by fire" that transforms them into women warriors of the new era.[117] This intense moment in the construction of the female warriors through gunplay is given further prominence when it is reintroduced as a "flashback" in act 5.

[The scene turns dark.
[Lights suddenly dim. The scene returns to the end of act 4].
. . . . . .
HU LIAOHONG: (struggles but gradually loses out) Help!
[Door opens, and Shujin drags out an ax]
QIN SHUJIN: You devil! (She swings the ax at Enemy Soldier B)
ENEMY SOLDIER B: Ah! (He fires)
HU LIAOHONG: (Like lightning, she quickly pushes Enemy Soldier B away) I dare you—
[A gun fires, and the enemy soldier falls under the ax, but Shujin also falls with the sound of the gunshot.]
HU LIAOHONG: [Abruptly picks up the torch and observes her; seeing no injury, she shouts] Shujin! Shujin!
QIN SHUJIN: [comes to herself a little] What happened? I did not die?
HU LIAOHONG: Shujin, you didn't die. I pushed the hand of the devil, and the bullet only scratched the skin of your face.
QIN SHUJIN: Liaohong, thank you so much.
HU LIAOHONG: It's you who saved me. The devil was cut dead by you.
. . . . . .
[Lights quickly change. The scene returns to Ziyu's home beside Lijiang. Ziyu, Dachun, Menghe, and Xiaojiang are enthusiastically reading the letter brought by Zhiqiang.][118]

Whether Tian Han was borrowing from "modern" cinematic technique or revisiting the retrospective narrator in "traditional" Chinese opera, the dramatic effect of this flashback is clear. Twice exposed to the physical confrontation between the two Chinese women and the Japanese soldiers, the audience is forced to reexperience Liaohong shooting the Japanese solider and Shujin chopping off another soldier's head onstage. The symbolic image of Salome, the icon of decadence in the European tradition, ironically found its most powerful expression during wartime in the Chinese hinterland city of Guilin. Here the audience was presented with an empowered Salome, who executes her own decapitations without asking favors.[119]

The final song in this "spoken drama" reinforces the theme of lovers and heroes. At their residence in Guilin, which the two modern women had left to work for the greater good, Xu Ziyu and his daughter notice a man and woman by the side of the river Lijiang. The daughter imagines them to be lovers so entranced in their mutual endearments (*jiang lian'ai*) that they turned into rocks. The conversation between father and daughter ends with Ziyu emphasizing that they all have found their own work in the service of the greater good. Indeed, the daughter takes on a part in a patriotic play. "Rhapsody on the Sounds of Autumn" ends with the nightingale-sounding "stone lovers" (*shitouban de nannü*) singing the "Autumn Love Song of the Silver River."

> Autumn wind brings the fire of hatred,
> Autumn insect sings the song of revenge.
> You come from the front, don't you know about the enemy's crimes?
> . . . . . .
> Let's mop up the enemies like the autumn wind sweeps the fallen leaves
> Floating and falling among the waves of the Dongting Lake.
> Only then can I embrace you, and you caress me,
> Like the cowherd and the weaver rendezvousing at the Silver River . . . . . .[120]

The enduring theme of the interrelatedness of love and war, romance and politics, achieves its final poetic expression in the hybrid genre of a patriotic love song. At the height of war in the hinterland, the lovers and heroes are operating under a single symbolic universe, where eroticism and heroism and nature and culture exist in an intertextual relationship. The movement of wind and the sound of insects are hence endowed with the fire of hatred and songs of revenge, and could usher in the realization of intimate contact between lovers. The culmination of the lovers' reunion in the style of the legendary weaving girl and cowherd along the iconic Silver River becomes the ultimate reward for their heroic engagement with the war in defeating their enemies.

"Memories of the South" or "The Lament of the South"

O Soul, come back! Alas for the Southern Land!

"THE SUMMONS OF THE SOUL"
(ATTRIBUTED TO QU YUAN), THIRD CENTURY BCE

Wasn't the imperial aura of the South,
to end in three hundred years?

"THE LAMENT OF THE SOUTH," YU XIN, SIXTH CENTURY

How can I not but remember, land to the south of the River?

"MEMORIES OF THE SOUTH," BAI JUYI, NINTH CENTURY

With the sight of the ruined land, dreams seem most real.
How can I leave behind the familiar scenery?
How can I believe the mapping of the land has changed?
I clumsily compose a set of songs to the tune of "The Lament of the South,"
to air my frustration and sing to my heart's content until old age.

"THE LAMENT OF THE SOUTH,"
IN *THE PEACE BLOSSOM FAN*, KONG SHANGREN, 1699

From the 1934 film story for "Lovers in Troubled Times" and the 1937 play "Marco Polo Bridge" to the 1947 film *Yi Jiangnan* (Memories of the South, or *Ai Jiangnan*, The Lament of the South), Tian Han maintained his obsession with performers and metaperformances. "Lovers in Troubled Times" depicts the female performer and her transformative power to inspire a young poet; "Marco Polo Bridge" features an Anti-Japanese Propaganda Troupe and its performances; "Memories of the South," again, concerns a similar propaganda troupe and the transformation of a "patriotic poet" during the vicissitudes of war.

The 1947 film "Memories of the South" follows this metadramatic trope with a focus on the romantic struggle between the body and the spirit (*ling yu rou*), enacted through the struggle between sexual indulgence and patriotism in the wartime context. For the first time, one sees the degeneration of an intellectual through the historical transformations of wartime China, rather than the regeneration of the self as embodied in the poet turned volunteer soldier in "Lovers in Troubled Times." As in many of Tian Han's early cinematic works, the feminine can manifest itself as both a "regime of authenticity" (the virgin) engaged in or inspiring revolution and a character antagonistic toward the revolutionary cause and possessing the power to erotically enslave the would-be revolutionary (the femme fatale).[121] The golden-throated Zhou Xuan of Shanghai played both a Westernized femme fatale, Huang Meigui (Yellow Rose), and a tea-picking girl, Xie Dai'e, who happens to be Huang's lost twin sister. The doubling of the virgin and the femme fatale develops the theme already presented in "Lovers in Troubled Times" and highlights the "blood relationship" between the two seemingly contrasting archetypes.

The film opens with a train heading from Shanghai to Hangzhou, crossing the fertile fields of Jiangnan (literally "South of the Yangtze River," or the South) in the late spring sun. A flag is hanging outside the train window, which reads "Shanghai Cultural Circles Anti-Japanese Propaganda Troupe." The young male and female youths (*nannü qingnian*) of the troupe are passionately singing "The Lament of the South," a six-stanza lyrical poem in the tradition of Qu Yuan, Yu Xin, Bai Juyi, and Kong Shangren (as quoted in the epigraphs above). Five of the six stanzas are seven-character regulated poems (*qiyan lüshi*), while the fourth is in the style of *ci*, also known as *changduanju*, referring to its irregular length. *Ci* is written to the tune of a specific *cipai* (melody), making it the equivalent of what we call lyrics today. Each stanza of this set of songs ends with a heartfelt lamentation: "Alas, the lamentable South" (*Ah, ke'ai de Jiangnan*)![122]

Long shots outside the train windows and close-ups of people inside are interpolated into the song. Scenes of peasant women working in the spring fields, Japanese soldiers walking past ruined homes, and views of the faraway station buildings are juxtaposed with close-ups of an old scholarly gentleman lamenting and sighing and a young man showing his anger and hatred through contrived and theatrical facial expressions on the train. As in many forms of Chinese opera, especially the *zaju* (variety play) of the Yuan dynasty, which opens with an important song introducing key characters and setting up the main thematic focus of the whole performance, this opening song not only foregrounds the lamentation of the South as the central theme of the film but also serves as a prophetic voice foreshadowing the fate of the male protagonist. He, as the last stanza of the lyrics tells us, will be lured away from national salvation into temporary enjoyment of personal pleasure (*naihe gouqie tan zanhuan*), rendering him a lamentable and dishonored figure in the end.[123]

In the film, modernist poet Li Zhiyun joins the Nation-Saving Propaganda Team, which wins him the title of "patriotic poet." While carrying out propa-

A scene from *Yi Jiangnan* (Memories of the South), dir. Ying Yunwei, screenplay by Tian Han, and starring Zhou Xuan. Shanghai, 1947, Guotai yingye gongsi. (Courtesy of the Shanghai Library.)

ganda tours in Hangzhou, he meets the beautiful Xie Dai'e and uses the excuse of writing a ten-thousand-word poem to retreat from the team to live with Xie along the West Lake (allusions to the White Snake story are abundant in the script transcribed from the film), in a similar fashion to the poet retreating to the seashore of Qingdao in "Lovers in Troubled Times."[124] The Japanese bombing of Shanghai in the "August 13 Incident" awakens Li from his comfortable life with Xie in the countryside. But the weak intellectual poet cannot sustain his revolutionary zeal. When Li goes to Hong Kong to collect funds for publication of their newspaper, he is soon mesmerized by Miss Hong Kong Huang Meigui ("Yellow Rose," later recognized as Xie's twin sister), marries her, and stays on, safely removed from war and revolution.[125]

The sentimental poet and his rather feeble "patriotism" are thus twice trapped by female beauty. His constancy proves to be to the world of carnal desire rather than to the world of the "soul" and the ideals of revolution. This equating of the soul, or spirituality, with politics has corollaries in the West. In the Western tradition, one might abandon public political life for a private life of spiritual reflection, and one might also withdraw from political life into an alternative interiorized value system of feeling, the romantic retreat. But the wartime moment in China bears more kinship to classical Christian dualism, that is, that women and the erotic life represent the great temptation away from God (which in the case of wartime China equates to political ideals). The poet's identity as lover overtakes that of patriotic poet in the film, and that is considered a sin. The poet ultimately assumes the role of the villain in the film, and the two women are in turn trapped by their ability to trap him in the first place: Huang leaves Hong Kong after discovering her lover is cheating on his first wife (her sister) and betraying his friends and country (collaborating with the Japanese); and Xie treats him as if he had died when he returns to Hangzhou, as he is no longer the patriotic poet she cherished in her heart.[126]

"Memories of the South" deals with themes that can be traced back to the now familiar tropes highlighted in the 1927 silent film made in Shanghai, "Lakeshore Spring Dream." That film features a playwright and his erotic encounters with an enigmatic femme fatale along the West Lake in Hangzhou, the iconic *Jiangnan* where the tea-picking Xie Dai'e also resides. The struggle between erotic urban aesthetics and the revolutionary South is further explored in Tian's film story for *Muxing zhiguang* (Maternal Radiance, 1932), in which a popular musician's attempts to "package" her stepdaughter into a seductive "queen of song" are defeated by the girl's biological father, a revolutionary musician returned from Nanyang, literally the "South Seas."[127]

Conclusion

Tian Han's obsession with the South was consistent throughout his career, and the wartime hinterland provided an ideal outlet for his physical travels to the southern provinces in the interior. He took pride in his Hunanese identity and was under the influence of his uncle's Hunanese network of intellectuals, professionals, and revolutionaries in his early years. The hinterland of manual labor, material impoverishment, and conservatism was in a constant battle with the utopian Southland of lychee, pearl, southern beauty, and revolutionary fervor. Tian's artistic disposition lured him from the experiential hinterland to the archetypal South. The South gradually took on an amorous and artistic identity and became a utopian wonderland, functioning as Italy did for Goethe,[128]

The Nanguo she group in Guangzhou, published in *Nanguo yuekan* (1929). (Courtesy of the Shanghai Library.)

although in the case of Tian Han the South was at times a siren luring him away from political engagement and at times a muse aligning him with his higher self and revolutionary ideals.

As discussed in chapter 2, Tian's first artistic endeavor on his return from Japan was independently publishing *Nanguo banyuekan* (Southland Bimonthly) to "break the current languishing state of the literary circles, in order to stimulate a fresh and aromatic atmosphere."[129] He built on his Southland enterprise throughout the 1920s in Shanghai with performance tours of major southern cities, including Nanjing, Hangzhou, and Guangzhou, and the enterprise evolved into a full-fledged independent art college with departments ranging from drama and painting to literature.[130] Tian Han's "artistic South" constantly desires and searches for the "revolutionary South." In his creative works, Canton (Lingnan, or "South of the Ranges") was the land of lychees and pearls, as well as erotic and exotic beauties. At the same time, it was at the center of the Nationalist revolution since at least the Canton Uprising of 1911, written into Tian's planned *san huang* (three yellows) historical plays.[131] Throughout Tian's career, the South ranges from "South of the Lake," "South of the River," and "South of the Ranges" to the "South Seas," covering Southeast Asia and Taiwan in geopolitical terms and as imagined cultural landscapes. Throughout wartime, Tian Han toured some and imagined all as hybrids of light and darkness, regeneration and decadence, and ideal locales for his hybrid breed of lovers and heroes.

Tian Han's obsessions with enigmatic female figures and his visions of the amorous and revolutionary South cannot be understood only as a product of an idiosyncratic personal psyche. Such obsessions and visions are indicative of a broader trend pervasive not only in his generation of Chinese artists and activists but also in a generation of international avant-gardists who came of age between the two world wars. It taps into a larger cultural imagination influenced by the anarchist, feminist, and socialist trends of the post–World War I moment and speaks to a renewed sense of artistic avant-gardism and political engagement throughout the trying years of World War II. Tian Han's experiments from Tokyo and Shanghai to the wartime hinterland serve as case studies of larger entanglements between romance and ideology, art and politics, and the avant-garde and the popular. These entanglements will enter the making of the national anthem and the re-creation of socialist opera after the founding of the People's Republic of China and throughout the 1950s in an international context.

CHAPTER FOUR

The International Avant-Garde and the Chinese National Anthem

Alexander Portnoy, who grew up in Newark, New Jersey during World War II, remembers in vivid detail a song he learned in grade school.

> Just the rhythm alone can cause my flesh to ripple. . . . "Arise, ye who refuse to be bond-slaves, with our very flesh and blood"—oh, that defiant cadence! I remember every single heroic word!—"We will build a new great wall!" And then my favorite line, commencing as it does with my favorite word in the English language: "*In*-dig-*na*-tion fills the hearts of all of our coun-try-*men!* A-*rise!* A-*rise!* A-RISE!"[1]

Portnoy is the "lust-ridden, mother addicted young Jewish bachelor" in Philip Roth's *Portnoy's Complaint,* the novel that made its author a major celebrity in American literature. The fictive young man appears to have paid serious attention to the revolutionary message of both the music and the lyrics. At the same time, it is hard to ignore the fact that this seems to have something to do with his own private construal of "A-*rise!* A-RISE!" as sanctioning his youthful obsession with masturbation.

Portnoy referred to the song as "the marching song of the victorious Red Army," which his teachers referred to as the "Chinese National Anthem" during World War II. The music teachers in New Jersey were neither alone nor original in their mistake. A Dutch filmmaker on location in China in 1938,[2] as well as a Chinese music educator in its wartime capital, Chongqing, did the same.[3] What was, in fact, a popular film song entitled "March of the Volunteers" would indeed go on to be designated the provisional national anthem of the new Communist regime—but only a full decade later, in 1949.

"Yiyongjun jinxingqu" (March of the Volunteers), regarded by a host of international artists and activists as the Chinese national anthem long before its ascendance to that official status, offers a case study in the democratic energies and the experimental natures of both the revolutionary avant-garde and popular nationalism. The constant reenactment of the song during wartime by a great number of people in China, and around the world, is testimony to the complexity and dynamics of national politics as embodied experience in an international setting.

The song would eventually—most likely due to its popularity—be designated the provisional national anthem at the founding of the People's Republic of China (PRC) in 1949, but it would only be written into the Chinese Constitution as the official national anthem more than half a century later, in 2004.[4] The transformation of a popular film song into the Communist national anthem suggests the confluence of several distinct determinants: the emergence of the Shanghai commercial film industry and the creation of new sound reproduction technology by US-trained engineers, the legacy of the avant-garde and the role of the Communist Party, the alignment of mass culture and military volunteers, and the convergence of an internationalist imagination and Chinese nationalism.

Scholars of the interwar European avant-garde have argued for its shaping influence in the creation of new cultural institutions and meanings.[5] This chapter taps into the expressive energy of the interwar and wartime avant-garde in the context of modern China. Furthermore, in accordance with Craig Calhoun's attempt to rescue nationalism from history "as a conceptual framework, a discursive formation, a rhetoric, a structure of loyalties and sentiments," which not only takes shape within history but also informs history,[6] I emphasize the democratic impulse within popular nationalism that fuels the process of constructing a national identity. One cannot ignore war, famine, and other disastrous outcomes brought on by nationalism, but, as Calhoun contends, what also matters is "the cultural productivity that goes into nationalism—the symphonies and tangos, films and poetry." Most important, the idea of the nation makes possible the imagination of a collective actor—"We the people," a performative construct that simultaneously calls "the people" into existence and exerts on them a strong claim to cohesion and collective action.[7] The decades between the two world wars constituted a similarly formative and dynamic moment in the mutual formation of the international avant-garde and modern Chinese nationalism.

One Song, Many Renditions

The original version of "March of the Volunteers" was written by Tian Han for the 1935 Chinese feature film *Fengyun ernü* (Lovers in Troubled Times). Its opening lyrics, "Arise, ye who refuse to be bond-slaves," urged the Chinese to rise up in the face of the Japanese invasion. The music was composed by Nie Er (1912–35), a talented young musician who had been exposed to Russian émigré musicians in Shanghai but was largely self-taught, and who died under unclear circumstances in Japan on his way to the Soviet Union. In a diary entry written before his death in Tokyo, Nie Er recorded his impressions on watching a Japanese military display accompanied by a marching song while finalizing his composition for "March of the Volunteers."[8] So it is not inconceivable that Nie Er's final composition for the "March" had been influenced by a Japanese imperial march glorifying Japan's *mission civilisatrice* in China.

In the film "Lovers in Troubled Times," about the transformation of a poet into a volunteer soldier, the song ushers in the final climax when the poet Baihua and the young girl Xinfeng are joined by a group of volunteers marching toward the battlefield. The scene opens with close-ups of a beating drum and a blowing bugle,[9] and it initiates the music in the style of a military march. The poet and the young girl lead the crowd, their faces in close-up, glowing with determination and happiness. Their mixed-voice singing, especially the male voice, dominates the whole song. Everyone, man or woman, young or old, marches on to fight the Japanese in resolute unison, as shown in repeated close-ups of their marching feet.

Three years later Tian Han welcomed Joris Ivens to Wuhan under rather precarious conditions, when the Dutch filmmaker was on location in China shooting his documentary *The 400 Million*, only a few months before the temporary wartime capital fell to Japanese invaders in October 1938. Ivens, whom Walter Benjamin praised for an earlier documentary in a contemporary essay on the mechanical reproducibility of art,[10] would return to China numerous times after this fateful encounter. In Ivens's film, it was "March of the Volunteers," not the then provisional national anthem "Three Principles of the People," that accompanied the raising of the flag of the Republic of China. Again sung by a chorus of mixed voices, the song pervades a tightly edited one-minute sequence in the documentary. In it an opening close-up of the back of two military band members with their sousaphones, a low-angle shot of the rising Nationalist flag that cuts to a group of men gazing up at it, and female students in Red Cross uniforms shouting "Long Live the Republic of China" lead to a chorus leader rhythmically conducting a group of students singing, and actors tearing down the Japanese flag and shouting slogans with raised fists are replaced by a young girl on an elevated platform passionately urging her audience to donate money or join up to fight the Japanese on the war front.[11]

Another three years later Paul Robeson, the African American singer, actor, athlete, and activist, recorded *Chee Lai: Songs of New China* with a Chinese chorus in New York in 1941. The transition from Wuhan to New York was nothing less than dramatic. Moreover, the fact that Robeson identified with the song and its anti-Japanese message before the attack on Pearl Harbor and the United States' entry into the Pacific War, speaks to his activist role in harnessing the internationalist sentiment of the time.

"Chee Lai," or "Arise," was the first line of "March of the Volunteers." Robeson sang the song first in Chinese, then in English. The English translation was reportedly produced by the exiled Chinese conductor Liu Liangmo in consultation with the lyricist Tian Han, though it is likely that Robeson himself also contributed to some of the wording, including highlighting the keywords "freedom" and "true democracy," which brought into full play the democratic aspiration in the Chinese original.[12] Robeson would sing the song on many more occasions following the release of the album. His live performance at the World Peace Conference in April 1949 in Prague, with the lyricist Tian Han in the audience,[13] possibly contributed to the song's ascendance to the national stage in the newly founded PRC a few months later.

"March of the Volunteers" had traveled from the 1935 Shanghai film to the 1938 documentary supported by left-wing artists in Hollywood and made by a Dutch director.[14] It then entered the repertoire of an African American actor and activist in the United States, and his version reached Europe and other parts of the world via radio airwaves and live concerts in the 1940s. This cluster of voices and images suggests that the production, circulation, and consumption of this popular film song and its evolution into the Chinese national anthem had as much to do with the joint efforts of an international avant-garde as with the rise of nationalism in Chinese politics by way of embodied performance and popular participation.

The International Avant-Garde

Why did these various nationals come together for what turned out to be yet another "nationalist" project? What made this project so appealing to them? How was "national art" so intrinsically connected to international politics in this case? The rise of international socialism and the development of the avant-garde in the post–Russian Revolution and post–World War I world provided unlikely mechanisms to link what I call the "1898 generation" together. Tian Han, Joris Ivens, and Paul Robeson were all born in 1898, as was the German composer Hanns Eisler, who composed for Ivens and was a close collaborator of Bertolt Brecht (also born in 1898). The latter wrote lyrics for Ivens and "teaching plays" (*Lehrstücke*) set in China, of which *The Measures Taken* was a representative piece.[15] The Soviet filmmaker Sergei Eisenstein, whose *Battleship Potemkin* entered Tian's and Ivens's visions, and Yokomitsu Ruiichi, whose novel *Shanhai* (Shanghai) came to represent the leading avant-garde school of writers in Japan, were also born in 1898; so was the later Chinese premier Zhou Enlai, whom Ivens met in Wuhan in 1938 and who was the key reason that he frequently returned to China to film.[16] All of them belong to the generation that came of age in post–World War I Berlin, Tokyo, Paris, New York, London, Amsterdam, and Shanghai.

The interwar international avant-garde's search for alternative cultural resources against the decay of bourgeois societies led its members to a cluster of shared cultural texts. August Strindberg influenced both Ivens and Tian through translations in German and Japanese, and his *Spöksonaten* (Ghost Sonata) was performed by the Provincetown Players during Robeson's association with Eugene O'Neill and the Players. Strindberg's *Ett drömspel* (*A Dream Play*) was staged in Berlin in 1921 by Max Reinhardt's company, and Ivens recorded his excitement at seeing it.[17] Around the same time, Tian Han was creating one of his very first stage plays in Tokyo. He inserted a "dream scene" in his three-scene play "Spiritual Light," where the female protagonist, Meili, is led by Mephistopheles to bear witness to the suffering of the refugees much as the Christ-like female protagonist, Agnes, is led to experience in *A Dream Play*.[18]

Robert Wiene's *The Cabinet of Dr. Caligari* premiered in Berlin and Tokyo almost simultaneously in the early 1920s, where it was seen by Joris Ivens in Berlin and Tian Han in Tokyo. Sergei Eisenstein's *The Battleship Potemkin* was shown by Tian in Shanghai in 1926 and by Ivens's film group after its founding in Amsterdam in 1927.[19] In the same year, Tian founded the Southland Institute of Film and Drama to make his first film, *Dao minjian qu* ("*V Narod*" *or* "To the People"), with Russian and German motifs in Shanghai. Around the same time, Ivens was associated with a group of artistic friends in Berlin, Amsterdam, and Paris, who shared antibourgeois ideals and the desire for innovation. Hendrik Marsman, the Tian Han figure in this group, wrote, "Art and life are one, undivided and undistinguished."[20] This belief in social involvement is one that Ivens, Robeson, and Tian remained loyal to all their lives.

Their generation of the international avant-garde was deeply inspired by Russian literature and Soviet cinema. Maxim Gorky's novel, *Мать* (The Mother, 1907), influenced both Ivens and Tian, although Tian was mainly touched by the original story and rewrote it as a one-act play in Shanghai,[21] while Ivens was mainly influenced by Pudovkin's film adaptation of the story. Brecht most famously adapted the novel into his radically experimental *Die Mutter* in 1932 and enlisted Hanns Eisler to compose more than ten songs for the performance.[22] In the same year, Tian Han published his adaptation *Muqin* in Shanghai with a theme song composed by Lü Ji entitled "Bohui'er zhige" (Song of Pawel).[23] The October Revolution had ushered in a period of cultural freedom (mostly outside the Soviet Union) in which futurists, supremacists, constructivists, and other avant-gardists experimented with film, theater, music, literature, and the visual arts with a profound impact on Ivens and Tian as early as the late 1910s and on Robeson in the late 1920s.

Amid the fever of interdisciplinary cultural experimentation, the rise of sound and music as a dominating feature onscreen in the global film industry and the mechanical reproduction and circulation of film songs brought about revolutionary changes. Ivens's documentary *Philips Radio* became the first Dutch film with sound in 1931. He also joined the Communist Party of Holland in the same year. Tian joined the Chinese Communist Party in 1932 and went on to write lyrics for some of the most popular screen songs of the mid-1930s. Although Robeson was never a Communist Party member, his sympathy for the common people, originating in his humble beginning as the son of a runaway slave, intensified during his concert tours in Britain around 1928 to 1929.[24] Hence, the conversations about the making and propagating of popular songs, the shared experience of an interwar international avant-garde, and the making of socially engaged artists worked hand in hand.

One Country, Two "National Anthems"

In his handwritten notes on the "flag-raising scene" in *The 400 Million,* Joris Ivens included the lyrics of a "Volunteer March" written out for him in Chinese and referred to the song as the "Chinese National Hymn."[25] In so doing, he was mistakenly, but prophetically, conferring on it an identity it would only provisionally assume more than a decade later. Pao-ch'en Lee (Li Baochen), famous for his role in promoting a choral movement in China at the time, writing from its wartime capital Chongqing in a *New York Times* article in 1939, also regarded the song as "virtually the national anthem of China at war."[26] Why "March of the Volunteers," rather than "Three Principles of the People," the song newly designated by the ruling Nationalists as the Chinese national anthem?

Interestingly, more than one music notation accompanied Lee's *New York Times* article. "Three Principles of the People," subtitled the "Nationalist Party Song," was written in numerical notation with only Chinese lyrics, while "March of the Volunteers," crowned as "*virtually* the national anthem," was written in Western notation with lyrics in both Chinese and English, hence making its message accessible to readers of the English-language newspaper. However, the caption mistakenly noted that they were both "March of the Volunteers," only in different notations and different languages.[27]

The ascendancy of "March of the Volunteers" as the de facto national anthem of the Chinese Republic at war, at the very moment when the necessity arose for the Nationalists to designate their party song as the new provisional national anthem, raises questions not only about the politics of wartime songs but also about the musicality of wartime politics. Lee's article suggested that "March of the Volunteers" quickly eclipsed "Three Principles of the People" in representing the Chinese nation to the international community. The competitive advantage of "March of the Volunteers" was quite prominent in Joris Ivens's documentary *The 400 Million* as well, as the (mis)match between the national flag and the popular film song seemed most natural to all involved at the time.

Joris Ivens, who, together with Ernest Hemingway, made *The Spanish Earth* documenting the Spanish Civil War in 1936, arrived in China in February 1938 to make *The 400 Million,* a documentary about "the people's war in China against Japan."[28] The Dutch filmmaker visited Moscow in December 1929. He stayed in Sergei Eisenstein's apartment, and Eisenstein's assistant was assigned to him to help in preparing Russian subtitles for his films.[29] He would go back to Moscow in February 1932 with the earnest hope of making a documentary on behalf of Soviet workers. The finished film, *Song of Heroes* (Komsomol, 1932), was one of the ten films chosen to celebrate the successful conclusion of the Soviet First Five Year Plan.[30] If Ivens's background predisposed him to sympathize with the Communists rather than the Nationalists in a China at war, Pao-ch'en Lee, born into a family of Christians and educated in missionary schools in Shanghai and later in the United States, seemed more likely to do the opposite.[31] However, both the Chinese resident in its wartime capital, Chongqing, and the foreign observer in the similarly Nationalist-controlled Xi'an, gave "March of the Volunteers" their vote of confidence. Why was this the case?

Both "Three Principles of the People" and "March of the Volunteers" were included in *China's Patriots Sing*,[32] a bilingual songbook Lee edited for the Propaganda Department of the Nationalist Party in 1939 in Chongqing, the wartime capital of "Free China" after the fall of Wuhan. Prominently placed as the first of the eleven songs was "Three Principles of the People," now matter-of-factly entitled *Guoge*, with its English translation "Chinese National Anthem" in large type printed below. Here the song was presented in a bilingual fashion, with instrumental accompaniment by Chao Yüan-Jen (Zhao Yuanren), a famed linguist and foundational figure in music education in the Republic. The lyrics appeared as follows.

國歌 Chinese National Anthem
三民主義 吾黨所宗 San Min Chu I,* our aim shall be,
以建民國 以進大同 To found a free land, world peace be our stand.
咨爾多士 為民前鋒 Lead on, com-rades, van-guards ye are!
夙夜匪懈 主義是從 Hold fast your aim by sun and star!
矢勤矢勇 必信必忠 Be earn-est and brave, your coun-try to save.
一心一德 貫徹始終 One heart, one soul; one mind, one goal!
*Pronounced San Min Joo Ee, Three Principles of the People.[33]

The English translation of the lyrics re-created the Chinese original in a free manner. Some of these changes were occasioned by the attempt to translate each four-word line in Chinese into four syllables in English so the English version could be sung to the Chinese melody. It also demonstrates an attempt to enable the song to speak to the Republic's current crisis rather than faithfully following the classical Chinese words spoken by Dr. Sun Yat-sen a decade and a half before. "San Min Chu I" was vaguely described as "our aim," while the Chinese original explicitly stated "the aim of our group," namely, our community, or more specifically our party, the Nationalist Party. "Republic of China" was translated as "a free land," and "Great Harmony" became "world peace." The English translation attempted to avoid any mention of the Nationalist Party. Instead it highlighted the land, the country, and the world, shifting the focus from a "party anthem" to a "national anthem." It is likely that the Propaganda Department of the Nationalist Party, the sponsor of Lee's bilingual songbook in 1939, intended to announce the party song as the Chinese national anthem to the international community.

Lee positioned "March of the Volunteers" immediately after the ceremonial "Chinese National Anthem" and "National Flag Song," and described it in the notes as "still *the* most popular war song in China" (Lee's emphasis).[34] The lyrics, translated by Lee himself, are as follows.

義勇軍進行曲
起來! 不願做奴隸的人們!
把我們的血肉, 築成我們新的長城!
中華民族到了最危險的時一候,
每個人被迫着發出最後的吼聲!
起來! 起來! 起來———!
我們萬眾一心, 冒著敵人的炮火, 前進!
冒著敵人的砲火, 前進! 前進! 前進! 進!

March of the Volunteers
A-rise! ye who refuse to be bond slaves!
With our very flesh and blood let us build our new Great Wall.
Chi-na's masses have met the day of dan-ger,
In-dig-na-tion fills the heart of all of our country-men.
A-rise! A-rise! A-rise———!
Man-y hearts with one mind, Brave the en-e-my's gun-fire, March on!
Brave the en-e-my's gun-fire, March on! March on! March on! on![35]

The simple and colloquial expressions in the lyrics gave rise to some of the most "catchy" phrases of the time. Expressions such as "Great Wall made of flesh and blood" (*xuerou changcheng*), "final outcry" (*zuihou de housheng*), and "ten thousand with one mind" (*wanzhong yixin*),[36] simultaneously consolidated images already widely circulating in the popular imaginary and further established their canonical status in the Chinese national imagination, although the translation by Lee took a certain degree of liberty in matching the English words with the music.

The music, according to Lee, was "a good example of what some musicians are trying to do now—that is, in brief, to copy the good points from Western music without impairing or losing our own national color."[37] "This stirring 'cry of pain and rage' spread over the country like fire," Lee wrote in his explanatory notes.[38] The newly designated national anthem "Three Principles of the People," though prominently listed as the first patriotic song, paled in comparison.

Linguistically, the popularity of "March of the Volunteers" suggests the success of the vernacular over the literary,[39] as the lyrics of "Three Principles of the People" were composed in a highly regulated form, with grammatical structures not easily understood by the uneducated, while lyrics sung by the "400 million" are direct, simple, and easy both to follow and to memorize. Phonetically, "Three Principles of the People" assumes the form of an imperial edict that can be read aloud and sung in many dialects,[40] similar to the Kangxi emperor's Sacred Edict or the Imperial Rescript on Education in Meiji Japan,[41] while "March of the Volunteers" was written to be sung in Mandarin with accompanying lyrics on the film screen, an educational tool aimed at creating a common national language with uniform pronunciation (although in reality Mandarin may have excluded as much as it included).

However, the two lyrics share more structural similarities than their obvious linguistic differences would suggest. Originally an address given by Dr. Sun Yat-sen at the elite Whampoa Military Academy, "Three Principles of the People" was directed at "the vanguards" of the people, the highly select future military leaders of the Nationalist Party—hence, "lead on, comrades, vanguards ye are!" Similarly, "March of the Volunteers" addressed "ye who refuse to be bond slaves" and urged "China's masses" and "all of our countrymen" to be "volunteers" for the nation. One could argue that both songs were "vanguardist," that is, they both seemed "Leninist" in structure even if their politics were Nationalist and Communist respectively. What distinguishes Nationalist elitism from Communist avant-gardism in this context?

If the implied speaker in "Three Principles of the People" was Dr. Sun himself, the speaker multiplied into "the 400 million" in "March of the Volunteers." It was hoped that the person who cried out in the beginning could be any and every one of the 400 million and that the addressor and addressee could form a self-replicating coaching relationship: any Chinese who was addressed would be expected to rise and march and would then urge any other Chinese to follow suit.[42] In this multiplication of enunciating voices lies the potential for mass mobilization.

Thematically, "Three Principles of the People" identifies no clear external threats, while "March of the Volunteers" identifies the Japanese as a clear, if unnamed, "enemy"—a tactic that effectively concretizes the abstraction of imperialism. Here Japanese imperialism served to catalyze the consolidation of Chinese nationalism, which was most readily embraced as a bulwark against an external threat. In short, "March of the Volunteers" was an effective tool in marketing mass mobilization.

The same Japanese threat also brought various groups of vanguards together. The loss of Manchuria to Japan in 1931, and especially the acute sense of nostalgia and pain popularized by a group of talented young writers displaced from Manchuria to Shanghai,[43] triggered a renewed sense of urgency for national salvation. Rana Mitter has argued, "The Manchurian propagandists provided a new and popularly resonant image of resistance heroes . . . allowing nationalism to be expressed in a new and different way from 1931 onward and encouraging the replacement of 'imperialism' in general with Japan in particular as its chief target."[44]

China at war was what John Fitzgerald called a "nationless state," meaning that "the Chinese nation has been created and recreated in the struggle for state power, and it was ultimately being defined by the state as a reward of victory."[45] "March of the Volunteers" functioned as an important call to arms summoning a new Chinese nation and a new Chinese citizen into being. The global political climate between the two world wars, from the rise of anticolonial nationalism in Africa, Asia, and Latin America to the formation of an internationalist political solidarity, provided fertile ground for the reemergence of the "masses" and "volunteers" as important religious, political, and popular cultural categories.[46]

Given that "March of the Volunteers" was, from the start, linked to and dependent for its distribution on film, it follows that technological and commercial factors are crucial to understanding the popularity and mobilizing power of the song. More important, "March of the Volunteers" provides a structure of meaning in which participatory action can be anchored. In fact, each individual singer becomes, through the song, a meaning-making agent whose personal embodiment becomes the only way to realize, to incarnate, the significance of the song. In spite of that, the power of forceful repetition and mechanical reproduction may supply the link from individual embodiment to collective solidarity and group cohesion.

It is significant to put volunteers and mobilization against the Japanese in the context of the rising anticolonial nationalisms around the world. It makes a big difference that the imperial power here was Japan, that is, specifically not European. Given Japan's function as the cultural matrix of many of the more radically inclined Chinese avant-gardists at the time, as shown throughout Tian Han's Tokyo sojourn and Shanghai experimentation, it suggests that the European avant-garde, representing the international antifascist movement, was in a better position to intervene and contribute to China's fight against Japanese imperialism.[47]

However, Tian Han's enchantment with Taishō Tokyo and his deep engagement with Japanese literary and cultural figures throughout his Shanghai years did leave traces in the lyrics written by him. They contain phrases such as *wanzhong yixin,* or in Pao-ch'en Lee's translation, "many hearts with one mind,"[48] possibly borrowed from and now turned into a rhetorical weapon against the Japanese slogan "one hundred million Japanese beat as one heart" (*ichioku isshin*).[49] For Tian Han, imperialist Japan was not the Japan he admired, and at the time of national crisis, national survival came before individual predilection and sympathies.

The Japanese annexation of Manchuria after the Mukden Incident in 1931, like Italy's annexation of Abyssinia (now Ethiopia) after the Second Italo-Abyssinian War in 1936, produced many works of art representing the suffering and humiliation that resulted.[50] The sounds and images of the International Brigades in the Spanish Civil War, popularized by Joris Ivens, Earnest Hemingway, Robert Capa,[51] and Paul Robeson,[52] were similarly transformed into a fervent collective political aspiration concerning Japan's full-scale war in China.

"March of the Volunteers" embodied such a collective aspiration, at once a favorite among missionary church choruses and at informal gatherings among foreign correspondents in China. In March 1938, in Guide (now part of Shangqiu, Henan), W. H. Auden and Christopher Isherwood were invited by Dr. Brown, a Canadian mission doctor who worked with Dr. Norman Bethune, to attend a service in the hospital chapel.[53] "They were singing a hymn with the words 'Arise! Arise!' and in Chinese it sounded like 'Chee-ee-ee-ee Lai!'"[54] The resounding "Chee Lai" would enter Joris Ivens's memoir, *The Camera and I*, as follows.

> [A]fter dinner in an old barn, each of us sings songs from his country. John and I sing old Dutch songs, sailor songs, and love songs. Captain Carlson plays *Working on the Railroad* on the harmonica. In a hoarse, melancholy voice Capa sings songs of the Hungarian plains and then we all sing a Chinese war song we have learned: *Chi-Lai*.[55]

Here "March of the Volunteers," or "Chi-Lai," provides a common language and a common expression for the Dutch filmmakers, the American captain, and the Hungarian photojournalist in the "catchy tune" composed by the talented young composer Nie Er and in the original Chinese lyrics written by Tian Han. Music and simple lyrics became an international language that facilitated transnational and transcultural communication. Just as Esperanto had provided a common ground for communication in the cosmopolitan Cosmo Club in Tokyo, of which Tian Han had been an active member, so singing together brought about collective physical and imaginative solidarity. Given the disparity and discreteness of individual experience, the same song was variously described as a "hymn" and a "war song," embodying a wide rage of experience from religious to militant. However, the power of the song to evoke physical and emotional coherence in a chorus of people singing in unison is still undeniable.

Ivens reported again how, after the battle of Tai'erzhuang, "a volunteer song of North China, a war song" was sung during a night march: "[O]ne of the officers up front on the road starts a song, another picks it up, then a third, and then we all sing."[56] It is probable that this volunteer song was indeed "March of the Volunteers," and Ivens's description of the way the song was picked up by one person and then another until it became a unanimous chorus is a vivid illustration of the process of political subject making, as well as a metaphor for the individual-collective dynamic. Though Ivens called "March" a popular war song of North China and misread its originating context (film) and geographic location (Shanghai), he nonetheless captured its popularity and mobilizing power and its ability to reproduce collective identity via embodied performance.

Making "March of the Volunteers"

"March of the Volunteers" has produced a cottage industry in contemporary Chinese popular culture, including multiple commemorative films and TV soap operas.[57] Given that the song occupies a crucial position in the national iconography of the PRC as its current national anthem, the story of its creation and propagation has been portrayed in numerous official and semiofficial versions in popular media.

However, these depictions are loathe to acknowledge the avant-garde and internationalist roots of the national anthem—roots that are exposed if we step back to trace the conception of the song and its initial circulation through print, recordings, stage, and screen. Of central importance were the Film Group, headed by the leftist playwright and director Xia Yan under the leadership of the Communist Party Shanghai Central Bureau's Cultural Committee (Wenwei), and the Diantong (Denton) Film Company, founded in the spring of 1934 in Shanghai.[58] The Communist connection inevitably framed the story of the song ideologically, often as a leftist enterprise per se, which resulted in the dominance of a narrow political interpretation of its making. In practice the making of the song required a diverse group of "actors" and "singers" to form a grand "chorus." It thus should be interpreted from a range of possible perspectives: political, artistic, technological, and commercial. Here the technology of songs and the polyphonic cultural scene of the mid-1930s must be emphasized. Print advertisements, gramophone records, radio airwaves, stage and street performances, and film screenings were all important channels through which to market and propagate the song, written and composed in 1935 for the popular commercial film "Lovers in Troubled Times."

"March of the Volunteers" has to be understood in the context of the film. The development of the domestically produced "Three Friends" (Sanyou) recording device in 1933,[59] and the ascendance of the Denton Film Company to popular prominence in 1934–35 had much to do with the popularity of film songs in a revolutionary age. "The Graduation Song," popularized by the first Denton film, *Taoli jie* (The Plunder of Peach and Plum), also appeared onstage in Tian Han and Nie Er's experimental "new opera," *Yanzijiang de baofengyu* (Storm over the Yangtze).[60] It was followed by "March of the Volunteers," promoted through a second Denton production, "Lovers in Troubled Times."

While writing the film story for "Lovers in Troubled Times," Tian Han was undergoing a bout of "self-criticism" in 1930 before joining the Chinese Communist Party in 1932.[61] He was head of the Music Group of the Soviet Friends Society, a united front organization initiated by Madame Sun Yat-sen and Tian himself in early 1933.[62] Tian Han, Ren Guang, An E, and Nie Er were among the initial members of the group. Ren Guang, a French-educated composer, was, at the time, the music director at the leading music giant Pathé-EMI's Shanghai office. Living in a Western villa in the heart of the French Concession and equipped with a piano and high-quality radio, Ren provided not only a space for the gatherings of the Music Group but also the necessary technology for their direct contact with Soviet music and communication with the wider world via shortwave broadcasts.[63] The stage was now set for the members of the Music Group to exert their influence in producing popular songs.

An E (the pen name of Zhang Shiyuan), on whose articles Tian based his writing about the development of Soviet film and the future of Chinese film,[64] had returned from Moscow in 1929 to work as a secret agent for the CCP. She fell in love with Tian Han and bore him a child in 1931. She later collaborated with Ren Guang to produce one of the first popular screen songs in the film *Yuguang qu* ("Fisherman's Song," 1934), the first Chinese film to win an international film prize.[65] It can be concluded that when "Lovers in Troubled Times" was produced by the Denton Film Company, the popularity of its songs made the Music Group a core institution in reaching out to the masses; Liu Liangmo, the future active campaigner of mass-singing activities through the Shanghai YMCA, was recorded as a member of this group in 1935.[66]

"March of the Volunteers" was central to the making of "Lovers in Troubled Times," as Denton was determined to repeat or even go beyond its market success with "The Graduation Song." He Lüting, sound director at Denton at the time, was entrusted with the task of arranging an instrumental accompaniment for the song. He was in close contact with the community of Russian Jewish émigré musicians in Shanghai, among them Aaron Avshalomov, whose compositions were a fusion of Chinese scales and characteristics and Western forms and instruments in the tradition of eighteenth-century chinoiserie.[67] He Lüting invited Avshalomov to compose the orchestral accompaniment for "March of the Volunteers" in May 1935.[68] Wang Renmei, whose debut in *Ye meigui* ("Wild Rose," a Chinese-style Pygmalion story) as Little Phoenix had won her wide popularity and critical acclaim,[69] played another Little Phoenix in "Lovers in Troubled Times." A former student of Li Jinhui, the master of "yellow music" famous for its display of female sexuality, Wang's singing and dancing skills earned her the part.

From an unfinished poem to a full-fledged film song with highly sophisticated instrumental accompaniment, the "March of the Volunteers" was an essential component of the success of "Lovers in Troubled Times." Though orchestrated by the Denton Film Company, itself an enterprise based on the newly invented sound-recording device and supported by the underground Communist Party, this "chorus" could not have been formed without the coordinated efforts of all the technical, musical, and commercial personnel involved. The Moscow-educated, underground CCP member An E was an active journalist and had inside connections with various media.[70] The Paris-trained musician Ren Guang, as a director at the commercial giant Pathé-EMI, represented the music industry. The Sanyou recording enterprise provided professional technical support from US-trained engineers.[71] Finally, Tian Han and Xia Yan, the leading intellectual figures in theater, film, and music circles at the time, connected the Soviet Friends Society Music and Film Groups with the commercial film venture of the Denton Film Company. Many of the "singers" and "actors" in this "chorus" were closely associated with the post–World War I international avant-garde and its transformation in the early 1930s, and had a keen sense of product marketing in an increasingly sophisticated media environment.

Marketing "March of the Volunteers"

The marketing of the song as a commercial product and its dissemination as political propaganda beg the following questions. Was politics (as expressed through the lyrics) being instrumentalized to help market the commercial film? Or was the commercial product being used as a way to market politics? What was the relationship between the new commercial mass entertainment culture and the new mass political movement? With the politically engineered resurgence of "red songs" and "red films" in contemporary Chinese popular culture, these questions seem as relevant today, if not more so, than they were seventy years ago.[72]

On May 8, 1935, *Shenbao* and *Shibao*, the two leading Shanghai newspapers at the time, simultaneously published two musical scores, "Songstress under the Iron Hoof" and "March of the Volunteers," as a preview to the film "Lovers in Troubled Times," due to be released later that month.[73] The scores were published in both staff and numerical notations with Chinese lyrics, with the expectation that individuals and groups would want to sing or play them on their own.[74] The publication of sheet music was big business prior to World War II all around the world as gramophones and radios continued to be luxury items. Music had a central place in modern schools (and churches), and musical literacy was much more widespread than it is nowadays. Still, it is hard to gauge exactly how widespread musical literacy was at the time. The inclusion of numerical notation in these newspaper publications points to the democratizing and vernacularizing trend at the time in China. It also highlights the importance of nonwritten modes of disseminating music, since such notation can be more easily taught to people who are musically illiterate. Although Nie Er was listed as the composer of the song, Tian Han, the lyricist, was nowhere to be found, given that the Nationalist police had arrested him a few months earlier and his name was banned in public.[75]

In the days following its first appearance in print, "March of the Volunteers" would appear many more times in *Chenbao* (May 9), *Zhonghua ribao* (May 10), *Minbao* (May 10), and *Da wanbao* (May 19), all the way up to the film's premier on May 24, 1935. A further print advertising campaign was carried out when leaflets containing the two musical scores were widely distributed to the Shanghai public on May 10.[76] The publication and distribution of musical scores weeks before the film premiere ensured a receptive audience for the film, as familiarity with the songs antedated and facilitated its popularity.

The musical scores were followed by full-page advertisements for the film on May 23 and May 24 in *Shenbao.* The importance of sound was highlighted by emphasizing the domestically produced Three Friends recording device and by stressing the synchronized dialogue and "heroic and passionate" singing throughout the film. Indeed, "Songstress" seemed to be the more prominently featured song at the time, as the emphasis on the virgin girl and her bodily struggle would surely attract much audience attention; however, the later ascendancy of "March" to national popularity was not unexpected, as the combination of love and revolution in the latter (as least in the original film) fit well with the highly encouraged, yet often spontaneously enacted, youthful patriotism of the time.

This elaborate print advertisement for the film went on to list Situ Huimin, filmmaker, CCP member, and a contributor to his cousin Situ Yimin's Three Friends device, as one of the sound-recording technicians.[77] He Lüting was listed as in charge of musical accompaniments. It was also reported that Ren Guang had recorded "March," sung by the Denton chorus, on May 9, 1935, at Pathé-EMI. Hence, the advertisement also contained a line in small print advertising this gramophone record. Similar advertisements, albeit half the size of the *Shenbao* one, also appeared on the day of the premiere in *Zhonghua ribao* and *Shibao,* with equal emphases on the sound effects and musical elements of the film. The film was described as "the only grand sing-along film with live dialogue and passionate singing" (*quanbu yousheng duibai gechang weizhuang reqing weiyi jupian*),[78] attesting to the important fact that the songs were key to the film's success.

The musical elements of the film served as a key instrument of political mobilization. *Diantong huabao (*Denton Gazette), a biweekly with a circulation of some thirty to forty thousand per issue at the time, published a special issue on "Lovers in Troubled Times" on June 1, 1935, which included the original film story and musical scores for "Songstress" and "March." In fact, the publication of the journal's inaugural issue in mid-May and its forthcoming special issue on June 1 was listed on the full-page *Shenbao* advertisement on the day of the film's premiere.[79] The popularity of the film songs attracted people to the theater on opening night, which further popularized the forthcoming *Denton Gazette*. This advertising campaign and propaganda drive highlighting the sound effect of the film continued on the night of the premiere at the Golden City Grand Theater, located in the heart of the International Settlement on the South bank of the Suzhou River, from where the song spread all over the country.[80]

The sudden death of the young composer, Nie Er, in Japan added a background of human drama to the song, further boosting its popularity. Nie Er had been closely involved with the Star Film Company, recording music for early sound films as part of the Bright Moon Song and Dance Troupe led by Li Jinhui. Although he worked inside the industry through Li Jinhui and the Bright Moon Troupe, Nie was also a member of the intellectual Left who wrote under the pen name Hei Tianshi (Black Angel), critiquing Li's profit-driven display of female sexuality in the Shanghai press.[81] Nie Er was on his way to the Soviet Union when "Lovers in Troubled Times" premiered in Shanghai. He had enthusiastically introduced "Songstress under the Iron Hoof" and "March of the Volunteers," the latter his composition, to Chinese students in Japan as early as June 1935. Nie drowned while swimming in the Japan Sea only a month later, at age twenty-three. Chinese students in Japan sent his ashes back to Shanghai, and a memorial service was held in August. Nie Er's handwritten final composition for "March of the Volunteers" was published in *Nie Er jinian ji* (A Memorial Collection of Nie Er's Works), compiled by Chinese students in Japan, on October 31, 1935.[82]

Thus, by late 1935, a few months after the advertising campaign and propaganda drive to promote "March of the Volunteers" in print, on records, and onscreen, the time was ripe for the song to touch the hearts and minds of thousands of engaged crowds. As the Japanese threatened to move from Manchuria into northern China in mid-1935, and with Chahar and Hebei provinces on the brink of falling to them, thousands of Beiping students braved the harsh winter weather of December 1935 to protest the Nationalist government's plan to establish the Hebei-Chahar Political Committee, a compromise that would have led to the establishment of a separate regime controlled by the Japanese in northern China. The student demonstrations in Beiping, later known as the December Ninth movement,[83] inspired a second wave of citywide and nationwide demonstrations involving more than ten thousand workers and urbanites later in the same month—and provided the perfect occasion for the first mass singing of "March of the Volunteers" as an inspirational marching song by the passionate protesters. The journey of the song from Shanghai to Beijing (Beiping) attests to its national mobilizing power as early as 1935.

Performing "March of the Volunteers"

Alongside the technological distribution of the song through feature film, documentary, radio broadcast, and gramophone record, the more traditional media of stage performance and mass singing brought the popularity of and affective identification with the song to a new level under the conditions of war. Technology re-presented spectral bodies and sounds on the screen, on recordings, or via radio airwaves, while "conventional" stage performance and street singing engaged the living presence of flesh and blood bodies. Although "Songstress under the Iron Hoof" appeared together with "March of the Volunteers" in the 1935 film, it may have appeared onstage a year earlier. Tian Han was experimenting with a dynamic "spoken drama plus songs" formula in a "two-scene new opera," *Yangzijiang de baofengyu* (Storm over the Yangtze), first performed in June 1934 in Shanghai and written up as a finished play in 1935.[84] Echoing his keen interest in bringing sound to film, Tian inserted multiple songs into this "new opera," ranging from film songs to songs specifically written for the performance both in the 1930s and in the 1950s.[85] Tian's practice was contemporary with, and can be understood in light of, Benjamin's discussion of Brechtian "epic theater."

> Epic theatre, he [Brecht] explained, should not so much develop an action as present a situation. It attains that condition, as we shall soon see, by allowing

> the action to be broken up. Here I would remind you of the songs whose main function is to break the action. It is here—namely with the principle of breaking into the action—that the epic theatre takes up a process which, as you can clearly see, has become common in film and radio, press and photography, over the last few years. I am speaking of the process of montage: the element which is superimposed breaks into the situation on which it is imposed.[86]

Brecht and Benjamin worked together on their analysis of the democratic potential of media (most prominently expressed in Benjamin's famous essay "The Work of Art in the Age of Mechanical Reproduction"), from which emerges the Brechtian conception of "realism" as art that uses the most complex modern technology to address the widest popular public.[87] Tian Han would have found a kindred spirit in Brecht, who was not only the same age but also faced similar aesthetic and political challenges. From popular songs to expressionist theater to lyric poetry, their experimentation resulted in aesthetic and political practices that were truly alive to the shifting valences of artistic forms.

Avant-garde theater and opera performances of the period in China can be read along the lines of Brechtian theatrical interventions in the age of radio and film. The function of montage and the shock effect it generated can be illustrated with a focus on stage performances of the film song "March of the Volunteers." What is important at the cultural moment under discussion is the simultaneity of new technological modes of discourse with more conventional stage performance and mass singing. Instead of pointing in different directions or being aimed at different audiences, we observe the emergence of popular songs as quotable gestures and movable archives consolidating linkages among technology, genre experimentation, profit, and propaganda. Indeed, in the instance of "March of the Volunteers," the two kinds of media amplify each other and serve to universalize the content.

Tian Han's 1937 play *Lugou qiao* (Marco Polo Bridge), written soon after the outbreak of the full-scale war, provided a venue for the intersection of new media representation and stage performance of "March of the Volunteers." As was discussed in chapter 3, the story is told through songs, which function both to highlight and to interrupt the action, leading up to the final chorus singing of "March of the Volunteers" onstage.

The "old tale plus new song" formula was one of the major strategies utilized by Tian Han to modernize traditional forms but certainly not the only one. New songs were constantly created to enrich the wartime repertoire of popular songs. "Song of Seeing off Brave Soldiers" is such a song, again with mass singing of "March of the Volunteers" onstage as the much-anticipated climax in the performance of "Marco Polo Bridge." The song ends with the onstage chorus singing to see the soldiers off and completes the play within the play, which is followed by cheering from the onstage audiences—the Twenty-Ninth Army soldiers and the masses—who join in a heroic chorus of "March of the Volunteers." The earlier songs were created to usher in the final singing of "March of the Volunteers" in unison, and thus the 1935 film song reemerged in the 1937 stage representations of contemporary mass-singing activities.

This university-student-initiated "petit bourgeois" style of "performance within a performance" is buttressed by a mass chorus at the end of the third scene, when the whole city shows up to see off the departing soldiers in resolute unison. The small-scale chorus now develops into a grand chorus of enthusiastic masses. Such a scene would have been very effective pedagogically; the step-by-step formation of a mass-singing chorus reminds us of the multiplication of addressees implied in the lyrics of "March of the Volunteers." This scene would have served as a pedagogical, or "how-to," tool for the further conduct of such activities. Scenes depicting the masses seeing off or welcoming soldiers home with food and clothes permeate wartime imagery—in painting and woodblock,[88] onstage and onscreen. Added to this abundant visuality now was the sound effect—a slogan if you will, though an emotionally resonant one for its targeted audience, that could be spread, mouth to mouth, across the wartime nation.[89]

According to a contemporary account, during the "Marco Polo Bridge" performance, when performers shouted "defend North China, recover lost land, and drive out the enemies" onstage, audiences echoed their words offstage, and when characters sang "March of the Volunteers" onstage, audiences joined in the singing offstage.[90] Furthermore, the ingenuity of the Harvard-educated director, Hong Shen, was widely acknowledged. For the final scene, where Chinese and Japanese soldiers fight beside the Marco Polo Bridge, Hong planted actors playing soldiers behind audience seats. Once the fighting on stage started, soldiers from among the audience flooded the stage. The theater was filled with soldiers' cries; the stage was filled with smoke and fire, as if the whole venue was transformed into a battlefield; and all the audience members were thrown into the midst of the "fight."[91]

This account vividly illustrates what film scholar Jane Gaines calls "political mimesis," the "production" of the audience as politicized bodies through the interaction between bodies in two locations, in Gaines's case, on the documentary film screen and in the audience seats. Gaines borrows from film and rhetoric scholar Linda Williams's discussion of three film genres that "make the body do things" and insists on thinking of the body "in relation to films that make audience members want to kick and yell, films that make them want to do something *because of the conditions in the world of the audience*" (Gaines's emphasis).[92]

This intermingling of actors and audience and the emotional energy field created on- and offstage suggest a kinship with the principles of Brechtian epic theater. After all, Brecht developed his "alienation theory" after watching the leading Peking Opera female impersonator, Mei Lanfang, perform in Moscow in 1935,[93] and Peking Opera conventions dictate that actors frequently address the audience directly out of character. As Brecht would have it, the audience should always be aware of the theatricality of the performance, thus precluding the engenderment of illusion.[94] Although the Chinese plays and films under discussion here seem to invest themselves in the emotional involvement of the audience, they also provide an opportunity for reflection and critique of the situation presented onstage. Moreover, Tian shared with Brecht's more soberly reflective plays an obsession with music. On the one hand, in their mutual emphasis on musical forms and musical performance, inspired by Peking Opera, they use comic elements to distance the audience from the action depicted onstage; on the other hand, the interaction between actors and audience thus breaks the fourth wall of theatrical illusion and extends the performance from the stage into the audience seats.

This focus on the interaction between bodies on- and offstage reminds us of the ample emphasis on bodily dynamics in the lyrics of the songs on Chinese stage and screen at the time. "Songstress" presents the image of the bodily suffering and emotional outburst (through singing) of a virgin girl under foreign invasion, hence the iron hooves of the horses of the imperial army. "Seeing Off" leads the audience to human bodies and warm kisses, which rouse volunteering soldiers' patriotic zeal and steel their determination to die for their country. "March of the Volunteers," finally, aims to incite the marching feet of the participating bodies. Conventional wisdom could argue that these bodies are instrumentalized for purposes of war, and hence were made into national and political *objects*. Recognizing the dark side of wartime mobilization in the context of the international antifascist popular front, these stage and screen representations of bodily interactions aspire instead to make those bodies into national and political *subjects*.

Moreover, the circulation of "guerrilla drama troupes" throughout the country transgressed the boundary between the fictive and the real. "The spectator himself constitutes the basic material of the theatre," Eisenstein famously declared, and "the objective of any utilitarian theatre is to guide the spectator in the desired direction."[95] With his theater work in Proletkult as background,[96] Eisenstein defines an "attraction" as "any aggressive aspect of the theatre" that can "produce emotional shocks" in the spectator, that can "enable the spectator to perceive the ideological side of what is being demonstrated—the ultimate ideological conclusion."[97]

Following Eisenstein, Gaines highlights the role of popular music, "often rhythmically reinforced through editing patterns," or what Eisenstein calls the "emotive vibration" in montage, to produce a bodily effect on the audience. In the aforementioned film *The 400 Million,* made by Joris Ivens on location in China in 1938, voice and music intensified the "montage of attractions"; actors tear a Japanese flag into several pieces and shout slogans with the ragged flag in their fists. The narrator informs us that "actors leave their theatres, play on the street corner. They instruct the audience in how to resist the enemy." All the while, "March of the Volunteers" plays in the background, stitching the visual and the aural into a deliberate pedagogical statement, albeit an emotionally persuasive one.[98] "March of the Volunteers" can also be found as a concluding song inviting audience participation during a wide range of street theater performances in wartime China. For a 1938 version of the most popular street theater piece, *Fangxia ni de bianzi* (Lay Down Your Whips), "March" was suggested as one of the best songs to end the play with, as its popularity would guarantee audience participation and bring the play into a grand finale of mass singing.[99]

The performance of "March of the Volunteers" on stages and in the streets not only connected Eisenstein, Brecht, and Tian Han's avant-garde experiments as politically inspired social acts; it also linked Joris Ivens, Paul Robeson and Tian Han throughout the process of making the song popular. Liu Liangmo, the Shanghai YMCA secretary who taught the song to Robeson, had consulted Tian Han in translating the Chinese lyrics into English, and Robeson was said to have sent royalties to Tian Han in China. Ivens probably found the 1935 Denton record of the song during postproduction in Hollywood in late 1938, the only record of a Chinese song that he could locate there at the time.[100] Most important, on April 22, 1938, Tian Han himself, then the bureau chief in charge of propaganda in the United Front of the Nationalists and Communists in

Left to right: Robert Capa, John Ferno, Joris Ivens, Tian Han, Robin Hyde, Shen Junru, and Wang Ming, April 1938, Hankou, China. (Courtesy of European Foundation Joris Ivens, Nijmegen, the Netherlands.)

Wuhan, personally welcomed Joris Ivens when the Dutch filmmaker returned from the Tai'erzhuang war front to Hankou while shooting *The 400 Million.*[101]

"March of the Volunteers" dominates the soundtrack in the crucial mass-singing scene included in the aforementioned one-minute sequence in *The 400 Million.* Here one sees the physical embodiment of the metaphorical "building a new Great Wall with our flesh and blood," with the chorus members standing together as if building a human wall.[102] The scene opens with the camera panning from left to right through faces of singing young girls in medium shots in the front row. Behind the female students are boys in military uniform, possibly new recruits at this recruiting gathering in Xi'an, as the big banners in previous scenes indicate. The camera highlights the girls who prominently occupy the front row, with one of them holding a triangular flag with characters that read *xuanchuan dui.*[103] The scene then cuts to a longer shot from the opposite angle, revealing the chorus formation. The previous scene is indeed part of a chorus formed by two rows of female students in front and one row of male students in uniform in the back. The crowd is gathering, and the camera again pans from left to right to disclose the location of the chorus leader. Now surrounded by his chorus from the left, and the spectators on the right forming a half circle, a skinny young man, in a well-tailored Sun Yat-sen suit,[104] passionately conducts the chorus while leading the singing himself.

Accompanying this masterfully edited sequence is "March of the Volunteers" sung by a chorus of mixed voices, just like the enthusiastic onscreen chorus, although there is no attempt to synchronize the song with the movement of lips or the conductor's baton on the screen. Indeed, the technology that would allow synchronized sound recording did not yet exist in 1938, so the film shooting and the sound recording took place separately. Ivens had to add four to five sound tracks to this particular scene during postproduction in the United States. He may have used the Denton record "March of the Volunteers" for the singing. He most likely would have recorded the commentary, written by Dudley Nichols and narrated by Fredric March, and the original music composed by Hanns Eisler in Hollywood studios, where he also added Chinese dialogue and sound bites spoken by Chinese Americans and re-created according to recordings he made in Hankou and Xi'an.[105] Hence, the use of "March of Volunteers" in this scene can be read as both diegetic and nondiegetic: it speaks for all the human activities connected through this scene and can be issued from sources both on and off the screen; it is also part of the commentary and represents the filmmaker's deliberate choice.

After returning to the United States for postproduction of the film, Ivens gave a lecture in 1939 at the Museum of Modern Art in New York on subjectivity and montage in documentary film, in which he argued for documentary to be considered part of the avant-garde that emerged in Europe in 1927. He advocated for documentary as the means of imbuing the film medium with cultural value as a reaction both to Hollywood commercialism and to the dead end of pure aestheticism. For him it was crucial that films take political positions and ally themselves with social movements, and he openly announced, "Yes, we are propagandists! Artists must take sides!" (Robeson would say exactly the same in the 1950s under McCarthyism).[106] He highlighted the subjectivity of documentary filmmakers and their necessary emotional involvement with their subjects. In the true Eisensteinian tradition, he emphasized the crucial importance of montage in producing spectators and achieving emotional persuasion. The case of *The 400 Million* was used to illustrate the close collaboration between music and editing in producing an emotional effect.[107] Montage was used to achieve moments of interruption and reflection, which provided spaces in which the viewers could make conceptual and emotional connections. The use of the popular "war song" in *The 400 Million* contributed to the dramatic and subjective qualities of Ivens's documentary and its power of political persuasion through affective identification.

Mass Singing "March of the Volunteers"

What Joris Ivens captured in Xi'an in May 1938 was only a single note in a symphony of mass-singing activities throughout China at the time. A black and white picture documenting a similar mass-singing event shows an almost all female front row in a seven-hundred-person chorus: in their student gowns, some girls raise their heads to follow the elevated conductor, while others, songbooks in hand, concentrate on singing. The symbolism is unmistakable: embodying individual genius and agency amid the gigantic female collective is the skinny male figure of the conductor balancing on the high ladder, strikingly similar to the intellectual image of the passionate conductor in Ivens's film.

While the identity of the conductor in Ivens's film is uncertain,[108] the man leading the seven-hundred-person chorus in June 1936 in an outdoor stadium in Shanghai was none other than the well-known Liu Liangmo. Liu would be described in a November 1941 *New York Times* article, before the attack on Pearl Harbor, as "the Shanghai YMCA secretary who communicated his enthusiasm to many others and was called to teach at the front" and praised as the inspiration behind the movement of patriotic mass singing in China. As a result, the author quoted the bilingual writer Lin Yutang, popular in the United States at the time for his 1935 book *My Country and My People*, declaring that "China is finding her voice."[109]

This same *New York Times* article reviewed a new album, *Chee Lai*,[110] with "March of the Volunteers" as the title song sung in both Chinese and English by the African American singer Paul Robeson and conducted by Liu Liangmo with a Chinese chorus. Robeson had demonstrated his support for the Chinese fight against Japanese aggression as early as 1938, when he appeared together with Madame Sun Yat-sen at a Save China Assembly in London. He would return to his native United States in 1939 and meet Liu Liangmo, the Chinese conductor in exile, in New York in 1940.[111] The reviewer commends Robeson for performing the Chinese song "with power and passion," but he concludes, "The songs tell us more about China's valor than about her music, and at the moment her fight is more momentous than her art."[112] Such comments reflect the judgment, common in the West, that the strong ideological nature of the song is at odds with its aesthetic merit. However, in another review in the *New York Times* in June 1942, half a year after Pearl Harbor, the same author offered a more appreciative perspective on Liu Liangmo's appearance in a Town Hall concert under the auspices of the Negro Publication Society of America, with "March of the Volunteers" (Chee Lai) once again on the program. Liu was hailed as "singing and speaking for the valiant Chinese," who "fight for their liberty with songs on their tongues as well as with guns, tanks and planes," and are "true to the spirit of their songs and were delightful for that reason."[113] However, it seems clear that the reviewer is still presuming an intrinsic incompatibility between politics and aesthetics, a premise that is at odds with the *littérature engagée* milieu out of which the work itself emerged.

Indeed, for Liu himself, the aesthetic virtue of "March of the Volunteers" lay precisely in the power of its "catchy lyrics" to "spread resistance slogans from mouth to mouth."[114] As if to echo Liu's enthusiasm, a few days before the full-scale Japanese invasion in July 1937, a *Libao* article reported that the opening line of "March of the Volunteers" had become a collective roar of frontier soldiers and masses.[115] Indeed, echoes of "March of the Volunteers" were heard as far away as Paris as early as July 1937, immediately after the outbreak of the war. While in exile in France, Ren Guang, an active member of the Soviet Friends Society Music Group, which facilitated the birth of the song in Shanghai in 1935, mobilized overseas Chinese to organize a chorus to raise money for war refugees in China. Ren would bring the Chinese chorus to attend the Anti-fascist Conference in Paris, representing forty-two nations, and the song would spread far and wide on that spring day in 1938, possibly its first official appearance outside China,[116] as the official release of Ivens's *The 400 Million* would have to wait until March 1939.[117] By mid-November 1937, on a ship from Nanjing to Wuhan (both strong bases for the Nationalists), "a seven-year old daughter of a KMT [Nationalist] representative from the Chinese community of Madagascar, was lustily singing 'The March of the Volunteers,' so widely had the song now spread."[118]

At the time of the first anniversary of the war on July 7, 1938, more than ten thousand people sang "March of the Volunteers" during the *xuanchuan zhou* (propaganda week) in Wuhan, conducted by Xian Xinghai and Zhang

Shu. According to his handwritten notes in 1938, Ivens recorded "March of the Volunteers" with a male chorus conducted by Xian Xinghai on July 1, 1938, in Hankow, Wuhan, although he had already filmed another "propaganda week" in Xi'an two months earlier.[119] Three months later the Japanese had conquered Wuhan. Xian Xinghai, the author of "Huanghe dahechang" ("Yellow River Cantata," 1939), another popular wartime song that later gained an international reputation, in an essay commemorating the third anniversary of the composer Nie Er's death, wrote, "'March of the Volunteers' has been widely recognized internationally as the most majestic song in China."[120]

This brings us back to Pao-ch'en Lee, the enthusiastic promoter of "March of the Volunteers" in Nationalist-controlled Chongqing. We have seen the context out of which Lee could refer to the song as "virtually the Chinese national anthem at war" in his *New York Times* article, anointing it "the most popular patriotic song in China" in his bilingual songbook funded by the Propaganda Department of the Nationalist Party in 1939. The *Music Educators Journal* in the United States published Li's translation of the lyrics in its November–December 1942 issue,[121] the only English version to include the word *indignation,* and thus the most likely source for the fictive Alexander Portnoy's grade-school version of the song.

When the Pacific War broke out in 1941, "March of the Volunteers" was sung in Singapore, Malaysia, and other areas of Southeast Asia, and it became a major marching song in the international antifascist movement.[122] During World War II, radio stations in England, the United States, the Soviet Union, and India often broadcast the Robeson version of the song. In 1944 "March of the Volunteers" became the opening music of the Chinese-language broadcast at Delhi Radio Station, India, years before the founding of the People's Republic in 1949.[123]

As the Japanese army moved west into the Chinese mainland, the song also traveled from Shanghai to the north, west, and south of the Chinese hinterland, bringing with it the spirit of anti-imperialist and antifascist nationalism. The song did not stop at the threatened national borders but spread far and wide, in the Chinese hinterland, Hong Kong, Singapore, Paris, London, New York, Prague, and Moscow, among many other locations, where its nationalist message merged with and blossomed into an internationalist spirit.

A closer look at the English translation of the Robeson and Liu version of the song provides insights into the internationalist character and appeal of the song.

Arise! You who refuse to be bond slaves!
Let's stand up and fight for liberty and true democracy!
All our world is facing the chain of the tyrants,
Everyone who works for freedom is now crying:
Arise! Arise! Arise!
All of us with one heart, with the torch of freedom, March on!
With the torch of freedom, March on! March on! March on and on![124]

Here "all our world" replaces "China's masses." "Liberty," "freedom," and "true democracy" enter the lyrics for the first time for an English-speaking audience. Robeson and Liu advocated a contagious revolutionary internationalism as the spirit of both the artistic avant-garde and the revolutionary vanguard. It is a vision larger than Chinese nationalism. Nonetheless, it is anchored in and inspired by the patriotism so expressively conveyed in the Chinese original, now remolded into an international anthem of antifascism.

At the World Peace Conference in Prague in April 1949, and on the occasion of Pushkin's 150th anniversary in Moscow on June 6 of the same year, Robeson would twice sing "Chee Lai" in Chinese, months before "March of the Volunteers" became the provisional national anthem of the PRC at its founding. Tian Han himself, together with Guo Moruo, Ding Ling, Ma Yinchu, Jian Bozan, Xu Beihong, and other cultural luminaries, were members of the Chinese delegation at the Prague Conference and were in the audience when Paul Robeson sang "Chee Lai" in Chinese. Shortly afterward they participated in the discussion to select a national anthem for the new People's Republic.[125]

Conclusion

In making and propagating "March of the Volunteers," did Tian Han and his international collaborators leave their avant-garde sensibilities at the door in favor of the urgent political needs of China's fight against Japan? Such a question presumes a clear separation between an artistic avant-garde and a political vanguard, which in this study are closely intertwined. The story of the making of "March of the Volunteers" into the Communist Chinese national anthem argues for wartime China as the site of salvation and redemption for the "failed" Euro-American avant-garde, a kind of spiritual pilgrimage. It demonstrates that leading members of the avant-garde in Europe and America were aware of, and physically and intellectually in communication with, the Chinese avant-garde. In the phenomenon of "March of the Volunteers," the avant-garde finally achieves popularity, making nationalism fashionable and communism compelling in a China at war against Japanese fascism.

In this study, the circulation through newspapers of numerically notated musical scores,[126] the popularity of sound film, and the ubiquity of gramophone records and radio broadcasts, as well as stage performances and mass singing on streets and battlefields are some of the factors that effectively created a mass political movement in tandem with a mass culture, and enabled the avant-garde to simultaneously achieve popularity and forge a new democratic national identity.

Hence, the story of the making of the national anthem of the PRC from a Shanghai popular film song foregrounds the relationship between the aesthetic avant-garde and the political vanguard—how national politics made possible the popularization of the avant-garde and how popularity further ensured the success of the song as propaganda. It forces us to unpack the complex interactions among the international avant-garde, the Shanghai commercial film industry (and the moment of sound film), and nationalist politics.

Xiaobing Tang's important study on the "intertextuality" between the song "March of the Volunteers" and the woodblock print "Roar, China!" has demonstrated the formation of a "dynamically interactive field of cultural imagination" in late 1935 and the circulation of the song and print as "a multimedia project" and "a transnational political rallying call." Langston Hughes's 1937 poem "Roar, China!," as Tang suggests, links the volunteers in the International Brigades of the Spanish Civil War and the volunteers on the northeastern front in wartime China. Tang treats the "Roar, China!" phenomenon as "an impassioned artistic intervention on an unprecedented global scale, and an uplifting vision of political solidarity among the colonized and oppressed nations around the world."[127]

My study of the transnational journeys of "March of the Volunteers" from film, mass choral performance, and stage and street performance to its international reproductions in documentary films, gramophone records, and radio broadcasts shares Tang's global vision. Contrary to the conventional narrative of incompatibility among the avant-garde, the commercial, and the political, I demonstrate the existence of a robust exchange among international avant-garde performance, the commercial culture industry, and the Nationalist and Communist cultural politics of the time. I argue that the politics of national salvation and antifascism in China at the time conditioned the flourishing of a leftist commercial film industry, which in turn fostered the power of the song to mold the formerly passive recipients of a capitalist culture industry into active participants and future subjects of a bourgeoning communist nation. Notwithstanding the danger of political manipulation, the expressive subjectivity of the volunteers, as rendered in the original film song and its many later renditions, and the multiplication of the few avant-gardes into the "400 Million" and their international cohorts suggested a possible route to salvation for the "failed" European avant-garde in the context of an international antifascist cultural movement.

In this context, "March of the Volunteers" became the anthem of a post–World War I international avant-garde and cultural Left, whose "obsession with China," after the baptism of the Spanish Civil War, went hand in hand with their search for a political and artistic utopia. The story of how the international avant-garde fostered and propagated "March of the Volunteers," finally enabling it to represent a roaring China to the international audience, helps us unpack the seemingly monolithic entity of nationalism and enriches our understanding of the international dimensions of Chinese cultural productions under communism.

The producers of this mass entertainment and mass movement came from diverse national and professional backgrounds. This fact grants the seemingly abstract notion of nationalism and internationalism a specific composition, that of an affective self-identification with the other (real or imagined). That self-identification can take shape along various lines, often in association with one's class, gender, race, and age. By identifying with an international "class" of "the people" (in Chinese, *renmin*), one can start to formulate a more concrete sense of the nation, or "a people" (*minzu*).[128]

The CCP re-created the very idea of "people" (*renmin*) and "nation" (*minzu*), both of which now look very different from the way they appeared in the Republican era.[129] In particular, "class" has become an elastic container encompassing gender, race, and other considerations, ceasing to operate only within concrete socioeconomic logic and instead assuming meaning as a consciousness (rather than status), a project and a program to be achieved.

The journey of the national anthem demonstrates the mutually constructive energies circulating between what I call "the post–World War I international avant-garde" and "modern China." If orientalism was the West's use of the Orient for its own imperialist purposes, while modernists such as Ezra Pound used Chinese poetry as a raw material and instrument for their own experimentation and imagination, then here twentieth-century China has served as a utopian "other" for many avant-gardists in their social experiments.

The interwar international avant-garde, at the same time, is relevant for the coming of age of modern China in the twentieth century. It served as the cultural force that made the modern Chinese nation "happen." The simultaneous development and cross-fertilization of the players in various fields of art, in and outside China, and their mutual quest for a new vision of social transformation, not only used art to transform society but also utilized social movements to propagate art.

In the end, the making of the Communist national anthem is open to at least two possible readings: on the one hand, it provides a model for the possible redemption of the European avant-garde in that the avant-garde finally seemed to gain popularity in the context of a progressive vision; and, on the other, it raises the real or perceived danger of the reincorporation of the avant-garde by the bourgeois culture industry and, as the story of the last three decades suggests, the flattening out of the politics of the avant-garde and the resulting pure "*simulacrum*,"[130] which becomes "only" merely popular in a "postsocialist" China.

CHAPTER FIVE

A White Snake in Beijing: Re-creating Socialist Opera

> Art is the leap of soul, it leans towards idealism; while politics aims at maintaining the status quo . . . art as an indicator is more sensitive than politics, it is the vanguard of politics.
>
> TIAN HAN, "ON ART AND ITS RELATIONSHIP WITH ITS TIMES AND POLITICS," 1929.

In chapter 4, we examined the making of the modern, westward-looking national anthem with its assertion of the masculinist values of nation building. We turn now to the making of a seemingly inward-looking Chinese opera with a female protagonist. Uncannily, it is the similarities rather than the differences between the two that prevail. Both are avant-gardist projects with popular appeal and political significance. The making of the White Snake opera opens out from the war-conditioned national anthem to encompass the folk, the fantastic, and the operatic within the cultural embrace of the young People's Republic of China.

The reinvention of the White Snake opera in Communist Beijing demonstrates the relevance of Tian Han's two lifelong intellectual obsessions with "creating the new woman" and "going to the people," originating at the post–World War I moment and still asserting key influences in the post–World War II 1950s. Women's issues, workers' issues, nationalism, and international socialism converged, forging a sustained dialogue on these issues throughout the interwar period and well into the newly established Communist regime. Throughout Tian Han's half century of experiments with the image of the White Snake, its transformation from a folk demon to a modernist femme fatale, then to a female warrior, and finally to a female activist propagating socialism and feminism, attested to the relevance of both the avant-garde and the popular in the cultural productions from the early years of the Republic of China to the first decade of the People's Republic.

The Peking Opera *Baishe zhuan* (White Snake) is thus a key text linking socialist feminism, the image of the female warrior, and the modern femme fatale to Chinese folk and operatic traditions. Most versions of the story recount how a white snake spirit disguised itself as a beautiful woman and went to the West Lake in Hangzhou to experience the beauty of the human world. She formed a sexual relationship with a handsome young man and experienced human love and happiness. In the meantime, her violation of the boundary between human and nonhuman attracted the attention of Fa Hai, a Buddhist monk with the power to recognize and exorcise spirits. Feng Menglong's seventeenth-century vernacular story "Bai niangzi yongzhen Leifengta" (Lady White Forever Imprisoned under Leifeng Pagoda) was one of the most popular retellings of the tale, highlighting the "lust, caution" parable embedded in it and repudiating the lustful nature of the snake woman and her destructive power while upholding the monk Fa Hai as a defender of social norms and natural human relations.[1]

The legend subsequently went through a major transformation during the Qing dynasty, when a *chuanqi* version entitled *Leifeng ta* (Leifeng Pagoda) and a *tanci* version entitled *Yiyao zhuan* (Tale of a Righteous Spirit) rewrote the White Snake as an endearing character and recast Fa Hai as a destructive power separating lovers and families.[2] Other versions have since incorporated both the lustful and loving natures of the White Snake, rendering her the embodiment of the exotic and the erotic in the legend's countless renditions in no less than a dozen local dialects and operatic forms.

The image of Salome as a femme fatale packaged in glamorously exotic costumes attracted the attention of the young Tian Han studying in Tokyo because of its sexually charged and subversive overtones and also because it recalled the mystical seductresses abundant in the Chinese folk, literary, and operatic traditions as fox spirits and flower fairies.[3] Female sexuality and its transgressive power preoccupied Tian Han through a half-century-long love affair with the images of Salome and the White Snake. Metamorphosing from the seventeenth-century Chinese vernacular tale to the eighteenth-century Japanese rendering, Japanese modernist writer Tanizaki Jun'ichirō's cinematic re-creation in the early 1920s, Tian Han's creative borrowing in the 1927 silent film "Lakeshore Spring Dream," and the Peking Opera "White Snake," the Salome figure was finally reconfigured in the image of the White Snake, a female warrior reinvented under conditions of war and national regeneration.

Tian Han actively engaged in reforming Chinese opera in Beijing in the

1950s.[4] He was appointed the chief of the Opera Reform Bureau in the Ministry of Culture at the founding of the PRC in October 1949 and head of the bureau's Experimental Opera School during the first half of 1950. No longer the young bohemian wandering wide-eyed around Tokyo, he was now a middle-ranking bureaucrat in Beijing. Among other things, he finalized his revision of the White Snake story in the form of a Peking Opera during the first years of the People's Republic.[5]

The images of Salome and the White Snake as re-created by Tian Han share qualities that fit the stereotypes of both "oriental mystique" and "occidental modern." Intrinsic to both images were implications of the female as destroyer, the feminine as the enemy of reason and order, the *yin* of chaos. The biblical myth of Eve's affiliation with the snake in the Garden of Eden suggests a Western archetype of the snake-woman charged with transgressive sexuality and demonic energies. Thus there appears to be an archetypal association of woman with demon-snake in both the Judeo-Christian and Chinese traditions. However much he professed to hold feminist values, Tian Han was undeniably drawn to and seduced by this markedly regressive archetype. At the same time, he invested considerable energies into reclaiming it on behalf of a progressive and socialist vision.

The metamorphosis of the powerful female images from Salome to the White Snake and from Tokyo to Beijing hence should not be read as a simple return to the Chinese tradition. Both the Salomes of Tokyo and Shanghai and the White Snakes of the hinterland and Beijing are distinctively avant-gardist projects rooted in the early- to mid-twentieth-century Chinese experiments in art and activism. Joris Ivens, the Dutch filmmaker who met Tian Han in Wuhan while on location in China shooting *The 400 Million* during wartime, was similarly engaged in cultural productions in the newly established Communist regime at the post–World War II moment with an internationalist feminist vision. He was making documentary films on international women's and workers' movements in East Germany and collaborating with Paul Robeson, Bertolt Brecht, Dimitri Shostakovich, and Pablo Picasso across the "Iron Curtain."[6]

Obsession with Chinese Opera

Xiqu, loosely translated as "Chinese opera," was reinvented in the early to mid–twentieth century and represented the convergence of at least three of the preoccupations of modern intellectuals, Chinese or otherwise. Packaged as "traditional," it carried immediate cultural prestige for some but was just as reflexively suspected of being "feudal" by others; its "popularity" meant pedagogical value to some and vulgarity to others; and insofar as it was perceived as expressing the "national essence" (i.e., "Chineseness"), some lamented it as a "national humiliation," while others, like Tian Han, took inspiration from it for his avant-gardist experiments and endowed it with a contemporary spirit by re-creating the genre. In short, the genre of *xiqu* provoked strong emotions and fierce intellectual debates no matter which side one took.

The transitional generation (from empire to nation) of Chinese intellectuals who came of age in the early twentieth century had Peking Opera and various local operas in their veins, as they encountered these genres in provincial capitals as well as Peking (Beijing). While its subject matter, drawn from folk legends, religious parables, historical tales, and vernacular texts, was remote from contemporary affairs, what might be termed an "operatic mode" of being in the world (e.g., seeing the world through the archetypes of scholar and beauty, emperor and official, hermit and knight-errant, spirit and demon) formed the mental map of these intellectuals, if only subconsciously. More important, while Chinese opera was becoming commercialized and professionalized in urban centers in the twentieth century, the operatic mode of performance was alive and well in heterogeneous forms in the vast rural areas. It melted into the social fabric of daily practices, ritual observations, religious festivals, and amateur or professional traveling performances.

The relevance of Chinese opera to mid-twentieth-century Chinese politics and culture brings to mind Walter Benjamin's now canonical use of "the angel of history,"[7] a character with its head facing the past and its body propelled toward the future, created during the darkest months in Benjamin's personal history before he committed suicide in September 1940. Such a surrealist figure put in an appearance in the original version of Mao Zedong's "Lun xin minzhu zhuyi xianzheng" (On New Democratic Constitutional Politics), a speech given, only months after Benjamin's essay was written, to the Committee on the Promotion of Constitutional Politics, where he used the mythical character Shengong Bao in *Fengshen bang* (Investiture of the Gods), whose head was attached backward, to criticize the "recalcitrant elements" (*wangu fenzi*) in contemporary politics.[8] Although they held opposing views on historical "progress" in 1940, Benjamin and Mao's shared evocation of these mythical and tragicomic figures struggling against the tide of history suggests their mutual apprehension concerning the connections and tensions between tradition and modernity, historical progress and the violence of history.

The cultural politics of "traditional opera" in modern China links a generation of modern Chinese intellectuals to their theatrical and traditional roots, as exemplified in Tian Han's lifelong romance with the genre. The "opera question" in modern China provides a unique perspective from which to examine the intricate transactions between "tradition" and "modernity," and among performance, politics, and popularity. That "opera" became an issue of life and death during the 1960s and 1970s suggests the weight of this inquiry. Tian Han's imprisonment and death during the Cultural Revolution had much to do with his 1961 Peking Opera *Xie Yaohuan* being publicly denounced as a "poisonous weed" starting in 1964 and again in early 1966, one of the first political campaigns against a piece of artwork and a prelude to the Cultural Revolution.[9]

However, for Tian Han in the early 1950s, amid a new tide of socialist construction, his experimental opera was uniquely positioned to accommodate the folk cultural and local operatic practices in Changsha, the religiosity and politics of Taishō Tokyo, the revolutionary bohemianism of Republican Shanghai, and the nationalist traditionalism of the wartime hinterland in a new Beijing. As late as in the spring of 1962 at the Guangzhou conference on drama, opera, and children's play, Tian Han was still enthusiastically calling for a new spring of theater production. His avant-gardist experiments with "traditional" forms and subjects during the first decade of the PRC reveal crucial linkages among cultural practices in Changsha, Tokyo, Shanghai, the wartime hinterland, and Beijing and should not be relegated to the dustbin of history so easily.

Before Tokyo There Was Changsha

Tian Han, whose given name was Shouchang (literally, "longevity and prosperity"), was thirteen years old in 1911. He was then a junior high school student in Changsha, the provincial capital of the central southern province of Hunan. Known as "the cradle of revolution," Hunan was famous for its strong revolutionary tendencies in late Qing and early Republican China.[10] Chen Tianhua was one of the most influential spokesmen for democratic governance at the time.[11] When he committed suicide to protest the Qing and the Japanese government's suppression of the Chinese student movement in Japan in 1905,[12] the incident triggered a mass demonstration in his home province, with protesters demanding that a public funeral be held for Chen as a revolutionary martyr. To the young Shouchang, who at age seven had already heard Chen Tianhua's books recited in the countryside, the demonstration following Chen's suicide in the provincial capital deepened his interest in this enigmatic revolutionary figure.

The abolition of the imperial examination system in the same year, 1905, fundamentally changed the centuries-old bureaucratic recruitment system in China. Shouchang, as the first son of a family of declining gentry, was given the opportunity to go to "new-style" schools set up by the late Qing reformers after a period of "old-style" education close to home. In 1909, based on academic excellence, he was recommended as a candidate to enter a junior high school in Changsha on the eve of the 1911 Revolution. In Changsha many of the educators in the new-style schools had returned from studying in Japan to propagate revolutionary ideas.[13] In the spring of 1910 a rice riot broke out on the streets of Changsha, during which Tian witnessed firsthand the rising power of mass struggle.[14] The enlightened atmosphere in the provincial capital, in conjunction with the well-developed newspaper industry and distribution system in late Qing and early Republican China, made popular newspapers, both national and local, readily available to teachers and students alike.[15] The young Shouchang would soon publish his first literary works in two such newspapers.

In April 1911, the Yellow Flower Mound Revolt led by Huang Xing and his fellow revolutionaries against the Qing dynasty broke out in Guangzhou. Although about eighty revolutionaries died and the uprising failed, the martyrs' depositions, published prominently in local and national newspapers, spread all over the country. Students in Changsha, Shouchang included, competed to recite the martyrs' last words. Fired with revolutionary zeal, they cut off their queues, a symbol of the Manchu Qing dynasty. A meaningful naming ceremony took place when Shouchang and three other classmates decided to change their names, and it happened that the names collectively formed a sentence: "[We who are willing to be] heroes long for [the return of] the Han" (*yingqiong huaihan*), as if in testimony to their anti-Qing sentiments at the time. Shouchang took up the character *han* (which means both the *han* race and a young man) as his given name.[16] Together with his family name, Tian, he adopted Tian Han, literally, "a man in the field," as his new name. After acquiring their new modern identities, the students transferred to a more radically oriented junior high school in order to enter a wider arena of political activism.

Under the pen name Han'er (Son of Han), Tian Han published his first work, a Peking Opera libretto, *Xin jiaozi* (A New Version of Mother Teaches Her Son), in *Changsha ribao* (Changsha Daily),[17] while still a high school student at Changsha Normal School in 1913. He tailored a dialogue between a mother and son in the form of a Peking Opera to address some of the pressing issues after the 1911 Revolution. The female lead (*zhengdan*) begins her monologue (singing to the tune of *er'huang*) by introducing her deceased husband as a martyr of the Wuchang Uprising of October 1911, which led to the fall of the Qing dynasty; then the young male lead (*xiaosheng*), the son, returns from his new-style school (modeled on Tian's own Changsha Shifan) to introduce geopolitics to his mother. He describes, also to the tune of *er'huang*, how a certain teacher, Chen, displaying a world map in class, explained with tearful eyes the current national crisis and Russia's threat to China.[18] In real life, this type of "sentimental education" focusing on geopolitics succeeded in fostering a strong sense of nationalist zeal among students in Western-style schools throughout the country. At the time of his first literary endeavor, Tian Han was already engaged in popularizing political messages through performance and role-playing.

By the time Tian Han's Peking Opera was serialized in March 1913, *Changsha Daily* had become the party organ of Tongmenghui (The Revolutionary Alliance) in Hunan. This former Qing government-sponsored newspaper announced its independence from the Qing in October 1911 and was taken over by the revolutionaries. After being completely restructured, it was operated by members of Tongmenghui and of Nanshe.[19] The paper covered a wide range of issues and became the most popular newspaper in Hunan at the time. Tian Han was probably put into contact with the newspaper through his maternal uncle, Yi Xiang, himself a Nanshe poet, a Tongmenghui member, and an active revolutionary and friend of Huang Xing.[20]

Tian Han next published, this time a short opera in the form of *yuanben*,[21] in the literary supplement *Yuxing* (Aftertaste) of a Shanghai newspaper, *Shibao* (The Times), in May 1915, at the age of seventeen. The piece is entitled "Xin Taohua shan" (New Peach Blossom Fan).[22] It opens with the Ming loyalist Hou Fangyu's ghost revisiting Nanjing and discussing anti-Japanese strategies with his ghost friends, including the legendary storyteller Liu Jingting. The text shifts to the vernacular when Liu starts his *guci* (drum song) storytelling, the themes of which very much resemble the political speeches of the time: advocating schooling, strengthening industries, and building up the military. Through Liu's words, Tian aired his admiration for Xu Teli, the headmaster of the Changsha Normal School, who cut his finger to write a letter in blood encouraging his students to participate in anti-Yuan Shikai activities.[23] The choice of *The Times*

(Shanghai) was not accidental either. Yi Xiang, Tian's maternal uncle, probably had close contact with the newspaper at the time. Yi himself would become its chief editor in 1919 when Tian came back from Tokyo to visit him in Shanghai.[24]

When Tian Han started his creative career in 1913 as a fifteen-year-old student in the Changsha Normal School, he was very much influenced by *Xin Luoma* (New Rome), an unfinished *kunqu* (Kun Opera) written by Liang Qichao, who was at the forefront of both political reform and cultural experimentation at the time.[25] Tian claimed to have modeled his own writing on this visionary reformer, especially his conviction that literature should be used to usher in political change. Liang's opera presented an allegory of the founding of the modern nation. The existent prologue (the wedge act) of the opera explains that the dramatization of the unification of Italy was meant to serve as a model for the national regeneration of China.[26] Liang's attempt to enlist a distinctive Chinese and perceivably traditional dramatic form on behalf of decidedly Western and modern subjects inspired the young Tian Han.

The Chunliu she (Spring Willow Society) had staged two of the first modern drama performances in the history of Chinese theater in Tokyo in 1907. The first was a performance of the third act of *La Dame aux Camélias* by Alexandre Dumas in Chinese translation by Chinese students in the spring of 1907, followed by a Chinese adaptation of *Uncle Tom's Cabin* in June of the same year. Ouyang Yuqian, one of the active members of the Spring Willow Society in Tokyo, returned to his hometown of Changsha to initiate modern drama activities soon after the 1911 Revolution. Although the emerging new genre already had some influence in Changsha, Tian Han was said to have passed by without entering the gate of the venue where such modern drama was being performed.[27]

Indeed, instead of being immediately drawn to "modern drama," Tian Han established a lifelong tie with Chinese operas by way of his brief but intense flirtation with the military, as a member of the "student army" during the 1911 Revolution in Changsha. Tian Han reported enthusiastically years later that, as part of the military, soldiers were admitted to opera performances, especially Hunan Opera (*daxi*) and Peking Opera, for free.[28]

The Perseverance of Tradition

Although one might expect Tian Han to have turned away from Chinese operas during his Tokyo sojourn while he immersed himself in his newfound loves, cinema and modern drama, such was not the case. Tokyo opened new windows for Tian Han, but it did not necessarily close old doors. Closely involved with Shenzhou Xuehui (Divine Land Society) activities in Tokyo, Tian Han's associations with veterans of the 1911 and 1913 revolutions, such as Lin Boqu, in effect served to reinforce his earlier ties with Chinese opera. Even more important paradigmatically were the cultural politics of "tradition" in Taishō Tokyo and Japan's own quest to reform its own "traditional theater" in the face of challenges from modern Western drama and Hollywood film.

The modernist writer Tanizaki Jun'ichirō based his 1921 film scenario *Jasei no in* (The Lust of the Serpent) on Ueda Akinari's *Ugetsu monogatari* (Tales of Moonlight and Rain),[29] which was in turn borrowed from Feng Menglong's vernacular version of the White Snake story compiled in the early seventeenth century.[30] Tanizaki's experiment with the White Snake image was an expression of the Japanese obsession with Chinese folk legends as re-created in vernacular storytelling and operatic performances. During Tian Han's contacts with contemporary Japanese cultural figures such as Kuriyagawa Hyakuson, Satō Haruo, and Akita Ujaku in Japan, the common ground for their conversations and interactions was often, not surprisingly, traditional Chinese folk stories in operatic form. Recorded in detail, for example, in Tian Han's 1921 diary *Road of Roses* was his meeting with Satō Haruo.[31] Among other things they discussed the story of Huang Wuniang, a folk legend based on historical events, which would develop into the most popular Chaozhou opera (in Minnan dialect), *Chen San Wuniang* (aka *Lijing ji*, or "Story of Lychee and Mirror"), during the Communist era in the 1950s.[32]

Tian Han's experiments in modern drama in Tokyo were influenced by the most outspoken representative of the Japanese shingeki (new theater) movement, Osanai Kaoru, whose Jiyū Gekijō (Free Theater) and Tsukiji Shōgekijō (Tsukiji Little Theater) were important models for Tian's own theater movements during the 1920s and 1930s. He adopted the new theater principles of realism and westernized staging and lighting. At the same time, Tian Han was in sympathy with the principles of the less radical Engeki Kairyōkai (Theater Reform Association) and the practices of the influential playwright and critic Tsubouchi Shōyō at the time, namely, the reconciliation of traditional and modern forms of theater with a strong awareness of new technological developments.[33]

Drama, to the extent that it is intended for performance and aspires to popularity, is necessarily invested in the vernacular. Tian Han's use of the vernacular in traditional Chinese theatrical practices connected the folk and the avant-garde. Tian enlisted large portions of spoken parts and "drum storytelling" for his opera renditions of the 1911 Revolution published as early as the mid-1910s. His use of the vernacular must be understood from two distinct perspectives: vernacular oral storytelling throughout premodern China has deep roots in the unofficial folk cultural tradition, but at the same time the vernacular in written form, as advocated during the antitraditional May Fourth movement, though ostensibly aimed at popularization, was, in effect, elitist, Western, and transgressive of indigenous (oral) culture. In practice the literary revolution was not about the general use of the vernacular; rather, it was about the use of the vernacular in elite genres such as prose essays, poetry, and academic discourse.

Tian Han's experiments with the vernacular in the spoken dialogues in his early operas were thus indebted to the oral tradition of Chinese folk storytelling while at the same time they foreshadowed the modern, Western use of the written vernacular as advocated by Hu Shi a few years later, as Tian's operas on current affairs were printed in a new medium—popular newspapers—in the mid-1910s rather than sung onstage.

Not coincidentally, Tian's first experiment with the Western genre of modern drama, *Fan'elin yu qiangwei* ("The Violin and the Rose," written in Tokyo in September 1920), enlisted a singing girl, Liu Cui, and her Beijing-style "drum song" in a contemporary story set in Shanghai.[34] A distinctively traditional and Chinese storytelling genre entered the experimental and Western dramatic form to demonstrate the perseverance of tradition on the road to modernity. For Tian Han, the artificial boundaries between the classical and the modern genres of "theater," be it Peking Opera, *yuanben*, or spoken drama, were all subject to trespass—they were all hybrid and flexible genres combining sung and spoken features.

An important step in Tian Han's operatic evolution occurred in Shanghai where he became acquainted with Ouyang Yuqian. At the time of their meeting, Ouyang himself was going through a transformation from "modern" to "traditional," taking up Chinese operatic performance as an adult and experimenting with Peking Opera. Ouyang soon became Tian's close collaborator in his art education endeavor at the Shanghai Art University in 1927. Their mutual affinity for Chinese opera and their shared open-mindedness toward "tradition" crystallized in an experimental Peking Opera, *Pan Jinlian*.

Originating from *Shuihu zhuan* (The Water Margin) and *Jinping mei* (The Plum in the Golden Vase), two of the most celebrated pieces of vernacular fiction of late imperial China, the Pan Jinlian character gained new life in the twentieth century. The piece was originally written as a modern drama but was staged in 1927 by Tian Han's Nanguo she (Southland Institute) as a Chinese opera. What Ouyang did with the Pan Jinlian story was revolutionary in the history of Peking Opera; in his rendering (he both wrote the libretto and performed Pan Jinlian as a female impersonator), Pan Jinlian was no longer the emblem of adultery she had been in the earlier versions but was instead endowed with the humanist spirit of the May Fourth movement. In portraying her as a Salome who bravely pursues her desired sexual object, Wu Song,[35] Ouyang Yuqian and Tian Han set Pan Jinlian's sexual awakening against the long tradition of female sexual oppression and invested her pursuit with humanist values, regardless of the extremity of her means of achieving those values.

The Southland Institute performance of the Peking Opera *Pan Jinlian* suggests the relevance of the genre of Chinese opera to Tian Han's artistic experimentation in Shanghai and provides an intriguing connection between the images of Salome and the White Snake. In a 1927 essay "Woman and Snake," Tian Han approached the snake-woman figure through Ouyang Yuqian's film *Tianya genü* (Wandering Songstress),[36] in which the image of the singing girl was modeled after a painting, with flowers on one shoulder and a snake on the other. This description summons the famous illustrations by Aubrey Beardsley for Oscar Wilde's *Salome.* Beardsley's style was introduced into China first by Tian's own translation of *Salome* using Beardsley's original drawings as illustrations in 1921 and was further publicized by Ye Lingfeng's stylish re-creations in *Huanzhou* (Fantasy Land) magazine and numerous book illustrations. Lu Xun's 1929 introduction to Beardsley's collective works further publicized the original style in the years to follow.[37]

It is true that Tian Han focused his creative energy on spoken drama and film during his Shanghai years before the outbreak of the war in the 1920s and 1930s. However, as the *Pan Jinlian* performance demonstrated, Tian was sensitive to the position of "traditional opera" in modern China, even at the height of his cinematic experiments and modern drama movements. In an essay crowning Ouyang Yuqian's *Pan Jinlian* as the first cry of the "new national theater movement" (*xin guoju yundong*) in 1928, Tian Han gave his first theoretically articulated assessment of both the "new theater" and the "old theater" in contemporary Chinese life.

> Those engaged in the new theater movement criticize "old theater" as lifeless, claiming that it is going extinct. Those performing "old theater" look down on new theater, arguing that it has yet to take shape, that it is unable to compete

> with "old theater." For our part, we think one should not divide the new and the old. We only know that theater is divided into opera and drama. Branding opera as old, and drama as new, is not always fair. For we know that both opera and drama can take on new and old forms.[38]

This quotation provides a context for the creation of the term *spoken drama* in modern China. It is said that the Chinese term *huaju* was coined by Hong Shen at the suggestion of Tian Han earlier in the same year, 1928, as a revision to the term *xinju* (new theater), with its implicit derogation of Chinese opera as *jiuju* (old theater).[39] The *Pan Jinlian* performance Tian Han praised, for example, adapted the form of Peking Opera but added to it the modern division of acts (*fenmu*) from Western spoken drama.[40] The combination of Pan's seductive beauty and her humanist spirit as a "liberated woman" endowed the performance with new meaning for Tian; at the same time, the formal experiments made it representative of the new national theater movement.

At the time of his so-called turn to the left in the late 1920s and early 1930s, Tian Han had written operas that included *Lin Chong* and *Xue yu xue* (Snow and Blood) and had put *Salome* and *Carmen* on the Shanghai stage. How can one account for his writing "old opera" and "turning left" at the same time? Publicly, Tian Han had to echo the prevailing discourse critiquing Chinese traditional opera since the May Fourth movement, but his treatment of the form was not without sensitive understanding and a goal of preservation.[41] In an essay written in 1934, he points out that "feudal old operas" were natural targets of the anti-imperialist and antifeudal May Fourth movement, quoting *Xin qingnian* (La Jeunesse) as a representative journal replete with articles attacking traditional opera.[42] He charges the national theater movement (guoju yundong) with using European petit bourgeois aestheticism to construct a theoretical basis for the old form, emphasizing the need for the "purification" of old opera techniques.[43] One cannot help wondering: was this a self-critique of his own embrace of Ouyang Yuqian's *Pan Jinlian* as the first "new national theater" (*Xin guoju*) in 1928? Does Tian Han's critique of "petit bourgeois" aestheticism anticipate the same charges lodged against him two decades later?

In his follow-up article speculating on the Soviet Union's motives for inviting the Peking Opera master Mei Lanfang to perform in 1935, Tian came up with two possible explanations. One was that the Soviet Union intended to learn from the traditional Chinese art form; the other was that the Soviet Union intended to reform that "old" Chinese art form through socialist reinterpretation. Tian based his speculations on Japanese leftist dramatist Akida Ujaku and others, quoting from *Atarashiki Roshia* (New Russia), a Japanese leftist journal.[44] The strong ideological viewpoint of the journal reduced Chinese art forms to "feudal residue" and the whole of non-Russian European culture and its theater to "the stink of rotten, putrid degeneracy."[45] Hauptmann, whose *Sunken Bell* had been the occasion of Tian's first meaningful encounter with modern drama during his Tokyo sojourn, was now listed by the journal among the degenerate bourgeois playwrights.[46]

It is telling, however, that during that same year, 1934, Tian Han published a collection of his translations of the "great aesthetic" writer Tanizaki's stories and a biography of Tanizaki under an assumed name.[47] He thus retained his early identification with aestheticism, embodied by Hauptmann and Tanizaki, planted in him during his Tokyo sojourn, though now it was repressed beneath his public and political self. This divide between a submerged self and a public persona was a source of conflict throughout his life but one that fruitfully impelled Tian Han toward a resolution through art that combined aestheticism with political engagement, as the seemingly clear divide between the private and the public realms proved to be unstable in practice.

The Opera of War

With the outbreak of a full-scale war between Japan and China, Tian Han's operas became conditioned by war and violence. *Shagong* (Killing in the Palace) is said to be part of the second half of *Mingmo yihen* (Lingering Sorrow for the Fall of the Ming), written just before the outbreak of the war in July 1937. It is the first of Tian Han's experimental Peking Operas on record that was actually performed, a testament to the hinterland period as a seedbed for the popularization of the avant-garde. It was published in *Kangzhan xiju* (Anti-Japanese War Theater) in Hankou in January 1938 and performed in Wuhan, during the second propaganda week on the "Drama Day," just before Tian's meeting with the Dutch filmmaker Joris Ivens in April 1938.[48] The play depicts the Chongzhen emperor's killing of his wives, consorts, and children on the threat of Li Zicheng's army breaking into the palace.

An interesting twist occurs when the crown prince and two other princes are confronted by the murderous emperor. The emperor is so easily persuaded to stop killing that he not only allows the three male heirs to live but also embarks on a long speech on how they should "go to the people."[49] After letting his sons go, the Chongzhen emperor commits suicide onstage. In Tian Han's creative rendering, the suicidal emperor finally transcends himself to achieve a modern humanist reflection on the evils of the "feudal system."[50] Although such anachronisms later became the target of criticism by Tian himself and others at the height of the opera reform movement of the 1950s, Tian's experiments decades earlier fully bore out his independent spirit and avant-gardism in the late 1930s.[51]

But in keeping with his lifelong thematic preoccupation, the most memorable figure of all in Tian Han's wartime operas is still the female warrior. In *Tuqiao zhizhan* (The Fight at Tuqiao), an opera Tian wrote in Nanjing in 1937, Mrs. Xin, wife of general Gao, proves to be the wisest and most courageous of them all, a woman who not only saves her husband from committing a fatal error but also has a crucial connection to Shi Kefa, a famous general, and other important figures. Comic elements are abundant in this short piece, one of which occurs when Mrs. Xin, in warrior's armor, confronts her husband in the midst of an intense battle. The husband, not recognizing his own wife, demands her name. This encounter suggests a deeper connection between femininity and war. Mrs. Xin's dressing up in a warrior's armor speaks to the inherent theatricality of the battlefield, linking performance and war. The masculinization of the Chinese woman at war can be read as an expansion of the definition of femininity, in that it is both a violation of traditional notions of femininity and a celebration of feminism. This combination of nationalism and feminism continues to have a double-edged effect on women under state Communism during the People's Republic. The Maoist rhetoric claiming that "women hold up half of the sky" was liberating and restricting at the same time: in the process of lifting women from past oppression, it swiftly put them in service of the new patriarchally controlled project of nation building.

A more extreme case of "dressing up for war" occurs in *Jianghan yuge* (Yangtze Fisherman's Song) in the figure of Ruan Chunhua, daughter of a fisherman. First performed on October 10, 1938, in Hankou, this piece was adapted into an epic-scale work in Guilin in June 1939. It became one of the biggest stage successes of Tian Han's wartime operas. In scene 36 of the opera, Chunhua, literally "Spring Flower," dresses up in beautiful clothes and enters the stage to fight the enemies, proclaiming, "Fighting is the happiest thing on earth; of course I will put on my best clothes for this."[52] Chunhua's manipulation of the double meanings of "dressing up" refers simultaneously to the soldier's need for a uniform in order to "perform" his military duties and to the feminine custom of dressing up to please one's beloved or celebrate a special occasion.[53]

Another female icon, Pan Jinlian, the vampirish Salome reinvented by Ouyang Yuqian in 1926 in Shanghai, was re-created in a Hunan Opera, *Wu Song*, written by Tian Han in Guilin in 1942 and first performed by the Zhongxing Hunan Opera Troupe in October of the same year. It was again adapted as a Peking Opera in Duyun in Guizhou province in 1944, and performed by the Siwei Children's Theater Troupe. In his preface to the opera, Tian Han writes passionately about the performance of Ouyang Yuqian's *Pan Jinlian*, which he attended in 1927 at the Shanghai Art University. He describes the scene at the end of the play where, pressed by Wu Song about her murder of his brother, Pan tears open her clothes to reveal her "snow-white breasts" and shouts, "Take out my heart slowly, please! You will see how much I love you once you see my heart!" Tian comments simply, "What an incarnation of Salome!"[54]

The Return of the White Snake

Tian Han started to turn the White Snake story into a Chinese opera, naming it *Jinbo ji* (Story of the Golden Bowl), in 1943. He justified the legend's unrealistic form (*fei xianshi de xingshi*) by stressing its antifeudal spirit and its origin in Buddhist teachings. Writing during the Second Sino-Japanese War, Tian set the story during the time of the Jiajing reign of the Ming dynasty (1522–66) when the *wokou* ("dwarf pirates," in most cases referring to the Japanese invaders) invaded Jiangnan (South of the Yangtze). In Tian's wartime version, the White Snake adopts a human identity, as reflected in her given name, Suzhen, literally "pure and chaste," and upholds the principle of "love above all" (the 2011 version of the White Snake film is persistently titled *It's Love* in English), while Fa Hai is portrayed as stubborn, nosy, and antihumanist (*fan renxing*). The key theme, according to Tian Han, is that "the power of natural love (*ziranjie de aili*) cannot be suppressed by a golden bowl,"[55] the bowl being a symbol of religious and patriarchal oppression.

In 1950, as chief of the Opera Reform Bureau, charged with censoring operas found to be reactionary, Tian Han was nonetheless concerned with the prevailing rhetoric castigating the "feudal content" of the "old operas" and called for "clear principles" from higher authorities for determining what is harmful and what is not. "New democratic" theater is first "national, as in 'of the Chinese nation'" (*minzu de*), he claimed. Using Russian composer Avshalomov's *Meng Jiangnü* opera as supporting evidence for the validity of such themes (despite having criticized Avshalomov in a 1946 review), Tian emphasized that many of the themes in the Meng Jiangnü story fit the anti-Japanese nationalist spirit of the time. It proved the validity of "scientific certainty" rather than " 'fate' determined by Buddhist prophet" (*bingfei suming, ershi kexue de biran*) and transferred the prevalent concept of "fate" from personal to national, turning Meng Jiangnü's personal quest for her husband into a political condemnation of the tyranny of the First Emperor.[56]

In responding to criticism targeting "the unscientific aspect of the old opera" (*jiuju zhong fan kexue de yimian*), Tian Han surveyed more than 900 Peking Operas and claimed that only 109 (12 percent) dealt with ghosts, spirits, or other supernatural or superstitious subjects. Defending traditional opera, he pointed to the "profound humanity" (*shenhou de renxing*) of the water goddess Bai niangzi (Madame White or the White Snake) in contrast to the feudal stubbornness (*fengjian de wanzhi*) of the Monk Fa Hai, in explaining why the audience has always been sympathetic to her.[57] In essence he argued that the eternally enchanting White Snake, though nonhuman and "unrealistic," was a more humane and empathetic character for contemporary audiences than the "realistic" moralist Fa Hai.

Furthermore, Tian Han applied a historicist critique to attempts to revise the "superstitious" content out of the "old operas." Tian reasoned that social problems existed in the past, as they do in the present, leading the disempowered to seek illusory control through superstition. Rather than worrying about "correcting" the content of the old operas, one should focus on solving the invidious social problems that lead to false beliefs. Moreover, Tian found social utility in some of the apparently superstitious or fantastic elements. For example, he contended, Madame White could be used to push for contemporary reform of national medical care (*mizu baojian*) as she suffered from the lack of intensive postnatal care in the story as many ordinary women did in real life.[58] This literal approach to symbolic material was a fairly desperate attempt to preserve the currency and relevance of the symbolic realm in the face of socialist realist pressure. Furthermore, at a time when medical supplies were in short supply nationally, Tian Han saw practical utility in continued belief in magical healing powers such as those of the White Snake.[59]

Tian's seemingly contradictory stands—advocating freeing people from superstition by addressing their real problems while also treating myth as a source of comfort they should be allowed to keep—reflect the ambiguous and ambivalent relationship among members of the socialist regime, modern intellectuals, and the folk and operatic traditions still prevalent at the time. Among all the operas featuring spirits and monsters, Tian regarded some as full of "dramatic stories, vivid imagery, and ethnographic interest," such as the Monkey King, Chang E, Weaver and Cowherd, White Snake, and Mulian stories.[60] On this point, Tian's position is not far removed from that of today's anthropologists of Chinese folk cultures who value the preservation of cultural roots in local customs as an important component of a modern sensibility. Tian was an early proponent of applying this scholarly and scientific perspective to Chinese operas as an argument for their preservation and continued patronage.

Certain elements of myth and folklore were generally deemed acceptable if they could be made to comport with the reigning narrative of class struggle. The Monkey King, for example, was generally treated at the time as a "representative of the peasant class in resisting dictatorship," as later illustrated in the animation *Danao tiangong* ("Havoc in Heaven," 1961–64), featuring the monkey as a class rebel.[61] But Tian Han read the iconic character differently, describing him as a petit bourgeois liberal and an individualist hero without principles, dangerously similar to a portrait of himself as a heroic avant-gardist. It suggests Tian's consistent engagement with the identities of both the intellectual loner and the class representative of the people: he had highlighted the importance of social solidarity in the age of individualist aspiration from his Tokyo years onward, and he was able to be sensitive to the dilemma of the individual loner in the prevailing rhetoric of class struggle of the 1950s.

Tian noted that Soviet fiction, drama, and film were full of fairy tales, from which people could still learn progressive lessons. It was up to the leaders of mass culture to foster the tales' progressive characteristics while limiting their superstitious aspect. He proposed to develop this last point in future discussions on *minzhu* (democracy) although these promised future analyses were never finished.[62]

Metamorphosis of the White Snake

There was an obvious tension between the sociocultural trends of 1950s China and Tian Han's imaginary world of glamorous female images and fantastic love stories. Given the prevailing political rhetoric of "going to the people" and "learning from the masses," Tian Han's return to these eccentric love stories is quite idiosyncratic. What drew him back to the powerful female images during the war with Japan, when, in 1943 in Guilin, he started to rewrite the White Snake story? What motivated him to spend more than a decade crafting the White

Snake story into a Peking Opera libretto? Why did he choose the snake-woman as the protagonist of the "brave new world" created by the 1949 Revolution?

More to the point, how was Tian Han able to express his internationalism and spiritual vision in Communist Beijing? In fact, the post–World War II and post-Revolution milieu had much in common with the spiritual maelstrom of post–World War I international socialism and avant-gardism. The Faustian search for a utopian settlement that obsessed Tian Han in Tokyo gained concrete political and social manifestation in the Communist capital. There was a prevailing optimism that the new PRC was moving in the direction of a utopian society, and the combination of spiritual, artistic, and political experiments of the interwar international avant-garde remained at the center of cultural productions under communism in the People's Republic.

While I argued in chapter 1 that Tian Han's "Spiritual Light" performance in Tokyo exemplified the expression of experimental content through experimental form, it does not follow that in adopting the traditional Chinese form of Peking Opera Tian Han was committing himself to traditional and conservative content. For one thing, the antiestablishment spirituality expressed in "White Snake" continues the antiorthodox spiritual pursuit of "Spiritual Light." For another, its Daoist-turned-anarchist search for personal fulfillment challenges the atheism of the Communist regime. "White Snake" revisits "Spiritual Light" in that it connects the early play's Tolstoyan inspiration with its roots in Daoism,[63] and embodies an enduring populist spirit relevant to Tian Han's cultural experiments from Changsha to Beijing. In fact, in the act of returning to a form rooted in Chinese tradition, Tian Han manages to radically reinvent and reinterpret traditional content.

Tian Han's obsession with the legend of the White Snake throughout his cultural journey illustrates the relationship between male intellectuals and the strong female images they created,[64] as well as the relationship among textual, sexual, and political transgressions. In a short piece written before the opera's first public performance in Beijing in 1954, Tian quoted Zhou Yang, the minister of culture of the People's Republic, to highlight the White Snake's power.

> [The opera] strongly expressed the Chinese people, especially Chinese women's, invincible willpower in pursuit of *freedom and happiness,* and their *heroic* spirit of self-sacrifice. They dare to fight against those vicious oppressors whose powers are far superior to their own, without hesitation, without compromise, to the death. We can simply say that their love conquered death.[65]

This revolutionary female figure with unvanquishable willpower, who conquers death with her love, is strangely reminiscent of the femme fatale represented in Tian Han's early works, but with a twist. Although her pursuit of freedom and happiness was recognized in the new People's Republic as a heroic fighting spirit representative of the Chinese people in general and Chinese women in particular, that same pursuit also compels the femme fatale, a figure who brings death as a companion of lust, and who shares much in common with early versions of the White Snake archetype. Tian Han's artistic and political experiments were embodied in a series of female imageries from Changsha to Beijing: from the virgin girl turned female artist in Tokyo to Salome the Shanghai femme fatale, and from the female warrior of the wartime hinterland to the socialist builder and female activist in Beijing.

Tian Han's enchantment with the femme fatale during his Tokyo and Shanghai experiments already had much to do with the revolutionary quality of her agency: her identity as a seductress and her pursuit of sensual enjoyment, whether we name it love or lust, are considered heroic by Tian and contemporary artists active during and after the May Fourth movement from the mid-1910s onward. In the context of the 1950s, Tian Han reconfigured his femme fatale by packaging her in a culturally and politically acceptable form, at the same time rekindling his youthful love of the revolutionary seductress. He channeled female sexuality in a sanctioned direction and found redemption for the femme fatale in the image of the heroic female warrior and feminist activist, figures already at the center of his early experiments in Tokyo, Shanghai, and the hinterland.

The femme fatale had to be repackaged and relabeled to facilitate her reincarnation in the Communist capital of Beijing, as a reinvented tradition, in the form of Peking Opera and various local operas widely popular and deeply resonant with the ordinary Chinese. If Tian Han provided one of the earliest contemporary attempts to rewrite the White Snake story in "Story of the Golden Bowl" during wartime,[66] he was definitely not alone after the First National Congress of Theatrical Performance in October 1952. The performance ushered in a renewed interest in opera reform, and new adaptations of the White Snake story in various local opera forms mushroomed in the years to follow.[67] In artistic circles, serious debates on the rewriting of the White Snake story appeared in *Renmin ribao* (People's Daily) and *Wenyi bao* (Literature and Art Bimonthly), with participants such as A Ying, the mediator between Tian Han and the revolutionary writer Jiang Guangci in Shanghai in the 1930s and a fervent critic of Tian Han's "Story of the Golden Bowl" in Beijing in the 1950s.[68]

Tian Han's description of himself as a "fellow traveler" of communism in 1930 was challenged by a more rigid divide between communist and noncommunist orientations in the 1950s. Dai Bufan's review in the *People's Daily* can be boiled down to a criticism of Tian Han's "petite bourgeoisie" (*xiao zichan jieji*) perspective.[69] Dai reasoned that because of Tian's class orientation he could not properly manage this antifeudal story because he was not immune to the poison elements in the old opera, and thus did not grasp the main contradictions central to the antifeudal theme. Tian Han did work on the earlier version in an attempt to incorporate Dai's and others' criticisms into "White Snake" over the next couple of years.

It was a rather long and stubborn engagement, however, rewriting the White Snake story from the war period to the first several years of the People's Republic. The metamorphosis of "White Snake" from the wartime hinterland to the Communist capital provides an opportunity to examine the multivalent spiritual connections between wartime and the new People's Republic.

After a decade-long revision process, Tian finalized "White Snake" as a Peking Opera between 1953 and 1955. The publication date coincides with the All China Women's Federation's national promulgation of the new marriage law, which not only made monogamy the only legal form of marriage,[70] but also made working women eligible for paid maternity leave and subsidized child care.[71] At first glance, it might seem far-fetched to use the White Snake tale to promote a new marriage law, but in practice it served the party's propagandistic purposes quite well in its newly refined form. The free love between White Snake and Xu Xian, her restored virginity before their chance encounter, and her identity as a human savior not only inherited the spirit of the powerful female figures from the interwar period but also incorporated the female warrior of the war period and the female model worker of the 1950s.[72]

The image of the White Snake, humanized and revolutionized at the same time in the Peking Opera version, served an important thematic function in the intellectual climate of "women's liberation" in the new regime. The All China Women's Federation (Fulian) became a branch of the Women's International Democratic Federation (WIDF, founded in 1945) in 1949. A strong "state feminism" promoting Mao's call for women to "hold up half of the sky" formed a cultural and political milieu conducive to the coming of age of a new generation of independent-minded, strong-willed, and strong-bodied women. Such prevailing feminist rhetoric provided the platform for the PRC's international outreach, as in the case of the 1954 color film "Butterfly Lovers," which was shown during the Geneva Convention at Premier Zhou Enlai's suggestion. "White Snake," as finalized by Tian Han in its Peking Opera version, became a designated performance text used by the Women's Federation to garner support for the new marriage law in its promotion of monogamy and a legal, heterosexual relationship between man and woman based on love and mutual respect.

The Peking Opera "White Snake"

It may come as a surprise to many that the Peking Opera version of "White Snake" as we know it today, and what became a key foundation for later visual renditions, was only finalized in the mid-1950s. How did Tian Han, the modernist, avant-gardist, and leftist playwright, come to write the definitive version of the legend into a seemingly traditional Peking Opera in the new People's Republic? What might this fantastic and fearless female image and its decisively Chinese operatic form contribute to our understanding of "communist cosmopolitanism" in the 1950s?[73]

Emerging from the intense experience of "Taishō democracy" and carrying his Tokyo and Shanghai cultural experiments with him into wartime and the new Communist capital, Tian Han's approach to the White Snake legend in the 1950s must be understood in the context of a historical and global vision. The conventional view is that an artist working in the People's Republic in the early 1950s was isolated from the global scene. Many question whether there was anything resembling "cosmopolitanism" to speak of in China at the time, insulated as it was within the communist camp on one side of a rigid Cold War divide.

In actuality, however, the flow of personal and intellectual exchanges between China and the world was much more vital than this conventional narrative of isolation allows. Reading the "White Snake" opera together with poetic documentaries on the international women's movement and everyday Chinese life coordinated by Joris Ivens in the 1950s, especially *Das Lied der Ströme* ("The Song of the Rivers") and *Die Windrose* ("The Windrose"), forces us to rethink the relationship between the lyrical and the realistic, the mythical and the socialist, and communism and cosmopolitanism.

Writing several decades ago, Joseph Levenson focused on the rendition of Western plays on the Chinese stage in the 1950s and described the phenomenon as "communist cosmopolitanism." I would argue that the intellectual and political fixation on "national form" and "national style" from wartime China to the early People's Republic and the projection by the international Left of a poetic and lyrical China were similar cultural strategies with a global vision. Chinese and foreign intellectuals and politicians had thought about this local-global synergy and pursued a "glocal" synthesis in their cultural production, dissemination, and consumption in the new Communist regime from the 1950s onward. Highlights from Tian Han's work on "White Snake," for example, served important diplomatic functions as model pieces shown to visiting international cultural figures and touring foreign countries.[74]

According to an interview with Li Zigui, a famous Peking Opera singer, Li tried to enlist Tian's help writing an opera since Tian had already become a household name with his widely performed Peking Operas around 1942.[75] Given that "White Snake" was one of the most popular festival plays (*yingjiexi*) among the people (*laobaixing dou xiwenlejian*), Li suggested it as a subject to Tian. Tian based his writing on the performance text drafted by Li and others and named the opera *Jinbo ji* (Story of the Golden Bowl).[76] It was very long, divided into two volumes, and contained such popular folk plots as White Snake's stealing money, spreading an epidemic, and repaying debts to the handsome young man Xu. According to Li, Tian Han's written version was performed on many occasions between 1946 and 1954. It was finalized only after the 1954 performance, between its first publication in the journal *Juben* (Plays) in 1953 and the 1955 People's Press version, in which only sixteen scenes remained.[77]

Although it was the romantic and mythical elements that attracted Tian Han to the text, the White Snake story served multiple purposes: it connected his aesthetic vision to a folk morality and popular value system, and at the same time it allowed him to revisit the femme fatale preoccupation of his modernist experiments. His mode of composition likewise comprehended the traditional and the modern. On the one hand, he followed the convention of relying on orally transmitted texts and "consulting the masses," soliciting advice from veteran Peking Opera singers Wang Yaoqing, Li Zigui, and Du Jinfang and referencing extant local operas. On the other hand, he visited Mount Emei, where the mythical White Snake supposedly originated, to immerse himself in the local landscape and customs (*tiyan shenghuo*) and to find his own vision of the story as an individual auteur, bringing to bear the perspectives of a modernist, a realist, and an ethnographer.[78]

Formal Experiments

In the text finalized by Tian Han, the experimental and the traditional, and the cinematic and the operatic, often intermingle. Tian Han's stage instructions for the "White Snake" opera are remarkably wide ranging, specifying location, timing, characters' entrances and exits, singing styles, expressiveness of speech, physical actions, and psychological changes. More important, cinematic language enters the operatic narrative, where flashbacks, voice-overs, and montages heighten the shock effect of the dramatic mise-en-scène and the ideological persuasion of the didactic theater as practiced by Eisenstein, Brecht, and Tian himself from the early 1930s onward.

The stage instruction in the "Jiubian" (transformation after the wine) scene includes a full description of Monk Fa Hai's voice-over speaking directly to Xu Xian: "Xu Xian, behind the rouge curtain lies the remedy for your drunkenness! Dare you take a look at your alluring wife now?"[79] This powerful voice-over, perhaps a flashback, perhaps a warning from Heaven, hits the most sensitive nerve of the suspicious husband. It not only demonstrates Monk Fa Hai's transcendental power (*fali wubian*) but also serves an important narrative function, supplying Xu Xian with the necessary motivation to gather his courage and raise the curtain to confront the true form of his wife. Without the omnipresence of Fa Hai, even in this most intimate moment, the shock caused by the White Snake's transformation could not be achieved. Hence, it is not surprising that the cinematic adaptations I have been able to collect, from the late 1970s to the late 2000s, all adopt the visual cue in the opera, visualizing the voice-over by juxtaposing the image of Fa Hai as imagined by Xu Xian with that of Xu Xian in the same frame to intensify the dramatic visual effect.[80]

As in Tian Han's earlier theatrical experiments, the spoken and the sung also closely interpenetrate the "White Snake" opera. In opera terminology, *nianbai* refers to the speech style while *changqiang* refers to the singing style. The *bai* (spoken) part is divided into *dubai* (monologue) and *duibai* (dialogue) and prose (*sanbai*) and poem (*yunbai*). Tian Han's meticulously crafted poetic monologues and dialogues for "White Snake" often take the form of seven-character four-line poems. The juxtaposition of monologue and dialogue, prose and poem, adds dynamism to both the speech style and the characterization.

BOATMAN: (off)

I row visitors through the duckweed
To look at the fallen blossoms.

HSU (XU XIAN): It is raining harder than ever. Please don't stand on ceremony. I'll go and hire that boat.

BAI SUZHEN: Well—it's very good of you. (She takes the umbrella).

HSU: It's nothing.

(The boatman rows his boat in)

BOATMAN:

A pot of wine, a spot of cover—
I will drink until the storm is over.[81]

In the Chinese original, Tian crafts a seven-character *jueju* rhyming in *dui, mei,* and *hui* for the miraculously appearing boatman, having him chanting offstage in poetic monologue. Tian juxtaposes the boatman, who travels between Mount Wu (famous for its Goddess Peak at the Three Gorges along the Yangtze) and the West Lake, and the first encounter between Xu Xian and the White Snake (and the transfer of the umbrella as not only a phallic symbol but also an emblem of their love at first sight). The colloquial, naturalistic dialogue between the two lovers cuts the boatman's poetic and symbolic monologue into two halves. The scene succeeds in achieving its dramatic effect precisely because of the dynamism fostered by the contrast between poem and prose, onstage and off, and monologue and dialogue.

Tian Han's libretto for "White Snake" further bridges the elite and the popular through its combination of vernacular and literary Chinese, as necessitated by both its subject matter and its audience. The story is set in premodern times, while the audience consisted of people in 1950s China. From the point of view of the audience, Xu Xian was a petit bourgeois urbanite with a low scholar-gentry background, while the White Snake and Green Snake (another snake spirit serves as both her sister and maid in this version) were nonhuman spirits seemingly not subject to social conventions, although the apparently hierarchical mistress and maid relationship conditioned White Snake's speech to be more literary and Green Snake's more vernacular.[82]

In the "broken bridge" scene, the White Snake emerges as a loving wife, sister, and mother, and her image is further humanized through long, emotional, and seemingly irregular arias created by Tian Han.

你忍心將我傷，端陽佳節勸雄黃；
你忍心將我誑，才對雙星盟誓願，又隨法海入禪堂；
你忍心叫我斷腸，平日恩情且不講，怎不念我腹中懷有小兒郎？
你忍心見我敗亡，可憐我與神將刀對槍，只殺得我精疲力盡頭暈
目眩痛不可當，你袖手旁觀在山崗。
手摸胸膛你想一想，有和面目來見妻房？

You could bring yourself to harm me
By forcing me to drink on the festival;
You could bring yourself to deceive me,
After swearing by the stars to be true;
By going with Fa Hai to the monastery.
Though you no longer loved me,
At least you should have thought of our child—
Yet instead you left me to die.
I fought the Deities,
My sword against their spears,
Till I was exhausted,
Reeling in agony,
While you looked on from the abbey!
Think of yourself—
How dare you come back to me?[83]

The singing style is both rhythmic and harmonic, but it also frequently breaks from convention to heighten the dynamics by contrasting long and short lines and creatively alternating but also echoing rhythms. On the surface, most of the arias do not fit the regular rhythms (2-2-3, or 3-3-4) of Peking Opera,[84] but they obey an emotional rhythm that renders them highly singable. With Peking Opera master Wang Yaoqing's arrangements, the above aria written by Tian Han has become a classic. Furthermore, Tian dramatized the language of Peking Opera in that he endowed it with narrative, emotionally expressive, and character-building functions. As Tian himself argued, "The best way to restore the old operatic technique is not to passively preserve it as if it is an antique; instead, we need to actively absorb it into new operas and propagate it as an important component of the new."[85]

The Making of a Female Warrior

Tian Han wrought a telling change on the opening of the opera. Instead of the White Snake paying her debt to Xu Xian for having saved her life, the opera opens on a chance encounter between the two, similar to the opening of his 1927 film "Lakeshore Spring Dream."[86] The opening "Youhu" (encounter at the lake) scene serves to highlight the White Snake's sensational and sensual attraction to Xu Xian's physical beauty.

> GREEN: Look, sister! There is a young man with an umbrella coming this way.
> How handsome he is!
> WHITE: Where? (Green points him out to her.) Ah!
> This is like meeting Pan An[87]
> In the streets of Luoyang.
> GREEN: (Smiling to see her stare so raptly) It is raining, sister. Let us go on.
> WHITE: Yes, let us go on.
> After a thousand years of tranquility
> *My heart is in turmoil.*[88]

The White Snake and Xu Xian had no relationship whatsoever before their chance meeting, and Xu Xian's striking physical beauty constitutes the major stimulus for the White Snake's emotional turmoil after "a thousand years of tranquility." We thus begin with a typical scene of "love at first sight." The young man with the umbrella certainly invites Freudian interpretation. But more important, when the White Snake gradually recognizes Xu Xian's quality, saying, "I am happy about the young man's honesty,"[89] she invites him to visit her the next day (keeping the umbrella he lent her as an excuse). It is the White Snake who actively inquires into Xu Xian's world, the world of humanity; she is the real agent who pushes the plot forward.

Tian Han changed a small detail in the lakeshore encounter scene, having Xu Xian returning from visiting his mother's tomb (as in some early versions) instead of from "collecting debts." He thus shifts the focus from indebtedness and repayment to filial piety. Consequently, when the White Snake praises Xu Xian for this filial deed in the "Jieqin" (wedding) scene, sighing, "How I admire your true filial piety,"[90] her image changes into that of a loyal daughter-in-law rather than a supernatural snake spirit returning to repay her debts.

It is quite extraordinary when the Green Snake boldly speaks the White

Snake's mind and proposes marriage to Xu Xian, showing that their free will is independent of social norms (although it is not uncommon for the maid to voice the hidden desires of her mistress in Chinese opera). One might think that the snake-women's spiritual power stems from their nonhuman identity, although the textual emphasis here is on the spiritual power itself, regardless of its origin (nonhuman or human). The marriage between the White Snake and Xu Xian is endowed with a revolutionary spirit and portrayed as a brave break from family bondage, a heroic gesture of personal liberation practiced by the real life modern women in Tian's life, Yi Shuyu, Lin Weizhong, and An E alike. In this sense, the White Snake and Green Snake can be seen as incarnations of the "new women" fleeing from home for free love during the May Fourth movement. The White Snake and Xu Xian's love at first sight and their self-determined marriage can be read as "revolutionary" in relation to the 1920s' discourse about personal freedom and freedom of marriage. By rediscovering the image of the powerful women he had worshipped in his youthful years, Tian Han revisited his youth and the exciting 1920s in the "wedding" scene.

Tian Han made another critical gesture by changing the White Snake from a widow (or a married woman) to a virgin.[91] In traditional versions the White Snake claims to be a widow, but there is no reference to a prior marriage. Her widowhood, however, possibly explains why she was dressed in white and called Madame White. Although a virgin in Tian's version, she is still dressed in white. I leave it to your imagination how she must have appeared, drenched with rain, waiting for Xu Xian's attention under the willow tree when they first met.

The image of the virgin, however, invokes the "pure love" between Tian Han and his first wife, Yi Shuyu, during their Tokyo sojourn, as well as the image of the Chinese Virgin Mary in Tian Han's first performed play, "Spiritual Light." In short, the desire to purify and perfect the White Snake, in order to intensify the spiritual power of the female image, drove Tian Han to depict her as a virgin rather than a widow. The more humane and pure the White Snake's love of Xu Xian is, the more dramatic the effect when she directly confronts Monk Fa Hai to reclaim her husband. This talk of purity and virginity does seem to be at odds with Tian's endorsement of her sensuality in Tokyo and Shanghai; however, the transgressiveness of that sexual energy is now packaged as a positive, revolutionary spirit.

No longer an evil being, the White Snake was reimagined as a savior figure, just like Li Xinqun in *Liren xing* (Songs of Modern Women), the powerful female intellectual figure in a film story about a new version of "three modern women," re-created by Tian Han during the war.[92] The White Snake's metamorphosis from seductress to virgin savior seems to reverse the modern woman's transformation from virgin savior to seductress in many of Tian's early works. It nonetheless suggests the deep-rooted dualism of the virgin and the femme fatale and the need for purification in the contemporary political climate.

Far from being the source of disaster, the White Snake has become a loving goddess both for the common folk of the city and for Xu Xian, her husband. The two are depicted as loving wife and caring husband. When Xu Xian sighs with gratitude, "My wife's love is as deep as the sea,"[93] it foreshadows the White Snake's use of magic to control water to reclaim her husband in the later scenes. At the same time, it highlights Tian Han's attention to the spiritual (as well as the physical) power of the White Snake's love for Xu Xian, a love "as deep as the sea." The idealized female image for Tian, as well as for many other Chinese male writers, was both ultrafeminine and ultramasculine, both submissive and controlling, both ultradecadent and ultrarevolutionary, as in the case of Wilde's *Salome* as understood by Tian and his contemporary Chinese avant-gardists. She should be as gentle as water and as strong as iron. In the age of revolution, she would be the first to rebel against oppression and fight as a real warrior, although her weapon might still be water.

Although the *chuanqi* version of the White Snake story from the eighteenth century already mentions a water battle, Tian Han added a real fight scene, "Shuidou," in the 1955 Peking Opera version. In contrast to the absence of actual fighting in earlier versions,[94] the masses appeared onstage as sea spirits under the command of the White Snake and Green Snake. A more confrontational White Snake emerged as a result. She was transformed thereby into a female warrior, an ordinary wife pushed to the edge of rebellion, similar to those righteous rebels in *The Water Margin*. "Wearing grief and anger on her face, a commanding flag in hand, Bai Suzhen comes onto the stage;[95] thus begins the battle between Monk Fa Hai and the White Snake, the climax of the story and a full display of the White Snake's spiritual, as well as physical, power. The climax of the plot also provides an opportunity for the unleashing of sexual energy. It is not without deliberation that Li Bihua, the contemporary Hong Kong writer, in her novel *Qingshe quanxin ban* (A Brand New Version of Green Snake), made Monk Fa Hai an object of sexual desire for both the White and Green Snakes after intense fights between the monk and the snakes.[96]

How did the devouring snake spirit become a pure and chaste wife? If the

White Snake's image as a female warrior was partly a result of accommodating contemporary politics within the opera, her image as a pure lover tells a rather different story.[97] Tian Han poured his love and obsession into the White Snake image during his decade-long rewriting process, making her the most understanding wife in the most touching "Duanqiao" (broken bridge) scene. He greatly expanded this scene with long and refined arias, which served to intensify the conflict between the Green Snake and Xu Xian, between the White Snake and Xu Xian, and between the feelings of love and betrayal. White Snake's bold self-revelation—"As your wife, I am originally a snake-goddess of Mount Emei"—did not appear in any previous versions. The line "Though I am not human, I treated you with deep love, and I have the offspring of your Xu family in my belly" was followed by an equally touching line from Xu Xian: "My wife, you treated me with true feeling, deep love; you have a tender heart, and for the love of me, you endured thousands of difficulties, hundreds of adversities."[98] Here Tian Han presented the White Snake as more humane than human. She was the newly humanized, the new convert! The new humanism acquired by the snake spirit, though, is not without strong political implications. She must be a fervent believer in the goodness of humanity and do all that is expected of a good human being.

At the same time, the White Snake's image as a passionate lover-warrior defending her family was also highlighted, in the ending scenes "Hebo" (caught by the golden bowl) and "Daota" (the pagoda crumbles). Tian Han intentionally fostered an atmosphere of family harmony and happiness in the first part of "Hebo." At the time of their son's first month celebration, the whole Xu family is enjoying a moment of rare harmony after all the vicissitudes. Right at this moment, Fa Hai breaks into the house with the golden bowl, breaking the family harmony and separating wife from husband, and mother from son, with force.[99]

By so situating his characters, Tian Han created a much more intense dramatic effect in this scene than existed in any earlier versions, as the White Snake's separation from her baby is rarely featured in any eighteenth- and nineteenth-century versions. Xu Xian shouts at Fa Hai, "Nonsense! Xu Xian comes to understand today that it is Fa Hai who eats people, not my wife! I will break the golden bowl and set my dear wife free." And the White Snake declares, "Never talk about charity and love with a killer."[100] By highlighting the conflict between the moral universe of the two lovers and that of the religious authority, Fa Hai, Tian Han again celebrated the spiritual power of true love and its revolutionary vitality. This highlighting of conflict can, of course, be interpreted again as a gesture of political compromise aimed at intensifying the "major contradiction" (*zhuyao maodun*) between the feudal defender and the revolutionary masses. It proves how difficult and delicate Tian Han's situation was, and as such indicative of the ongoing struggle of modern Chinese intellectuals to achieve artistic expression while "dancing in chains."

Tian Han made the Green Snake a more radical substitute for the humanized White Snake from the very beginning of the story. She could speak out in a situation that was difficult for the White Snake to handle according to human norms, the marriage proposal being one of many examples. She would be the ultimate advocate of a fight against Fa Hai to win back Xu Xian, while the White Snake still pinned her hopes on Fa Hai's benevolence. Moreover, in Tian's final version, it is the Green Snake who goes back and defeats the pagoda god and sets the White Snake free. She becomes the ultimate substitute for the White Snake in the last scene, "The Pagoda Crumbles." The Green Snake's androgynous background in some of the earlier versions—originally a male and later transformed into a female—is suggestive of the power of gender transgression.[101] By foregrounding her in the narrative, Tian Han suggests the power of the lower class that she represents as the White Snake's maid. It is even more important that the Green Snake is said to be leading the masses of water creatures to topple the pagoda as it stresses that only grassroots collective action can prevail against an enemy.

Tian Han's reconfigurations of the White Snake in the 1950s functioned as a mirror reflecting his own shifting cultural identities in a turbulent world. Fantasizing about a female image that combines both feminine and masculine qualities, a hybrid of a strong-willed vampire woman and a passionate female warrior, Tian Han's own desire for transcendence amid historical chaos is finally revealed.

The female image was used as a locus of self-projection. Tian Han's obsession with the fantastic woman speaks ultimately to his fantasy about his own role as a male intellectual in modern China. His obsession with powerful femininity is thus a self-obsession that reveals his deep concern with intellectuals' shifting identities in the turbulence of modern Chinese history. The discourse of women's liberation, together with the discourse of "going to the people," not only pushed intellectuals to construct their own identities in relation to these two sets of strong "others" but also provided them with a convenient rhetorical framework through which to express their anxieties and concerns about the fate of the intellectual and the nation as a whole. This situation, however, was not a new one. Tian Han's dual obsessions with "creating the new woman" and "going to the people" had occupied his avant-gardist experiments from the first decades of the twentieth century to their myriad transformations in the process of popularizing the avant-garde throughout the past decades.

A Profound Propaganda: the International Avant-Garde in the 1950s

Artistry and popularity are the means of creating a "profound propaganda" according to Joris Ivens, writing in 1958 about his poetic and lyrical representations of the Great Leap Forward in *Zaochun* ("Early Spring"), before the Beijing premiere of *The Windrose,* now renamed *Wu zhi ge* ("Five Songs").[102] Both Tian and Ivens were simultaneously poets and propagandists throughout their experiments in art, life, and politics, from the post–World War I moment in pursuit of social democracy to the post–World War II moment calling for democratic socialism.

Joris Ivens provides a case study in the relationship between art and political engagement that intersects interestingly with Tian Han's case. Each was attacked for his political alignment, but from opposite directions. Ivens wrestled with a single review throughout the second half of his long film career. Cynthia Grenier regards his *La Seine a rencontré Paris* (The Seine Meets Paris, 1957) as one of "the most tender, charming, moving and accurate pictures ever made about Paris," comparable to the poetic lyricism of one of his earliest films, *Rain* (1929). At the same time, she dismissed the social realist pictures he had made during the intervening thirty years as "easy propaganda . . . unworthy of his intelligence."[103] In Tian Han's case, the critic Dai Bufan accused him not of sacrificing artistic creativity for political propaganda but rather of being insufficiently rigorous in his socialist realism and indulging in petit bourgeois lyricism.[104]

Ivens and his DEFA (Deutsche Film-Aktiengesellschaft) colleagues founded the Leipzig Documentary Film Festival in 1955,[105] the same year in which Tian Han's Peking Opera "White Snake" was published as a single volume. Underlying the seemingly coincidental timing of Ivens's documentary activities and Tian's opera was a deeper intellectual connection. Ivens, Eisler, and Brecht all worked in East Germany at the time, and Ivens's panoramic documentaries on workers' and women's lives on different continents of the world always highlighted the PRC as a key representative.

When observing Tian Han's work on opera reforms in the PRC together with Joris Ivens's work on documentaries in East Germany, we become aware of the interconnected nature of their experiments. Tian Han's work was filled with a strong desire to maintain his avant-gardist spirit while boosting the international reputation of the new Communist China. Ivens and his network of international avant-garde artists worked together to propagate a strong sense of internationalism, socialism, and feminism through his panoramic documentaries. Hence Tian Han's reinvention of the White Snake tale in the 1950s is not only about a Chinese avant-gardist's transformation under communism; rather, it is a story of the dialogue between the 1920s and 1950s, on a scale much larger than China, which includes a spectrum of utopian artists and activists in the context of the Cold War.

As part of his description of himself as a "fellow traveler" of communism in 1930 in his famous epic-scale self-criticism, Tian Han narrated his self-proclaimed transformation from a formalist to a social realist. Joris Ivens told a similar story in his 1932 reflection during his stay in the Soviet Union, where he emphasized his own development and transformation "from a representative of the leftist avant-garde movement into an active fighter in the class struggle." However, both Tian's and Ivens's "self-criticism" also served as self-promotion: in Ivens's case, he described his first film, *Bridge*, made in 1928 before his Soviet experience, as, while "not a class conscious film," nevertheless a "protest against the middle-class cinematography of Hollywood, Paris, and Berlin."[106] He of course could not foresee that he would arrive in Hollywood in 1936 and that his two most acclaimed films made in the late 1930s, *The Spanish Earth* and *The 400 Million*, would be made with money and support gathered from progressive intellectuals and artists centered in Hollywood. In fact he would write about Hollywood during his first stay there in 1936 in the following terms: "To my mind, Hollywood is the world's greatest centre of agitation and propaganda. Here independent film groups are already engaging in courageous pioneering work."[107]

A similar self-proclaimed rhetoric of identity "transformation" and "remolding" occurred in the cases of Hanns Eisler and Bertolt Brecht. The development of these three avant-gardists shows striking parallels. Not only were Eisler, Brecht, and Ivens all born in 1898 into middle-class families, but they were also all in Berlin during the post–World War I moment when revolution and counterrevolution were the order of the day. Their artistic and political growth mirrored each other's and that of Tian Han: they seemed to have begun as avant-garde formalists, an identity they came to denounce as bourgeois after their association with the labor movement and international socialism. In theoretical terms, the views of Brecht, Eisler, and Ivens closely paralleled that of two famous essays by Walter Benjamin: "The Author as Producer" (1934) and "The Work of Art in the Age of Mechanical Reproduction" (1936), in which he used precisely these three avant-gardists as examples for presenting his ideas, especially in response to Lukács's Marxist theory of art (notion of realism) and Lenin's theory of reflection.[108]

Tian Han's artistic and political development from the late 1910s to the 1950s followed a similar trajectory. Like the trio of Ivens, Brecht, and Eisler, Tian Han was inside the communist camp at the height of the Cold War and had finalized his Peking Opera version of the White Snake story in Beijing in the mid-1950s while serving as chief of the Opera Reform Bureau, a middle-ranking artistic and bureaucratic position in the PRC. Yet, despite his self-criticism and renunciation of his prior work, the rhetoric of transformation did not translate so neatly into real life. Both Ivens's films and Tian Han's plays produced during the 1950s quote extensively from their previous materials. Ivens used footage from his previous films, and Tian Han injected elements of the femme fatale and female warrior into the reimagining of the White Snake.

Both Ivens's *The Song of the Rivers* and *The Windrose* and Tian's "White Snake" were produced at the height of the Cold War with a utopian vision of harmony and love. In other words, in the larger context of social realism both artists continued to produce deeply personal and psychologically meaningful work and continued to explore subjects of abiding personal import, with which they had long been engaged in their previous works: for Joris Ivens, the river as the container of life, culture, and social movement; for Tian Han, the image of strong-willed and strong-bodied women as social agents. And indeed their personal obsessions overlap since the White Snake is very much the embodiment of water, and as a water goddess she contains both the primitive power of the river and the contemporary political symbolism of its changing tides.

The controversy in East Germany concerning Ivens's first film made after World War II in Western Europe, *The Seine Meets Paris,* parallels the situation in which Tian Han found himself in the late 1950s in the PRC. When Ivens returned to the Leipzig Documentary Film Festival in 1960 with this 1957 film, his East German colleagues found his change of style from revolutionary to poetic incomprehensible: "The poetry is beautiful, but nowadays the political and historical movements are in the foreground. And that does not happen in *La Seine. . . . Song of the Rivers* is profound, and *La Seine. . .* is just a babbling brook according to so many people; it is very beautiful, but it is no river." One of the colleagues, Karl Gass, asked simply, "Where is the fist, Joris?" Three years later, Gass explained his behavior at the time, stating that "for me documentary film is a weapon and that is how I got to know it with Joris. It did surprise me and many others, that film could mean something else to him as well: poetry."[109]

Indeed, for Ivens, documentary film was the only way for the avant-garde filmmaker to stand up to the film industry, and only independent film had the capacity for self-criticism that leads to progress. In 1931 he wrote about the avant-garde documentary film as a representative of the masses, a mouthpiece of the people, and at the same time a way to tell personal stories.[110] Spiritually echoing Tian Han's "self-criticism" of the same time, Ivens differed from Tian in his technical superiority: as the heir of a photographic equipment company, he was literally born with a camera in his hand and equipped with the best knowledge and practice of his time. If Ivens was a poet-cameraman in one, with a better understanding of materials and techniques, Tian Han was more of a poet-director, who, while he lacked the technical and material resources of Ivens, nonetheless meticulously gathered a group of young people with shared aspirations to form a film institute and make his first independent film in Shanghai in 1926, as Ivens did in Amsterdam a year later.

Joris Ivens defended himself against both Cynthia Grenier's 1958 description of him as an "easy propagandist" and the East Germans' criticism of him for losing his fighting spirit: "It is not so that Ivens has two guises: the leftist and the esthete. Some people say that only the purely esthetic films are artistic; the rest are not art. Others see me exclusively as a militant filmmaker. Both are incorrect. When I made *The Seine Meets Paris,* my views were just as left-wing as they were when making political films. With political films I have often been just as rigorous about finding the best artistic form."[111]

Tian Han similarly used the leading Soviet avant-gardist poet and propagandist Vladimir Mayakovsky as a positive example of one who uses art as propaganda. He praised Mayakovsky's use of poetry and painting to promote the leather shoes made by state-owned companies during the era of the new economic policy in Russia. The praise was aimed not just at the message but at the medium: "What is most unparalleled is that his propaganda poetry and painting for leather shoes not only represents political views but also expresses moving artistic power." Following Mayakovsky, Tian Han argues that during the Sino-Japanese War, some people called anti-Japanese drama "propaganda theater" while calling drama that did not engage with anti-Japanese war "artistic theater." However, any theater that truly functioned as anti-Japanese propaganda must have had its distinctive artistic quality. He proclaims, "We must achieve both 'propaganda' and 'artistry'; it is only through artistry that one can propagate!" [112]

The documentaries coordinated by Joris Ivens in East Germany with the support of filmmakers in the PRC, the Soviet Union, Brazil, France, Italy, and many other countries cut across the Cold War divide and linked the modernist 1920s to the socialist 1950s. Even after a pronounced identity shift from lyric poets to social realists, members of the interwar international avant-garde kept experimenting with form. The intricate relationship among commissioned work, individual creation, popular participation, and social movement suggests a complex network of actors and subjectivities rather than a monolithic, hegemonic system. The juxtaposition of Chinese opera and documentary film reveals their connections beyond their apparent differences as stylized and realistic, abstract and concrete, and fantastic and reflective.

Feminine performances are central to both Tian Han's opera and Joris Ivens's film. The images of beautiful, powerful, and independent women come to stand in for the newly founded communist regimes. The fantastic White Snake joins hands with her international sisters as humane, loving, and working women contributing to a greater good and a new society. Both the Chinese opera and the internationalist documentary produced in the 1950s continue Tian Han's and Ivens's avant-gardist and socialist obsessions of "going to the people." The masses enter "White Snake" partly to demonstrate the snake-woman's magic power to control "water troops," but, more important, the fighting scene is used to portray the fighting spirit of the oppressed against an oppressor, Monk Fa Hai. Similarly, the women in the film *The Windrose* masterminded by Ivens come from all walks of life, including a teacher, a farmer, a worker, and a cadre.[113] The fact that these "real" women are played by beautiful actresses suggests the power of the fictional in representing the real, and the collaboration of fantasy and reality.

Situated in the communist camp in the PRC and East Germany, both Tian Han and Joris Ivens operated under the conditions of the Cold War, and the politics of isolation and containment pushed both artists to venture beyond the confines of their immediate political environment. Tian Han's reinvention of a "traditional" genre and return to a folk heroine in effect bridged his communist present and populist and socialist past. "White Snake," together with "Butterfly Lovers" and "The Western Chamber," helped to present the image of a feminine, nonthreatening China to the wider world through film screenings and performance tours not only within the communist camp but also at international conventions and venues.

The transnational documentaries produced by DEFA in East Germany allegedly reached more than 250 million viewers throughout the world (possibly through free screenings to workers' and women's groups), while the "White Snake" opera became one of the most widely adapted and lastingly popular works produced in the PRC. On the one hand, the popular impact reveals the power of performance in service of political propaganda. On the other hand, governmental and institutional support for these works in effect legitimized eccentric love stories and seductive female images and secured the production, circulation, and consumption of works of art that were universally appealing and profoundly visionary but might not have been made in the first place due to lack of funds and institutional support. Our current preoccupation with the rise of state capitalism in the PRC and other "latecomers" to modernity is but one manifestation of a profoundly ambiguous attitude toward these powerful states and their complex impact on our economic and civic lives in the contemporary world.[114]

Epilogue

Endings, Happy and Otherwise

Tian Han and *Guan Hanqing*

On June 28, 1958, fifteen hundred professional theater troupes performed plays by one single playwright simultaneously in some one hundred different theatrical venues all over the People's Republic of China in celebration of the seven-hundredth anniversary of his theatrical activities. Outside China the playwright's works were known through translations into English, French, German, Japanese, and other languages. The playwright, Guan Hanqing, lived in the thirteenth century under the Mongol Yuan dynasty. His newfound fame throughout the PRC and abroad had to do with the World Peace Conference's recent designation of him as one of the ten "world cultural figures" of the year.[1]

Tian Han decided to write a play about Guan Hanqing while preparing a speech in his honor, as required by his position as chairman of the Dramatist Association. During his preparation, Tian read Guan's lyrics to a song "not giving in to old age" (*bu fu lao*), where the playwright celebrated his bohemian lifestyle in the entertainment quarters as "the leader of all the prodigals in the country" and proudly declared himself "a copper bean, which can't be made soft by cooking nor flattened by beating."[2] Guan's sexually explicit reference to his life in the pleasure quarters—"I've plucked every bud hanging over the wall, and picked every roadside branch of the willow. The flowers I plucked had the softest red petals, the willow I picked were the tenderest green"—may well have excited and troubled Tian Han at the same time.[3] How to write a play that would celebrate Guan's social criticism while satisfying, or concealing, Tian's own fascination with the bohemian lifestyle of the playwright of seven hundred years ago? In a key confrontation between Guan Hanqing and Ye Hefu, the antagonist in the play, Tian speaks through Guan in defense of both his character and himself: "I am not a master of depicting prostitutes and songstresses! I did write stories about them: I sang praises for the chivalric courtesan Zhao Pan'er because she helps others when they are in danger,"[4] thus justifying, conditionally, the artist's freedom by claiming an ethical component to his art.

Tian Han, at the age of sixty (*jiazi*) in 1958, in effect wrote himself into the Guan Hanqing character. He saw in Guan a mirror of himself as a playwright, an artistic bohemian, and a leader of theater circles who harbored the intellectual desire to be the spokesman of the people. Tian found Guan's *Dou E yuan* (Injustice to Dou E) particularly close to his heart, as the strong-willed female characters echoed the centrality of female resistance in his own works. He praised Guan's "feminist and class consciousness" and recognized the quality of Guan's works as avant-garde despite the seven-hundred-odd years separating them. Guan's formal experiments in *Dou E yuan* again attracted Tian's attention, as they share a strong affinity with folk storytelling genres, which he himself exploited in works such as the "White Snake" opera. Traces of the legend genre of the Tang dynasty, as well as the storytelling of the Song, entered Guan's play, where, according to Tian Han, realism, romanticism, humanism, and an avant-gardist fighting spirit converge.[5]

Tian's play *Guan Hanqing* premiered on June 28, 1958, in Beijing and was met with great success. Three leading theater troupes in Japan staged joint performances of the play in Osaka, Yokohama, Kyoto, and Tokyo, among other locations, in 1959. Many audience members bought copies of the play in Japanese translation. At the Tokyo premiere of the play in Shinjuku, the performance was broadcast live through NHK via radio and television.[6] *Guan Hanqing*'s success in Japan attested to Tian Han's strong presence in and impact on this neighboring country as late as 1959. Given the overwhelming reception of *Guan Hanqing* in Japan at its premiere, it only seems natural that senior Japanese scholars of Chinese literature whom I met in Tokyo in 2003 would be able to vividly recall the sensation of watching the play in Japanese as young men.

I remember vividly how I was first reminded of the iconic position of *Guan Hanqing* for a whole generation of students and scholars growing up in the PRC soon after encountering these Japanese scholars in Tokyo. It was in the spring of 2004 on the campus of Beijing Normal University (BNU). I was doing fieldwork for my dissertation and had just relocated from Tokyo to Beijing. Professor Liu Xiangyu, my adviser during my undergraduate and masters studies at BNU, on hearing of my current research on Tian Han, spontaneously started singing a song from *Guan Hanqing*, his eyes half closed, accompanied by fervent hand gestures. The song had taken him back to his student years.

The song, "Shuangfei die" (A Pair of Butterflies), was written by Tian Han to be sung by the character Guan Hanqing as a declaration of love to his lead actress when both of them were wrongly imprisoned. Written in the classical style but imitating the vernacular in Guan's works, it forms the emotional climax and formal pinnacle of the 1958 play and deserves to be quoted in full here.

將碧血，寫忠烈，
作厲鬼，除逆賊，
這血兒啊，化做黃河揚子浪千疊，
長與英雄共魂魄！
強似寫佳人繡戶描花葉；
學士錦袍趨殿闕；
浪子朱窗弄風月；
雖留得綺詞麗語滿江湖，
怎及得傲幹奇枝鬥霜雪？
念我漢卿啊，
讀詩書，破萬冊，
寫雜劇，過半百，
這些年風雲改變山河色，
珠簾捲處人愁絕!
都只為一曲《竇娥冤》，
俺與她雙瀝長弘血；
差勝那孤月自圓缺，
孤燈自明滅；
坐時節共對半窗雲，
行時節相應一身鐵；
各有這氣比長虹壯，
哪有那淚似寒波咽！
提什麼黃泉無店宿忠魂，
爭說道青山有幸埋芳潔。
俺與你發不同青心同熱；
生不同床死同穴；
待來年遍地杜鵑花，
看風前漢卿四姐雙飛蝶。
相永好，不言別！[7]

We shall lay down our lives like the martyrs of old,
  whose spirit keeps haunting the wicked.
And our blood shall flow
  eternally like the Yellow River,
  like the Youngtse [Yangtze] mingling with the souls of the
  heroes of times bygone.
This is something nobler than writing about maidens
  embroidering in their chambers,
Or scholars in their silks
  visiting the royal court,
Or philanderers romancing by brightly painted windows.
These embellished lines may give the country
  something to read and think about,
  but to survive the rigors of a snowstorm
  takes the strength of a pine.
I studied thousands of volumes of the classics;
I wrote more than fifty plays.
And all these years the nation has been crushed,
  people have suffered untold misery everywhere.
We saw, and we fought,
  till "Tou Ngo" [Dou E] sped us to our deaths.
The moon wanes by itself,
  the single wick flickers out alone,
  but we shall die together.
Resting, we share
  the same glimpse of the clouds
  through our barred windows.
Walking, our chains clank in unison,
But like the rainbow,
  our hearts are bright with faith and strength.
Who would waste tears?
If there is no place for martyrs
  in the nether world,
  are there not green vales reserved
  in which the pure and great may rest?
Years divide us, but our hearts are one.
Unwedded, we shall lie in the same grave.

Behold! When the fields again
are red with azalea blossoms,
how two butterflies, you and I,
will flutter in the breeze, loving each other,
never to part![8]

Almost forty years prior to 1958, while a student in Tokyo, Tian Han had already written about the moonlight, the clouds, and the rainbow in the classical style with a hint of the vernacular and the youthful enthusiasm of the May Fourth era. In the excerpt from his 1921 Tokyo diary that opened chapter 1, Tian Han presented an illuminated urban landscape where glass windows reflected both natural light and modern technology and music drifted from unseen singers. The young Chinese roamed the city enchanted by the sights and sounds of the modernity of everyday urban life. Similar imagery entered the 1958 song, but with some twists: the lonely moon (*guyue*) does not seem to be within reach, and the single wick (*gudeng*) seems far too fragile to supply any light or heat. Although the clouds are divided by barred windows and the protagonists are in chains, the rainbow "bright with faith and strength" does bring to mind radiating light from the Tokyo scene.

However, the kind of "faith and strength" expressed here is quite different from the utopianism of Tian Han's Tokyo. It centers on the love between the imprisoned thirteenth-century playwright and his lead actress, as well as their mutual determination to die for their art and its popularization as a living performance form among the people, speaking their minds against official corruption and social injustice. Their willingness to martyr themselves for this cause brings to mind the star-crossed lovers in Tian Han's Shanghai play "The Night a Tiger Was Captured," although that May Fourth era play pales in comparison in terms of the characters' devotion to the common good.

A fighting spirit runs through the song, but is gradually transformed into a heart-wrenching love that aspires to conquer death. Through Guan's voice, Tian Han celebrates the "pure and great" (*fangjie*) quality of the lovers, in spite of the unconventionality of their liaison, divided by years (*fabu tongqing*) and unwedded (*shengbu tongchuang*). The song ends with the fictive Guan imagining his lover and himself as two butterflies rising above their shared grave like the lovers in "Butterfly Lovers," "never to part" in their afterlives.

These lyrics can be regarded as the culmination of the literally thousands of lyrics and poems (in both classical and modern styles) written by Tian Han throughout his writing life of a half a century. The song and its meticulously crafted lyrics exemplify Tian's lifelong engagement with both the spoken and the sung in performance, as expressed in his continual experiments with combinations of opera, drama, and film from Changsha to Beijing. The fact that about half of Tian's spoken dramas contain songs and poems demonstrates his special attention to musicality in his plays. The songs and poems function, as discussed throughout this book, as quotable gestures and movable archives for the purpose of popularization.

Tian Han composed the lyrics for the song with great attention to both its classical style and its vernacular quality contemporary with Guan Hanqing's time. He followed the rather difficult rhyme syllable *e*, which limited the characters he could use. Literally "dancing in chains" and reflective of Guan's and his own increasingly restrictive conditions for cultural production in 1958 during the Anti-Rightist Campaign,[9] Tian was nonetheless able to miraculously mobilize a whole range of Chinese characters, from *xue* (blood), *lie* (martyr), *zei* (possibly pronounced *ze* at the time, "the wicked"), *die* (layers of waves), *ye* (leaves), *que* (palaces), *yue* (moon), *xue* (snow), *se* (color), *jue* (deepest), *que* (waning of the moon), *mie* (flickering out of the wick), *tie* (iron chains), *ye* (tearing up), *jie* (clean and pure), *re* (warmth in the heart), *xue* (grave), *die* (butterfly), and *bie* (part) to compose an elegant poem that was at the same time accessible to ears accustomed to the vernacular songs in Guan's works. It is significant that both "White Snake" and *Guan Hanqing*, often considered Tian Han's best works, were products of the new Communist regime and a result of socialist cultural production in the 1950s.

We have seen that Tian Han's avant-gardism was that of a bohemian populist, in whom romanticism coexists with a deep concern for social injustice, as expressed in his early works such as "A Night in a Café" and "The Night a Tiger Was Captured." Even after his so-called turning to the left in the 1930s, Tian's works were still saturated with such romantic tropes as the wandering poet and parting between lovers. Tian Han projected onto the character of Guan Hanqing in this 1958 play the qualities of such a romantic bohemian populist.

Guan Hanqing is depicted as an avant-gardist in the play, in a direct reflection of Tian Han's own continued avant-gardist experiments well into the first decade of the PRC. In act 4 of the play, Tian sets up a discussion between Guan and his playwright friends on changing tunes according to emotions and their desire to throw theatrical conventions overboard.[10] Their free spirit in reshaping the very genre of the *zaju* (variety play) echoes Tian Han's own creative remolding of Peking Opera in "White Snake," discussed in chapter 5.

Guan Hanqing is another instance of Tian Han's abiding preoccupation with the depiction of artists in general and performers in particular. His first published play, "Violin and Rose," featured a female performer of drum storytelling (*gushu*); *Mingyou zhisi* (Death of a Famous Actor) again focused on the fate of performers of Chinese opera in modern Shanghai, where backstage at the opera house became center stage for modern drama performance. *Erbaiwu xiaozhuan* (Anecdotes of an Actor), a film based on Tian Han's script, further manifests Tian's love of Chinese opera, his insider's knowledge of the workings of the theater circles, and his suggestions for opera reform, at a key transitional moment from the Republic of China to the People's Republic, as it was filmed in the spring of 1949 and opened in Shanghai after the Communist seizure of power. In *Guan Hanqing* Tian bases his female protagonist on the real life actress Zhu Lianxiu, a contemporary of Guan's for whom he wrote a song.[11] In Tian's creative rendering of the female performer Zhu, her performance of the role of Dou E in Guan's play endowed her with the spirit of the wrongly executed woman and dressing up as Dou E at the same time allowed her to assume Dou's fighting spirit.[12]

Tian Han was keenly aware of the need to reevaluate and reconnect with the tradition of critical realism and May Fourth avant-gardism at the 1958 moment. Guan Hanqing's position as a Han literati under the Mongol Yuan dynasty appealed to Tian's own anti-Manchu nationalism as a Han student in the late Qing and early Republican years. Tian presented Guan through the words of his lead actress, Zhu Lianxiu, as someone who "hasn't quite outgrown the 'childlike heart' (*tongxin*),"[13] a not so subtle and rather ahistorical reference to Li Zhi's theory of the childlike heart (*tongxin shuo*) from the sixteenth century. Li's insistence on spontaneous feelings and the virtue of desire formed some of the most iconoclastic views on tradition in Chinese history,[14] and it is no surprise that he became a favorite source of inspiration for the May Fourth avant-gardists in the early twentieth century.[15]

Although the actress Zhu to some extent conformed to the stereotype of female characters who took inspiration from their male lover/mentor, she also represented a more radically feminist position and often "helped" Guan in the discovery of his own power as an avant-garde artist, as in the following scene.

KUAN HAN-CH'ING (Guan Hanqing): In ancient times, when one traveler saw another being attacked, he would unsheathe his sword and go to the rescue. In my case, I have no sword to unsheathe, only a worn-out brush.

CHU LIEN-HSIU (Zhu Lianxiu): Isn't your brush as good as a sword? Isn't your script your sword?[16]

Here Guan Hanqing emerges as a left-wing writer in the style of Lu Xun and Tian Han, who used his drama as a weapon to expose and revolt against those who abuse power. Guan's agitation incited violence against the powerful and achieved concrete political results in Tian's idealist rendering of the real life effect of socially engaged writing. In Tian's play *Guan Hanqing*, Wang Zhu, a character resembling Robin Hood or the heroes of *The Water Margin*, inspired by the call to "eradicate evil for all commoners" in Guan's play *Dou E yuan*, assassinated the representative of the evil forces—the powerful minister Akham. Here writing becomes a potent weapon of inspiration and attack. Hence *Guan Hanqing* can be read as Tian Han's tribute to the social impact of leftist writing since the May Fourth era; at the same time, it lends itself to interpretations that bring contemporary politics under critical scrutiny.

Ye Hefu, the antagonist who was himself a playwright, warns Guan Hanqing of the danger of writing historical plays to critique contemporary politics: "Listen to me," he says, "regardless of in which dynasty you set your story, as long as it is performed, everyone will know who you are writing about."[17] After the premiere of *Dou E yuan*, Guan is ordered to change his play in accordance with a list of revisions, a not so subtle reference to theater censorship under the Yuan, but equally applicable to other historical conditions, including Tian Han's own. Tian speaks through Guan in the play: "I'm afraid I can't [change the play]. If all this is to be changed, it won't be a play anymore."[18] With Ye as the perfect foil, "the wicked one" who should be hunted down, as in the song "A Pair of Butterflies," Guan emerges as a true intellectual hero in Tian's play. This characterization was defiantly far from the portrayals of intellectuals in the mainstream ideology at the time, given that the timing was *after* the start of the Anti-Rightist Campaign, which targeted intellectuals; however, it did rekindle the fire of avant-gardism and critical realism of the May Fourth era and helped to restore left-wing intellectuals' self-assumed role as representatives of the people.

Guan Hanqing attracted the attention of Zhou Enlai, himself a performer of modern drama in his student days and now the PRC's prime minister, through the Cantonese Opera version of the play. It was said that Zhou had watched the Cantonese Opera and was extremely taken by the performance of its star actress, Hong Xiannü, as the determined female lead Zhu Lianxiu, although he suggested that they change the ending of the play to the separation of the playwright and his actress lover, rather than having them reunited in exile as it currently stood. Zhou's reasoning behind the need to present a more tragic ending, according to Tian's recollection, likely had to do with accentuating the realism of the play: the harsher the reality the protagonists face, the more effective the critique of the Mongol Yuan rulers.[19]

Tian Han did change the ending according to Zhou's suggestion to the separation of the playwright and his lover in the 1960 version of the play, but he insisted on keeping the original at the same time as an alternative ending.[20] Deep in his heart, Tian couldn't bear to give up the union of the two as was planned from the beginning. Moreover, any sudden change in the ending would render many details in the previous acts superfluous. Tian insisted that a "happy ending" could still be realistic; moreover, popular sentiment demanded it.[21] As a popular avant-gardist, he always had both his artistic integrity and his popular audience in mind.

Tian Han re-created Guan Hanqing as the ideal embodiment of an avant-garde, political, and popular playwright. The historical and allegorical parallel between Tian's portrayal of Guan's mission as spokesman of the people and his own self-projected image as a left-wing intellectual representing the voice of the people, is striking. With *Guan Hanqing*, Tian Han was able to paint a final bold stroke in his self-portrait as a modern Chinese avant-garde who actively and effectively engaged with the popular and the political through his art and activism.

Only a few years later that confident and positive portrayal of the artist in relation to society would come to seem overly optimistic. In 1966 Tian Han's 1961 Peking Opera *Xie Yaohuan* was harshly and openly criticized for its alleged "feudal" and "counterrevolutionary" tendencies and was indicted, together with Wu Han's Peking Opera *Hairui baguan* and Meng Chao's Kun Opera *Li Huiniang*, as "three poisonous weeds" in a *People's Daily* article. Indeed, *Xie Yaohuan* was one of the first literary works to come under attack during the Cultural Revolution,[22] hence ushering in the tragic end of Tian Han, an avant-garde who had engaged in a lifelong pursuit of the political and the popular throughout the vicissitudes of twentieth-century Chinese revolutions.

In Tian's idealistic re-creation of Guan Hanqing's thirteenth-century China, the playwright imprisoned for his outspoken critique of the government was able to avoid death and even reunite with his lover and lead actress and embark on a journey to the South to start a new life. In his own very real twentieth-century China, Tian Han would remain in solitary confinement throughout the last two years of his life from late 1966 to late 1968. The tragic ending of Tian's life echoes the ending of *Guan Hanqing* suggested by Zhou Enlai and rejected by Tian himself, as he insisted on retaining the reunion of the two lovers as one possible ending. An E, the "Red Salome" of Tian's Shanghai years and his lifelong companion in Beijing, would not be able to reunite with him as his imagined Zhu Lianxiu did with Guan Hanqing.

Ai Wei Wei and the Transformation of the Chinese Avant-Garde

I have treated avant-garde performance as an important political force in an intricate dance with popular culture from early- to mid-twentieth-century China. Such an approach facilitates a creative rereading of the cultural dynamics and political tensions at work during both the Cultural Revolution and the postsocialist transformations in contemporary China. Ai Wei Wei presents a case study for such a rereading.

The political campaigns that conditioned Tian Han's creation of *Guan Hanqing* in the late 1950s traumatically impacted the lives of a whole generation born amid such intense political change. In 1957 Ai Wei Wei's life both started and, in a sense, ended, that is, he was born in mid-1957 and exiled from Beijing in early 1958. His father, the leading Chinese avant-garde poet Ai Qing (1910–96), was designated a rightist and sent to Beidahuang (The Great Northern Wilderness), and the family followed him. The family was transferred to Xinjiang in the far Northwest of China in less than two years, where they settled in Shihezi in the winter of 1959. According to Ai Wei Wei's mother, Gao Ying, they were protected by the minister of agriculture, Wang Zhen, throughout these years. Sending Ai Qing to Beidahuang in 1958 was in a way removing him from the cultural circle in Beijing so as to protect him. Ai Qing was appointed associate head of the 852 Farm when they stayed in the Northeast, and when Wang Zhen found out that his health was deteriorating, he made it possible for them to transfer to Xinjiang, where the economy was more robust and a better living standard could be guaranteed. The family lived in Shihezi, one of the settler cities of the Bingtuan, where demobilized soldiers were sent to improve production.[23]

As Ai Wei Wei began to remember things, Ai Qing's situation started to worsen with the beginning of the Cultural Revolution. He was assigned to clean public toilets, and the family was sent farther down to the village, from Shihezi to Balian (Eighth Company) in 1967. The whole family lived in a cellar for five years, and they could only return to Shihezi city in 1972. Ai Wei Wei returned to

Beijing with his family in May 1975 to seek treatment for his father's eyes.[24] For two years he taught himself painting as a way to avoid having to leave Beijing to find work (as his household registration was still in Xinjiang).[25]

It was during this time that Ai Wei Wei was first introduced to postimpressionist painters such as Van Gogh, Cezanne, and Gauguin through a book he received as a gift from Yang Xianyi, a friend of his father. An Oxford graduate and a leading figure in translating Chinese classics into English together with his Oxford-educated English wife Gladys Yang in the PRC, Yang Xianyi had access to rare copies of books originally published abroad. Ai Wei Wei treated this little album of paintings as his Bible and started copying every single painting in it.[26]

Again through his father's artistic network, Ai Wei Wei befriended Zhao Zhenkai, the aspiring young poet known as Bei Dao, who brought his poems to the Ai residence in search of recognition from the veteran poet Ai Qing. Ai Wei Wei lent Bei Dao the impressionist album, and it circulated widely among the young artists in Bei Dao's circle. It was through Bei Dao that Ai Wei Wei was put in touch with the poet Mang Ke and the artist Huang Rui, the latter being the organizer of the Xingxing meizhan (Stars Art Exhibition), widely regarded as the first outcry of avant-garde art in contemporary China.[27]

It was also at this time, in 1978, that the very first college entrance examination since 1966 was held. High school seniors of the class of 1966 (people like my father, then in their thirties with children) took the examination together with students ten years their junior such as Ai Wei Wei. With the encouragement of Professor Zheng Ke of the Central Academy of Craft Art, Ai Wei Wei registered to take the examination to enter the Beijing Film Academy (BFA) with "design" as his major and was accepted as part of the very first class of incoming college freshmen after the Cultural Revolution.[28]

Ai Wei Wei's father, Ai Qing, had traveled at the age of nineteen to study painting in Paris, where he stayed from 1929 to 1932, returning to China as an avant-gardist poet and political activist. He was jailed by the Nationalists for his left-wing activism and was only released in 1935. He met Tian Han and Joris Ivens in April 1938 in Wuhan at a meeting in honor of the Dutch filmmaker, who was on location for his documentary *The 400 Million*. During the same month of the same year, in the same city, Ai composed a captivating four-hundred-line poem in praise of the sun, in which he endowed it with the spirit of the French and American revolutions and the principles of love, peace, freedom, and democratic ideals, among other symbolic meanings.[29] Like Tian Han and many other artists and activists of the time, Ai Qing moved west to the wartime capital Chongqing after the fall of Wuhan. Unlike Tian Han, he went even farther northwest to Yan'an, the base where Mao Zedong was building the Communist resistance, in 1941. Importantly, like the leading Shanghai feminist writer Ding Ling, Ai Qing was critical of the Communist bureaucracy in Yan'an. In 1957, shortly after the birth of his son Ai Wei Wei, Ai Qing would be designated a rightist partly due to his outspoken support of Ding Ling.[30]

Some twenty-two years later, in 1979, soon after entering the Beijing Film Academy, Ai Wei Wei participated in the Stars Art Exhibition outside the National Museum of Fine Arts in Beijing, an outdoor exhibition that challenged the official exhibition inside the museum commemorating the thirtieth anniversary of the founding of the PRC. The young artists' works, largely experimental in nature, were hung along the walls and fences of the compound for passersby and spectators to see, for free. Among the entries in the exhibition were Ai Wei Wei's paintings in imitation of the postimpressionist album he had received from Yang Xianyi. The young artists' pursuit of formal experimentation was widely regarded by scholars as avant-gardist. They characterized the Stars Art Exhibition as part of a post–Cultural Revolution reaction against the politicization of art during the socialist era and its artists as seeking to reclaim art from politics, as also expressed by the poetry group Jin Tian (Today), with Bei Dao at the center.[31]

However, this characterization itself should be open to scrutiny. It is significant to situate Ai Wei Wei and the Stars Art Exhibition of 1979 in the context of Tian Han's and Ai Qing's generation of early-twentieth-century Chinese avant-garde artists and activists. Using Tian Han's intellectual journey as a case study, I have demonstrated that the post–Cultural Revolution use of the term *avant-garde* to denote art reclaimed from politics represented an almost total inversion of the original meaning of the term, which denoted art that was deeply intertwined with political purposes and aspirations. As discussed in the introduction to this volume, the term is in need of realignment with its historical roots to better reflect the artistic and political aspirations of both the early-twentieth-century and late-twentieth-century Chinese avant-gardists. The literature and art that aspired to political engagement with society in the context of twentieth-century Chinese revolutions can serve as a model for a reenergized avant-garde, one practitioner of which is Ai Wei Wei.

The "birth" of the avant-garde in China in the late 1970s indeed first saw the "Democracy Wall" movement, starting in 1976, which culminated with Wei

Jingsheng's advocacy of a "fifth modernization," namely, democracy, and his resulting public sentence and imprisonment. Wei received intellectual support from avant-gardist groups such as the Stars and Today, which in turn brought these groups under government surveillance. It was in this atmosphere that Ai Wei Wei quit the Beijing Film Academy and, following his then girlfriend, left China for the United States in 1981.[32]

A nationwide avant-garde movement was fomenting in the mid-1980s for the first time in Chinese history, according to Gao Minglu, curator of the China/Avant-Garde Exhibition at the National Art Gallery in Beijing in 1989, in his recent study on this subject.[33] Many practitioners in this movement visited Ai Wei Wei in New York's East Village where he photographed many of them during his decade-long stay there.[34] These photos constitute a kind of unofficial "who's who" of a new generation of Chinese avant-gardists, people who shared the artistic self-consciousness and sense of social mission with Tian Han and his generation, at least in the 1980s.[35]

I have attempted to redraw the lines among avant-garde art, commercial popular culture, and political propaganda throughout this study. I have argued that in order to understand propaganda in the Chinese context we need to free ourselves of the preconception of an intrinsic antinomy between art and ideology, between art and propaganda, and thus between the avant-garde and the popular. Instead of focusing chiefly on the intrinsic aesthetic value of the work of art, we need to also be asking: is this art *effective*? Does it make things happen in the real world?

Ai Wei Wei returned to China in 1993 to visit his father, who was in critical condition at the time. After bumming in New York for twelve years,[36] he decided to return to China for good, partly due to his obligation to his father and partly propelled by a desire to be relevant, to make *consequential* art.

> I refuse to forget. My parents, my family, their whole generation and my generation all paid a great deal in the struggle for freedom of speech. Many people died just because of one sentence or even one word. Somebody has to take responsibility for that. If a nation cannot face its past, it has no future.[37]

But Ai Wei Wei returned to a changed China—a post-1989 and post–Deng Xiaoping "Southern Talks" China, where "to get rich was glorious" and economic development had become the ultimate touchstone. Young artists bumming in Beijing, as depicted in Wu Wenguang's documentary *Liulang Beijing*

(Bumming in Beijing) and Wang Xiaoshuai's feature film around this time, were dreaming of making the opposite journey of leaving Beijing for New York. Liu Xiaodong, the artist protagonist in Wang Xiaoshuai's 1992 film *Dongchun de rizi* (The Days), went to New York in 1993 and stayed in Ai's East Village apartment, at the time when Ai was attempting to transplant himself from New York to Beijing.[38]

The changed political conditions in China called for a politically reengaged art. Since his return, Ai Wei Wei has been conscious of himself as an artist working in a relationship with, and on behalf of, "the people," those whose voice is not as loud as his, those who may not have any voice at all. For Ai, art, politics, and life are mutually interpenetrating and inseparable.

> My definition of art has always been the same. It is about freedom of expression, a new way of communication. It is never about exhibiting in museums or about hanging it on the wall. Art should live in the hearts of the people. Ordinary people should have the same ability to understand art as anybody else. I don't think art is elite or mysterious. I don't think anybody can separate art from politics. The intention to separate art from politics is itself a very political intention.[39]

Thus, like Tian Han and his cohorts, Ai is an avant-gardist who strives for political relevance and popularity. "As an artist, finding a way to communicate with people is the core activity."[40] Ultimately, his "cyberactivism" has made him who he is today, just as the new technology of radio and sound film made Tian Han and his generation of the post–World War I international avant-garde who they were. Before his high-profile consultation on the design for the Bird's Nest stadium, and his subsequent withdrawal of support from the Olympics, Ai's international visibility was very limited. Since his engagement in "citizen activism," which includes collecting the names of the children who died in the 2008 Sichuan Earthquake, and his extremely savvy use of social media, in particular Twitter, he has become omnipresent, the "Ai God" (Ai shen). In the end it is technology, be it the telegraph, radio, sound film, or the Internet, that determines the role and function of a modern artist, according to a rather thoughtful and reflective Ai Wei Wei, speaking to his Danish host in his deceptively gentle English, which sounds extremely funny to anyone familiar with his curse-laden Chinese.[41] Ai reinvigorates the central premise of this study, the idea that performance, politics, and popularity converge in the image of a popular avant-garde.

Notes

Prologue

1. *The People's Republic of Capitalism with Ted Koppel,* dir. Ted Koppel and Robert Goldsborough, Discovery Channel documentary series, 2008, four episodes on DVD.

2. Yasheng Huang, *Capitalism with Chinese Characteristics: Entrepreneurship and the State* (New York: Cambridge University Press, 2008).

3. The normal school system was indeed inherited from Tian Han's time and earlier, and many students from poor families took the opportunity for professional education to become self-supporting scholars and teachers.

4. Talal Asad, "The Concept of Cultural Translation in British Social Anthropology," in *Genealogies of Religion: Discipline and Reasons of Power in Christianity and Islam* (Baltimore: Johns Hopkins University Press, 1993), 194–95.

5. Tu Wei-ming, "Cultural China: The Periphery as the Center," *Daedalus,* vol. 120, no. 2, The Living Tree: The Changing Meaning of Being Chinese Today (Spring 1991), 1–32; Shu-mei Shih, "The Concept of the Sinophone," *PMLA,* vol. 126, no. 3 (May 2011), 709–18.

6. Jaroslav Průšek, "Basic Problems of the History of Modern Chinese Literature: A Review of C. T. Hsia, *A History of Modern Chinese Fiction,*" *T'oung Pao,* no. 49 (1962), 357–404; C. T. Hsia, "On the 'Scientific' Study of Modern Chinese Literature: A Reply to Professor Průšek," *T'oung Pao,* no. 50 (1963), 428–74.

7. Jaroslav Průšek, *The Lyrical and the Epic: Studies of Modern Chinese Literature,* edited by Leo Ou-fan Lee (Bloomington: Indiana University Press, 1980).

8. Leo Ou-fan Lee, *The Romantic Generation of Modern Chinese Writers* (Cambridge, MA: Harvard University Press, 1973).

9. Jaroslav Průšek, "A Confrontation of Traditional Oriental Literature with Modern European Literature in the Context of the Chinese Literary Revolution," *Archiv Orientální,* no. 32 (1964), 365–75, included in Průšek, *The Lyrical and the*

Epic, 74–85, see especially 83–84; and Leo Ou-fan Lee, *Shanghai Modern: The Flowering of a New Urban Culture in China, 1930–1945* (Cambridge, MA: Harvard University Press, 1999), 134–35.

10. Liang Luo, "Weimei yishi yu nüxing huanxiang: Zai chuantong yu xifang zhijian qunxun de Shi Zhecun" (Aesthetic Consciousness and Feminine Illusion—Shi Zhecun: A Writer Roaming between Tradition and the West) (MA thesis, Department of Chinese Lanuage and Literature, Beijing Normal University, 1999).

11. Ibid., 4.

Introduction

1. In this study, the boundary between the cosmopolitan and the international is not as clear-cut as is often presumed. The distinction between a "bourgeois" cosmopolitanism and a "proletarian" internationalism will be challenged throughout Tian Han's intellectual journeys as detailed in the following chapters.

2. Penato Poggioli, *The Theory of the Avant-Garde*, translated from the Italian by Gerald Fitzgerald (Cambridge, MA: Belknap Press of Harvard University Press, 1968); Peter Bürger, *Theory of the Avant-Garde*, translated from the German by Michael Shaw, foreword by Jochen Schulte-Sasse (Minneapolis: University of Minnesota Press, 1984).

3. Mary Gluck, *Popular Bohemia: Modernism and Urban Culture in Nineteenth-Century Paris* (Cambridge, MA: Harvard University Press, 2005). For a Chinese translation, see *Liuxing de boshi miya: Shijiu shiji Bali de xiandai zhuyi yu dushi wenhua*, translated with an introduction by Liang Luo (Hefei: Anhui jiaoyu chubanshe, 2009).

4. Karen Smith's *Nine Lives: The Birth of Avant-Garde Art in New China*, updated ed. (Hong Kong: Timezone8, 2008) is a recent example.

5. On *xianfeng*, see Xun Yue, "Hanji: Gaozu ji'er," in *Hanyu dacidian*, CD 2.0 version (Hong Kong: Shangwu yinshuguan, 2002).

6. See Tian Han's letter to Zuo Shunsheng, May 12, 1919, in *Tian Han quanji* (Shijiazhuang: Huashan wenyi chubanshe, 2000), vol. 20, 4.

7. On *qianwei*, see "Xu wenxian tongkao, bing wu," in *Hanyu dacidian*, CD 2.0 version (Hong Kong: Shangwu yinshuguan, 2002).

8. See Tian Han, "Xiju yu shehui," in *Jukan*, a literary supplement of *Beiping chenbao*, no. 263 (January 19, 1936), in *Tian Han quanji*, vol. 15, 281.

9. See Haun Saussy, "Mei Lanfang in Moscow, 1935: Familiar, Unfamiliar, Defamiliar," in "Modernisms' Chinas," edited by Eric Hayot, special issue, *Modern Chinese Literature and Culture*, vol. 18, no. 1 (Spring 2006), 14.

10. Ibid., 8–29, especially 23.

11. Pierre Bourdieu locates this process in the socialization of the flesh, and *embodiment* became a keyword in such discussions. See Pierre Bourdieu, *The Logic*

of Practice, translated from the French by Richard Nice (Stanford, CA: Stanford University Press, 1990).

12. See Ban Wang, *The Sublime Figure of History: Aesthetics and Politics in Twentieth-Century China* (Stanford, CA: Stanford University Press, 1997).

13. Sascha Bru, "The Phantom League: The Centennial Debate on the Avant-Garde and Politics," in *The Invention of Politics in the European Avant-Garde (1906–1940)*, edited by Sascha Bru and Gunther Martens (Amsterdam and New York: Rodopi, 2006).

14. See Sascha Bru's discussion in ibid., 21.

15. David Porter, "China Is Not a Foreign Country: The Promises and Perils of Cross-Cultural Comparison," in "China," special issue, *Michigan Quarterly Review*, vol. 47, no. 2 (Spring 2008).

16. Chen Sihe, "Lun Wusi xinwenxue yundong de xianfengxing," *Fudan xuebao* (social science edition), no. 6 (2005), 1–17; Chen Sihe, "Xianfeng yu changtai: Xiandai wenxueshi de liangzhong jiben xingtai," *Wenyi zhengming*, no. 3 (2007), 59–68; Tang Xiaobing, "Women zenyang xiangxiang lishi (dai daoyan)," *Zai jiedu: Dazhong wenyi yu yishi xingtai*, rev. ed. (Beijing: Beijing daxue chubanshe, 2007), 1-17; Xiaobing Tang, *The Origins of the Chinese Avant-Garde: The Modern Woodcut Movement* (Berkeley: University of California Press, 2007).

17. André Stufkens, "Lust for Life: An Introduction to Ivens and the 20th Century," in *Cinema without Borders* (Nijmegen, the Netherlands: European Foundation Joris Ivens, 2002), 14.

18. Georg Lukács, *History and Class Consciousness: Studies in Marxist Dialectics* (Cambridge, MA: MIT Press, 1972), xxvii.

19. Arif Dirlik, *The Origins of Chinese Communism* (New York: Oxford University Press, 1989), 8, 29.

20. For more on Tian Han's association with his fellow Hunanese writers and activists in Japan, see Li Yuejin, "Hunan xiandai liuri zuojiaqun jiqi tedian," *Zhongguo wenxue yanjiu*, vol. 4 (2005), 66–70. Zhou Fohai was a founding member of the Communist Party but later was treated as a "traitor" because of his high-profile position in the Wang Jingwei government in Nanjing during the Second Sino-Japanese War. He was sentenced to death (commuted to life in prison) after the fall of the Nanjing government in 1945 and died in prison in Nanjing in 1948. For more on Zhou Fohai, see Song Jiayang and Jin Mingquan, "Zhou Enlai yu Zhou Fohai tongqi shixue Heshang zhao (Kawakami Hajime) de chayi," *Chongqing daxue xuebao* (social science edition), vol. 12, no. 2 (2006), 79–81.

21. Pan Hannian, for his Communist underground activities in the Wang Jingwei government during the Second Sino-Japanese War, was singled out in 1955 as a *neijian* (internal traitor) and was sentenced to life in prison in 1976. Pan died in 1977, and his name would only be cleared in 1982. For more on Pan Hannian, see

Yin Qi, *Pan Hannian de qingbao shengya* (Beijing: Renmin chubanshe, 1996). Zeng Xubai, the son of Zeng Pu, was a key figure in the two Zengs' Francophile salon located in the Shanghai French concession. Tian Han associated with the Francophiles, including Fu Yanchang and Zhang Ruogu, as he was himself a Francophile in Tokyo and continued to imagine Paris as a cultural capital while in Shanghai. See Liang Luo, "Reality Supplements Fantasy: Imagining Paris in a Shanghai Salon," paper presented at the Seventeenth Congress of the International Comparative Literature Association, Hong Kong, August 10, 2004.

22. "Popular, adj. and n.," *Oxford English Dictionary,* 3rd ed., December 2006, online version, December 2011, http://www.oed.com.ezproxy.uky.edu/view/Entry/147908 (accessed March 8, 2012). An entry for this word was first included in the *New English Dictionary* in 1907.

23. Tao Dongfeng, "Liuxing wenhua huhuan xin de yanjiu fanshi," *Wenyi yanjiu,* no. 5 (2001), 10–14; Tao Dongfeng, "Yanjiu dazhong wenhua yu xiaofei zhuyi de sanzhong fanshi jiqi xifang ziyuan," *Hebei xuekan,* vol. 24, no. 5 (Spring 2004), 86–92.

24. David Johnson, "Communication, Class, and Consciousness in Late Imperial China," in *Popular Culture in Late Imperial China,* edited by David Johnson, Andrew J. Nathan, and Evelyn S. Rawski (Berkeley: University of California Press, 1985), quoted at 47; Peter Burke, *Popular Culture in Early Modern Europe,* 3rd rev. ed. (Farnham and Burlington: Ashgate, 2009); George Rudé, *Ideology and Popular Protest,* with a new foreword and updated bibliography by Harvey J. Kaye (Chapel Hill: University of North Carolina Press, 1995).

25. Leo Ou-fan Lee and Andrew J. Nathan, "The Beginning of Mass Culture: Journalism and Fiction in the Late Ch'ing and Beyond," in *Popular Culture in Late Imperial China,* edited by David Johnson, Andrew J. Nathan, and Evelyn S. Rawski (Berkeley: University of California Press, 1985), 360–95.

26. Chang-tai Hung, *War and Popular Culture: Resistance in Modern China, 1937–1945* (Berkeley: University of California Press, 1994), 9.

27. Barbara Mittler, "Popular Propaganda? Art and Culture in Revolutionary China," *Proceedings of the American Philosophical Society,* vol. 152, no. 4 (December 2008), 466–89. Also see a relevant earlier study by Marja Kaikkonen, *Laughable Propaganda: Modern Xiangsheng as Didactic Entertainment* (Stockholm: Institute of Oriental Languages, Stockholm University, 1990).

28. "Propaganda, n.," *Oxford English Dictionary,* 3rd ed., June 2007, online version, December 2011, http://www.oed.com.ezproxy.uky.edu/view/Entry/152605 (accessed March 8, 2012);. An entry for this word was first included in the *New English Dictionary* in 1908.

29. *Xuanbu chuanda* (to announce and to spread), as in *xuanchuan zhaozhi* (announcing an imperial edict), in "Biography of Ma Zhong, Record of Shu," in

*Sanguo zhi (*Record of the Three Kingdoms). See the first entry for *xuanchuan* in *Hanyu dacidian*, CD 2.0 version (Hong Kong: Shangwu yinshuguan, 2002).

30. Zhou Dunyi, *Zhouzi tongshu* [eleventh century], with guided reading by Xu Hongxing (Shanghai: Shanghai guji chubanshe, 2000).

31. Poggioli, *The Theory of the Avant-Garde.*

32. See Randy Barbaba Kaplan, "The Pre-Leftist One-Act Dramas of Tian Han (1898–1968)" (PhD diss., Ohio State University, 1986); Liang Luo, "The Theatrics of Revolution: Tian Han (1898–1968) and the Cultural Politics of Performance in Modern China" (PhD diss., Harvard University, 2006).

33. See Xiaomei Chen, "Tian Han and the *Nanguo* Phenomenon: Networking the Personal, Communal, and Cultural," in *Literary Societies of Republican China*, edited by Kirk A. Denton and Michel Hockx (Lanham, MD: Lexington Books, 2008); Xiaomei Chen, "Reflections on the Legacy of Tian Han: 'Proletarian Modernism' and Its Traditional Roots," *Modern Chinese Literature and Culture*, vol. 18, no. 1 (Spring 2006), 155–215; Dong Jian, *Tian Han zhuan* (Beijing: Shiyue wenyi chubanshe, 1998); Kotani Ichirō, "Nichū gindai bungaku kōryūshi no naka ni okeru Den Kan: Den Kan to onaji jidai nihonjin saka no ōrai," *Chūgoku bunka: Kenkyū to kyōiku*, vol. 55 (1997); and Rudolf G. Wagner, *The Contemporary Chinese Historical Drama: Four Studies* (Berkeley: University of California Press, 1990).

34. Andreas Huyssen, "The Hidden Dialectic: Avantgarde-Technology-Mass Culture," in *After the Great Divide: Modernism, Mass Culture, Postmodernism* (Bloomington: Indiana University Press, 1986); Malte Hagener, *Moving Forward, Looking Back: The European Avant-Garde and the Invention of Film Culture, 1919–1939* (Amsterdam: Amsterdam University Press, 2007); Sascha Bru and Gunther Martens, eds., *The Invention of Politics in the European Avant-Garde (1906–1940)* (Amsterdam and New York: Rodopi, 2006).

35. For a wonderful analysis of the dialectics between the country and the city in English literature, see Raymond Williams, *The Country and the City* (New York: Oxford University Press, 1973).

36. Charles Russel, *Poets, Prophets, and Revolutionaries: The Literary Avant-Garde from Rimbaud to Postmodernism* (New York: Oxford University Press, 1985), 25.

37. Andreas Kalyvas, *Democracy and the Politics of the Extraordinary: Max Weber, Carl Schmitt, and Hannah Arendt* (Cambridge: Cambridge University Press, 2008), 297.

38. See Geremie R. Barmé, *An Artistic Exile: A Life of Feng Zikai (1898–1975)* (Berkeley: University of California Press, 2002); Theodore Huters, *Bringing the World Home: Appropriating the West in Late Qing and Early Republican China* (Honolulu: University of Hawai'i Press, 2005); Erez Malena, *The Wilsonian Moment: Self-Determination and the International Origins of Anticolonial Nationalism* (New

York: Oxford University Press, 2007); Alexander C. Y. Huang, *Chinese Shakespeares: Two Centuries of Cultural Exchanges* (New York: Columbia University Press, 2009); and Karen Laura Thornbor, *Empire of Texts in Motion: Chinese, Korean, and Taiwanese Transculturations of Japanese Literature* (Cambridge, MA: Harvard University Asia Center, 2009).

39. On March 13–14, 1965, when writing self-criticism became a daily routine and only a few years before his death, Tian Han reread Tanizaki Jun'ichirō's *Chijin no ai* and criticized Tanizaki's portrayal of the male protagonist as he was conquered by the beauty of the femme fatale, Naomi, and tolerated all her mistakes. The very fact, however, that Tian Han revisited Tanizaki and the image of Naomi in 1965 and recorded it in his dairy attests to the central importance and remarkable endurance of this Japanese connection. See Tian Han, "1965 nian riji," in *Tian Han quanji*, vol. 20, 344–45.

40. Ban Wang, *The Sublime Figure of History: Aesthetics and Politics in Twentieth-Century China* (Stanford, CA: Stanford University Press, 1997); Kirk A. Denton, *The Problematic of Self in Modern Chinese Literature: Hu Feng and Lu Ling* (Stanford, CA: Stanford University Press, 1998); Peter Button, *Configurations of the Real in Chinese Literary and Aesthetic Modernity* (Leiden: Brill, 2009).

41. See Chen Sihe, "Lun Wusi xinwenxue yundong de xianfengxing"; Chen Sihe, "Xianfeng yu changtai"; Xiaobing Tang, *The Origins of the Chinese Avant-Garde;* and Gao Minglu, *Total Modernity and the Avant-Garde in Twentieth-Century Chinese Art* (Cambridge, MA: MIT Press, 2011).

42. Ono, Shinji, *Goshi undō zai Nihon* (Tokyo: Kyūko Shoin, 2003).

43. See David Der-wei Wang, *The Monster That Is History: History, Violence, and Fictional Writing in Twentieth-Century China* (Berkeley: University of California Press, 2004); Leo Ou-fan Lee, *Shanghai Modern: The Flowering of a New Urban Culture in China, 1930–1945* (Cambridge, MA: Harvard University Press, 1999); and Michel Hockx, *Questions of Style: Literary Societies and Literary Journals in Modern China, 1911–1937* (Leiden: Brill, 2003).

44. Tian Han, "Nü yu she" (1927), in *Tian Han sanwen ji* (Shanghai: Jindai Shudian, 1936).

45. Mao Zedong, "On New Democracy," in *Mao Zedong xuanji* (Beijing: Renmin chubanshe, 1964). Turning the "new democratic" rhetoric on its head, Tian Han proposed to develop and advocate national, scientific, and democratic (for the widest number of people, i.e., popular) content, and he used that as criteria in striving for a new democratic theater, *minzu gewuju*, or "national musical". See Tian Han, "Zenyang zuo xigai gongzuo?–gei Zhou Yang tongzhi de shi feng xin," in *Tian Han quanji*, vol. 17, 99.

46. See Wang Hui, *The Politics of Imagining Asia*, edited by Theodore Huters

(Cambridge, MA: Harvard University Press, 2011); and He Guimei, *"Xin qimeng" zhishi dang'an: 80 niandai Zhongguo wenhua yanjiu* (Beijing: Beijing daxue chubanshe, 2010).

47. Zhong Xueping, *Mainstream Culture Refocused: Television Drama, Society, and the Production of Meaning in Reform-Era China* (Honolulu: University of Hawai'i Press, 2010).

Chapter 1

1. Tian Han, *Qiangwei zhilu* (Shanghai: Taidong tushuju, 1922), 2; all translations, except where otherwise noted, are my own.

2. Bruce Brooks Pfeiffer, *Frank Lloyd Wright, 1867–1959: Building for Democracy* (Cologne: Taschen, 2004).

3. A strikingly similar passage dealing with the transition from natural to man-made light can be found at the opening of Mao Dun's *Ziye* (Midnight), where the working together of light and music again foster a distinctively urban milieu, that of Shanghai in the early 1930s. A key difference between Mao Dun's 1933 portrayal of Shanghai and Tian Han's 1921 reflection on Tokyo, however, lies in Mao Dun's critical view of the darkness of the metropolis, which will be echoed by Tian Han in the next chapter. See Mao Dun, *Ziye* (Beijing: renmin wenxue chubanshe, [1933] 1960), 1.

4. Tian Han, "Eguo jinci zhi geming yu pinfu wenti," *Shenzhou xuecong*, no. 1 (September 20, 1917).

5. Tian Han, "Xin Jiaozi," *Changsha ribao*, March 14–16, 1913; Han'er (Tian Han), "Xin Taohua Shan," *Shibao* (Shanghai), May 26, 1915.

6. Li Yongchun, *"Shaonian zhongguo" yu wusi shiqi shehui sichao* (Changsha: Hunan renmin chubanshe, 2005); Henry DeWitt Smith II, *Japan's First Student Radicals* (Cambridge, MA: Harvard University Press, 1972); Matsuo Takayoshi, "Kosumo kurabu shōshi," *Kyoto Nōtorudamu Joshi Daigaku kenkyū kiyō*, no. 26 (March 2000).

7. Edward Seidensticker, *Low City, High City: Tokyo from Edo to the Earthquake: How the Shogun's Ancient Capital Became a Great Modern City, 1867–1923* (New York: Alfred A. Knopf, 1983), 259; Henry D. Smith, "Tokyo as an Idea: An Exploration of Japanese Urban Thought up to 1945," *Journal of Japanese Studies*, vol. 4, no. 1 (1978): 45–80; Fujii Shōzō, *Erosenko no toshi monogatari: 1920 nendai Tokyo, Shanhai, Pekin* (Tokyo: Misuzu Shobō, 1989).

8. Tian Han, *Sanye ji* (Shanghai: Yadong tushuguan, 1920); Tian Han, *Qiangwei zhilu* (Shanghai: Taidong tushuju, 1922), in *Tian Han quanji*, vol. 20, 240–42.

9. Seidensticker, *Low City, High City*, 283–84.

10. Departing from previous scholarship, a recent treatment of *Chuangzao she*

highlights Tian Han's activist role in it, see Xiaobing Tang, with Michel Hockx, "The Creation Society (1921–1930)," in *Literary Societies of Republican China,* edited by Kirk A. Denton and Michel Hockx (Lanham, MD: Lexington Books, 2008).

11. Kotani Ichirō and Liu Ping, eds., *Tian Han zai Riben* (Beijing: Renmin wenxue chubanshe, 1997), is a notable exception.

12. Tian Han, "*Kafeidian zhi yiye,*" *Chuangzao jikan,* vol. 1, no. 1 (May 1922).

13. Guo Moruo, trans., *Shaonian weite zhi fannao, 10th ed.* (Shanghai: Taidong tushuju, 1926); Guo Moruo, trans., *Fushide* (Shanghai: Chuangzaoshe chubanshe, 1928).

14. Tian Han, "Preface to *Lingguang*: A Letter to Mr. Li Jiannong," *Taiping yang,* vol. 2, no. 9 (January 1921). Solecisms are in the original.

15. Hong Shen's play *The Wedded Husband,* performed at the Ohio State University in English in 1919, provides an intereting contemporary case of representing China in the diaspora. I thank Professor Kirk A. Denton for inviting me to contribute to the Hong Shen Symposium and for the opportunity to watch a revival of the play directed by Siyuan Liu and produced by Man He at the Ohio State University from November 17 to 18, 2013. *Huaju* (spoken drama) is a term allegedly invented as late as 1928 by a group of Chinese playwrights, including Hong Shen and Tian Han, to designate the "spoken" quality of Western-style drama as practiced in China then and to differentiate it from traditional Chinese theatre, which was mostly "sung." The first performance of spoken drama in Chinese was said to be a performance of the third act of *La Dame aux camélias* by Alexandre Dumas fils and a short adaptation of *Uncle Tom's Cabin,* by Chunliu she (Spring Willow Society), in Tokyo in 1907. For more on Chunliu she, see Iizuka Yutori et al., *Bunmeigi kenkyū no genzai: Shunryūsha hyakunen kinen kokusai shinpojūmu ronbunshū* (Tokyo: Tōhō Shoten, 2009).

16. Wang Benchao, *Ershi shiji zhongguo wenxue yu jidujiao wenhua* (Hefei: Anhui jiaoyu chubanshe, 2000), 30.

17. Gaimushō gaikō kiroku, "Ryūni Shina gakusei saikin ni okeru shisō oyobi dōsei ni kansuru ken," Japanese Foreign Ministry Office, Diplomatic Archives, document no. 20-1770, 1921, unpaginated; "Zairyū Shinajin to honpō tokubetsu yō-shisatsunin no kankei," in *Zairyū gaikokujin gaikyō,* marked as "top secret," Japanese Foreign Ministry Office, Diplomatic Archives, document no. 4-2-2, 1921, 73–75; "Shina kankei jimu gaiyō," Japanese Foreign Ministry Office, Diplomatic Archives, document no. 3-10-5-17-2, 1922, 22–25.

18. Leo Ou-fan Lee, *The Romantic Generation of Modern Chinese Writers* (Cambridge, MA: Harvard University Press, 1973); Jianmei Liu, *Revolution Plus Love: Literary History, Women's Bodies, and Thematic Repetition in Twentieth-Century Chinese Fiction* (Honolulu: University of Hawai'i Press, 2003); Haiyan Lee, *Revolution of the Heart: A Genealogy of Love in China, 1900–1950* (Stanford, CA: Stanford University Press, 2007).

19. An almost identical scene, except for the sound of the church bell, opens the 1935 film *Fengyun ernü* (Lovers in Troubled Times), written by Tian Han, when the camera pans into the window of a Western-style villa showing a "femme fatale" playing piano in her sitting room. For a detailed analysis of the opening scene of the film, see Laikwan Pang, *Building a New China in Cinema: The Chinese Left-Wing Cinema Movement, 1932–1937* (Lanham, MD: Rowman & Littlefield, 2002), 96.

20. *Zhongxi hebi* can also be taken as a key phrase summarizing Tian Han's spiritual, aesthetic, and political philosophy at the time.

21. Phrases such as "Good evening" and "Sit down, please" were inserted in their English originals in the Chinese text. See Tian Han, *Lingguang,* in *Taiping yang,* vol. 2, no. 9 (January 1921), 6.

22. Guo Moruo translated *Faust* into Chinese in 1920, and Tian Han quoted Guo's translation in "Spiritual Light." Guo's translation, however, was not published until 1928. See Guo Moruo, *Fushide.*

23. Marshall Berman, *All That Is Solid Melts into Air: The Experience of Modernity* (New York: Penguin Books, 1988), 44.

24. Henrik Ibsen, *Et dukkehjem* ("A Doll's House," 1879); August Strindberg, *Ett drömspel* ("A Dream Play," 1901), Tian Han, *Lingguang* ("Spiritual Light," 1920–21).

25. See Tian Han, *Lingguang,* in *Taiping yang,* vol. 2, no. 9 (January 1921), 9; and Johann Wolfgang von Goethe, *Faust* (part I), New German-English ed., translated by Peter Salm (New York: Bantam Books, 1985), 70–71.

26. See Guo Moruo, *Nüshen* (Shanghai: Taidong tushuju, 1921).

27. See Tian Han, *Lingguang,* in *Taiping yang,* vol. 2, no. 9 (January 1921).

28. In the original edition published in *Taiping yang* in 1921, Tian Han used the two Chinese terms interchangeably. Later editions only use *leichuan.* It may be a technical mistake resulting from insufficient editorial support in early magazine publishing. See Tian Han, *Lingguang,* in *Taiping yang,* vol. 2, no. 9 (January 1921), 20, 25. "River of tears" may also be a reference to *Henhai* (The Sea of Regret), a melodramatic story by Wu Jianren written around the turn of the twentieth century. It was quoted in *Lingguang* as a representative of *romance* as against officially sanctioned *history.*

29. See Tian Han, "Chile 'zhiguo' yihou de hua," in *Shaonian shijie,* vol. 1, no. 8 (August 1, 1920).

30. Although socialist feminism can be readily identified with the avant-garde here, it appeared to many to have been "tainted" by the Communist regime in the 1950s, and Tian's avant-gardism had to take refuge in the folk and the fantastic in the image of the White Snake in the People's Republic.

31. See Lu Xun, "Zixu," in *Nahan* (Beijing: Xinchao she, 1923).

32. Tian Han, *Lingguang,* in *Taiping yang,* vol. 2, no. 9 (January 1921), 21. Lu Xun's preface to his first short story collection, *Nahan* (Call to Arms), where he

recounts his decision to give up medicine for literature in order to save the soul rather than the body of the Chinese people after watching a slide show in Japan, has been canonized in modern Chinese literary history as a ritualistic moment in the birth of modern Chinese literature. For discussions of the "slide incident" from a range of perspectives, see Lee Ou-fan Lee, *Voices from the Iron House: A Study of Lu Xun* (Bloomington: Indiana University Press, 1987), 17–19; Lydia Liu, *Translingual Practice: Literature, National Culture, and Translated Modernity—China, 1900–1937* (Stanford, CA: Stanford University Press, 1995), 62, 71; Yomi Braester, *Witness against History: Literature, Film, and Public Discourse in Twentieth Century China* (Stanford, CA: Stanford University Press, 2003), 34–40; and Eileen J. Cheng, "Recycling the Scholar-Beauty Narrative: Lu Xun on Love in an Age of Mechanical Reproductions," *Modern Chinese Literature and Culture*, vol. 18, no. 2 (Fall 2006), 7–8.

33. See Tian Han, *Lingguang*, in *Taiping yang*, vol. 2, no. 9 (January 1921). Meili's attitude foreshadows the coming together of romance and a higher level of reality in Tian Han's and Joris Ivens's works in the 1950s.

34. Ellen Key considered love a religion and treated love (not marriage) as the foundation for the morality of sex. See Honma Hisao, "Xing de daode zhi xin qingxiang," a Japanese essay introducing Ellen Key's theory of love and marriage, quoted in Chinese translation in Tian Han, "Mimi lian'ai yu gongkai lian'ai," *Shaonian zhongguo*, vol. 1, no. 2 (August 15, 1919).

35. See Tian Han, *Lingguang*, in *Taiping yang*, vol. 2, no. 9 (January 1921), 21. Here Tian Han based his rendering of Ibsen's extremely popular play on Hu Shi's Chinese translation. For more on the Nora trope in modern China and Tian Han's personal encounter with it, see Rachel Hsu, *"Nuola" zai Zhongguo: Xin nüxing xingxiang de suzao jiqi yanbian, 1900s-1930s* (Taipei: National Chengchi University Press, 2003); and Liang Luo, "Modern Girl, Modern Men, and the Politics of Androgyny in Modern China," *Michigan Quarterly Review*, vol. 47, no. 2 (Spring 2008), 290, 306, n23.

36. Tian Han mentioned watching a play entitled *Shenzhu zhinü* (The Daughter of Gods) as among one of his first encounters with modern drama performances on the Tokyo stage in 1918. Although Magda was mentioned as the female protagonist of the play, suggesting it may be an adaptation of Hermann Sudermann's *Magda*, it also brought to mind the leading female role of Agnes in Strindberg's *A Dream Play* as the daughter of Gods. Both plays were adapted and performed in Japanese on Tokyo stages at the time.

37. August Strindberg, *Ett drömspel* (Stockholm: Albert Booniers Förlag, [1901] 1917), 60.

38. August Strindberg, *Ett drömspel*, in *Plays by August Strindberg*, translated with an introduction by Edwin Bjorkman (London: Duckworth, 1913), 80.

39. Tian Han, "Chile 'zhiguo' zhihou de hua," *Shaonian shijie,* vol. 1, no. 8 (August 1920), in *Tian Han quanji,* vol. 14.

40. Tian Han, "Chile 'zhiguo' zhihou de hua," in *Tian Han quanji,* vol. 14, 197.

41. Tian Han, "Disi jieji de furen yundong," *Shaonian zhongguo,* vol. 1, no. 4 (October 15, 1919), in *Tian Han quanji,* vol. 18, 269–71.

42. Stephen A. Kent, "Weber, Goethe, and the Nietzschean Allusion: Capturing the Source of the 'Iron Cage' Metaphor," *Sociological Analysis,* vol. 44, no. 4 (1983), 302–3.

43. Berman, *All That Is Solid Melts into Air,* 118.

44. Karl Marx, *Capital: A Critique of Political Economy,* vol. 1, part II: *The Process of Capitalist Production as a Whole,* edited by Friedrich Engels (New York: Cosimo, Inc., 2007), 650.

45. Walter Benjamin, "Theses on the Philosophy of History," in *Illuminations: Essays and Reflections,* edited and with an introduction by Hannah Arendt, translated by Harry Zohn (New York: Harcourt, Brace & World, 1968).

46. Marcus Hitch, *Goethe's Faust: A Fragment of Socialist Criticism* (Chicago: Charles H. Kerr, 1908), 13–14; C. T. Hsia, *C. T. Hsia on Chinese Literature* (New York: Columbia University Press, 2004), 121–22.

47. See the discussion in Berman, *All That Is Solid Melts into Air,* 72.

48. See Berman's treatment of the image of the halo in Marx in "The Loss of a Halo," in *All That Is Solid Melts into Air.*

49. *Third World* is a term coined during the Cold War to refer to countries that were unaligned with either the communist camp (the Soviet Union) or the capitalist bloc (the United States). However, the Chinese Communist leader Mao Zedong defined *Third World* differently. He considered China part of the Third World while in the West China is often considered as having been part of the Soviet camp. China participated in the first large-scale Asian-African conference in 1955 in Bandung, Indonesia, where the nonalignment movement was consolidated.

50. Leo Ou-fan Lee, *The Romantic Generation of Modern Chinese Writers* (Cambridge, MA: Harvard University Press, 1973), 279–93.

51. Tian Han, Guo Moruo, and Zong Baihua, *Sanye ji* (Kleeblatt) (Shanghai: Taidong tushuju, 1920).

52. For a recent study on Zong Baihua, see Tang Yonghua, *Zong Baihua yu "Zhongguo meixue" de kunjing: Yige fansixing de kaocha* (Beijing: Beijing University Press, 2010).

53. Berman, *All That Is Solid Melts into Air,* 116–18.

54. The protest movements worldwide since the 1960s can be understood as the brainchild of the interwar international avant-garde. Their combination of spiritual, artistic, lifestyle, and political experimentation was an inheritance from the

early twentieth century revived under postmodern, postsocialist, and postcolonial conditions.

55. See a relevant recent study, Karen Laura Thornber, *Empire of Texts in Motion: Chinese, Korean, and Taiwanese Transculturations of Japanese Literature* (Cambridge, MA: Harvard University Asia Center, 2009).

56. For more on the cultural background and contemporary representation of Edo-Tokyo, see Seidensticker, *Low City, High City;* Theodore C. Bestor, *Neighborhood Tokyo* (Stanford, CA: Stanford University Press, 1989); Jinnai Hidenobu, *Tokyo: A Spatial Anthropology,* translated by Kimiko Nishimura (Berkeley: University of California Press, 1995); and Donald Richie, *Tokyo: A View of the City* (London: Reaktion Books, 1999).

57. Joshua Fogel's discussion of the "Sinosphere" as a China-centered regional order in premodern East Asia is instructive here. See his *Articulating the Sinosphere: Sino-Japanese Relations in Space and Time* (Cambridge, MA: Harvard University Press, 2009).

58. See Andrew Gordon, *A Modern History of Japan: From Tokugawa Times to the Present* (New York: Oxford University Press, 2003).

59. Ibid, 168.

60. See Erez Manela, *The Wilsonian Moment: Self-Determination and the International Origins of Anticolonial Nationalism* (New York: Oxford University Press, 2007).

61. See "Mei zongtong zhi yihe tiaojian," *Shibao* (Shanghai), January 11, 1918, 2.

62. Kwŏn was regarded as "a Korean of Chinese nationality" in Ono Shinji's book on the May Fourth movement in Japan. See Ono Shinji, *Goshi undō zai Nihon* (Tokyo: Kyūko Shoin, 2003). As far as I know, there is no biographical information on him available in either Korean or English. At an Asian Modernities seminar at the University of Kansas, Professor Kyoim Yun suggested that Kwŏn Hŭi-guk (instead of Kwŏn Hŏi-guk) might be the correct spelling of his name. The phenomenon of "Sinicized" Koreans fighting Japanese colonialism in Tokyo while in close contact with Japanese and Chinese radicals deserves a separate study.

63. "Zairyū gaikokujin gaikyō," December 1921, marked as "top secret," Japanese Foreign Ministry Office, Diplomatic Archives, document no. 4-2-2, 73–75. The Cosmo Club was a manifestation of the influence of late Meiji and early Taishō anarchism in Japan, which climaxed in "the great treason affair" of Kōtoku Shūsui. See Ira L. Plotkin, *Anarchism in Japan: A Study of the Great Treason Affair, 1910–1911* (Lewiston, NY: Edwin Mellen Press, 1990). For an informative account of the Cosmo Club and Tian Han's involvement with it, see Matsuo Takayoshi, "Kosumo kurabu shōshi," *Kyōto Nōtorudamu Joshi Daigaku kenkyu kiyō,* no. 26 (March 2000); and Ono Shinji, *Goshi undō zai Nihon,* 250.

64. Ono Shinji, *Goshi undō zai Nihon,* 250; "Zairyū gaigokujin gaikyō," 73–75.

65. "Zairyū gaigokujin gaikyō," 73–75.

66. See Tian Han, "Pingmin shiren huiteman de bainianji," *Shaonian zhongguo,* vol. 1, no. 1 (July 15, 1919).

67. See Tian Han's letter to Zuo Shunsheng, May 12, 1919, in *Tian Han quanji,* vol. 20, 4. For more on Tian's association with Zuo, see Zuo Shunsheng, "Tantan wo suo renshi de jige gongchan dangren: Zhang Wentian, Tian Han, Li Da, ji qita," in *Zhengxin xinwenbao* (Taipei, July 23, 1966).

68. See Tian Han's letter to Zuo Shunsheng, May 12, 1919, in *Tian Han quanji,* vol. 20, 7.

69. Ibid.

70. It is still relevant today with regard to China's rise as a leading power of the twenty-first century and the competing cultural imperialisms exhibited by the United States and China.

71. For more on Saint Simonian socialism and its connection to feminism and romanticism, a topic very much at the center of Tian Han's Tokyo experiments, see Claire Goldberg Moses and Leslie Wahl Rabine, *Feminism, Socialism, and French Romanticism* (Bloomington: Indiana University Press, 1993).

72. See Fredrik Fällman, *Salvation and Modernity: Intellectuals and Faith in Contemporary China* (Lanham, MD: University Press of America, 2008), 4.

73. See Ban Wang, "Discovering Enlightenment in Chinese History: *The Rise of Modern Chinese Thought,* by Wang Hui," *boundary 2,* vol. 34, no. 2 (2007), 217–38.

74. "Datongxue," *Wanguo gongbao,* nos. 121–24 (February–April 1899).

75. Fällman, *Salvation and Modernity,* 16.

76. See Bing Xin, *Fanxing* (Shanghai: Shangwu yinshuguan, 1933).

77. See the website of World Student Christian Federation, http://www.wscf-global.org/WSCFGlobalMeetings.php (accessed October 28, 2010).

78. See the discussion in Wang Benchao, *Ershi shiji zhongguo wenxue yu jidujiao wenhua* (Hefei: Anhui jiaoyu chubanshe, 2000), 121.

79. See the discussion of the five professors in Geremie R. Barmé, *An Artistic Exile: A Life of Feng Zikai (1898–1975)* (Berkeley: University of California Press, 2002), 9.

80. See Konishi Sho, "Translation and Conversion beyond Western Modernity: Tolstoian Religion in Meiji Japan," in *Converting Cultures: Religion, Ideology, and Transformations of Modernity,* edited by Dennis Washburn and A. Kevin Reinhart (Leiden: Brill, 2007), 244–55.

81. See Tian Han, *Qiangwei zhilu,* in *Tian Han quanji,* vol. 20, 264.

82. Tian Han, "Shiren yu laodong wenti," *Shaonian zhongguo,* vol. 1, no. 8 (1920), 1–36, and vol. 1, no. 9 (1920), 15–104, in *Tian Han quanji,* vol. 14 (see page 116 in particular).

83. For more on the Boxer Uprising, see Paul A. Cohen, *History in Three Keys: The Boxers as Event, Experience, and Myth* (New York: Columbia University Press, 199); and Anthony E. Clark, *China's Saints: Catholic Martyrdom during the Qing (1644–1911)* (Bethlehem, PA: Lehigh University Press and Lanham, MD: Rowman & Littlefield, 2011).

84. See Yoshiko Ashiwa and David L. Wank, eds., *Making Religion, Making the State: The Politics of Religion in Modern China* (Stanford, CA: Stanford University Press, 2009), 3; and Thomas David DuBois, *Religion and the Making of Modern East Asia* (Cambridge: Cambridge University Press, 2011).

85. See Rebecca Nedostup, "Civic Faith and Hybrid Ritual in Nationalist China," in *Converting Cultures: Religion, Ideology, and Transformations of Modernity,* edited by Dennis Washburn and A. Kevin Reinhart (Leiden: Brill, 2007), 31.

86. See Tian Han, *Qiangwei zhilu* (Shanghai: Taidong tushuju, 1922); and Dong Jian, *Tian Han zhuan* (Beijing: Shiyue wenyi chubanshe, 1996), 101.

87. There is a scarcity of biographical information on Zhang Difei. We only know him through Mao Zedong's criticism of him in 1943: "I have to question the KMT members, did the world and China only witness the 'bankruptcy' of Marx-Leninism, while the other 'isms' were all good? How about Wang Jingwei's three-people-ism that I mentioned before? How about Hitler, Mussolini, and Tojo Hideki's fascism? How about Zhang Difei's Trotskyism?" Mao Zedong, "Zhiwen Guomindang," *Jiefang ribao* (Yan'an), July 12, 1943. For Mao, Zhang Difei the Trotskyist was as bad as or worse than Wang Jingwei and the fascists in the context of 1943. In a telegram sent on July 9, 1943, from Yan'an, Zhang Difei was described as a "leading anti-CCP secret agent, head of the educational bureau in Xi'an, and a famous Trotskyist traitor." Anon., "Yan'an minzhong kangzhan liuzhounian jinian dahui guanyu huyu tuanjie fandui neizhan tongdian," *Jiefang ribao* (Yan'an), July 10, 1943.

88. For more on Yoshino Sakuzō, see Tetsuo Najita, "Some Reflections on Idealism in the Political Thought of Yoshino Sakuzō," in *Japan in Crisis: Essays on Taishō Democracy,* edited by Bernard S. Silberman and H. D. Harootunian (Princeton, NJ: Princeton University Press, 1974); and Peter Duus, "Yoshino Sakuzō, The Christian as Political Critic," *Journal of Japanese Studies,* vol. 4, no. 2 (Summer 1978), 301–26. For Shinjinkai, see Henry DeWitt Smith, *Japan's First Student Radicals* (Cambridge, MA: Harvard University Press, 1972).

89. Shinjinkai's official journal changed its name four times between 1918 and 1922: it was first published as *Demokurashii* (Democracy), vol. 1, nos. 1–8 (March–December 1919); then was changed to *Senku* (Pioneer), from February 1920 to August 1920; then was changed again to *Dōhō* (Brothers), from October 1920 to May 1921; and finally was changed to *Narōdo* (Narod, Russian for "the people"), from July 1921 to April 1922. The changing names of Shinjinkai's official journal reflect its vibrant intellectual atmosphere, as well as the constant shift of its political focus. Tian Han's

interactions with Shinjinkai spanned the publication of all four journals. See Hōsei Daigaku Ōhara Shakai Mondai Kenkyūjo, ed., *Shinjinkai kikanshi: Demokurashii, Senku, Dōhō, Narōdo* (Tokyo: Hōsei Daigaku Shuppankyoku, 1969).

90. There is a tendency to reduce the myriad threads of thought active in the association to a prelude to the founding of the CCP in the official discourse of the People's Republic. For recent scholarship on Shaonian zhongguo xuehui, see Wu Xiaolong, *Shaonian zhongguo xuehui yanjiu* (Shanghai: Sanlian shudian, 2006); and Chen Zhengmao, *Lixiang yu xianshi de chongtu: "Shaonian zhongguo xuehui" shi* (Taipei: Xiuwei zixun keji gufen youxian gongsi, 2010).

91. Evan Dawley discusses this debate from the perspective of international history. See Evan Dawley, "Changing Minds: American Missionaries, Chinese Intellectuals, and Cultural Internationalism, 1919–1921," *Journal of American-East Asian Relations*, vol. 12, nos. 1–2 (spring-summer 2003), 1–21.

92. Zeng Muhan (Zeng Qi) was born in Sichuan, and his early training was Confucian, but with the abolition of the examination system in 1905, he also obtained a Western education. He attended Aurora University (Zhendan daxue) in Shanghai where he formed attachments to lifelong political compatriots Li Huang and Zuo Shunsheng, with whom he would cofound the Young China Association after a period of study in Japan in 1918–19. During his sojourn in Europe (1919–24), Zeng was a prolific journalist and also kept a diary. He was a leading figure of the Young China Association's Paris branch and contributed to *Young China* regularly from Paris during this time. See Marilyn Avra Levine, *The Found Generation: Chinese Communists in Europe during the Twenties* (Seattle: University of Washington Press, 1993), 179.

93. Although a constitution regulates the relationship between the state and the citizen, not between organizations and the citizen, and Tian's application of the national constitution to nongovernmental organizations may not be valid in legal terms, it is nonetheless an emotionally persuasive statement. See Jessie Gregory Lutz, *Chinese Politics and Christian Missions: The Anti-Christian Movements of 1920–1928* (Notre Dame, IN: Cross Cultural Publications, Cross Roads Books, 1988), 33; and Yamamoto Tatsuro and Yamamoto Sumiko, "The Anti-Christian Movement in China, 1922–1927," *Far Eastern Quarterly*, vol. 12, no. 2 (February 1953), 133–47. Christianity also had much to do with warlord politics at the time. Tian Han's personal connection to Feng Yuxiang, the so-called Christian warlord, invites further exploration.

94. Here "young man" and "new man" are used interchangeably, denoting both the young in age and the new in mind.

95. See Tian Han, "Shōnen to shinjin tono mondō," *Dōhō*, no. 4 (January 1, 1921), reprinted in *Shinjinkai kikanshi* (Tokyo: Hōsei Daigaku Shuppankyoku, 1969), 396.

96. Tian Han, "Shaonian zhongguo yu zongjiao wenti: Zhi Zeng Muhan yifeng xin," *Shaonian zhongguo*, vol. 2, no. 8 (February 1921), 57–61.

97. They all claimed to be pantheists; in particular, Zong Baihua, in his second letter to Guo Moruo, referred to Guo as a pantheist. See Tian, Guo, and Zong, *Sanye ji*, 4–5.

98. For more on deism, see Peter Byrne, *Natural Religion and the Nature of Religion: The Legacy of Deism* (New York: Routledge, 1989).

99. See Ono Kazuko, *Chinese Women in a Century of Revolution, 1850–1950*, edited by Joshua A. Fogel, translated by Kathryn Bernhardt et al. (Stanford, CA: Stanford University Press, 1989), 72, 77. Zhang Zhujun (1876–1964) was an influential female Christian and one of the first women to open a hospital in China. Tian Han may very well have been inspired by the real life Zhang Zhujun when conceiving the character of the same given name in his play.

100. *Mei* (plum), *lan* (orchid), and *zhu* (bamboo), often referred to together as *suihan sanyou* (three friends in the cold season), are iconic symbols of male intellectual integrity in Chinese and Japanese literary traditions. At the end of the published play, Tian Han recorded in English the following: "Produced at the Kanda Chinese YMCA Theatre, Tokyo, on Jan. 16, 1922 with the following cast—Miss S. Y. Fang as Miss Chiouchuen (Zhujun) Chiang, Miss K. C. Kang as Miss Nanchuen (Lanjun), Miss S. Y. Yi as Miss Maichuen (Meijun), directed by the author himself." see Tian Han, *Piyaluo zhigui* (The Ghost of the Piano), *Shaonian zhongguo* (Young China), vol. 3, no. 9 (April 1922), 40–41. So far I have not been able to identify Miss Fang, who played the oldest sister. Kang Jingzhao, for whom Tian Han wrote at least a "biography" and a published love letter addressing her as *jiejie* (elder sister), performed the second sister. See Tian Han, "Kang Jingzhao nüshi xiaoshi" (A Brief Biography of Ms. Kang Jingzhao), *Shanghai huabao* (Shanghai Pictorial), June 6, 1927; Tian Han, "Youchou furen yu jiejie—liangge butong de nüxing" (Ms. Melancholy and Sister—Two Kinds of Women), *Nanguo yuekan*, vol. 1, no. 1 (May 1, 1929), while the nineteen-year-old Yi Shuyu (1902–25), Tian Han's cousin, lover, and later first wife, played the younger sister.

101. Tian Han, "Shiren yu laodong wenti," *Shaonian zhongguo*, vol. 1, nos. 8–9 (February–March 1920). In *Tian Han quanji*, vol. 14, 105.

102. Willard Wolfe, *From Radicalism to Socialism: Men and Ideas in the Formation of Fabian Socialist Doctrines, 1881–1889* (New Haven, CT: Yale University Press, 1975), 146.

103. Tian Han's *Wufan zhiqian* was first published in *Chuangzao jikan* in August 1922. He revised the play in 1932 after his self-proclaimed "turning left" around 1930, changing the title to *Zimei* (Sisters), and included it in the first volume of his drama collection. See Tian Han, *Wufan zhiqian*, in *Chuangzao jikan*, vol. 1, no. 2

(August 1922), 53–73; and Tian Han, *Zimei*, in *Tian Han xiquji* (Shanghai: Xiandai shuju, 1932), vol. 1.

104. *Shoes*, dir. Lois Weber, performed by Mary MacLaren and Harry Griffith, United States, 1916, 60 min., 35 mm.

105. Cai Chusheng, in his now canonical film *Xin nüxing*, also used this technique, showing intertitles "wo yao huo" (I want to live) issuing from the mouth of the dying "new woman," one character bigger than another, even when the film already incorporated sound. The intriguing residue of showing intertitles in a sound film suggests the effectiveness of the graphic and other visual elements and their perceived impact on the film audience. See *Xin nüxing*, dir. Cai Chusheng (Shanghai: Lianhua yingye gongsi, 1933). The cry "I want to live" survived the 1930s film and formed a key moment in *Baimao nü* (The White-Haired Girl) when the female protagonist Xi'er anounces, "I will not die! I want to live! I want revenge!" *Baimao nü*, dir. Wang Bin, Shui Hua (Changchun dianying zhipianchang, 1950).

106. See Jeffery A. Dym, *Benshi, Japanese Silent Film Narrators, and Their Forgotten Narrative Art of Setsumei: A History of Japanese Silent Film Narration* (Lewiston, NY: Edwin Mellen Press, 2003). Also see Kyoko Omori's argument on the avant-gardism of *benshi setsumei*, "The *Benshi* Live Narrator as Modernist: Pyschological Films of the Early Twentieth Century in Japan," paper presented at the "Modernist Media and the Pacific Rim" stream, organized by Michael Coyle and Steven Yao, at the Twelfth Modernist Studies Association Conference, Victoria, British Columbia, November 11–14, 2010.

107. For more on Changsha Normal School's English education, see Wang Fengye et al., eds., *Hunan sheng Changsha Shifan Xuexiao xiaozhi, 1912–1992* (Changsha: Hunan jiaoyu chubanshe, 1993); and Li Yu, *Changsha de jindaihua qidong* (Changsha: Hunan jiaoyu chubanshe, 2000).

108. See Tian Han, *Qiangwei zhilu*, in *Tian Han quanji*, vol. 20, 266; and *Kume Masao: Hito to sakuhin* (Kōriyama: Kōriyama Seinen Kaigisho, 1991), 151–52.

109. See Tian Han, "Shoes," in *Tian Han quanji*, vol. 18, 20. Before he left Japan for China, Tian Han's uncle, Yi Xiang, gave him three hundred yen for living expenses for the next year. Tian Han deposited the money in a local bank. See Tian Han, "Zizhuan" (1967), in *Tian Han quanji*, vol. 20, 515. The reliability of this account, written almost half a century later, is open to discussion.

110. See Michael Budd, "Moments of Caligari," in *Cabinet of Dr. Caligari: Texts, Contexts, Histories* (New Brunswick, NJ: Rutgers University Press, 1990). Robert Wiene's *The Cabinet of Dr. Caligari* premiered in February 1920 in Berlin, in April 1921 in New York City, and in May 1921 in Tokyo.

111. See Budd, "Moments of Caligari," 7–14.

112. For a discussion of the frame structure and political implications of the

ending of the film, see Siegfried Kracauer, *From Caligari to Hitler: A Psychological History of the German Film* (Princeton, NJ: Princeton University Press, 1966).

113. See Tian Han, "Kaligeli boshi de sishi," *Yinxing* (1927), in *Yinse de meng* (Shanghai: Liangyou tushu gongsi, 1928).

114. *Hubian chunmeng*, dir. Bu Wancang, conceived and with intertitles written by Tian Han (Shanghai: Mingxing dianying gongsi, 1927).

115. See Joanne Bernardi, *Writing in Light: The Silent Scenario and the Japanese Pure Film Movement* (Detroit, MI: Wayne State University Press, 2001), 165; Chiba Nobuo, *Eiga to Tanizaki* (Tokyo: Seiabō, 1989), 150; and Thomas LaMarre, *Shadows on the Screen: Tanizaki Jun'ichirō on Cinema and "Oriental" Aesthetics* (Ann Arbor, MI: Center for Japanese Studies, University of Michigan, 2005).

116. See Yamamoto Kikuo, *Nihon eiga ni okeru gaikoku eiga no eikyō: hikaku eigashi kenkyū* (Tokyo: Waseda Daigaku Shuppanbu, 1983), 135.

117. See Tanaka Eizo, *Meiji Taishō shingekishi shiryō* (Tokyo: Engeki Shuppansha, 1964). Only two years later Tian Han would stage his own play "Spiritual Light" on the same stage.

118. Ibid. It is most likely that what the Japanese translated as "Sacrifice" was *Den Fredslöse*, 1871 (*The Outlaw*, translated by Edith and Wärner Oland), a rewrite of a historical tragedy, *Sven the Sacrificer*, as a one-act play in prose.

119. See Kamiyama Sōjin, *Sugao no Hariuddo* (Tokyo: Jitsugyō no Nihonsha, 1930).

120. See Tian Han, "Zhi Guo Moruo de xin," in *Tian Han quanji*, vol. 14, 150; and Gerhart Hauptmann, *The Sunken Bell, a Fairy Play in Five Acts*, translated by Charles Henry Meltzer, in *Seven Contemporary Plays*, selected and edited by Charles H. Whitman (Boston: Houghton Mifflin, 1959).

121. See Emma Goodman, *The Social Significance of the Modern Drama* (Boston: Richard G. Badger, 1914), 115.

122. See Shimamura Hōgetsu, *Torawaretaru bungei* (Tokyo: Hokkō Shobō, 1948).

123. It is likely that Tian Han had access to English translations of the German play, which were widely available in Tokyo at the time, such as an edition "freely rendered into English verse" by Charles Henry Meltzer, *The Sunken Bell, a Fairy Play in Five Acts* (Garden City, NY: Doubleday, Page & Company, 1911).

124. See Tian Han, *Qiangwei zhilu*, in *Tian Han quanji*, vol. 20, 274; and Ayako Kano, *Acting Like a Woman in Modern Japan: Theater, Gender, and Nationalism* (New York: Palgrave, 2001).

125. For more on Oscar Wilde's *Salome*, see Françoise Meltzer, *Salome and the Dance of Writing: Portraits of Mimesis in Literature* (Chicago: University of Chicago Press, 1987); and Petra Dierkes-Thrun, *Salome's Modernity: Oscar Wilde and the Aesthetics of Transgression* (Ann Arbor: University of Michigan Press, 2011). For

an intriguing case of male World War I prisoners of war impersonating Salome, see Alon Rachamimov, "The Disruptive Comforts of Drag: (Trans)Gender Performances among Prisoners of War in Russia, 1914–1920," *American Historical Review* vol. 3, no. 2 (April 2006), 362–82.

126. See Guo Yanli, *Zhongguo jindai fanyi wenxue gailun* (Wuhan: Hubei jiaoyu chubanshe, 1998). The congruence of sexuality and death does have deep roots in Chinese culture itself, as we shall see later throughout Tian Han's interaction with the White Snake legend, although at the time, in the late 1910s, Tian's cultural orientation can best be understood in terms of a post-Freudian consciousness about eros and thanatos as exemplified by the European models, which brought to the surface elements already in his "folk" consciousness. Perhaps it's best to see it as a matter of foreign exemplars granting permission to his articulation of repressed material (repressed in the unconscious of the culture).

127. Here I translate *gaizaoli,* literally "the power to reform," as "tranformative power." I am tempted to translate it as "transgressive power," as I believe that Tian Han was referring to the power of transgression here as well, but "transformative" is closer to the Chinese original in this instance.

128. See Tian Han, "Meiyu," in *Tian Han quanji,* vol. 11, 1–4. Italicized words appeared in their original languages.

129. For the use of the foreign in the context of Yu Dafu, see a recent PhD dissertation, Valerie Levan, "Forbidden Enlightenment: Self-Articulation and Self-Accusation in the Works of Yu Dafu (1896–1945)" (PhD diss., University of Chicago, 2010).

130. See Tian Han, *Qiangwei zhlu,* in *Tian Han quanji,* vol. 20, 267–68.

131. See Tian Han, "Zhi Guo Moruo de xin," in *Tian Han quanji,* vol. 14, 130; For more on the prevalence of the confessional mode of writing in Japanese literature at the time, see Edward Fowler, *The Rhetoric of Confession: Shishōsetsu in Early Twentieth-Century Japanese Fiction* (Berkeley: University of California Press, 1992).

132. See Tian Han, *Sanye ji* (Shanghai: Yadong tushuguan, 1920).

133. Tian's definition was heavily indebted to that of Madame de Staël's definition in her history of 19th century English romanticism. See Tian Han, "Shiren yu laodong wenti," *Shaonian zhongguo,* vol. 1, nos. 8–9 (February–March 1920), in *Tian Han quanji,* vol. 14, 92.

134. Ibid., vol. 14, 93–94.

135. Tian Han, "Xin luoman zhuyi ji qita: Fu Huang Rikui xiong yifeng changxin," *Shaonian zhongguo,* vol. 1, no. 12 (June 1920), in *Tian Han quanji,* vol. 14, 168–69.

136. Born in the same year as Tian Han in 1898, Huang Rikui went to Japan to study in the same year Tian Han did, 1916. The two most probably met in Tokyo between 1916 and 1918. Huang was one of the first members of the CCP. He died of

illness in 1930 in Shanghai. For more on Huang and Beijing University, see *Huang Rikui wenji* (Guilin: Guangxi renmin chubanshe, 1989); Timothy B. Weston, *The Power of Position: Beijing University, Intellectuals, and Chinese Political Culture, 1898–1929* (Berkeley: University of California Press, 2004), 220, 230–31; and Mechthild Leutner, ed., *The Chinese Revolution in the 1920s: Between Triumph and Disaster* (New York: RoutledgeCurzon, 2002).

137. "To see a world in a grain of sand / And a heaven in a wild flower / Hold infinity in the palm of your hand / And eternity in an hour." William Blake, *Auguries of Innocence* (New York: Grossman Publishers, 1968).

138. Tian Han had a close personal relationship with Abbot Juzan, and he published in *Shizi hou,* an anti-Japanese Buddhist journal edited by Juzan during the Second Sino-Japanese War. See Tian Han, "Fu Juzan fashi" (A Reply to Abbot Juzan), *Shizi hou* (Roar of the Lion), no. 1 (December 15, 1940); and Tian Han, "Guanyu xin fojiao yundong" (On the New Buddhist Movement), *Shizi hou,* nos. 8–9 (September 15, 1941). For more on Abbot Juzan, see Abbot Xinrong and Jiang Canteng, *Juzan fashi yanjiu* (Taipei: Xin wenfeng chuban gongsi, 2006).

139. Gustave Le Bon, *The Psychology of Socialism* (New York: Macmillan, 1899), ix–x, xii, as quoted in Wolfe, *From Radicalism to Socialism,* 1975, 13.

140. See Tian Han, "Baimei zhiyuan de neiwai," *Shaonian zhongguo,* vol. 2, no. 12 (June 15, 1921), in *Tian Han quanji,* vol. 13, 332–47.

141. See *Kindai sakka tsuitōbun shūsei,* supervised by Inamura Tetsugen (Tokyo: Yumani Shobō, 1987). Writing this in the immediate aftermath of the Japanese earthquake near Sendai in 2011, where Lu Xun studied, and close to Furukawa, birthplace of Yoshino Sakuzō, which I visited in 2003, I cannot help contemplating this unfolding tragedy's long-term cultural impact on Japan and the world. Would this, like the 1923 Great Kantō Earthquake, become the starting point for another intellectual shift from Kantō to Kansai? With the tsunami and the nuclear issue affecting everyone in such an interconnected world, could this event have a global economic, environmental, cultural, and political impact beyond our wildest imagination?

142. See Tanizaki Jun'ichirō, "Shanhai kōyūki," *Josei* (May, June, and August 1926); and Tian Han, "Women de ziji pipan," *Nanguo yuekan,* vol. 2, no. 1 (1930).

Chapter 2

1. Tian Han, *Shanghai* (1927–29), in *Tian Han quanji,* vol. 13, 19–20.

2. 旋律的世界，/沉默的大海？/嘍嘍的是什麼聲音？/悠悠的是什麼情緒？/我自己也難索解！/像一枝蘆葉臨風：/時而歌舞，/時而悲哀，/時而驚駭。Tian Han, "Ye" ("Night," 1920), in *Tian Han quanji,* vol. 11, 11.

3. 火，火，火！/火的笑，火的怒，火的悲哀，火的跳躍！/朦朧的火，蓬勃的火，熱烈的火，/薔薇細徑的火，/象牙宮殿的火，/是現實的火，/是神祕的火，/是剎那的火，/是永劫的火；/現在的焰中，湧出神秘的蓮花，/剎那的閃光，照見永劫的寶座！/照見草，/照見木，/照見人，/照見我，/什麼是草？/什麼是木？/什麼是人？/什麼是我？/在這黑暗無明的裡面，/營了幾千年相斫的生活！/哦！哦！薔薇的火，象牙的火，/願借你藝術的光明，引見我們最大的父母！ Tian Han, "Huo" ("Fire," 1920), in *Tian Han quanji*, vol. 11, 20–21.

4. Tian Han quoted this in Chinese as the epigraph to *Shanghai*, in *Tian Han quanji*, vol. 13, 7. Tian identifies the quote as "From 'Song of Mary the Mother of Christ'" in English after quoting the hymn in Chinese. The words are in fact a conflation of two hymns, "Jerusalem My Happy Home" and "O Mother Dear Jerusalem."

5. Joshua A. Fogel, *Articulating the Sinosphere: Sino-Japanese Relations in Space and Time* (Cambridge, MA: Harvard University Press, 2009), 99.

6. For a relevant recent study, see Pär Kristoffer Cassel, *Grounds of Judgment: Extraterritoriality and Imperial Power in Nineteenth-Century China and Japan* (New York: Oxford University Press, 2012).

7. For example, Stefan Tanaka reminds us that for the Japanese intellectuals, Tōyō (the Eastern Sea) always excluded Japan, and that special knowledge of Tōyō was termed *tōyōshi* (oriental history) and was used to construct a new Japanese nation-state in the late nineteenth and early twentieth centuries. In a similar spirit, Nishihara Daisuke argues that Tanizaki Jun'ichirō, looking to China to fulfill his orientalist fantasy, was the representative Taishō intellectual. See Stefan Tanaka, *Japan's Orient: Rendering Pasts into History* (Berkeley: University of California Press, 1993); and Nishihara Daisuke, *Tanizaki Jun'ichirō to orientarizumu: Taishō Nihon no Chūgoku gensō* (Tokyo: Chūō Kōron Shinsha, 2003).

8. Liu Jianhui (Ryū Kenki), *Mato Shanhai: Nihon chishikijin no kindai taiken* (Tokyo: Kōdansha, 2000).

9. Wen-hsin Yeh, *Provincial Passages: Culture, Space, and the Origins of Chinese Communism* (Berkeley: University of California Press, 1996), 172–73.

10. Tian Han is listed in a Japanese police record, dated December 28, 1921, as one of the sympathizers of Shi Cuntong. See "Shinajin Shi Sontō tsuihō shobun ni taisuru zairyū Shinajin no kansō," Japanese Foreign Ministry Office, Diplomatic Archives, document no. 4-2-6, 1921, unpaginated.

11. Tian Han, "Zui'e" ("Evil," 1919), in *Tian Han quanji*, vol. 11, 7–8.

12. Satō Haruo was one of the very first modern Japanese writers with whom Tian Han had close contact in Tokyo, although Tian Han did visit Kuriyagawa Hakuson earlier in Kyoto during the spring break of 1920. Tian Han's 1921 visit to Satō Haruo as portrayed by himself can be read as a representative piece of intellectual self-fashioning. See the October 16, 1921, entry in Tian Han, *Qiangwei zhilu* (Shanghai: Zhonghua shuju, 1922). Zhonghua shuju (China Books) was the second

most important publishing house at the time in China. Thanks to Zuo Shunsheng, a friend at the Changsha Normal School and Young China Association, Tian Han secured a position as an editor in this publishing house on his return from Tokyo.

13. In his travel account, "Mato" (Demon Capital), Muramatsu Shōfū gives a detailed account of his meeting with Tian Han in Shanghai. Muramatsu published his account in book format soon after. See Muramatsu Shōfū, *Mato* (Tokyo: Konishi Shoten, 1924). Muramatsu established his personal journal *Sōjin* in April 1926; many of his articles portraying his association with Tian Han were published in this journal. I could not locate the journal in its originally published format. A limited number of Muramatsu's articles and Tian Han's letters to him are reprinted in different formats. *Tian Han zai Riben* (Tian Han in Japan) is an important source among them. See Kotani Ichirō and Liu Ping, eds., *Tian Han zai Riben* (Beijing: Renmin wenxue chubanshe, 1997).

14. In the letter, Tian Han writes, "[U]nfortunately China is decisively not transforming into a new China; instead, it has been influenced by the trend of worldwide capitalist restoration, and it is turning old day by day. Not to mention Marx, even Sun Yat-sen was crying bitterly. . . . [S]oon the cry of Sun will become the cry of the Chinese people, and it will only do you good if you can hear it." In *Tian Han quanji*, vol. 20, 42. The letter is originally published in *Sōjin*, vol. 3, no. 10 (October 1928), and is translated from Japanese into Chinese by Liu Ping and included in *Tian Han quanji*.

15. See Joanne Bernardi, *Writing in Light: The Silent Scenario and the Japanese Pure Film Movement* (Detroit: Wayne State University Press, 2001). Tian Han watched *Lady Windermere's Fan*, a play by Oscar Wilde, translated by Tanizaki Jun'ichirō, in Tokyo in 1918. Tanizaki's film scenarios also influenced Tian Han, especially *Jasei no in* ("The Lust of the Serpent," Taikatsu, 1921), a story based on the legend of the White Snake as re-created by Ueda Akirari (1734–1809) in his now canonized *Ugetsu Monogatari* ("Tales of Moonlight and Rain," 1776).

16. Ouyang Yuqian was born in Liuyang, Hunan province. He went to Japan to study as a teenager. He was one of the most prolific cultural figures of his time who crossed boundaries among Peking Opera, spoken drama, and film. Ouyang was attracted to Tian Han's cultural endeavors in the early 1920s, and the two joined forces thereafter around their mutual love for the performing arts and film. Ouyang later would part with Tian to pursue a drama movement supported by the government, while Tian would insist on an "unofficial drama movement." The two would go on to be personally related through their children's marriage later in their lives. For more on Ouyang, see Ouyang Yuqian, *Ziwo yanxi yilai* (Taipei: Longwen chubanshe, 1990).

17. Tian Han's affiliation with the Nanjing government (a short-lived career serving as a "Nanjing government film officer") became an issue of debate in Japanese leftist circles during Tian Han's visit to Tokyo in 1927.

18. The photo was published in *Tanizaki Jun'ichirō ten* (Yokohama: Kanagawa Kindai Bungakkan, 1998), 30. The book also includes a picture of a page from Oscar Wilde's *The Picture of Dorian Gray,* a copy Tanizaki borrowed from a friend and on which he made notes. He told the friend "it was fascinating" (22). Another series of four pictures includes illustrations from Tanizaki's novels *The Sigh of the Mermaid* and *The Magician,* influenced by Aubrey Beardsley's illustrations in Wilde's *Salome* (24). Although there were mutual sources of influence for both the Japanese and the Chinese writers, Tanizaki and Tian came up with their own artistic expressions. Tian Han used Tokyo as a mediating ground, but he also reached out to Europe and America directly through the network of diasporic Chinese students.

19. In "Wo de Shanghai shenghuo," Tian Han wrote "Melancholia," with a capital M, in its English original and translated it as *youyuzheng* later in the same essay. Here Tian Han was quoting Tanizaki's description of him. The self-fashioning gesture is evident in his textual performance. See Tian Han, "Wo de Shanghai shenghuo," *Shanghai shenghuo,* inaugural issue (December 15, 1926), in *Tian Han quanji,* vol. 13, 231.

20. Ibid., 228–31.

21. Yokomitsu Ruiichi, *Shanghai,* translated by Dennis C. Washburn (Ann Arbor: Center for Japanese Studies, University of Michigan, 2001).

22. Tanizaki Jun'ichirō, "Shanhai Kōyūki," translated by Paul D. Scott, *Chinese Studies in History,* vol. 30, no. 4 (Summer 1997), 89.

23. Tanizaki Jun'ichirō, *Shen yu ren zhijian* (*Kami to hito no aida,* or "Between God and Man"), translated by Li Shuquan (Tian Han) (Shanghai: Zhonghua shuju, October 1934).

24. Satō Haruo, *Tianyuan zhi youyu* (*Den'en no yūutsu,* or "Rural Melancholy"), translated by Li Shuquan (Tian Han) (Shanghai: Zhonghua shuju, July 1934).

25. See Tanizaki Jun'ichirō's memoir as serialized in *Bungei shunjū,* June–November 1942, excerpted in *Tian Han zai Riben,* edited by Kotari Ichirō and Liu Ping (Beijing: Renmin wenxue chubanshe, 1997), 180–95.

26. Tian Han, "Letter to Tanizaki Jun'ichirō" (1928), originally published in *Nanguo,* vol. 5 (August 1928), in *Tian Han quanji,* vol. 20, 51.

27. For more on Tian Han's intimate connection with Uchiyama Kanzō, see Paul Scott, "Uchiyama Kanzō: A Case Study in Sino-Japanese Interaction," *Sino-Japanese Studies,* vol. 2, no. 2 (May 1990), 53.

28. Tian Han, "Du *Hunan niu,*" in *Tian Han quanji,* vol. 13, 92–102.

29. According to the brief biography appended to the end of Karashima's book *Chūgoku no Shingeki* (Chinese New Drama), Karashima graduated from the department of Chinese literature at Tokyo Imperial University in 1928. He became a lecturer at Kyoto Imperial University the same year. When Karashima came to China in 1928–29, he most likely was teaching at Kyoto Imperial University as a lecturer. "Professor" was used in both Uchiyama's postcard and Tian Han's account in

a general sense. Karashima Takeshi, *Chūgoku no Shingeki* (Tokyo: Shōheidō, 1948), 232.

30. For more on Zhou Xinfang, see Zhou Xinfang, *Zhou Xinfang wutai yishu*, interviewed by Wei Ming and Lu Zhong (Beijing: Zhongguo xiju chubanshe, 1961).

31. As an established figure in Peking Opera, Zhou Xinfang joined Tian Han's Nanguo she and became an important participant of his transmedia experiments in Shanghai in the late 1920s. See Shen Hongxin and He Guodong, *Zhou Xinfang zhuan* (Shijiazhuang: Hebei jiaoyu chubanshe, 1996).

32. See *Fengshen bang* (Beijing: Renmin wenxue chubanshe, 1992).

33. Tian Han, "Du *Hunan niu*," in *Tian Han quanji*, vol. 13, 96.

34. Jin Shengtan was one of the most acclaimed commentators on Chinese vernacular literature in the seventeenth century. Tian Han and his Japanese contemporary's mutual admiration for this Chinese literary figure suggests the deep bond fostered between modern Japanese and Chinese intellectuals out of their mutual esteem for late imperial Chinese literature.

35. Tian Han's autograph (1928), in Karashima Takeshi, *Chūgoku no Shingeki* (Tokyo: Shōheidō, 1948), first page of the book, unnumbered.

36. Karashima Takeshi, *Chūgoku no Shingeki*, 4–5.

37. Kotani and Liu, *Tian Han zai Riben*, 541.

38. See Tanizai Jun'ichirō, "Shanhai Kōyūki," translated by Paul D. Scott, *Chinese Studies in History*, vol. 30, no. 4 (Summer 1997), 94.

39. Tian Han used the term *ziji pipan*, instead of *ziwo piping*, to mean "self-criticism," linguistic evidence of the strong Japanese influence at the level of terminology. The Japanese original that Tian Han had in mind should be *ware ware no jiko hihan*, and the use of first person plural "our" rather than singular "my" suggests an emphasis on group solidarity rather than individual identity. See Tian Han, "Women de ziji pipan," *Nanguo yuekan*, vol. 2, no. 1 (1930).

40. Gion is a famous geisha quarter in Kyoto. It has been used as a site for Shinto festivals and theatrical performances since the eighteenth century. See an account contemporary with Tian Han's visit, Akiyama Aisaburō, *The Gion Festival* (Kyoto: Akiyama Aisaburō, 1924).

41. Tian Han, "Women de ziji pipan," *Nanguo yuekan*, vol. 2, no. 1 (1930), 46–47.

42. Tian Han's practice of quoting his diary in criticizing himself deserves some scrutiny. This diary appears to have been written retrospectively as Tian Han looked back from the perspective of 1930 and pointed out instances ripe for self-criticism during his 1927 visit. It is possible that Tian Han in fact fabricated this diary for the express purpose of this self-criticism: contextualizing his visit to Japan within the immediacy of a diary granted authenticity to his memories. The diary helped to publicize the image of Tian Han in 1930 as radically different from that of Tian Han

in 1927. The performative undertone of this piece of self-criticism is thus strong: Tian Han is both revealed and concealed. In particular, the conflicts between Tian Han and the Japanese leftists during his Tokyo visit are intentionally dramatized.

43. Tian Han's encounter with the Tsukiji Little Theater during his 1927 visit to Japan and later watching Zen'ei za's production of *Prince Hargen* provided a timely stimulation for his own little theater movement in Shanghai. See Tian Han, "Women wei shenme yao jianshe women de juchang: AB duihua," *Minguo ribao*, March 29, 1928; and Tian Han, "Xiaojuchang zhi yiye," in the local supplement of *Shenbao*, June 14, 1928.

44. It is significant that the Japanese avant-garde theater group Zen'ei za was scheduled to stage Upton Sinclair's *Prince Hagen*, a fantasy about greed and power, at the time of Tian Han's visit. Both Tian and the group shared Sinclair's concern for social liberty and his socialist experiments in art. For more on Sinclair, see Anthony Arthur, *Radical Innocent: Upton Sinclair* (New York: Random House, 2006).

45. On June 28–29, 1927, Tian Han met more than thirty prominent Japanese cultural figures, including Satō Haruo, Muramatsu Shōfū, Akutagawa Ryūnosuke, Nakagawa Yoichi, Kaneko Mitsuharu, Akita Ujaku, Kikuchi Kan, Yamamoto Sanehiko, Yokomitsu Ruiichi, Kawabata Yasunari, Kataoka Teppei, and Jūichiya Gisaburō, among others (June 28), and Mushanokōji Saneatsu, Muramatsu Shōfū, Satō Haruo, Akita Hōdō, Takata Yasuma, and Tanizaki Jun'ichirō, among others (June 29). See "Tian Han yu tong shidai Riben zuojia jiaoliu dashiji," in *Tian Han zai Riben*, edited by Kotani Ichirō and Liu Ping (Beijing: Renmin wenxue chubanshe, 1997), 455.

46. Tian Han, "Women de ziji pipan: Women de yishu yundong zhi lilun yu shiji, shangpian," in *Tian Han quanji*, vol. 15, 80.

47. Ibid., 81.

48. Tian Han, "Shiren yu laodong wenti," *Shaonian zhongguo*, vol. 1, nos. 8–9 (February–March 1920).

49. See Ōmi Komaki and Satomura Kinzō, "Seiten hakujitsu no kuni e," *Bungei sensen*, June 1926, in *Tian Han zai Riben*, edited by Kotari Ichirō and Liu Ping (Beijing: Renmin wenxue chubanshe, 1997), 226; and, in the same volume, Kotani Ichirō, "Tian Han yu Riben" (540).

50. Although the play was not published until January 1924, Tian Han started to conceive and write it in 1923. See "Huohu zhiye," *Nanguo banyuekan*, 1 (January 1924).

51. The image of the lotus flower has long been used to symbolize the purity and chastity of a young girl, as well as southern literary sentimentality. The closely related literary convention of the *cailian qu* (lotus-picking song) most prominently embodies the sexual energy surrounding the lotus-picking activity, through which the lotus as virgin trope is consolidated. See Xiaofei Tian, "The Cultural Construc-

tion of the 'North' and 'South' in Medieval China," talk given on May 8, 2006, at Harvard University.

52. See Randy Barbara Kaplan trans., "The Night a Tiger Was Captured," *Asian Theater Journal,* vol. 11, no. 1 (Spring 1994), 4; and Randy Barbara Kaplan, "The Pre-leftist One-Act Dramas of Tian Han (1898–1968)" (PhD diss., Ohio State University, 1986). For a recent translation, see Tian Han, "The Night the Tiger Was Caught (1922–1923)," translated by Jonathan S. Noble, in *The Columbia Anthology of Modern Chinese Drama,* edited with an introduction by Xiaomei Chen (New York: Columbia University Press, 2010).

53. The whipping scene may have influenced one of the most popular street plays during the war with Japan (1937–45), entitled *Fangxia ni de bianzi* (Put Down Your Whip). It was partly developed from Tian Han's miniature play *Meiniang,* which is based on the character Mariana in Goethe's *Wilhelm Meister.* For more on the transformation of this most popular anti-Japanese one-act street play, see Li Jianli, "'Zaizao' de qimeng yu jiuwang: Dui jietou ju 'Fangxia ni de bianzi' de kaocha," in *Zhongshan daxue xuebao* (social science edition), no. 4 (2007).

54. Tiger and tiger hunter are important plot elements in the fourteenth-century Chinese vernacular fiction *Shuihu Zhuan* (The Water Margin). Tian Han would rewrite *The Water Margin* in different performance genres with a focus on the tiger-fighting hero Wu Song and the femme fatale Pan Jinlian in his later years. In Southeast Asia, it was believed that the tiger is able to call the souls of the dead and take the form of human beings so as to walk and live among people. This was also the case in Yunnan province, Southwest China, and was widely believed in Japan. See Robert Wessing, *The Soul of Ambiguity: The Tiger in Southeast Asia,* Special Reports, no. 24 (De Kalb: Center for Southeast Asian Studies, Northern Illinois University, 1986). In China the image of the tiger as a mythic animal goes back to foundational myths of the land and the people. See Barend J. ter Haar, *Telling Stories: Witchcraft and Scapegoating in Chinese History* (Leiden: Brill, 2006). In the Indian tradition, see K. Brittlebank, "Sakti and Barakat: The Power of Tipu's Tiger, an Examination of the Tiger Emblem of Tipu Sultan of Mysor," *Modern Asian Studies,* vol. 19, no. 2 (1995), 257–69. I thank members of the H-Asia discussion list for providing this bibliographic information.

55. Leo Ou-fan Lee, in *Shanghai Modern,* attributes the first modern Chinese usage of the term *decadence* to Lu Xun's 1924 translation of Kuriyagawa Hakuson's *Kumon no shōchō* (Symbols of Agony). Lu Xun translated the term as *tuitang* (dejection), while Kuriyagawa's original term was *tuifei* (dilapidation), in fact a borrowed term from the classical Chinese literary vocabulary. In his play, written as early as December 1921 in Tokyo, Tian Han had already used the Chinese term *tuifei* to describe the mental state of his male protagonist, a young student struggling between "flesh and spirit" years before the publication of Lu Xun's translation. Tian

Han visited Kuriyagawa at his home in Kyoto as early as in April 1920 and discussed with him various contemporary cultural issues concerning Japan and China. Most important, Tian Han translated Oscar Wilde's *Salome* and published it in *Shaonian zhongguo* (*Young* China) in 1921, which must have familiarized him with the issue of "decadence" through writings on Oscar Wilde, Aubrey Beardsley, and the *Yellow Book*. For more on decadence and its relevance to modern Chinese literary culture, see Leo Ou-fan Lee, *Shanghai Modern: The Flowering of a New Urban Culture in China, 1930–1945* (Cambridge, MA: Harvard University Press, 1999), 232–33.

56. According to the second entry for the character *tui* in *Hanyu dacidian*, it refers to ruined and decayed structures. The first entry for the character *fei* echoes that of the *tui*, denoting a building that is ruined and useless. See *Hanyu dacidian*, CD 2.0 version (Hong Kong: Shangwu yinshuguan, 2002).

57. In traditional Chinese literature, as well as the Western literary tradition, the "fool" can often be divided into the "jester" and the "simpleton": the former a kind of truth teller and the latter a sort of holy person.

58. The first entry for *sha* in *Hanyu dacidian* reads *tounao chunben, bukan shili*, meaning "someone is stupid and not understanding earthly affairs and reason." The first entry for *dian* echoes *sha*, but it clearly refers to mental illness or craziness.

59. See Lu Xun, "Kuangren riji," in *Lu Xun zhuyi biannian quanji*, edited by Wang Shijia and Zhi An (Beijing: Renmin chubanshe, 2009), vol. 3.

60. See "The Night a Tiger Was Captured," in Randy B. Kaplan, "The Pre-leftist One-Act Dramas of Tian Han" (PhD diss., Ohio State University, 1986), 189. I have modified the quoted text slightly. Kaplan's dissertation, the only book-length study on Tian Han available in the English-speaking world before my own, consists of a collection of her translations of Tian Han's nine one-act dramas, together with her introduction to each drama. For a new translation, see Tian Han, "The Night the Tiger Was Caught (1922–1923)," translated by Jonathan S. Noble, in *The Columbia Anthology of Modern Chinese Drama*, edited with an introduction by Xiaomei Chen (New York: Columbia University Press, 2010).

61. For insightful discussions of Yanagita Kunio and the issue of *jōmin* (the eternal folk) in modern Japan, see Harry Harootunian, "Figuring the Folk," in *Mirror of Modernity: Invented Traditions in Modern Japan*, edited by Stephen Vlastos (Berkeley: University of California Press, 1998).

62. See Kaplan, "The Night a Tiger Was Captured," 175.

63. *Xin nüxing*, dir. Cai Chusheng and starring Ruan Lingyu as the female protagonist Wei Ming (Shanghai: Lianhua yingye gongsi, 1933). Ruan committed suicide soon after the release of the film in 1935, a sad reminder of the tremendous difficulties "new woman" faces in real life.

64. Kaplan, "The Night a Tiger Was Captured," 191–93.

65. Tian Han translated Oscar Wilde's *Salome* in 1920. Themes such as the con-

flict between flesh and soul, and the sweet bitterness of love and death, had also already entered Tian Han's play *Kafeidian zhi yiye* (A Night in a Café), written in Tokyo in 1921.

66. See Tian Han, "Eluosi wenyi sichao zhi yipie," *Minduo zazhi* (The People's Tocsin), vol. 1, nos. 6–7 (May and December 1919). I could not locate these two issues of the magazine and had to use the version included in the complete works of Tian Han. See *Tian Han quanji*, vol. 14, 1–78, especially 48.

67. Tian Han, "Women de ziji pipan," *Nanguo yuekan*, vol. 2, no. 1 (1930), in *Tian Han quanji*, vol. 15, 82–86.

68. *Nanguo banyuekan* (Southland Bimonthly), embodies Tian Han's search for a land of romanticism, a land of sexual ecstasy, a land of nonconformity, and a land of unofficial ideology. Here the lotus flower symbolizes the pure and authentic folk spirit, as well as the bohemian, avant-garde, and eternally beautiful. See Zhou Zuoren, "Ziji de yuandi," in *Ziji de yuandi* (Shanghai: Beixin shuju, 1927), 1–4.

69. See "Nanguo xuanyan," *Nanguo banyuekan* (January 5, 1924), quoted in Liu Ping, *Xijuhun: Tian Han pingzhua* (Beijing: Zhongyang wenxian chubanshe, 1998), 134.

70. Arthur Symons, *William Blake* (London: A. Constable, 1907). According to Bonnie McDougall, the books for which Arthur Symons (1865–1945) was known in China and Japan include *Studies in Prose and Verse* (1904) and *The Symbolic Movement in Literature* (1899). The former includes a short review article entitled "What Is Poetry?," which Tian Han quoted in his 1920 article for *Young China*. The latter was perhaps more widely known through quotations in essays by the Japanese critic Kuriyagawa Hakuson. See Bonnie McDougall, *The Introduction of Western Literary Theories into Modern China, 1919–1925* (Tokyo: Center for East Asian Cultural Studies, 1971), 67, 111–12. Also available in Japan at the time was Archibald G. B. Russell, *The Engravings of William Blake* (London: G. Richards, 1912). As a student of English in Tokyo, Tian Han possibly read Blake in English, as well as Arthur Symons's and others' books on Blake. As far as I can determine, the first Japanese writer who systematically introduced Blake is Sangū Makoto, in his volume *Selected Poems of William Blake*, credited to him in 1925 and published by Kenkyusha in Tokyo. Thus, Tian Han's striving to be "the William Blake of China" in the year 1924 was a pioneering endeavor in both Japan and China at the time.

71. See "Nanguo xuanyan," quoted in Liu Ping, *Xijuhun*, 134.

72. See William Blake, *Songs of Experience* (London: The Author and Printer, W. Blake, 1794).

73. For more on Chinese literary societies, see Michel Hockx, *Questions of Style: Literary Societies and Literary Journals in Modern China, 1911–1937* (Leiden: Brill, 2003); and Kirk A. Denton and Michel Hockx eds., *Literary Societies of Republican China* (Lanham, MD: Lexington Books, 2008).

74. See Pierre Bourdieu, *The Field of Cultural Production: Essays on Art and Literature*, edited and introduced by Randal Johnson (New York: Columbia University Press, 1993).

75. There are, of course, examples of "independent publishing endeavors" before those of Tian Han. Lun Xun and Zhou Zuoren published their first translations of stories from Eastern European and other "oppressed nations" in a collection entitled *Yuwai xiaoshuo ji* (Stories from the Outside World), as early as 1909 in Tokyo. There were also many endeavors after Tian Han's, including Shao Xunmei's *Jinwu yuekan*, published by his own Jinwu Bookstore; Liu Na'ou, Shi Zhecun, and Mu Shiying's *Wugui lieche* (Trackless Train), published by their Shuimo Bookstore; and Tian Han's Japanese friend Muramatsu Shōfū's personal journal *Sōjin*.

76. Tang Huaiqiu (1898–1954) was another legendary and often overlooked figure in the field of the performing arts and film in modern Chinese cultural history. Tang was a central figure in Tian Han's Nanguo she, acted in films such as *Shennü* ("Goddess," dir. Wu Yonggang, 1934), and became the leading figure in the Zhongguo lüxing jutuan (China Travel Drama Troupe), the first professional drama troupe in modern China. See Chen Yueshan et al., eds., *Tang Huaiqiu yu zhongguo lüxing jutuan* (Beijing: Zhongguo xiju chubanshe, 2000).

77. For more on the Shanghai Francophiles and the artistic group situated around Fu Yanchang, see Fu Yanchang, Zhu Yingpeng, and Zhang Ruogu, *Yishu sanjiayan* (Shanghai: Liangyou tushu gongsi, 1927).

78. See Zuo Ming, "'Nanguo' dao nanguo," in *Nanguo de xiju*, edited by Yan Zhewu (Shanghai: Mengya shudian, 1929), 165–66.

79. Tang Lin is pictured with and mentioned by Tanizaki in his 1926 Shanghai travelogue, see Tanizaki, "Shanhai kōyūki."

80. See Tian Han, *Dao minjian qu* (To the People), originally published in *Nanguo tekan, Xingshi zhoubao*, 23–24 (1926), in *Tian Han quanji*, vol. 10, 9–17. *Xingshi zhoubao* connected Tian Han with the *Guojia zhuyi pai* (Nationalist School) thinkers, a faction of the Young China Association, whose members, including Tian's friends Zeng Qi and Zuo Shunsheng, parted ways with the newly founded Communist Party and founded the Zhongguo qingnian dang (Chinese Youth Party) instead. Tian's association with *Xingshi zhoubao* became a major liability when he had to revisit this episode and offer self-criticism of his political insensibility close to the end of his life in the late 1960s. See Tian Han, "Zuo Shunsheng he *Xingshi zhoubao*," in *Tian Han quanji*, vol. 20, 573–74.

81. Li Chuli, born in Jiangjin, Chongqing, was one of the earliest theorists of romanticism in the Creation Society. This may explain his contribution to "revolutionary literature" later. See Li Chuli, *Zenyang jianshe geming wenxue* (Shanghai: Jiangnan shudian, 1930).

82. See Leon Trotsky, *Literature and Revolution* (Ann Arbor: University of

Michigan Press, 2000). Boris Pilnyak (1894–1937) wrote about his own travels in China. See Boris Pilnyak and Vera T. Reck, *Chinese Story and Other Tales,* translated from the Russian by Michael Green (Norman: University of Oklahoma Press, 1988). It could be argued that Tian Han's fate during the Cultural Revolution to some extent mirrored Pilnyak's fate under Stalinism.

83. Jiang Guangci (1900–1931), a talented poet with a Soviet background, is famous for his "revolution plus love" formula in writing popular fiction at the time. For more on the "revolution plus love" fiction in modern China, see Jianmei Liu, *Revolution Plus Love: Literary History, Women's Bodies, and Thematic Repetition in Twentieth-Century Chinese Fiction* (Honolulu: University of Hawai'i Press, 2003).

84. Xu Xiacun (1907–86) is the Chinese translator of Daniel Defoe's *Robinson Crusoe.* A prolific translator, writer, and critic, Xu studied in both Tokyo and Paris and in short stories such as "Modern Girl" wrote about a transnational femme fatale making a living as a café waitress between Shanghai and Tokyo. See Xu Xiacun, "Modern Girl" (original title in English), *Xin wenyi* (New Literature and Art), vol. 3 (December 1929), 406–13.

85. See Tian Han, "Women de ziji pipan," *Nanguo yuekan,* vol. 2, no. 1 (1930).

86. See Tian Han, *Dao minjian qu,* originally published in *Nanguo tekan,* in *Xingshi zhoubao,* vols. 23–24 (1926), in *Tian Han quanji,* vol. 10, 9–17.

87. See Zhou Zuoren, "Riben de xincun," *Xin qingnian,* vol. 6, no. 3 (1919); and Zhou Zuoren, "Fang riben xincun ji," *Xinchao,* vol. 2, no. 1 (1919).

88. Natsume Soseki, *Kokoro* (Tokyo: Iwanami Shoten, 1914).

89. The urbanite's ethnographic image of village people as primitive and pure would emerge as a hallmark of post-Mao Chinese avant-garde filmmaking, as in the case of *Huang tudi* (Yellow Earth) and *Hong gaoliang* (Red Sorghum), two of the earliest endeavors in the mid- to late 1980s. *Yellow Earth* (dir. Chen Kaige, 1984) and *Red Sorghum* (dir. Zhang Yimou, 1988) are among the representative pieces from the "fifth generation" of Chinese filmmakers, many of them graduates of the Beijing Film Academy in 1982.

90. Tian Han, "Dao minjian qu," *Yinxing* (1927), in *Tian Han sanwenji* (Shanghai: Jindai shudian, 1936), 118.

91. Tian Han, *Yinse de meng,* serialized in *Yinxing* starting in February 1927 (from no. 5 to no. 13).

92. See Zuo Ming, "'Nanguo' dao nanguo," in *Nanguo de xiju,* edited by Yan Zhewu (Shanghai: Mengya shudian, 1929), 165–66.

93. See Mary Gluck, *Popular Bohemia: Modernism and Urban Culture in Nineteenth-Century Paris* (Cambridge, MA: Harvard University Press, 2005), 28; and Joseph Donohue, "Distance, Death, and Desire in Salome," in *The Cambridge Companion to Oscar Wilde,* edited by Peter Raby (Cambridge: Cambridge University Press, 1997), 127. As discussed in Donohue's piece, the green flower can be

read as a covert sign of homosexuality in Paris at the time. The Nanguo group's outlandish costumes might also have something to do with the homosocial and homosexual energies circulating among the young people of the group. For more on cultural representations of same-sax desire in Republican China, see Tze-lan D. Sang, *The Emerging Lesbian: Female Same-Sex Desire in Modern China* (Chicago: University of Chicago Press, 2003).

94. For an important study on the Leifeng Pagoda on West Lake, see Eugene Y. Wang, "Tope and Topos: The Leifeng Pagoda and the Discourse of the Demonic," in *Writing and Materiality in China: Essays in Honor of Patrick Hanan,* edited by Judith T. Zeitlin and Lydia H. Liu, with Ellen Widmer (Cambridge, MA: Harvard University Asia Center, 2003), 489–552. For more on the significance of the West Lake in Chinese literary and cultural traditions, see Xiao Xinqiao, *Xihu gudai baihua xiaoshuoxuan* (Hangzhou: Zhejiang renmin chubanshe, 1982); and A. C. Graham, *Poems of the West Lake, Translations from the Chinese by A. C. Graham* (London: Wellsweep, 1990).

95. Tian Han, "Fanpaiya de shiji," *Yinxing* (1927), in *Tian Han sanwenji,* 147-49.

96. Ibid.

97. *Honglou meng* (Dream of the Red Chamber) has long been regarded as the most important novel on romantic love in the Chinese literary tradition. See Wai-yee Li, *Enchantment and Disenchantment: Love and Illusion in Chinese Literature* (Princeton, NJ: Princeton University Press, 1993). The red chamber, or bloody chamber, is also a marker of female sexuality in the Western tradition. See Angela Carter, *The Bloody Chamber* (New York: Harper & Row, 1979).

98. The dream framework of the film brings to mind the unreliable narrator Frances in *The Cabinet of Dr. Caligari,* whose sanity remains an open question at the end of the expressionist classic.

99. Tian Han, "Shanghai," in *Tian Han quanji,* vol. 13, 13.

100. Yamaguchi Shin'ichi, "Wakaki no Den Kan no koto," in *Tian Han zai Riben,* edited by Kotani Ichirō and Liu Ping (Beijing: Renmin wenxue chubanshe, 1997), 397–98.

101. Tian Han, "'Lingguang' xuyan: Zhi Li Jiannong xiansheng de yifeng xin," *Taiping yang,* vol. 2, no. 9 (1921), in *Tian Han quanji,* vol. 16, 280.

102. Tian Han, "Diyici gongyan zhihou," *Minzhong ribao,* December 22, 1928.

103. Tian Han, *Qiangwei zhilu* (Shanghai: Taidong tushuju, 1922), in *Tian Han quanji,* vol. 20, 242.

104. Tian Han, *Sun Zhongshan zhisi,* in *Tian Han quanji,* vol. 2, 1–29.

105. For Nationalist censorship of the planned performance of Tian Han's *Sun Zhongshan zhisi,* see Tian Han, "Nanguo yu guanfu," *Nanguo zhoukan* (inaugural issue), August 1929, in *Tian Han quanji,* vol. 15, 54–55.

106. For Tian Han's translation of *Salome,* see Tian Han, trans., *Shalemei, Shaonian zhongguo,* vol. 2, no. 9 (March 1921). It was published in book form by Zhonghua shuju in 1923 in Shanghai. For Tian's adaptation of Prosper Mérimée's novella *Carmen* into a six-act play, see Tian Han, *Carmen, Nanguo yuekan,* vol. 2, nos. 2–3 (May–June 1930). Tian used the original name Carmen, instead of a Chinese transliteration, as the title of the play. He would revisit the play in 1955, and a revised version was published in book form in 1955 in Beijing.

107. Tian Han, *Shuofeng,* Part I: "So This Is Paris," *Fanbao* (Shanghai), vol. 1, no. 1 (January 1, 1927), in *Tian Han quanji,* vol. 13, 81–82.

108. Known in the film world as the "Lubitsch Touch," Lubitsch's style was characterized by "a compression of ideas and situations into single shots or brief scenes that provided an ironic key to the characters and to the meaning of the entire film." Ephraim Katz, *The Film Encyclopedia, 4th ed.* (New York: HarperCollins, 2001). Lubitsch subsequently alternated between escapist comedies and grand-scale historical dramas; he enjoyed great international success with both. Tian Han referred to the Lubitsch Touch when describing the special "taste" of the film, showing his familiarity with contemporary developments in the film world.

109. See Ushihara Kiyohiko, *Kiyohiko eigafu 50-nen* (Tokyo: Kagamiura Shobō, 1968).

110. Tian Han, "I Stand Alone" (original title in English), in *Tian Han sanwenji,* 155-60.

111. Most of these films are Hollywood productions. Tian Han also watched European and Soviet movies. His essays, such as "Yun" (Cloud), "Xing guniang" (Apricot Girl), and "Xue zi" (Shoes) are important sources documenting his moviegoing experience in Tokyo, although one does have to take into account the mediated nature of these essays, which were written years after his Tokyo sojourn and served as a nostalgic gesture commemorating past grandeur.

112. Lee, *Shanghai Modern,* 23.

113. Tian wrote the story and the script was developed by Xia Yan. I have placed the term *leftist* in quotation marks to emphasize its problematic nature. A similar qualification of *left-wing* is called for in the term *left-wing cinema.* see Vivien Shen, *The Origins of Left-Wing Cinema in China, 1932–1937* (New York: Routledge, 2005).

114. A Ying (1900–1977) is remembered in Chinese literary history for his pioneering contribution to studies of Late Qing literature and the history of the "new literary movement" in the first decades of twentieth century. See, for instance, A Ying, *Wanqing wenyi baokan shulue* (Beijing: Gudian wenxue chubanshe, 1958); and A Ying, *Zhongguo xinwenxue yundongshi ziliao* (Shanghai: Shanghai shudian, 1982).

115. Tian Han, "Women de ziji pipan," in *Tian Han quanji,* vol. 15, 103.

116. Dong Jian, *Tian Han zhuan* (Beijing: Shiyue wenyi chubanshe, 1996), 365-69.

117. An E, *An E wenji* (Beijing: Zhongguo wenlian chuban gongsi, 2008); see volume 1 for her song lyrics.

118. Legend has it that Jiang changed his given name from ci 慈, "mercy," to chi 赤, "red," showing his revolutionary determination around this time. Also see Wu Sihong, "Diary of a Bohemian Girl," *Nanguo yuekan*, vol. 2 (June 1929).

119. The Duncan Dancing Troupe's German background further complicates this Soviet connection. It's debatable whether one can call Irma Duncan's dance troupe or movement Soviet. It was essentially European and in some ways essentially American, mediated through the Soviet Union. Certainly this represents an encounter with international modernism. Tian Han intentionally represented this encounter as specifically Soviet in spirit.

120. Irma Duncan was born Irma Dorette Ehrich-Grimme on February 26, 1897, in Schleswig-Holstein near Hamburg. She became a pupil of Isadora Duncan in January 1905 at her Grunewald School near Berlin, and later, along with five other original pupils, she was adopted by Isadora. Her name was legally changed to Irma Duncan in 1917. In 1918 the six formed an independent group known as the Isadora Duncan Dancers. Irma's debut as such occurred at Carnegie Hall on June 27 of that year. In 1921 she accompanied Isadora to Russia to found, at the government's invitation, a school of dance. Irma served as a teacher in Moscow for seven years, making her solo debut there on April 29, 1923. From Isadora's death in 1927 until 1930, Irma directed the Moscow school. She toured with her students to Europe, Asia, and the United States. When her group, known as the Isadora Duncan Dancers of Moscow, was forced to return to Russia, Irma chose to remain in the United States. She authored several books on Isadora Duncan and her technique and died on September 20, 1977. New York Public Library, http://digilib.nypl.org/dynaweb/dhc/findaid/duncan/@Generic__BookTextView/135, accessed June 20, 2005. Her China tour inspired another young Chinese, the legendary female soldier Xie Bingying, who watched the same troupe performing in Wuhan in 1926. See Xie Bingying, *A Woman Soldier's Own Story: The Autobiography of Xie Bingying*, translated by Lily Chia Brissman and Barry Brissman (New York: Columbia University Press, 2001), 71.

121. Tian Han, "Shuofeng," in *Tian Han quanji*, vol. 13, 83–84.

122. Tian Han was referring to Kuriyagawa Hyakuson's influential work *Kumon no shōchō* (Symbols of Agony) and his visit to Kuriyagawa in Kyoto in the spring of 1921.

123. Tian Han, "Shuofeng," in *Tian Han quanji*, vol. 13, 83–85.

124. Tian Han, "Kafei dian zhi yiye," *Chuangzao jikan*, vol. 1, no. 1 (1922), in *Tian Han quanji*, vol. 1, 109-10.

125. Quoted in Linda Wong, "'Undecadent' Representations of Oscar Wilde's *Salome* in Modern China," in *Decadence (Fin de Siècle) in Sino-Western Literary Confrontation*, edited by Marián Gálik (Bratislava: Institute of Oriental and African

Studies, Slovak Academy of Sciences, 2005), 103. I thank Professor Wilt L. Idema for bringing this book to my attention.

126. Even more fitting than the Salome parallel, this "unnamed beauty" and her "world-saving" teachings bring back a canonical figure in the Buddhist tradition, the Yulan Guanyin (Fish Basket Guanyin), who transforms herself into a beautiful woman to speak Buddhist teachings to the fishermen and finally converts a fisherman surnamed Ma into a believer. For more on the female Guanyin in the Chinese cultural tradition, see Wilt L. Idema, "Introduction," in *Personal Salvation and Filial Piety: Two Precious Scroll Narratives of Guanyin and Her Acolytes* (Honolulu: Kuroda Institute and University of Hawai'i Press, 2008).

127. Shi Nai'an and Luo Guanzhong, *Shuihu zhuan* (Beijing: Renmin wenxue chubanshe, 1975); Xiaoxiao sheng and Mei Jie, *Jin ping mei cihua: Mengmeiguan jiaoben* (Taipei: Liren shuju, 2007).

128. Ouyang Yuqian, *Pan Jinlian,* in *Twentieth-Century Chinese Drama: An Anthology,* edited by Edward M. Gunn (Bloomington: Indiana University Press, 1983). Wei Minglun, a contemporary Sichuanese writer, further re-created Pan Jinlian in a postmodern fashion in the late 1980s. Wei brought people of different times and cultures together and provided them with a common forum for discourse. Lu Shasha, a modern young woman, blasts Shi Nai'an, the author of *Water Margins,* who created Pan Jinlian, for his deep-rooted traditional bias against women and laments that Pan Jinlian could not file for a divorce. In Wei's vision, Tolstoy's Anna Karenina pleads with Jinlian to run away from home like her or commit suicide, as she did later, instead of homicide. As the drama unfolds and Jinlian meets her tragic end, a contemporary female judge finally penalizes Wu Song for his lawlessness and cruelty in killing his sister-in-law Jinlian. See Wei Minglun, *Pan Jinlian: Juben yu juping* (Beijing: Sanlian shudian, 1988).

129. Tian Han, "Guanyu Wu Song yu Pan Jinlian," *Pinglun bao* (Kunming), May 12, 1945, in *Tian Han quanji,* vol. 17, 335–37.

130. *Dianying* was edited by Lu Mengshu, the editor of the film magazine *Yinxing* (Movie Guide) where Tian Han published his essay series "Yinse de meng" (Silver Dreams).

131. Tian Han, "Sulian dianying yishu fazhan de jiaoxun yu woguo dianying yundong de qiantu," *Nanguo yuekan,* vol. 2, no. 4 (July 20, 1930), in *Tian Han quanji,* vol. 18, 74–95.

132. Tian Han mentions an American production, *Dangren hun,* that portrays a counter image of a male Red Army officer and a female White Army soldier's love story with a happy ending. Tian again makes the point that capitalist film shows no sympathy for the proletariat. He quotes Iwasaki Akira's (1903–81) writings on film to underscore the point that cinema can no longer be pure art because of the nature of its production, distribution, and consumption, all of which are controlled by

huge capitalist enterprises. See *Tian Han quanji*, vol. 18, 81–84. For more on *Sorok pervyy* and its translation and adaptation history in China, see Cao Jinghua, trans., *Di sishi yi* (Beiping: Weiming she, 1929), a translation of Boris Lavrenyov's 1924 novel *Sorok pervyy*. An E adapted the novel as a three-act play, *Matejia* (Maryutka), based on Cao's translation. The play was performed in March 1931 by the Left-Wing Dramatist Association at Daxia University in Shanghai, with participation by Liu Baoluo, Zhou Boxun, Zheng Junli, Hu Ping, and Zhou Yang. With the advent of the "thaw" (1955–56) in the Soviet Union, Grigori Chukhrai's 1956 remake of this 1927 silent film won him a special jury award at the Cannes International Film Festival in 1957. I thank Enhua Zhang for sharing her research notes on this film.

133. It is not difficult to see why this story captured Tian's imagination, given all the warlord conflicts of his day.

134. Tian Han, "Sulian dianying yishu fazhan de jiaoxun yu woguo dianying yundong de qiantu," *Nanguo yuekan*, vol. 2, no. 4 (July 20, 1930), in *Tian Han quanji*, vol. 18, 80.

135. See *ibid.*, 80–81.

136. Tian Qinxin's 2001 stage play about Tian Han's love relationships with four modern women, *Kuangbiao* (Hurricane), took the Chinese and international stages by storm. It re-creates An E, Tian Han's lifelong companion in art, revolution, and love, as a Red Salome. See Tian Qinxin, *Tian Qinxin de xiju ben* (Beijing: Beijing daxue chubanshe, 2010).

137. Yu Shan (1908–68) came from the prominent Yu family in Shanyin (Shaoxing), Zhejiang. Her uncle Yu Dawei was a high-ranking official in the Nationalist government at the time, with a joint appointment as minister of defense and minister of transportation. Yu Shan herself studied at the Shanghai Conservatory of Music and later graduated from Jinling University in Nanjing and was fluent in English. Tian Han discovered Yu when he went to Jinling University to direct *Hushang de beiju* (Tragedy at the Lake) and invited her to join Nanguo she. Yu made her name acting as Salome and Carmen in Tian's productions in 1929 and 1930, respectively. Yu is now remembered for her charm and her close association with Tian Han, Zhao Taimou, Xu Zhimo, Wen Yiduo, and Liang Shiqiu, among other prominent cultural figures of Republican China. See Wang Mingjian, "Yu Shan: Minguo caizi milian de jiaren," *Wenshi bolan*, no. 5 (2009).

138. According to Tian Han's public letter to Chen Ningqiu (Sai Ke), Chen broke from Tian and Nanguo she and left for the North shortly after the *Salome* performance. See Tian Han, "Bieyi, yuan zi'ai: Song Chen Ningqiu jun," *Shenbao* (Shanghai supplement), August 15, 1929, in *Tian Han quanji*, vol. 15, 47–50. For more on Chen Ningqiu and his reputation as an anti-Japanese poet, lyricist, dramatist, and film worker, see Han Sanzhou, "Yan'an 'guairen' Sai Ke de 'guaishi,'" *Gejie*, no. 3 (2011), 32.

139. For an informative discussion of masculinity in contemporary Chinese literature, see Xueping Zhong, *Masculinity Besieged? Issues of Modernity and Male Subjectivity in Chinese Literature of the Late Twentieth Century* (Durham, NC: Duke University Press, 2000).

140. Tian Han, "Gongyan zhiqian: Ti ziji hanjiao, ti minzhong hanjiao," in *Tian Han quanji*, vol. 15, 174–77.

141. See Tang Shaohua, *Wentan wangshi jianzheng* (Taipei: Zhuanji wenxue chubanshe, 1996).

142. See Zhou Zhaokuan, ed., *Yiwei rensheng: Wu Zuoren de yisheng* (Xi'an: Shanxi renmin meishu chubanshe, 1998).

143. Tian Han, "Yishu yu shidai ji zhengzhi zhi guanxi," in *Tian Han nianpu*, edited by Zhang Xianghua (Beijing: Zhongguo xiju, 1992), 129.

144. For an insightful discussion of Bizet's *Carmen*, see Susan McClary, "Structure of Identity and Difference in Bizet's *Carmen*," in *The Work of Opera: Genre, Nationhood, and Sexual Difference*, edited by Richard Dellamora and Daniel Fischlin (New York: Columbia University Press, 1997), 115–30. For more insights into cinematic adaptations of *Carmen* and the intrinsic connections between the two genres (of opera and film) in light of Walter Benjamin's essay "The Work of Art in the Age of Mechanical Reproduction," see Jeremy Tambling, "Ideology in the Cinema: Rewriting *Carmen*," in *Opera, Ideology, and Film* (Manchester, UK: Manchester University Press, 1987), 13–40.

145. Tian Han, "Bianji houji," *Nanguo yuekan*, vol. 2, no. 3 (June 1930).

146. Tian Han, *Carmen*, in *Tian Han quanji*, vol. 2, 162.

147. Ibid., 165.

148. Ibid., 167.

149. Ibid., 206.

Chapter 3

1. See David Der-wei Wang, *Fin-de-Siècle Splendor: Repressed Modernities of Late Qing Fiction, 1848–1911* (Stanford, CA: Stanford University Press, 1997), 156–71.

2. See Tian Han's discussion of the idea of *minjian* and how it is related to the Russian populist and Japanese new village movements in "Dao minjian qu," in *Yinse de meng* (Shanghai: Zhonghua shuju, 1928).

3. For informative analysis on Herder's thought and the development of anthropology as a discipline, see John H. Zammito, *Kant, Herder, the Birth of Anthropology* (Chicago: University of Chicago Press, 2002).

4. Tian Han arrived in Changsha, the capital of his home province of Hunan, in early 1938. He worked with others to establish *Kangzhan ribao* (Anti-Japanese War Daily) there. He left Changsha for Wuhan to work with the "Third Bureau," in

charge of art and propaganda, but returned after "the great fire of Changsha" and established the first newspaper, *Xin Changsha bao* (New Changsha Daily), to be published after the fire.

5. During his two-year forced stay in Nanjing, Tian Han was actively engaged in the city's artistic circles. See Tian Han, "Baofengyu zhong de Nanjing yitan yipie," *Xinmin bao* (Nanjing), June 9, 10, 12, 14, and 29, 1936, in *Tian Han quanji*, vol. 15, 282–96.

6. See Mao Zedong, *Zai Yan'an wenyi zuotanhui shang de jianghua* (Yan'an: Jiefang she, 1943).

7. See Ed Jocelyn and Andrew McEwan, *The Long March: The True Story behind the Legendary Journey That Made Mao's China* (London: Constable, 2006); and Helen Praeger Young, *Choosing Revolution: Chinese Women Soldiers on the Long March* (Urbana: University of Illinois Press, 2001).

8. See Charles W. Hayford, *To the People: James Yen and Village China* (New York: Columbia University Press, 1990); and Chang-tai Hung, *Going to the People: Chinese Intellectuals and Folk Literature, 1918–1937* (Cambridge, MA: Harvard University Press, 1985).

9. See Yanagita Kunio, *Tōno monogatari* (Tokyo: Yanagita Kunio, Meiji 43 [1910]).

10. See Lu Xun, "Nahan zixu," in *Lu Xun zhuyi biannian quanji*, edited by Wang Shujia and Zhi An (Beijing: Renmin chubanshe, 2009), vol. 4.

11. See Leo Ou-fan Lee, *Voices from the Iron House: A Study of Lu Xun* (Bloomington: Indiana University Press, 1987); and Carolyn Brown, "The Paradigm of the Iron House: Shouting and Silence in Lu Xun's Stories," *Chinese Literature: Essays, Articles, Reviews*, vol. 6, nos. 1–2 (1984), 101–20.

12. See *Mao Zedong Zhuan (1886–1949)* (Beijing: Zhonggong zhongyang wenxian yanjiushi, 1996); and Maurice Meisner, *Mao Zedong: A Political and Intellectual Portrait* (New York: Polity Press, 2007).

13. See Tian Han, "Dao minjian qu," *Yinxing* (1927).

14. Tian Han, "Xiju yu shehui," in *Jukan*, a literary supplement of the *Beiping chenbao*, no. 263, January 19, 1936, in *Tian Han quanji*, vol. 15, 281.

15. Zhao Shuli, "Wenhua yu xiao huozi," originally published in *Zhongguo wenhua jianshe xiehui Shanxi fenhui yuekan*, vol. 2, no. 2 (February 16, 1936), under the pseudonym Chang Zhai.

16. Ibid.

17. See Yang Baichou, "Yi Zhao Shuli," *Da xinan wenxue*, vol. 1 (1988); and Zhao Shuli, "Huiyi lishi, renshi ziji" (1966), in *Zhao Shuli wenji*, vol. 4. One needs to take into account the mediated nature of these personal reflections written decades after the events took place.

18. See Chen Huangmei, "Xiang Zhao Shuli fangxiang maijin," in *Zhao Shuli*

yanjiu ziliao, edited by Huang Xiuji (Taiyuan: Beiyue chubanshe, 1985), 200; and Zhao Shuli, "'Ya' de moyun," *Zhongguo wenhua jianshe xiehui Shanxi fenhui yuekan,* vol. 2, no. 2 (February 16, 1936), written under the pseudonym Chang Zhai.

19. For more on Zhao Shuli, see Jiang Hui, "From Lu Xun to Zhao Shuli: The Politics of Recognition in Chinese Literary Modernity" (PhD diss., New York University, 2007); and G. Andrew Stuckey, *Old Stories Retold: Narrative and Vanishing Pasts in Modern China* (Lanham, MD: Lexington Books, 2010).

20. Zhao Shuli, *Li Youcai banhua* (Pingshan: New China Bookstore, North China Branch, 1943).

21. See Jack Belden, *China Shakes the World* (New York: Harper, 1949), 87.

22. Zhao Shuli, "Yesuan jingyan," in *Zhao Shuli quanji* (Taiyuan: Beiyue wenyi chubanshe, 2000), vol. 4, 186.

23. See Leo Ou-fan Lee, *The Romantic Generation of Modern Chinese Writers* (Cambridge, MA: Harvard University Press, 1973).

24. See Dong Jian, *Tian Han zhuan* (Beijing: Shiyue wenyi chubanshe, 1996), 3.

25. Mao Zedong, "Zhongguo shehui ge jieji de fenxi," in *Mao Zedong xuanji* (Beijing: Renmin chubanshe, 1964), 3–11.

26. Mao Zedong, "Qingnian yundong de fangxiang" (May 4, 1939), in *Mao Zedong xuanji,* 525–33.

27. Mao Zedong, "Daliang xishou zhishi fenzi" (December 1, 1939), in *Mao Zedong xuanji,* 581–83.

28. Mao Zedong, "Zhongguo geming he zhongguo gongchandang" (December 1939), in *Mao Zedong xuanji,* 584–617.

29. Mao Zedong, "Zai Yan'an wenyi zuotanhui shang de jianghua" (May 1942), in *Mao Zedong xuanji,* 804–35.

30. Lycian Pye made a similar point in his book on Mao, *Mao Tse-Tung: The Man in the Leader* (New York: Basic Books, 1976).

31. Leon Trotsky, "What Is Proletarian Culture, and Is It Possible?" (1923), included in Leon Trotsky, *Literature and Revolution* (Ann Arbor: University of Michigan Press, 1960), as chapter 6, "Proletarian Culture and Proletarian Art."

32. Although Mao may not have known about Trotsky's essay, it is likely that he was familiar with the kind of argument put forward by Trotsky in his 1923 essay, as there were many "Trotskyites" among the ranking members of the Chinese Communist Party, with none other than Chen Duxiu, one of the founders of the CCP, emerging as a leading Trotskyite.

33. The idea of transformation also closely resembles the idea of "self-cultivation" (*xiushen, xiuyang*) in neo-Confucianism. Liu Shaoqi, in particular, would use the term *xiuyang* in his 1939 speech on how to be a good communist. See Liu Shaoqi, "Lun gongchan dangyuan de xiuyang," speech given at Marxist-Leninist College in Yan'an, July 1939, and first published as a monograph by the People's Press in 1962.

34. See Stephen R. Platt, *Provincial Patriots: The Hunanese and Modern China* (Cambridge, MA: Harvard University Press, 2007).

35. See, for example, Hu Yingjian, "Lun Kangzhan shiqi jiuti shige de fuxing," *Kangri zhanzheng yanjiu*, January 2001.

36. Mao Zedong, "Cong qunzhong zhong lai, dao qunzhong zhong qu," in *Mao Zedong xuanji* (Beijing: Renmin chubanshe, 1991), vol. 3, 899.

37. See Joshua Goldstein, *Drama Kings: Players and Publics in the Re-creation of Peking Opera, 1870–1937* (Berkeley: University of California Press, 2007); and Jin Jiang, *Women Playing Men: Yue Opera and Social Change in Twentieth-Century Shanghai* (Seattle: University of Washington Press, 2009).

38. As early as 1927, Tian Han had written in "Nü yu she" about his ambition to make the White Snake tale into a film. See *Tian Han sanwenji* (Shanghai: Jindai shudian, 1936). While the cinematic obsession had always been there, wartime conditions both intensified the desire and presented obstacles to its materialization under difficult economic conditions.

39. See Tang Tao, *Zhongguo xiandai wenxueshi* (Beijing: Renmin wenxue chubanshe, 1979); Kirk A. Denton, *The Problematic of Self in Modern Chinese Literature: Hu Feng and Lu Ling* (Stanford, CA: Stanford University Press, 1998); and Wang Hui, *Xiandai zhongguo sixiang de xingqi*, 2nd ed. (Beijing: Sanlian shudian, 2008).

40. Chang-tai Hung, "Historical Plays," in *War and Popular Culture* (Berkeley: University of California Press, 1994), 78–85.

41. Tian Han, *Tian Han cizuo gequji*, edited by Sun Shen, Li Yinghai, and Xiang Yansheng (Beijing: Renmin yinyue chubanshe, 2003).

42. Tian Han, "Review of Zhan Jingtang," *Lianhua huabao* (Shanghai), vol. 9, no. 5 (July 1, 1937), in *Tian Han quanji*, vol. 17, 371–77.

43. Li Suyuan, *Zhongguo xiandai dianying lilunshi* (Beijing: Wenhua yishu chubanshe, 2005), 142.

44. Tian Han, *Yingshi zhuihuai lu* (Beijing: Zhongguo dianying chubanshe, 1981), 3.

45. Tian Han, "Review of Zhan Jingtang," in *Tian Han quanji*, vol. 17, 371–77.

46. Tian Han had already called for the making of 3-D films in 1937 in Shanghai. See ibid., 372. Had Tian Han lived to see films in movie theaters today, he might not have been surprised to see that 3-D films have become the new standard in the film industry.

47. Ibid., 371–77.

48. See Zhang Xianghua, *Tian Han nianpu* (Beijing: Zhongguo xiju chubanshe, 1992), 198.

49. Wu Yigong et al., eds., *Shanghai dianying zhi* (Shanghai: Shanghai shehui kexueyuan, 1999).

50. David Robinson's article on Maxu Weibang's *Yeban gesheng* obscured Tian

Han's great contribution to the film while he was under house arrest by the KMT in Nanjing. Robinson considered the film to be arguably the most fascinating and creative of all interpretations of Gaston Leroux's horror tale. According to Robinson, part of the film's huge success on its first release was the popularity of the songs, at least one of which remained a favorite long after the film itself had been forgotten. The lyrics were written by Tian Han, who also contributed extensive revisions to the script. At Tian's suggestion, the composer was Xian Xinghai, who deliberately combined elements of popular and folk songs with idioms of both Western and traditional Chinese opera. Robinson considers it a compilation in the manner of a silent film score, "recklessly juxtaposing popular classics, from 'Night on Bare Mountain' to 'Orpheus in the Underworld,' Händel's 'Largo,' and 'Rhapsody in Blue.'" Although skillfully chosen, these melodies were still quite unfamiliar to the general Chinese public in 1937; hence it is hard to gauge their impact on their audience at the time. See David Robinson, "Return of the Phantom," *Film Quarterly*, vol. 53, no. 2 (Winter 1999–2000), 43–46.

51. I treat this song's fascinating afterlife in the 2007 Ang Lee film *Lust, Caution* in an article in progress entitled "*Lust, Caution*: An Epilogue to the Twentieth Century."

52. For more on Manchukuo and the Chinese resistance to it, see Prasenjit Duara, *Sovereignty and Authenticity: Manchukuo and the East Asian Modern* (Lanham, MD: Rowman & Littlefield, 2003); and Norman Smith, *Resisting Manchukuo: Chinese Women Writers and the Japanese Occupation* (Vancouver: University of British Columbia Press, 2007).

53. See Zhang Yaojie, *Yingju zhiwang Tian Han: Aiguo weimei de langman rensheng* (Taiyuan: Shanxi jiaoyu chubanshe, 2003), 279. Xiaomei Chen questions Zhang's approach in her article on Tian Han, "Reflections on the Legacy of Tian Han: 'Proletarian Modernism' and Its Traditional Roots," *Modern Chinese Literature and Culture,* vol. 18, no. 1 (Spring 2006), 155–215.

54. See the opening sequence of *Fengyun ernü* (story by Tian Han, screenplay by Xia Yan), dir. Xu Xingzhi, and starring Yuan Muzhi and Wang Renmei (Shanghai: Diantong yingye gongsi, 1935).

55. Ban Wang, *The Sublime Figure of History: Aesthetics and Politics in Twentieth-Century China* (Stanford, CA: Stanford University Press, 1997), 125.

56. Laikwan Pang, *Building a New China in Cinema: The Chinese Left-Wing Cinema Movement, 1932–1937* (Lanham, MD: Rowman & Littlefield, 2002), 98.

57. See Xu Xingzhi dir., *Fengyun ernü* (Shanghai: Diantong yingye gongsi, 1935).

58. Qingdao was a significant locale for Tian Han. The seaside resort may have revived fond memories of his summer vacation in Kamakura in 1920 with Yi Shuyu and Kang Jingzhao, the two most featured female figures in his early writings. The

seashore is also reminiscent of the West Lake in "Lakeshore Spring Dream," in which the "vampire" woman and sadistic femme fatale abuses the male protagonist for sexual enjoyment. I discussed this film in detail in chapter 2, in which I treat the female figure in the film as an incarnation of the image of the White Snake, an image mediated by Tanizaki's 1921 film scenario for *Jasei no in* and one that combines the mysterious folk spirit with that of the modern femme fatale.

59. Tanizaki Jun'ichirō, *Jasei no in*, *Shufu no tomo*, April 1922.

60. I thank Professor Theodore Fiedler for pointing out that the singing girl's costume strongly resembles that of women performers in Weimar Germany.

61. Tian Han contributed to the iconography of the "Red Detachment of Women" with his own Peking Opera adaptation of the film. See Tian Han, *Hongse niangzi jun* (1964), in *Tian Han quanji*, vol. 9.

62. Writing in the late 1950s, Tian Han reflected on the film's story as follows: "This is a process through which young men and women develop from wavering lovers to anti-Japanese heroes under urgent political situations." Although colored by its contemporary political circumstances, Tian's insistence on the theme of youthful transformation and intellectual metamorphosis should be taken seriously as an enduring concern throughout his artistic experiments. See Tian Han, "Yingshi zhuihuai lu," originally published in *Zhongguo dianying* and *Dianying yishu* from 1958 to 1959, in *Tian Han quanji*, vol. 18, 199.

63. Tian Han, "Yiyongjun jinxingqu," in *Fengyun ernü*, transcribed from the film by Li Suyuan, originally published in *Tian Han dianying juben xuanji*, in *Tian Han quanji*, vol. 10, 259–60.

64. Guo Moruo, "Fenghuang niepan," in *Guo Moruo daibiaozuo* (Beijing: Huaxia chubanshe, 2009).

65. Tian Han died under the name Li Wu, assigned by the committee in charge of his case in No. 301 Hospital in Beijing on December 10, 1968. For more details of the circumstances leading up to his death, see Tian Han, "1968 nian riji canpian," in *Tian Han quanji*, vol. 20, 509–10.

66. Lu Xun, "Da Xu Maoyong bing guanyu kangri tongyi zhanxian wenti," *Zuojia*, vol. 1, no. 5 (August 1936).

67. See Tian Han, *Lugou qiao* (Chengdu: Xiemei yinshuaju, 1937), in *Tian Han quanji*, vol. 4.

68. David Drasner, ed., *Theatre in Theory, 1900–2000: An Anthology* (Malden, MA: Blackwell, 2008), 169.

69. See Tian Han, "Kangzhan yu xiju," in Tian Han, *Kangzhan yu xiju* (Changsha: Shangwu yinshuguan, December 1937), in *Tian Han quanji*, vol. 15, 310–33; and Tian Han, "Guanyu kangzhan xiju gaijin de baogao," *Xiju chunqiu*, vol. 1, no. 6, and vol. 2, nos. 2–3 (April, July, and September 1942), in *Tian Han quanji*, vol. 15, 388–93.

70. Ang Lee's film *Lust, Caution* re-creates such a scene, with the female protagonist Wang Jiazhi kneeling in front of her male counterpart and the audience during a stage performance to urge them to join the fight against the Japanese. It is likely that Ang Lee was inspired by plays like Tian Han's *Lugou qiao* (Marco Polo Bridge) when conceiving the stage play scene in his film.

71. Tian Han, *Lugou qiao,* in *Tian Han quanji,* vol. 4.

72. *Qin Qiong fangyou,* like *Jinlian xishu* (Pan Jinlian Flirts with Her Brother-in-Law), is a canonized excerpt from an established Peking Opera repertoire. Qin Qiong's story originated in *Shuo Tang quanzhuan* (A Full Version of Tang Stories). Qin was said to be the sixteenth hero of the Sui dynasty (581–618), which preceded the Tang (618–907). Like that of another Sui dynasty hero Yuchi Gong's story entered Lu Xun's *Ah Q zhengzhuan* (The True Story of Ah Q) as a quotation from an established theatrical repertoire, Qin Qiong's story here also functions as a marker of the significance of established opera repertories in modern Chinese life, personal and political. Qin became one of the great generals in the founding of the Tang dynasty, together with Yuchi Gong. People in traditional China all knew Qin and Yuchi, as they became canonized as the door gods, whose pictures had to be renewed every year.

73. The tale was popularized via Pathé-EMI records of Peking Opera highlights sung by the leading opera singer, Tan Xinpei, before World War I. See Guo Tao, "Baidai fuchen: Jindai Shanghai Baidai changpian gongsi shengshuaiji," *Shilin,* no. 5 (2008), 26–41, 127.

74. Tian Han, *Lugou qiao,* in *Tian Han quanji,* vol. 4, 143.

75. See Walter Benjamin, "The Author as Producer," *New Left Review,* vol. 1, no. 62 (July-August 1970), 91. Brecht's and Eisler's play *Die Maßnahme* ("The Measures Taken," 1930), set in China in the 1930s, lends itself to rich comparative possibilities with Tian Han's contemporary plays and Ang Lee's twenty-first-century reinvention in *Lust, Caution:* the themes of China in the 1930s, the Soviet connection, the missionary impulse in revolutionary work, the justification of revolutionary violence, sentimentalism in revolution, internationalism, and the function of the singing and chorus.

76. Tian Han, *Lugou qiao,* in *Tian Han quanji,* vol. 4, 147.

77. Here the color black suggests "sunburnt" and serves as a class marker to distinguish intellectuals from people who have to work in the open. It may also be interpreted in similar ways as in Zhao Shuli's *Xiao erhei jiehun* (The Marriage of Young Blacky), suggesting a peasant identity with its original wildness and honesty, very much working within the intellectual tradition of exoticizing the folk.

78. Tian Han, *Lugou qiao,* in *Tian Han quanji,* vol. 4, 155.

79. Tian Han, *Zuihou de shengli* (Hankou: Shanghai zazhi gongsi, 1938).

80. The Communist International facilitated the coming together of the first united front (1923–27), when Nationalists and Communists tried to work together to fight the warlords, which ended with Chiang Kai-shek's cleansing of the Communists from the Nationalist Party on April 12, 1927, in Shanghai. For more on the second united front (1935–41), with the invading Japanese as a mutual enemy, see John K. Fairbank and Albert Feuerwerker, eds., *The Cambridge History of China* (Cambridge and Taipei: Cambridge University Press and Caves Books, 1986), vol. 13, *Republic China, 1912–1949*, pt. 2, 220–29.

81. For more on the Third Bureau and its transformation into a nominal "Cultural Committee" from the late 1930s to the 1940s, see Yang Hansheng, "Huiyi wenhua gongzuo weiyuanhui," in *Chongqing kangzhan jishi* (Chongqing: Chongqing chubanshe, 1985).

82. I have placed "tradition" in quotation marks to highlight the invented nature of "traditional opera" in modern China.

83. Tian Han, "Lun zhanshi xiju de xin yu jiu," in Tian Han, *Kangzhan yu xiju* (Chongqing: Duli chubanshe, 1939).

84. Dong Jian, *Tian Han zhuan* (Beijing: Shiyue wenyi chubanshe, 1996), 558.

85. Tian Han, *Xin ernü yingxiong zhuan*, in *Tian Han quanji*, vol. 7, 333–35. This song echoes some lyrics by Qiu Jin, especially as expressed in the image of the woman warrior. For more on Qiu Jin's writings in English translation, see Wilt L. Idema and Beata Grant, *The Red Brush: Writing Women of Imperial China* (Cambridge, MA: Harvard University Asia Center, 2004), 765–808.

86. Cross-dressing is an enduring theme in the making of the female scholar-warrior, from the story of Mulan, the legend of the butterfly lovers, and the female royal son-in-law (*nü fuma*) to the real life wartime female solider Xie Bingying. For a discussion of cross-dressing and androgyny in the works of Tian Han in particular and modern Chinese performance in general, see Liang Luo, "Modern Girl, Modern Men, and the Politics of Androgyny in Modern China," in "China," special issue, *Michigan Quarterly Review*, vol. 47, no. 2 (April 2008).

87. Tian Han, *Xin ernü yingxiong zhuan*, in *Tian Han quanji*, vol. 7, 388.

88. Ibid., 395.

89. Tian Han, "Fanpaiya de shiji," in *Tian Han sanwen ji* (Shanghai: Jindai shudian, 1936).

90. For more on female same-sex desire in Chinese literature, see Tze-lan D. Sang, *The Emerging Lesbian: Female Same-Sex Desire in Modern China* (Chicago: University of Chicago Press, 2003).

91. See Tian Han, *Xin ernü yingxiong zhuan*, in *Tian Han quanji*, vol. 7, 435.

92. See *Dong Jieyuan Xixiang ji*, 8 vols. (Beijing: Renmin wenxue chubanshe, 1962); and Wang Shifu, *Xixiang ji* (Shanghai: Shanghai guji chubanshe, 1978). The

two versions have been studied together, although the Wang version enjoys wider popularity. See Wang Zhiyong, ed., *Dong Wang hekanben Xixiang ji yanjiu lunwenji* (Gaoxiong: Fuwen tushu chubanshe, 1991).

93. See Tian Han, *Xin ernü yingxiong zhuan*, in *Tian Han quanji*, vol. 7, 421.

94. See Yuan Jiao, "Hongxian," in *Ganze yao*, edited by Tao Zongyi (Shanghai: Shangwu yinshuguan, 1927); and Pei Xing, "Nie Yinniang," in Pei Xing, *Chuanqi* (Taipei: Shijie shuju, 1959).

95. See David Der-wei Wang, *Fin-de-Siècle Splendor: Repressed Modernities of Late Qing Fiction, 1848–1911* (Stanford, CA: Stanford University Press, 1997), 157.

96. Ibid., 156.

97. The theater is named after the Shanghai theater that premiered "Lovers in Troubled Times" in 1935. See *Tian Han quanji*, vol. 7, 314. The use of *Pingju* to refer to *Jingju* (due to the renaming of Beijing as Beiping) should not be confused with *Pingqiang bangzixi*, popular in North China and renamed Pingju (Ping Opera) in Shanghai in the 1930s. For more on Ping Opera, see Hu Sha, *Pingju jianshi* (Beijing: Zhongguo xiju chubanshe, 1982).

98. Tian Han gave this speech on drama and opera at the welcoming party hosted by Ma Yanxiang in his honor on April 23, 1939 in Guilin, as reported in *Jiuwang ribao* (Guilin), April 24, 1939, quoted in Dong Jian, *Tian Han zhuan* (Beijing: Shiyue wenyi chubanshe, 1996), 558.

99. Ouyang Xiu, "Rhapsody on the Sounds of Autumn," translated by A. C. Graham in *The Anchor Book of Chinese Poetry*, edited by Tony Barnstone and Chou Ping (New York: Anchor Books, 2005). Tian Han quoted lengthy excerpts from Ouyang Xiu's rhapsody in his play of the same name, in *Tian Han quanji*, vol. 4, 265–66.

100. Tian Han, *Qiusheng fu*, in *Tian Han quanji*, vol. 4, 251.

101. Ibid., 253.

102. Tian Han quoted the diary of a student, Chen Mingzhong, to lend a sense of authenticity to his new lyrics for "Volga Boatmen's Song," their boat song on the West Lake. See Tian Han, "Women de ziji pipan," in *Tian Han quanji*, vol. 15, 145.

103. Tian Han, *Qiusheng fu*, in *Tian Han quanji*, vol. 4, 284.

104. Ibid.

105. Ibid., 313–14.

106. Tian Han, "Xuezi," in *Yinse de meng* (Shanghai: Liangyou tushu gongsi, 1928).

107. Tian Han, *Qiusheng fu*, in *Tian Han quanji*, vol. 4, 322.

108. Ibid. The theme of falling leaves returning to their roots gained new life in 2007, when the Taiwanese American popular singer Leehom Wang, inspired by his role as the patriotic student leader K'uang Yu-min in Ang Lee's 2007 film *Lust, Caution*, composed a song, "Luoye guigen," and wrote lyrics for it with the borrowed identity of Kuang Y. M. Although the political meaning of returning to the masses is

nowhere to be found in the 2007 song, the music video, directed by Leehom Wang himself, nonetheless employs images of childhood to convey the sense of unfulfilled love, tragedy, and loss. See the "Luoye guigen" music video, inspired by *Lust, Caution,* lyrics and music by Kuang Y. M., dir. and performed by Leehom Wang, Taipei: Hito Radio, June 20, 2007.

109. As Lijiang is a stand-in for Guilin, Xiaoxiang stands in for the city of Changsha, the capital of Hunan province and the home province of both the fictive Xu Ziyu and the real Tian Han.

110. Tian Han, *Qiusheng fu,* in *Tian Han quanji,* vol. 4, 343.

111. Here *ernü* literally means "sons and daughters." In the specific context, it refers to young people from the northeastern provinces. It can also be translated as "lovers" as it fits what Tian Han had in mind when naming his film story *Fengyun ernü,* which I translate as "Lovers in Troubled Times" rather than "Children of Troubled Times" to highlight the transition from lovers to heroes throughout the story.

112. This is reminiscent of the *shimbei shugi* (pro-Americanism) for which the Japanese secret police condemned the YMCA activities in Taishō Tokyo. See Gaimushō gaikō kiroku, "Shina kankei jimu gaiyō," Japanese Foreign Ministry Office, Diplomatic Archives, document no. 3-10-5-17-2, 1922, 108–26.

113. See Evans Fordyce Carlson, *Twin Stars of China: A Behind-the-Scenes Story of China's Valiant Struggle for Existence by a U.S. Marine Who Lived and Moved with the People* (New York: Dodd, Mead & Company, 1940).

114. Tian Han, *Qiusheng fu,* in *Tian Han quanji,* vol. 4, 340.

115. Ibid., 347.

116. Ibid.

117. See Bao Weihong, "Baptism by Fire: Spectatorship and Aesthetic Affect in Chinese Cinema from Shanghai to Chongqing (PhD diss., University of Chicago, 2005).

118. Tian Han, *Qiusheng fu,* in *Tian Han quanji,* vol. 4, 363–64.

119. It is worth noting that Tian Han's construction of female soldiers was not without real life models. The Chinese writer Lin Yutang, famous for introducing Chinese culture to the English-speaking world at the time, presented Xie Bingying as a real life Chinese woman soldier by translating and publishing (abroad) her "Army Diary." One needs to acknowledge the *packaged* nature of the image of Xie Bingying, both by herself and by her enthusiastic male translator. For recent scholarship on Lin Yutang, see Shuang Shen, *Cosmopolitan Publics: Anglophone Print Culture in Semi-colonial Shanghai* (New Brunswick, NJ: Rutgers University Press, 2009); and Qian Suoqiao, *Liberal Cosmopolitan: Lin Yutang and Middling Chinese Modernity* (Leiden: Brill, 2010).

120. Tian Han, *Qiusheng fu,* in *Tian Han quanji,* vol. 4, 369–70.

121. See Prasenjit Duara, "The Regime of Authenticity: Timelessness, Gender,

and National History in Modern China," *History and Theory,* vol. 37, no. 3 (October 1998), 287–308.

122. Ying Yunwei dir., *Yi Jiangnan,* screenplay by Tian Han, starring Zhou Xuan (Shanghai: Guotai yingye gongsi, 1947). Tian Han, *Yi Jiangnan,* original screenplay lost, transcribed from the film by Zi Qing, in *Tian Han dianying juben xuan* (Beijing: Zhongguo dianying chubanshe, 1983), in *Tian Han quanji,* vol. 10, 321–24.

123. Ibid., 323.

124. See, for example, ibid., 331, where the poet Li Zhiyun borrows an umbrella from a beautiful girl in the rain along the West Lake in the style of Xu Xian in *Baishe Zhuan* (The White Snake).

125. The wartime cartography of revolution, on the other hand, points to how Chinese patriots being forced to go to other parts of the country and forging a new nation through artistic activities. See ibid., 369.

126. Ibid., 378–85.

127. See Tian Han, *Muxing zhiguang* (film story), *Chenbao* (Shanghai), July 21–25, 1933, 10, published under Bu Wancang, in *Tian Han quanji,* vol. 10, 21–31; and Tian Han, *Muxing zhiguang* (screenplay), transcribed from the film by Lei Ting, in *Tian Han dianying juben xuanji* (Beijing: Zhongguo dianying chubanshe, 1983), in *Tian Han quanji,* vol. 10, 35–65.

128. See Johann Wolfgang von Goethe, *Italian Journey: 1786–1788,* translated by W. H. Auden and Elizabeth Mayer (New York: Penguin Classics, 1992).

129. See "Nanguo xuanyan," *Nanguo banyuekan,* January 5, 1924, quoted in Liu Ping, *Xijuhun: Tian Han pingzhuan* (Beijing: Zhongyang wenxian chubanshe, 1998), 134.

130. See Yan Zhewu ed., *Nanguo de xiju* (Shanghai: Mengya shudian, 1929); Jiang Biwei, *Wo yu Beihong: Jiang Biwei huiyilu* (Nanchang: Yuelu shushe, 1986); and Ouyang Yuqian, *Dianying banlu chujiaji* (Beijing: Zhongguo dianying chubanshe, 1984).

131. Tian Han planned to write a series of three historical plays each named after a locale in South China bearing the character *huang* (yellow), hence the "three yellows." The planned plays are *Huanghua gang* ("The Yellow Flower Mound," written between 1925 and 1930 in commemoration of the Canton Uprising of 1911), *Huanghe lou* ("The Yellow Crane Tower," in commemoration of the Wuchang Uprising of 1911), and *Huangpu chao* ("The Tide of the Yellow Bank River," reflecting "the Nanjing Road Incident," part of the May Thirtieth movement in Shanghai in 1925). The first play is unfinished, and the latter two never materialized. See Tian Han, "Women de ziji pipan," in *Tian Han quanji,* vol. 15, 86.

Chapter 4

1. Philip Roth, *Portnoy's Complaint* (1969), in *Philip Roth, Novels, 1967–1972* (New York: Library of America, 2005), 395.

2. See Joris Ivens's handwritten shooting notes for *The 400 Million,* shot on location in China during 1938. Kees Bakker, "Inventory of the Joris Ivens Archives," European Foundation Joris Ivens, Nijmegen, the Netherlands, 1998, Inv. no. JIA 2.3.02.39.01-238.

3. See Pao-ch'en Lee, ed., *China's Patriots Sing* (Chungking: China Information Publishing Company, 1939).

4. See *Zhonghua renmin gongheguo xianfa* (Beijing: Quanguo renmin daibiao dahui, 2004), chap. 4, item 136.

5. Malte Hagener analyzes the establishment of the documentary as a genre and film studies as a discipline and the creation of film archives with government funding in various European countries. See Malte Hagener, *Moving Forward, Looking Back: The European Avant-Garde and the Invention of Film Culture, 1919–1939* (Amsterdam: Amsterdam University Press, 2007), 16.

6. Craig Calhoun, *Nations Matter: Culture, History, and the Cosmopolitan Dream* (New York: Routledge, 2007), 7–9.

7. Ibid., 45–48.

8. According to Nie Er's diary, he started to learn English at age fourteen in 1926 in Kunming, if not earlier. An entry on Karl Marx was recorded in the tenth month of 1927. A full "Winter Vacation Daily" was written in English by the end of 1927, where he recorded his activities as follows: practicing piano, participating in drama performances, painting, copying music notes, studying English at the YMCA, attending concerts at the Educational Association, and going to movies. He started to study Japanese in 1930, and "*The Internationale*" first appeared in an entry in the same year. Nie Er went to Shanghai later in 1930 and recorded fascinating details of his intimate contact with the film industry, in particular his role in bringing music into film after joining the Lianhua (United China) film company. A striking entry on April 21, 1935, days before he finalized his composition for "March of the Volunteers" in Tokyo, suggests that he most likely had been directly influenced by Japanese imperial marches lauding Japan's colonial presence in Manchuria. See Nie Er, *Nie Er riji* (Zhengzhou: Daxiang chubanshe, 2004).

9. Tian Han may be referring to a famous American painting, *The Battle Hymn of the Republic,* in which a drummer, a fife player, and a flag bearer join the American Revolution.

10. Benjamin mentioned Ivens's *Borinage,* a 1933 documentary about coal miners' strikes in the Borinage region of Belgium, as a representative case that "offers everyone the opportunity to rise from passer-by to movie extra. In this way any man might even find himself part of a work of art." Walter Benjamin, "The Work of Art in the Age of Mechanical Reproduction" (1936), in Walter Benjamin, *Illuminations: Essays and Reflections,* edited and with an introduction by Hannah Arendt, translated by Harry Zohn (New York: Harcourt, Brace & World, 1968), 233.

11. Joris Ivens, dir., *The 400 Million*, 1939, 53.51 min., 35 mm, black and white, New York: History Today Inc. "March of the Volunteers" appeared from minutes 20:20 to 21:20, lasting a full minute.

12. These terms were not alien to contemporary political discourse in China. In the Civil War that followed World War II, the CCP focused heavily on its "new democratic" strategy against the KMT.

13. Guo Moruo led a delegation representing China at the conference. Tian Han was a member of the Chinese delegation.

14. Joris Ivens went to China to film as a member of "History Today Inc., Motion Picture Production," a New York and Hollywood venture that had Ernest Hemingway, Lillian Hellman, and Ivens himself as members of board of directors. Hans Wegner Archive, document no. 91, European Foundation Joris Ivens, Nijmegen, the Netherlands.

15. Walter Benjamin relied on Ivens, Eisler, and Brecht in developing some of his most celebrated theoretical pieces, with a special focus on the pedagogical quality and democratic participation of Ivens's documentary, Eisler's music, and Brecht's theater. See Benjamin, "The Work of Art in the Age of Mechanical Reproduction," 219–54; and Walter Benjamin, "The Author as Producer," *New Left Review*, vol. 1, no. 62 (July-August 1970), 83-96.

16. Ivens met Madame Sun Yat-sen in Hong Kong in February 1938 before arriving in Hankow. Madame Sun may have introduced him to Zhou Enlai in Hankow. See Joris Ivens, *The Camera and I* (New York: International Publishers, 1969), 149.

17. Hans Schoots, *Living Dangerously: A Biography of Joris Ivens* (Amsterdam: Amsterdam University Press, 2000), 24.

18. Tian Han, "Lingguang," *Taiping yang*, vol. 2, no. 9, (January 1921), 5–28; August Strindberg, *Ett drömspel* (1901) (Stockholm: Norstedt, 1988).

19. Schoots, *Living Dangerously*, 25.

20. André Stufkens, "The Song of Movement: Joris Ivens's First Films and the Cycle of the Avant-Garde," in *Joris Ivens and the Documentary Context*, edited by Kees Bakker (Amsterdam: Amsterdam University Press, 1999), 54.

21. Tian Han, *Muqin*, based on Gorky's novel, in *Tian Han daibiaozuo* (Shanghai: Santong shuju, 1941), vol. 1.

22. Bertolt Brecht wrote *Die Mutter* (The Mother) from 1930 to 1931 in collaboration with Hanns Eisler, Slatan Dudow, and Günter Weisenborn. The play combined different genres ranging from agitprop, *Lehrstück*, and the biography play to historical drama. The songs composed by Eisler heightened the play's political impact and were played separately at concerts and rallies in 1932. See Laura J. R. Bradley, *Brecht and Political Theater: The Mother on Stage* (New York: Oxford University Press, 2006), 8–11.

23. See "Bohui'er zhige" (1932), lyrics by Tian Han, music by Lü Ji, in *Tian Han cizuo gequji*, edited by Sun Shen, Li Yinghai, and Xiang Yansheng (Beijing: Renmin yinyue chubanshe, 2003), 1.

24. See Paul Robeson, *Here I Stand*, with Lloyd L. Brown and an introduction by Sterling Stuckey (Boston: Beacon Press, 1988), 32–35; and Martin Duberman, *Paul Robeson, A Biography by Martin Duberman* (New York: New Press, 1989), 113–24.

25. See Joris Ivens's notes, handwritten in Hankow (Hankou) in 1938, on sound effects recording for *The 400 Million*, Joris Ivens Archives, JIA 2.3.02.39.01-238.

26. Pao-ch'en Lee, "China's War Songs: Everybody Sings Them and Many Are Being Written and Distributed," *New York Times*, December 24, 1939, 9. For more on Pao-ch'en Lee (Li Baochen, 1907–79), see Zhao Qin, *Li Baochen*, Taiwan yinyue-guan zishen yinyuejia congshu, no. 23 (Taipei: Shibao wenhua, 2003).

27. Pao-ch'en Lee, "China's War Songs," *New York Times*, December 24, 1939, 9.

28. Joris Ivens, *The Camera and I* (New York: International Publishers, 1969), 141.

29. Ibid., 51.

30. Komsomol is a syllabic abbreviation of the Russian Kommunisticheskii Soyuz Molodyozhi, or All-Union Leninist Young Communist League. See ibid., 67–74.

31. See Zhao Qin, *Li Baochen*, 18–25, 53–63.

32. Pao-ch'en Lee, ed., *China's Patriots Sing* (Chungking: China Information Publishing Company, 1939).

33. See Lee's "explanatory notes," included in the ibid., unpaginated, placed before page 1.

34. Ibid.

35. Ibid., 4–5. The lyrics appeared in Lee's songbook exactly as quoted above. The syllabic hyphenation in transcribing the lyrics represents the musical rhythm. It also demonstrates Lee's attentiveness in matching his English translation with the original music.

36. Given Tian Han's background, it is possible to read *wanzhong yixin* as borrowed from, and now used as an implicit polemic against, the Japanese slogan "one hundred million Japanese beat as one heart" (*ichioku isshin*).

37. Lee, "China's War Songs," 9.

38. Ibid.

39. Popularity is hard to measure, although it seems hard to imgine that Lee used the claims of popularity as a way to promote "March" in his songbook, which was sponsored by the Nationalists in Chongqing.

40. S. Wells Williams et al., eds., *A Syllabic Dictionary of the Chinese Language* (Tung chou [Tongzhou]: North China Union College, 1909).

41. See Marius B. Jansen, *The Japanese and Sun Yat Sen* (Cambridge, MA: Harvard University Press, 1954); and Marius B. Jansen, *The Making of Modern Japan* (Cambridge, MA: Harvard University Press, 2002).

42. Robert Chi's analysis of the addressee in "March of the Volunteers" is helpful here. See Robert Chi, "'The March of the Volunteers': From Movie Theme Song to National Anthem," in *Re-envisioning the Chinese Revolution: The Politics and Poetics of Collective Memories in Reform China,* edited by Ching Kwan Lee and Guobin Yang (Stanford, CA: Stanford University Press, 2007), 222.

43. See Xiao Hong, *The Field of Life and Death and Tales of Hulan River* (Bloomington: Indiana University Press, 1979).

44. Rana Mitter, *The Manchurian Myth: Nationalism, Resistance, and Collaboration in Modern China* (Berkeley: University of California Press, 2000), 3. See also Rana Mitter's historiographical review, "Modernity, Internationalization, and War in the History of Modern China," *Historical Journal,* vol. 48, no. 2 (2005), 523–43.

45. John Fitzgerald, "The Nationless State: The Search for a Nation in Modern Chinese Nationalism," *Australian Journal of Chinese Affairs,* no. 33 (January 1995), 76.

46. For an in-depth discussion of the rise of anticolonial nationalism, see Erez Manela, *The Wilsonian Moment: Self-Determination and the International Origins of Anticolonial Nationalism* (New York: Oxford University Press, 2007).

47. On the point of antifascism, there is one complication here: Chiang Kai-shek did not completely break with the Nazis until 1941, although he did have Soviet support until 1939. The Germans maintained a diplomatic presence in Chongqing until they switched their support to Wang Jingwei in 1941.

48. See Lee, *China's Patriots Sing.*

49. See Barak Kushner, *The Thought War: Japanese Imperial Propaganda* (Honolulu: University of Hawai'i Press, 2007), 29.

50. See Tian Han, "Abixiniya de muqin," in *Limin zhiqian* (Shanghai: Beixin shuju, 1937).

51. Robert Capa ascended to world fame through his expressive photographs taken at the war front during the Spanish Civil War. Invited by Joris Ivens, he went to China as a photographic assistant and reporter for *Life* magazine in 1938. See Alex Kershaw, *Blood and Champagne: The Life and Times of Robert Capa* (New York: Thomas Dunne Books, St. Martin's Press, 2002).

52. Paul Robeson went to Spain in 1938 in support of the International Brigades. He also appeared, together with Madame Sun Yat-sen, in London in a Save China Assembly later the same year. See Duberman, *Paul Robeson,* 217–22.

53. See Ivens, *The Camera and I;* and W. H. Auden and Christopher Isherwood, *Journey to a War* (New York: Octagon Books, 1972).

54. Auden and Isherwood, *Journey to a War,* 88.

55. Ivens, *The Camera and I,* 158.

56. See Ibid. Both Shangqiu and Tai'erzhuang are testimonials to the shifting borders of war.

57. *Guoge* (feature film, dir. Wu Ziniu, 1999) and *Guoge* (TV series, 2010) are two examples.

58. See Ren Dong, "Xia Yan dui sanshi niandai zhongguo zuoyi dianying yundong de gongxian," *Dianying wenxue,* no. 3 (2008), 12–13.

59. See Wang Xufeng, "Zhongguo yousheng dianying chuqi de guochan dianying luyinji: Jinian Situ Huimin xiansheng danchen 100 zhounian," *Xiandai dianying jishu,* no. 6 (2010); Li Wenbin, "Situ Huimin," in *Zhongguo dianyingjia liezhuan* (Beijing: Zhongguo dianying chubanshe, 1992), vol. 1; and Situ Lian and Guan Hui, eds., *Situ Huimin zhuanlue,* in *Guangdong wenshi ziliao* (Guangzhou: Guangdong renmin chubanshe, 1989), vol. 60.

60. See Tian Han, "Yangzijiang de baofengyu," in *Tian Han quanji,* vol. 3, 37–71.

61. See Tian Han, "Women de ziji pipan," in *Tian Han quanji,* vol. 15, 80–186.

62. Boris Pilnyak, Tian Han, and Jiang Guangci had been involved in the founding of the Sino-Russian Society for Cultural Relations as early as in 1926 amid Tian Han's independent filmmaking endeavor "To the People". It was also Tian Han who arranged the first screening of *Battleship Potemkin* in Shanghai as early as in 1926. These episodes are significant as they serve as reminders of the "Sino-Russ" (Pilnyak's term) intellectual connections that existed a decade before the creation of Soviet Friends Society and the making of "March of the Volunteers" in the early to mid-1930s. See Boris Pilnyak, *Chinese Story and Other Tales,* translated and with an introduction and notes by Vera T. Reck and Michael Green (Norman: University of Oklahoma Press, 1988), 57, 90.

63. *Dianying yishu,* issues 1–12 (Beijing: Zhongguo dianying chubanshe, 1988), 64.

64. Tian Han, "Sulian dianying yishu fazhan de jiaoxun yu woguo dianying yundong de qiantu," *Nanguo yuekan,* vol. 2, no. 4 (July 20, 1930), in *Tian Han quanji,* vol. 18, 74–95.

65. The film won an honorary mention at the 1935 Moscow International Film Festival.

66. See Xia Yan, "Letter to Zhou Weishi," especially on Liu Liangmo's involvement in the Soviet Friends Society in 1935, *Xin wenhua shiliao* (Sources on the New Culture Movement), no. 6 (1994).

67. Aaron Avshalomov (1894–1965) was a composer and conductor of the Shanghai Symphony Orchestra from 1943 to 1946. See Jacob Avshalomov and Aaron Avshalomov, *Avshalomovs' Winding Way: Composers Out of China—a Chronicle* (Bloomington, IN: Xlibris, 2002).

68. Sun Jinan, *Zhongguo yinyue tongshi jianbian* (Jinan: Shandong jiaoyu chubanshe, 1991), 470.

69. See *Ye meigui* (Wild Rose), dir. Sun Yu, starring Jin Yan and Wang Renmei (Shanghai: Lianhua yingye gongsi, 1932). For more on Wang Renmei, see Wang Renmei, with Xie Bo, *Wo de chengming yu buxing: Wang Renmei huiyilu* (Shanghai: Shanghai wenyi chubanshe, 1985).

70. An E worked as a journalist in Shanghai while engaging in underground activities as a Communist. For more on this episode in An E's life, see An Yu, "Zhanhuo zhong zouchu de hongse cainü: An E," *Dangshi bocai,* no. 2 (2008), 44–46.

71. See Wang Xufeng, "Zhongguo yousheng dianying chuqi de guochan dianying luyinji—jinian Situ Huimin xiansheng danchen 100 zhounian."

72. For Bo Xilai and his "Chongqing model" for singing red songs, see Ye Sishi and Yang Yan, "Xin shiqi zhuliu wenhua jiequ dazhong wenyi de lujing: Cong 'chaoji nüsheng,' 'hongge hui,' dao 'chang hong se' huodong," *Xinwen zhishi,* no. 7 (2011), 15–17. For a recent study on mainstream culture as manifested in contemporary Chinese television drama, see Zhong Xueping, *Mainstream Culture Refocused: Television Drama, Society, and the Production of Meaning in Reform-Era China* (Honolulu: University of Hawai'i Press, 2010).

73. See Guo Chao, *Guoge licheng* (Beijing: Zhongguo guoji guangbo diantai chubanshe, 2002), 33.

74. See ibid., 19.

75. Nationalist censorship was a central topic in Joris Ivens's diary, written during his shooting of *The 400 Million* in China in 1938. See Ivens, *The Camera and I.*

76. See Guo Chao, *Guoge licheng,* 34.

77. Situ Huimin served as an important contact for the Dutch filmmaker Joris Ivens when he went to the PRC to teach and film in the 1950s. Situ Huimin's sons' New Year's card to Ivens in 1958 in China is preserved at the European Foundation Joris Ivens in Nijmegen, the Netherlands. Sihu's centennial was commemorated in the official magazine of the foundation, the caretaker of Ivens's archives in his birthplace, Nijmegen. See "Commemoration of Huimin Situ's 100th Birthday," in *The Ivens Magazine,* no. 16 (October 2010), 15.

78. See Guo Chao, *Guoge licheng,* 20–21.

79. See ibid., 21.

80. Ibid., 34. The last scene of *Center Stage* (dir. Stanley Kwan, 1993) vividly visualizes the introduction of sound devices in Chinese filmmaking, when China's great actress of the silent era, Ruan Lingyu, expresses her determination to learn to speak Mandarin onscreen (she grew up speaking Cantonese). Her performance, especially that of a speaking female subject, became an act of enunciation and an embodied experience of subject making, both for the performers and for their audience.

81. See Hei Tianshi (Nie Er), "Zhongguo gewu duanlun," *Dianying yishu*, no. 3, (1932).

82. See Guo Chao, *Guoge licheng*, 34; and Joshua H. Howard, "The Making of a National Icon: Commemorating Nie Er, 1935–1949," *Twentieth Century China*, vol. 37, no. 1 (2012), 5–29.

83. For the relevance of the December Ninth movement in modern Chinese literature, see Su Guangwen, "Wenxue yu lishi: Zhongguo xiandai wenxue shiye li de '12.9 yundong,'" *Guizhou shehui kexue*, no. 6, (2005).

84. It is possible that Tian Han have incorporated "Songstress under the Iron Hoof" into the stage performance of "Storm over the Yangtze" during the making of "Lovers in Troubled Times" in 1934–35. However, as I was not able to locate any published version of the play before the version included in *Dazhong juxuan*, and this 1938 version only retains one act and four songs without the appearance of "Songstress," I really cannot say for sure whether Tian included the song either in performance or in print earlier. The version widely available now is a result of Tian's revision of 1955, which contains many more songs (including "Songstress") and much more elaborate plot elements, reflecting the politics of the mid-1950s. See Tian Han, "Yangzijiang de baofengyu," in *Dazhong juxuan*, edited by You Jing (Hankou: Shanghai zazhi gongsi, 1938), vol. 1, 41–65; and Tian Han, "Yangzijiang de baofengyu," in *Tian Han quanji*, vol. 3, 37–71.

85. Tian Han rewrote "Storm over the Yangtze" in 1955. The 1955 version includes a prelude, namely, a poem to be recited. The keywords *heping* (peace), *minzhu* (democracy), *shehui zhuyi* (socialism) in the last line of the poem are markers of the new edition. The first scene of the new version includes "Maibao ge" (Newspaper-Selling Song), "Biye ge" (Graduation Song), "Tieti xia de genü" (Songstress under the Iron Hoof), "Matou gongren ge" (Song of Dock Workers), and "Dazhuan ge" (Song of Hitting Bricks). Only the last song was in the 1938 version. Songs in the second scene include "Dalu ge" (Song of the Big Road) and "Dazhuang ge" (Song of Hitting Pickets), which was in the 1938 version, among other, unnamed songs. See Tian Han, "Yangzijiang de baofengyu," in *Tian Han quanji*, vol. 3, 37–71.

86. Walter Benjamin, "The Author as Producer," *New Left Review*, vol. 1, no. 62 (July-August 1970), 93–94. ,

87. Bertolt Brecht, "On the Formalistic Character of the Theory of Realism," in *Aesthetics and Politics*, with Theodor Adorno, Walter Benjamin, Ernst Bloch, and Georg Lukács, with an afterword by Fredric Jameson (London and New York: Verso, 1980), 72–76; and Bertolt Brecht, "Popularity and Realism," in *Aesthetics and Politics*, 79–85.

88. See, for example, *Kangzhan banian muke xuanji* (Shanghai: Kaiming shudian, 1946).

89. Xiaobing Tang, "Echoes of Roar China! On Vision and Voice in Modern

Chinese Art," *positions: east asia cultures critique*, vol. 14, no. 2 (2006), 467–94; Xiaobing Tang, *Origins of the Chinese Avant-Garde: The Modern Woodblock Movement* (Berkeley: University of California Press, 2007).

90. This slogan brings to mind Sun Yat-sen's slogan "recover China and chase away the Tartars." See Liu Ping, "Kangzhan paohuo zhong de xiju chuangzuo yu yanchu," http://www.china001.com/show_hdr.php?xname=PPDDMV0&dname=HLPO741&xpos=36, accessed July 15, 2009.

91. Ibid.

92. "Horror makes you scream, melodrama makes you cry, and porn makes you 'come.'" Jane M. Gaines, "Political Mimesis," in *Collecting Visible Evidence*, edited by Jane M. Gaines and Michael Renov (Minneapolis: University of Minnesota Press, 1999), 90.

93. For more on the encounter between Bertolt Brecht and Mei Lanfang in Moscow, see Haun Saussy, "Mei Lanfang in Moscow, 1935: Familiar, Unfamiliar, Defamiliar," *Modern Chinese Literature and Culture*, vol. 18, no. 1 (Spring 2006), 8–29.

94. Bertolt Brecht, *Brecht on Theatre: The Development of an Aesthetic*, edited by John Willett (New York: Macmillan, 1964), 122.

95. Sergei Eisenstein, "Montage of Attractions," translated by Daniel Gerould, in *Re: Direction—a Theoretical and Practical Guide*, edited by Rebecca Schneider and Gabrielle H. Cody (New York: Routledge, 2002), 303–4.

96. See Lynn Mally, *Culture of the Future: the Proletkult Movement in Revolutionary Russia* (Berkeley: University of California Press, 1990).

97. Eisenstein, "Montage of Attractions," 304.

98. See Ivens, dir., *The 400 Million*. 20:50-21:20.

99. See You Jing ed., *Dazhong juxuan* (Hankou: Shanghai zazhi gongsi, 1938), vol. 1, 19.

100. According to Ivens's retrospective account, written in 1945, he probably obtained a copy of the Denton record in Hollywood. It was recorded by Ren Guang with the Denton chorus in 1935 in Shanghai. The availability of "March of the Volunteers" in Hollywood in 1938 and its prominence in *The 400 Million* reminds us of the rather unusual flow of mechanically reproduced sound bites from China to the United States, which then came to represent the "real" China in 1938 via a European filmmaker who connected China and Hollywood artists and activists through his filmmaking. See Joris Ivens, "How I Filmed *The 400 Million*," in *Joris Ivens and China* (Beijing: New World Press, 1983), 29.

101. Ivens's concluding words at the welcome meeting were recorded as "I represent countless people in Europe and North America, who sympathize with the anti-Japanese war in China. In order to defend truth and humanity, I am filming a true record of the courageous war effort in China, so as to have it spread all over the world." *Wenhui bao* (Shanghai), April 30, 1938, 3.

102. The Great Wall symbolism also brings to mind the troubled Southern Song and the Ming dynasties, when those situated within the Great Wall had to fight Jurchens, Khitans, Japanese, and Manchus.

103. As discussed in the introduction to this volume, propaganda is an inadequate, if not incorrect, translation of the Chinese word *xuanchuan,* which literally means "to announce and then to spread." *Xuanchuan dui,* in the Chinese context, is often understood as a singing and dance troupe with a mission, without the negative connotation attached to the English usage. Rather than avoiding the term, I consider it more constructive to confront the use of the term in the English language and to use it in the Chinese context with qualification.

104. The same style of modern Chinese tunic suit, first developed by the Nationalist leader Sun Yat-sen soon after the founding of the Republic, became widely known as the Mao suit in the West, after it became the standard male attire in the PRC for official occasions and hence came to be associated with communism. For more on fashion and national perception in modern China, See Antonia Finnane, *Changing Clothes in China: Fashion, History, Nation* (New York: Columbia University Press, 2008).

105. See Joris Ivens's notes, handwritten in Hankow in 1938, on sound effect recordings for *The 400 Million,* Joris Ivens Archives, JIA 2.3.02.39.01-238; and Ivens, "How I Filmed *The 400 Million,*" 29.

106. See Joris Ivens, "Documentary: Subjectivity and Montage," lecture given at the Museum of Modern Art, New York, December 13, 1939, in *Joris Ivens and the Documentary Context,* edited by Kees Bakker (Amsterdam: Amsterdam University Press, 1999), 250; and Robeson, *Here I Stand, 30.*

107. Ivens, "Documentary," 250–60.

108. According to Ivens's shooting notes from Hankow in 1938, the conductor featured in this Xi'an scene may be either Zhang Shu or Xian Xinghai, who together conducted the chorus singing "March of the Volunteers" in Hankow a few months later. A member of Tian Han's Nanguo she troupe in the 1920s, a member of the CCP since 1933, and a member of the Soviet Friends Society Music Group led by Tian Han, Zhang Shu worked closely with Tian up until his untimely death in a plane crash during the Second Sino-Japanese War in 1938. For more on Zhang Shu, see Huang Jishi, *Zhang Shu zhuan* (Beijing: Tuanjie chubanshe, 1994). Xian Xinghai, like Ren Guang a decade earlier, arrived in Paris to study music in 1929. Two years later he was admitted to the Paris Conservatory to study composition with both Vincent d'indy and Paul Dukas. Xian returned to China in 1935 and composed many popular songs for stage and screen. He worked closely with Zhang Shu in Wuhan during the war with Japan from 1935 to 1938. Xian went to Yan'an in October 1938, joined the CCP in 1939, and went to the Soviet Union to compose music for the documentary *Yan'an and the Eighth Route Army* in 1940. He died in Moscow in 1945, his health having suffered after an attempt to leave for China after

the 1941 German invasion of the Soviet Union (he was stranded in Alma Ata in Kazakhstan from 1943 to 1945). For more on Xian Xinghai, see Ma Ke, *Xian Xinghai zhuan* (Beijing: Renmin wenxue chubanshe, 1980).

109. Howard Taubman, "Songs That Chinese People Are Singing These Days: Other Releases," *New York Times,* November 30, 1941, 6.

110. *Chee Lai,* Keynote, 1941, three 10-inch records.

111. Duberman, *Paul Robeson,* 222.

112. Taubman, "Songs That Chinese People Are Singing," 6.

113. Howard Taubman, "'Firing Line' Songs Thrill Audience: Folk Ditties, Workers' Chants, War Songs Given under Negro Group's Auspices," *New York Times,* June 27, 1942, 9.

114. Luo Weihong, "Liu Liangmo and Anti-Japanese Mass singing Activities," *Shiji,* no. 5 (2005), 12.

115. Ibid., 12. Founded on September 20, 1935, in Shanghai, *Libao* was established as a direct response to the Japanese aggression in China. It catered to middle- to lower-class readers, promising to inform them of world affairs in five minutes and at the cost of only a dollar for a three-month subscription. Its focus on anti-Japanese resistance was highly popular among its readers, and its highest sales figures reached two hundred thousand per day.

116. Guo Chao, *Guoge jicheng,* 35.

117. According to Ivens's autobiography, however, he had shown *The 400 Million* at a Hollywood screening for the American Friends of the Chinese People in 1938. See Ivens, *The Camera and I,* 181.

118. See Israel Epstein, *My China Eye: Memoirs of a Jew and a Journalist* (San Francisco: Long River Press, 2005), 81.

119. See Joris Ivens's notes, handwritten in Hankow in 1938, on sound effect recordings for *The 400 Million,* Joris Ivens Archives, JIA 2.3.02.39.01-238.

120. Xian Xinghai, "Nie Er, Zhongguo xinxing yinyue de chuangzao zhe" (1938), in *Xian Xinghai quanji* (Guangzhou: Guangdong gaodeng jiaoyu chubanshe, 1989), vol. 1, 30.

121. T'ien-Han (Tian Han) and Nieh Erh (Nie Er), "March of the Volunteers," *Music Educators Journal,* vol. 29, no. 2 (November–December 1942), 26–27. The two-page article includes "March of the Volunteers" in staff notation with both English translation and accompaniment by Lee Pao-ch'en. Below the musical score, Lee included both his own translation and Liu Liangmo's translation side by side so readers could compare the two versions.

122. When visiting a museum in Singapore in 2009, I encountered a recording of "March of the Volunteers," sung by ethnic Chinese fighting the invading Japanese, in an exhibition booth, demonstrating its relevance to local history. "March of the Volunteers" is part of a permanent exhibition in the Singapore History Gallery of the National Museum of Singapore.

123. Guo Chao, *Guoge licheng,* 36.

124. T'ien-Han (Tian Han) and Nieh Erh (Nie Er), "March of the Volunteers," 27.

125. "Yiyongjun jinxingqu dashiji," in Guo Chao, *Guoge licheng* 36. "Yiyongjun jinxingqu dashiji" presents a chronological record of "March of the Volunteers."

126. The history and usage of numerical musical notations can be read as part of an attempt to vernacularize culture in modern China and Japan. One major reason for the popularity of the numerical notation in China must have been that few printing facilities in China could print staff notation while many could manage numerical notation.

127. See Tang, "Echoes of Roar China!," 467–94.

128. Joseph Levenson, in his *Revolution and Cosmopolitanism,* used "a people" (*minzu*) and "the people" (*renmin*) to distinguish the nation-based nationalism of the Nationalists and the class-based internationalism of the Communists, who consolidated their influence on the national "people" by means of their emphasis on an internationalist class of "peoples." See Joseph R. Levenson, *Revolution and Cosmopolitanism: The Western Stage and the Chinese Stages,* with a foreword by Frederic E. Wakeman Jr. (Berkeley: University of California Press, 1971), 6–7.

129. Scholars of "minority studies" have engaged with this topic for years. For a recent example, see Thomas S. Mullaney, *Coming to Terms with the Nation: Ethnic Classification in Modern China* (Berkeley: University of California Press, 2010).

130. See Fredric Jameson, *Postmodernism; or, the Cultural Logic of Late Capitalism* (London and New York: Verso, 1991), 16–18.

Chapter 5

1. The full-fledged legend of the White Snake cannot be traced back before the early sixteenth century, so it is the youngest of the four great folktales of China, that is, *Baishe zhuan* (White Snake), *Niulang zhinü* (The Weaver and the Cowherd), *Liangzhu* (The Butterfly Lovers), and *Mengjiangnü* (Lady Mengjiang). Over the centuries it continued to undergo extensive development, and Tian Han based his retelling on the late-nineteenth-century version of the tale, not on Feng Menglong's version. See Feng Menglong (1574–1646), "Bai niangzi yongzhen Leifengta," in Feng Menglong, *Jingshi tongyan* (Beijing: Renmin wenxue chubanshe, 1956), chap. 28; and Wilt L. Idema, *The White Snake and Her Son, A Translation of the Precious Scroll of Thunder Peak, with Related Texts* (Indianapolis: Hackett Publishing, 2009).

2. See Fang Chengpei (fl. 1771), *Leifeng ta chuanqi, 4 vols.* (Shanghai: Shanghai guji chubanshe, 1995); and Chen Yuqian, Chen Shiqi, and Yu Xiushan, *Yiyao zhuan,* 12 vols. (block print, double leaves, oriental style, in case, 1869).

3. See Pu Songling (1640–1715), *Quanben xinzhu Liaozhai zhiyi,* edited and annotated by Zhu Qikai (Beijing: Renmin wenxue chubanshe, 1989).

4. Tian Han also became the chief editor of *Renmin xiju* (People's Theater)

magazine, newly founded in Shanghai. He published "How to Conduct Opera Reform," "The Spoken Drama Movement in the Past Year," and a play entitled *Chaoxian fengyun: Jiawu zhizhan sanbuqu zhiyi* (Storms over Korea: One of the Jiawu War Trilogy) during 1950. He organized and attended the National Opera Work Conference. He served as the vice chairman of the conference and gave a speech entitled "Struggle for Patriotic People's New Opera." See "Tian Han nianbiao jianbian," in *Tian Han quanji,* vol. 20, 603–4.

5. See Tian Han, *Baishe zhuan,* first published in *Juben,* August 1953. Also see Tian Han, *Baishe zhuan* (Beijing: Baowentang shudian, October 1953); and Tian Han, *Baishe zhuan* (Beijing: Zuojia chubanshe, June 1955).

6. Examples include *Das Lied der Ströme* (The Song of the Rivers), dir. Joris Ivens, DEFA, 1954, 90 min., sound, black and white, 35 mm, commissioned by the World Federation of Trade Unions; and *Die Windrose* (The Windrose), dir. Alberto Cavalcanti et al., artistic director Joris Ivens, DEFA, 1957, commissioned by the Women's International Democratic Federation.

7. Walter Benjamin, "Theses on the Philosophy of History," in *Illuminations: Essays and Reflections,* edited and with an introduction by Hannah Arendt, translated by Harry Zohn (Boston: Houghton Mifflin Harcourt, 1968).

8. Tian Han quoted Mao Zedong's use of Shengong Bao to demonstrate the need to push such characters forward in an article on opera reform; see Tian Han, "Zenyang zuo xigai gongzuo?," in *Tian Han quanji,* vol. 17, 140-41; and Mao Zedong, "Lun xin minzhu zhuyi xianzheng," in *Mao Zedong xuanji* (Beijing: Renmin chubanshe, 1964).

9. Kang Sheng attacked *Xie Yaohuan* as a "big poisonous weed" at the National Modern Peking Opera Festival in June 1964; and *Renmin ribao* published an article openly criticizing *Xie Yaohuan* as "an antiparty and antisocialist big poisonous weed" in February 1966. See "Tian Han nianbiao jianbian," in *Tian Han quanji,* vol. 20, 610.

10. For more on the role of the Hunanese in the making of modern China, see Stephen R. Platt, *Provincial Patriots: The Hunanese and Modern China* (Cambridge, MA: Harvard University Press, 2007).

11. See Chen Tianhua, "Lun zhongguo yi gaichuang minzhu zhengti," in *Chen Tianhua ji* (Shanghai: Minzhi shuju, 1928).

12. Chen Tianhua's suicide was Tian Han's first indirect encounter with the body politic of modern China. A decade later, in Tokyo, Matsui Sumako's love suicide would reinforce Tian Han's sense of the aestheticism of death, youth, and artistic perfection from a different perspective.

13. Qiu Jin, Tang Qunying, and many other female revolutionaries were educated in Changsha, the provincial capital of Hunan, and returned to Hunan after their sojourns in Japan. Xu Teli, headmaster of the Changsha Normal School, from

which Tian Han graduated, was another representative educator at the time in Hunan.

14. See He Yintai and Li Dasan, *Tian Han pingzhuan* (Changsha: Hunan renmin chubanshe, 1984), 8.

15. Liang Qichao's *Xinmin congbao* and *Guofeng bao* were two prominent examples. *Minbao, Changsha ribao,* and *Shanghai shibao* were other popular newspapers, both local and national.

16. See Dong Jian, *Tian Han zhuan* (Beijing: Shiyue wenyi chubanshe, 1996), 54.

17. *Changsha ribao* became the most popular revolutionary newspaper in Hunan at the time. Its daily issue consisted of three large sheets and twelve pages, six of them devoted to news, one to a supplement, and five to advertisements. See *Changsha shizhi* (Changsha: Hunan chubanshe, 1996), vol. 13, 485.

18. Han'er (Tian Han), "Xin jiaozi," *Changsha ribao,* March 14–16, 1913.

19. Nanshe, the South Society, famous both for its elegant literary style and for its anti-Manchu politics, was founded by Chen Qubing, Xu Tianmei, and Liu Yazi in November 1909; all three were also members of Tongmenghui, led by Sun Yatsen. Fu Xiongxiang, a Nanshe poet, became the chief editor of *Changsha Daily,* and Kong Zhaoshuo, a Tongmenghui member, acted as editor. See *Changsha shizhi,* vol. 13, 485.

20. Only three of Yi Xiang's poems were collected in the 1936 edition of *Nanshe shiji,* vol. 2, 258–59. Judging from the dozens of Yi Xiang's poems published in *Taiping yang* magazine from March 1917 to October 1917, this collection only included a small fraction of Yi Xiang's poetic writings.

21. *Yuanben* evolved from *canjunxi. Canjunxi* (adjutant plays) in their simplest form are comic dialogues between two men, somewhat comparable to the modern *xiangsheng.* According to ancient anecdotes, *canjuxi* performances at court included political satire. In some cases, apparently, the term *canjuxi* was also applied to longer plays with more than two actors. In the twelfth century, *canjunxi* evolved into farce, which was referred to in the North, under the Jin, as *yuanben* and in the South, under the Southern Song, as *zaju.* Wilt Idema and Lloyd Haft, *A Guide to Chinese Literature* (Ann Arbor: Center for Chinese Studies, University of Michigan, 1997), 172. But *yuanben* is also used as a general term meaning "play" and is often used to describe one-act plays. Tian Han might simply be referring to a short opera here.

22. Han'er (Tian Han), "Xin Taohua shan," *Yuxing* literary supplement, *Shibao* (Shanghai), May 25–26, 1915.

23. Ibid.

24. It is likely that *The Times* in which Tian Han published his work was the same newspaper closely connected with Kang Youwei and Liang Qichao from 1904

onward. For more on the publishing history of *The Times* in Shanghai, see Huang Hu, *Zhongguo xinwen shiye fazhanshi* (Shanghai: Fudan daxue chubanshe, 2007).

25. See Xiaobing Tang, *Global Space and the Nationalist Discourse of Modernity: The Historical Thinking of Liang Qichao* (Stanford, CA: Stanford University Press, 1996).

26. For a recent analysis of "New Rome," See Alexander C. Y. Huang, *Chinese Shakespeares: Two Centuries of Cultural Exchange* (New York: Columbia University Press, 2009), 57–60.

27. See Dong Jian, *Tian Han zhuan,* 65-66.

28. Ibid, 60.

29. Joanne R. Bernardi, "The Literary Link: Tanizaki and the Pure Film Movement," in *A Tanizaki Feast: The International Symposium in Venice,* edited by Adriana Boscaro and Anthony Hood Chambers (Ann Arbor: University of Michigan Press, 1998), 82–84.

30. See Pu Songling, *Liaozhai zhiyi* (Shanghai: Shanghai guji chubanshe, 2005). Female performance using a borrowed body, key to the Japanese adaptations of the White Snake tale, is a common trope in Chinese literary tradition as well, as in *Huapi* (Painted Skin) from *Liaozhai zhiyi*, where a ghost paints the skin of a beautiful woman daily to maintain its beautiful appearance.

31. Tian Han, *Qiangwei zhilu* (Shanghai: Taidong tushuju), 1922.

32. Chaozhou as a dialect is closely linked to the Minnan dialects of southern Fujian, so Chaozhou is culturally much closer to Quanzhou and Zhangzhou (Xiamen) than to Canton. The romance of Chen San and Wuniang was already known from sixteenth-century printings of *chuanqi* plays written in Minnan. Ballads recounting the romance can be traced back to the eighteenth, and perhaps even the seventeenth, century. So the rewritings of the 1950s are only the latest incarnations of a tradition of more than four hundred years. There is a considerable body of scholarship on this legend in Taiwan. See Chen Xiang, *Chensan Wuniang yanjiu* (Taipei: Taiwan Shangwu yinshuguan), 1985.

33. For more on Osanai Kaonu, see Gioia Ottaviani, "'Difference' and 'Reflexivity': Osanai Kaonu and the Shingeki Movement," *Asian Theater Journal,* vol. 11, no. 2 (Autumn 1994), 213–30.

34. Tian Han, "Fan'elin yu qiangwei," *Shaonian zhongguo,* vol. 2, nos. 5–6 (November–December 1920).

35. For detailed discussion of Ouyang Yuqian's *Pan jinlian* and the intertextual tensions between premodern and modern texts it embodies, see Yomi Braester, *Witness against History: Literature, Film, and Public Discourse in Twentieth-Century China* (Stanford, CA: Stanford University Press, 2003), 56-80.

36. It is likely that Tian Han's lyrics for "Tianya genü," a theme song in the 1937 film *Malu tianshi,* were inspired by Ouyang's film of a decade earlier.

37. Lu Xun, "Biyacilai huaxuan xiaoyin," *Yiyuan zhaohua,* vol. 1, no. 4 (May

1929). See also *Lu Xun quanji* (Beijing: Renmin wenxue chubanshe, 1958), vol. 7, 547–49.

38. Tian Han, "Xin guoju yundong de diyisheng," *Liyuan gongbao* (Shanghai), nos. 22–23 (November 8 and 11, 1928), in *Tian Han quanji,* vol. 17, 1–2.

39. See Zhang Xianghua, *Tian Han nianpu* (Beijing: Zhongguo xiju chubanshe, 1992), 107.

40. See *Tian Han quanji,* vol. 15, 118.

41. Bo Hong (Tian Han), "Zhongguo jiuxi yu Mei Lanfang de zai pipan," *Zhonghua ribao* (Shanghai), October 21, 1934.

42. *Xin qingnian,* vol. 5, no. 4 (October 15, 1918).

43. The national theater movement had a strong backing from the Nationalist Party and achieved spectacular success with the foreign tours of Mei Lanfang, with the aid of Qi Rushan's theorizing of the new national opera in his writings.

44. Tian Han, "Sulian wei shenme yao qing Mei Lanfang qu yanxi," in *Tian Han quanji,* vol. 17, 35.

45. Tian Han was quoting Soviet playwright Vladimir Kirshon's writing on his impressions of Western European theater. See *ibid.,* 35.

46. See ibid. For an excellent analysis of Mei Lanfang's 1935 Soviet visit in the context of the multiple modernisms involved, see Haun Saussy, "Mei Lanfang in Moscow, 1935: Familiar, Unfamiliar, Defamiliar," in "Modernisms' Chinas," edited by Eric Hayot, special issue, *Modern Chinese Literature and Culture,* vol. 18, no. 1 (Spring 2006), 8–29.

47. Li Shuquan (Tian Han), *Shen yu ren zhijian,* translated from Tanizaki Jun'ichrō, with a biography of the author up to 1927 (Shanghai: Zhonghua shuju, 1934).

48. Tian Han welcomed Joris Ivens to Hankou in April 1938 at a gathering of some two hundred people, with the Dutch filmmaker, his group, and the New Zealander female journalist Robin Hyde as guests of honor. See *Wenhui bao* (Shanghai), April 30, 1938, 3. Also see the letter from Robin Hyde (Iris Wilkinson) to her father, Eddie Wilkinson, describing the meeting in detail in Derek Challis and Gloria Rawlinson, *The Book of Iris: A Life of Robin Hyde* (Auckland: Auckland University Press, 2002), 573–74. I thank Duncan Campbell for bringing this letter to my attention.

49. Tian Han, *Shagong,* in *Tian Han quanji,* vol. 7, 160.

50. Li Wei, "Zailun jingju gaige de Tian Han moshi," *Tongji daxue xuebao* (social science edition), vol. 16, no. 6 (December 2005), 95–99.

51. It is not impossible that Joris Ivens may have told Tian Han about *Zungchin,* by the seventeenth-century Dutch playwright Joost van den Vondel, which also deals with the suicide of Chongzhen. I thank Professor Wilt L. Idema for bring this possibility to my attention.

52. Tian Han, *Jianghan yuge,* in *Tian Han quanji,* vol. 7, 279–81.

53. For an investigation of this uncanny resonance, see Aranzazu Usandizaga and Andrew Monnickendam, eds., *Dressing Up for War: Transformations of Gender and Genre in the Discourse and Literature of War* (Amsterdam and New York: Rodopi, 2001).

54. Tian Han, "Guanyu Wu Song yu Pan Jinlian," in *Tian Han quanji,* vol. 17, 335.

55. Tian Han, "Zenyang xie *Jinbo ji*," in *Tian Han quanji,* vol. 17, 333–34. The bowl referenced in the title is the begging bowl, a key symbol indicating that a monk has cut himself off from all earthly attachments.

56. See Tian Han, "Zenyang zuo xigai gongzuo?–gei Zhou Yang tongzhi de shifeng xin," in *Tian Han quanji,* vol. 17, 103.

57. Ibid., 117.

58. Ibid., 122-23.

59. Ibid., 120–24.

60. Ibid., 157.

61. *Da'nao tiangong,* dir. Wan Laiming (Shanghai: Shanghai meishu dianying zhipianchang, 1961–64).

62. Tian Han, "Zenyang zuo xigai gongzuo?–gei Zhou Yang tongzhi de shifeng xin," letter 3, in *Tian Han quanji,* vol. 17, 158.

63. See Konishi Sho, "Translation and Conversion beyond Western Modernity: Tolstoian Religion in Meiji Japan," in *Converting Cultures: Religion, Ideology, and Transformations of Modernity* (Leiden: Brill, 2007), 244–55.

64. It is very likely that Tian Han learned the legend of the White Snake as a child in Changsha.

65. Tian, Han, "*Baishe zhuan* xu" in *Baishe zhuan,* (Beijing: Zuojia chubanshe, 1955), 1–5.

66. Tian Han, *Jinbo ji* (Shanghai: Zhonghua shuju, 1951); Dai Bufan, "Ping *Jinbo ji,*" *Renmin ribao,* September 12, 1952.

67. Chen Youming et al. (South China Opera Reform Committee), *Baishe zhuan* (Cantonese opera) (Guangzhou: Huanan renmin chubanshe, 1954); Cheng Rong et al. (East China Opera Research Institute), *Baishe zhuan* (Yue opera) (Beijing: Zuojia chubanshe, 1955).

68. Yang Gang, Zhang Geng, and A Ying, "Guanyu *Baishe zhuan* de taolun," *Wenyi bao,* no. 23 (1952), 8–13; Dai Bufan, "Shilun *Baishe zhuan* gushi," *Wenyi bao, no.* 13 (1953), 18–23.

69. Use of the term *petite bourgeoisie* has gained new life in China today, where it is often used to refer to white-collar workers and their lifestyle in the city.

70. The new marriage law was important, but one should not forget that the Civil Code of 1930 already required that the rights of both husband and wife be protected after the dissolution of marriage and established the autonomy of women.

See *The Civil Code of the Republic of China* (Shanghai: Kelly & Walsh, 1930), article 143; and *Li Fengjin: How the New Marriage Law Helped Chinese Women Stand Up* (Portland, OR: Opal Mogus Books, 2005), edited and translated by Susan L. Glosser. The original was edited by Dong Jianzhi, illustrated by Cheng Shifa and published by New Tide Publishing Company, Shanghai, November, 1950. The book includes the 1950 New Marriage Law in the Appendix.

71. One could argue that women were liberated from their men and subordinated to the party and other work units. Instead of parents approving of marriage, it was the work unit that gave approval. However, one could not deny the sense of empowerment and the material benefits working women (especially working mothers) gained in this process.

72. Such a female model worker was the protagonist of the Chinese episode in the documentary *The Windrose* conceived by Joris Ivens and produced in East Germany in 1957, where the female protagonist won over a male competitor in the democratic election to become the village head! See *Die Windrose.*

73. Joseph Levenson, *Revolution and Cosmopolitanism: The Western Stage and the Chinese Stage* (Berkeley: University of California Press, 1971).

74. Tian Han accompanied visiting Soviet puppet master Sergey Obraztsov and his wife, Gulina Ulanova, during their visit to the PRC in 1951. Tian had watched Obraztsov's performance at a farewell party before leaving Moscow, where he had been part of the delegation to the World Peace Conference in May 1949. Obraztsov's identity as a poet and a master puppeteer greatly impressed Tian. He invited the Soviet couple to visit the Chinese Opera Research Institute and Experimental Opera School, which he was heading. After watching two scenes from "White Snake" ("stealing the magic mushroom" and "water battle") performed by students from the school, Obraztsov was deeply impressed. The next day Gulina Ulanova watched the "water battle" scene and had her picture taken with Liu Xiurong (as the White Snake) and other students. See Tian Han, "Women bici faxian le shi," *Renmin ribao,* November 17, 1951, in *Tian Han quanji,* vol. 18, 617–20.

75. It is important to point out that Tian Han gained wide popularity among the people during the war largely because of his popular film songs and his widely performed Peking Operas, including the widely popular *Jianghan yuge* (Yangtze Fisherman's Song), first written as *Yufu jiuguo* (Fisherman Saves the Country) in October 1938 in Wuhan and performed at the Grand Stage in Hankou and later adapted into an epic forty-four-scene Peking Opera, which premiered at the Golden City Grand Theater in Guilin in July 1939. See *Jianghan yuge,* in *Kangzhan wenyi,* vol. 5, nos. 2–3 and 4–5 (December 1939 to January 1940).

76. Tian Han, *Jinbo ji* (Shanghai: Zhonghua shuju, 1951).

77. This is according to Li Zigui's oral narration, recorded by Jiang Jianlan in "Tianlao xie 'baishe zhuan' shimo," *Zhongguo xiju,* no. 7 (1988), 40.

78. For an informative study of Tian Han's opera writing in his later years, see Liu Fang, "Zai kunhuozhong xunqiu tupo: Tian Han houqi xiqu chuangzuo xinli tanmi," *Zhongguo xiqu xueyuan xuebao,* vol. 30, no. 3 (August 2009), 21–27.

79. See Tian Han, *Baishe zhuan* (sixteen-scene Peking Opera), in *Tian Han quanji,* vol. 9, 80. Tian Han revised the "White Snake" opera in 1952 based on *Jinbo ji,* first performed at the First National Opera Performance Conference by the experimental opera school of the National Opera Research Institute headed by himself. See *Juben,* no. 8 (1953). The play was published by the Writer's Press as a single volume in 1955. Tian Han wrote a few new lines especially for actress Zhao Yanxia's performance of the White Snake role as late as in June 1964, only a few years before his death, see *Tian Han quanji,* vol. 9, 115-116.

80. See *Baishe zhuan* (Shanghai: Zhongguo changpian shanghai gongsi, 1996), VCD, with Li Bingshu as the White Snake; *Baishe zhuan* (Tianjin: Tianjinshi wenhua yishu yinxiang chubanshe, 2004), VCD, with Zhao Yanxia as the White Snake; *Baishe zhuan* (Beijing: Beijing wenhua yishu yinxiang chubanshe, 2005), DVD, with Diao Li as the White Snake; and *Baishe zhuan* (Beijing: Beijing wenhua yishu yinxiang chubanshe, 2007), DVD, with Zhang Huoding as the White Snake.

81. Tian Han, *The White Snake,* translated from the Chinese by Yang Hsien-yi and Gladys Yang (Beijing: Foreign Languages Press, 1957), 11–12.

82. The literary speech of the mistress and more vernacular speech of the maid reflect an established stage convention. See Tian Can, "*Baishe zhuan* yuyan tedian shuolüe," *Xiqu yishu,* no. 3 (2001), 35–41.

83. Tian Han, *The White Snake,* 65.

84. In some cases ten-syllable lines also follow the 3-4-3 model, and a seven-syllable line can easily be replaced with a 3-3 line.

85. Tian Han, "Zhou Xinfang xiansheng yu pingju gaige yundong," in *Tian Han quanji,* vol. 17, 526.

86. See *Hubian chunmeng,* dir. Bu Wancang, conceived and with intertitles written by Tian Han (Shanghai: Mingxing dianying gongsi, 1927). The following analysis of *Baishe zhuan* is based on the 1955 single-volume edition published by the Writer's Press, the "final" version Tian Han himself claimed to have accomplished after more than a decade's rewriting. There are many differences between the 1953 *Juben* version and the 1955 Writer's Press version. The former has twenty-six scenes while the latter has only sixteen. Tian Han opened the 1955 version with a scene at the West Lake, for example, omitting the prologue of leaving Mount Emei. The 1955 version is much more condensed and polished; many details are omitted.

87. The translators describe Pan An as "A man famous for his good looks. It is said that when he walked through Luoyang women gathered round and tossed fruit to him." Tian Han, *The White Snake,* 10.

88. Ibid.

89. The line in Chinese is "Zhe junzi laocheng lingren xi." Tian Han, *Baishe zhuan* (Beijing: Baowentang shudian, 1957), 8.

90. The line in Chinese is "Junzi ruci chunxiao, zhennai kejing." Ibid., 13.

91. The White Snake was widowed in many earlier Chinese versions, Japanese renditions, and Tian Han's own script for the 1927 film. See, for example, "Li Huang," in Li Fang ed., *Taiping guangji wubaijuan* (Shanghai: Saoye shanfang, 1924), vol. 458; and Feng Menglong, "Bai niangzi yongzhen Leifengta," in *Jingshi tongyan,* chap. 28.

92. *Liren xing,* dir. Chen Liting, written by Tian Han (Shanghai: Kunlun yingye gongsi, 1949).

93. Tian Han, *The White Snake,* 23.

94. In Tian Han's *Jinbo ji,* for example, the actual fighting is absent, although the eighteenth-century versions of the White Snake story appear to have contained elaborate fighting scenes. In *Jinbo ji,* the White Snake and Fa Hai's dialogue and singing constitute the whole scene in which she comes to reclaim her husband. See Tian Han, *Jinbo ji,* in *Tian Han quanji,* vol. 9, 162-166.

95. Tian Han, *Baishe zhuan* (Beijing: Baowentang shudian, 1957), 56.

96. See Li Bihua, *Qingshe quanxin ban* (Taipei: Huangguan wenxue, 1993).

97. The portrayal of the marriage between the lovers, however, did align with the new marriage law and its elevation of monogamy.

98. Tian Han, *Baishe zhuan* (Beijing: Baowentang shudian, 1957), 71–72.

99. Moreover, iconic phrases as "qin er de lian, wen er de sai" (kissing again and again my dear son's face) were added in 1963 specifically for Zhao Yanxia's performance a year later. See *Guangming ribao,* April 29, 1979.

100. Tian Han, *Baishe zhuan* (Beijing: Baowentang shudian, 1957), 82.

101. See Hsu Wen-hung, "The Evolution of the Legend of the White Snake," *Tamkang Review,* vol. 4, no. 1 (1973), 134.

102. Joris Ivens, "Five Countries: Five Songs," handwritten essay, 1958, Beijing. Huub Jansen, Inventory of the Hans Vegner Collection, European Foundation Joris Ivens, Nijmegen, the Netherlands, 2004, Inv. nr. HVA 2.3.02.56.01-294; and Joris Ivens Archives, JIA 2.3.02.56.02-311.

103. Cynthia Grenier, "Joris Ivens: Social Realist versus Lyric Poet," *Sight and Sound,* vol. 27, no. 4 (Spring 1958), 204.

104. Dai Bufan, "Ping *Jinbo ji*"; Yang Gang, Zhang Geng, and A Ying, "Guanyu *Baishe zhuan* de taolun," 8–13; Dai Bufan: "Shilun *Baishe zhuan* gushi," 18–23.

105. DEFA (1946-1992) was the state-owned film studio in the former East Germany. Ivens's half-century engagement with China led me to the Leipzig Documentary Festival and its Ivens retrospective in October 2009 featuring many of Ivens's DEFA productions.

106. Joris Ivens, "Zur Methode des dokumentarischen films: In besondern des films *Komsomol*," Joris Ivens Archives, JIA 2.3.02.32.02-190, translated from the German by Kees Bakker.

107. Joris Ivens, "Notes on Hollywood," in *Joris Ivens and the Documentary Context*, edited by Kees Bakker (Amsterdam: Amsterdam University Press, 1999), 240–46.

108. See André Stufkens, "The Song of Movement: Joris Ivens's First Films and the Cycle of the Avant-Garde," in *Joris Ivens and the Documentary Context*, 69.

109. "Ivens and the DEFA," in *Joris Ivens and the Documentary Context*, 100–101.

110. Joris Ivens, "Quelques réflections sur les documentaires d'avant-garde," *La revue des vivants*, no. 10 (1931), 518–20.

111. Joris Ivens, quoted in Hans Shoots, *Living Dangerously: A Biography of Joris Ivens* (Amsterdam: Amsterdam University Press, 2000), 253.

112. Tian Han, "Yong liangtiao tui maixiang xiju de xin jieduan" (1958), in *Tian Han quanji*, vol. 17, 279.

113. See *Die Windrose*.

114. "The Rise of State Capitalism: The Spread of a New Sort of Business in the Emerging World Will Cause Increasing Problems," *Economist*, January 21, 2012.

Epilogue

1. Lu Shouping, "Zaju bantou Guan Hanqing," *Dangdai ren*, no. 1 (2009).

2. Li Zhiyan, *Tian Han chuangzuo ceji* (Chengdu: Sichuan wenyi chubanshe, 1994), 72.

3. Guan's lyrics in Steven Owen, *An Anthology of Chinese Literature, Beginnings to 1911* (New York: W. W. Norton, 1997), 739.

4. Tian Han, *Guan Hanqing*, in *Tian Han quanji*, vol. 6, 136.

5. Tian Han, "Weida de yuandai xiju zhanshi Guan Hanqing," in *Tian Han quanji*, vol. 14, 614–19.

6. Li Zhiyan, "Tian Han tongzhi de huaju *Guan Hanqing* zai Riben de wutai shang," *Juben*, no. 7 (1959), 104.

7. Tian Han, *Guan Hanqing*, in *Tian Han quanji*, vol. 6, 170–71.

8. T'ien Han (Tian Han), "Kuan Han-ch'ing" (Guan Hanqing), translated by the Foreign Languages Press, Peking, in *Twentieth-Century Chinese Drama: An Anthology*, edited by Edward M. Gunn (Bloomington: Indiana University Press, 1983), 361.

9. For a relevant recent study on the political culture of the first decade of the Maoist era, see Chang-Tai Hung, *Mao's New World: Political Culture in the Early People's Republic* (Ithaca, NY: Cornell University Press, 2011).

10. Tian Han, *Guan Hanqing,* in *Twentieth-Century Chinese Drama,* edited by Edward M. Gunn (Bloomington: Indiana University Press, 1983), 340–41.

11. Zhu Lianxiu was suggested to Tian Han by the historian Jian Bozan as the female protagonist for *Guan Hanqing.* See Xiong Kunjing, "Huaju *Guan Hanqing* chuangzuo shimo," *Dangshi wenyuan,* no. 11 (2009), 55.

12. Tian Han, *Guan Hanqing,* in *Tian Han quanji,* vol. 6, 168.

13. Ibid., 116.

14. Pauline Lee, *Li Zhi, Confucianism, and the Virtue of Desire* (Albany: State University of New York Press, 2012).

15. Zhou Zuoren, *Zhongguo xinwenxue de yuanliu* (Beiping: Renwen shudian, 1934).

16. Tian Han, *Guan Hanqing,* in Gunn, *Twentieth-Century Chinese Drama,* 334.

17. Tian Han, *Guan Hanqing,* in *Tian Han quanji,* vol. 6, 137.

18. Tian Han, *Guan Hanqing,* in Gunn, *Twentieth-Century Chinese Drama,* 345.

19. Or perhaps the tragic ending echoes more readily Zhou's own choices in his revolutionary youth, when he abandoned his first lover for Deng Yingchao. See Gao Wenqian, *Zhou Enlai, the Last Perfect Revolutionary* (New York: PublicAffairs, 2007).

20. To respect Tian's choice, the current *Tian Han quanji* (Complete Works of Tian Han) remarkably kept both endings, that is, the reader can choose to read either or both of the endings and make up his or her own mind regarding the fate of the protagonists. See *Guan Hanqing,* in *Tian Han quanji,* vol. 6.

21. Zou Yanjiu, "*Guan Hanqing* de ziwo shuqing jiegou," *Lilun yu chuangzuo,* no. 4 (2001), 55.

22. See "Tian Han de 'Xie Yaohuan' shi yike da ducao," *Renmin ribao,* February 1, 1966. Culminating in his Peking Opera *Xie Yaohuan,* Tian Han's theatrical and cinematic experiments instantiate the dynamics animating Chinese cultural productions from the 1910s to the 1960s. Based on *Nü xun'an* (The Female Inspector General), in a Shanxi local opera genre, *wanwanqiang,* Tian Han wrote *Xie Yaohuan* in 1961. It was premiered by the Zhongguo jingjuyuan (Peking Opera Institute of China) in Beijing in the same year. Using the courageous female officer Xie Yaohuan and the powerful empress Wu Zetian as his mouthpieces, Tian Han resurrected the powerful female images prominent in his stage and screen experiments since the early twentieth century. At the same time, he endowed the female characters with a contemporary feminist spirit.

23. Gao Ying, *Ai Wei Wei de muqin Ai Qing de qizi: Gao Ying zishu* (Hong Kong: Dashan wenhua chubanshe, 2012), 64, 79.

24. Ibid., 97, 102, 107, 124.

25. Zhang Yingguang, "Ai Wei Wei, zuiju 'xingxing' jingshen de ren," *Xin jingbao,* October 27, 2004.

26. Ibid.

27. Ibid.

28. Ibid.

29. 太陽/它使我想起 法蘭西 美利堅的革命/想起 博愛 平等 自由/想起 德謨克拉西/想起《馬賽曲》《國際歌》/想起 華盛頓 列寧 孫逸仙/和一切把人類從苦難裡拯救出來的/人物的名字/是的/太陽是美的/且是永生的. See Ai Qing, *Xiang taiyang* (Shanghai: Haiyan chubanshe, 1940).

30. Gao Ying, *Ai Wei Wei de muqin Ai Qing de qizi,* 69.

31. Kong Lingwei, "Zhongguo xiandai yishu de gouxing: Chongsi xingxing meizhan, 85 xinchao ji 90 niandai yilai de 'xifang zhuyi,'" *Yishu pinglun,* no. 9 (2009).

32. Ai Wei Wei, "Ai Wei Wei de shijieguan," interview by Zhao Zilong, Kang Xueru, and Du Xiyun, December 19, 2009, *Huxian weiquan,* http://fzh999.net/show.asp?id=971, accessed March 8, 2013.

33. Gao Minglu, *Total Modernity and the Avant-Garde in Twentieth-Century Chinese Art* (Cambridge, MA: MIT Press, 2011).

34. Selections from Ai's photographs were exhibited in the Three Shadow Studio designed by Ai himself in the early 2000s. Among Ai's subjects, Chen Kaige, a classmate at the BFA, emerged as the leading figure of the fifth generation of Chinese avant-gardist film directors from the mid-1980s onward. So was Gu Changwei, who became a famed cinematographer and worked closely with Zhang Yimou, another classmate from the BFA and himself a leading fifth generation director, on many of his films. Feng Xiaofang, the box office king of contemporary Chinese filmmaking, who revolutionized the comedy genre of "New Year Film" from the 1990s onward, though seemingly just an interesting outlier in this scenario, in effect embodied the convergence of the avant-garde and the popular.

35. For a good grasp of the cultural milieu of the 1980s in Mainland China, see Zha Jianying, *Bashi niandai fangtanlu* (Hong Kong: Oxford University Press, 2006).

36. Wu Wenguang's 1990 documentary *Liulang Beijing* (Bumming in Beijing), depicting five young artists and their floating life in Beijing, can be read side by side with Ai Wei Wei's bumming in New York around the same time, although the artists in Wu's documentary all dream of trading places with Ai as New York symbolized artistic freedom for them at the time.

37. Ai Wei Wei, "Shame on Me, Part 1: 'Shame on Me,'" interview in *Der Spiegel,* November 24, 2011, http://www.spiegel.de/international/world/ai-weiwei-shame-on-me-a-799302.html, accessed March 6, 2013.

38. "Huajia Liu Xiaodong: Wo dui huahua yizhi you jikegan," *Waitan huabao,* February 20, 2008.

39. Ai Wei Wei, "Shame on Me; Part 2: 'Do They Want Me to Leave?'," interview in *Der Spiegel,* November 24, 2011, http://www.spiegel.de/international/world/ai-weiwei-shame-on-me-a-799302–2.html, accessed March 6, 2013.

40. Tania Branigan, "Ai Weiwei: Everyday I think, this will be the day I get taken in again . . . ," *The Guardian*, Friday 25 November 2011, http://www.theguardian.com/artanddesign/2011/nov/26/ai-weiwei-china-situation-quite-bad, accessed March 6, 2013.

41. Ai's artworks were on display at the Louisiana Museum of Modern Art in Denmark from November 18, 2011, to February 12, 2012, in an exhibition entitled "Louisiana Contemporary: Ai Wei Wei." Ai visited Louisiana on December 21, 2010, and was interviewed by Christian Lund as part of the "Louisiana Talks" series. See http://www.youtube.com/watch?v=xR6BcfmgVh0&feature=related, accessed March 8, 2013. Extracts from the interview, produced by Marie Friis Forchhammer and Martin Kogi and copyrighted by the Louisiana Museum of Modern Art, 2011, were also shown at the exhibition.

Glossary

A Ying 阿英
Ai Jiangnan 哀江南
Ai Qing 艾青
Ai Wei Wei 艾未未
Akita Ujaku 秋田雨雀
An E (Zhang Shiyuan) 安娥（張式沅）
An E wenji 安娥文集
Atarashiki mura 新しき村
Atarashiki Roshia 新しきロシア
"Bai niangzi yongzhen Leifengta" 白娘子永鎮雷峰塔
Baishe zhuan 白蛇傳
baishi 稗史
benshi 弁士
bieqiu xinsheng yu yibang 別求新聲于異邦
Bing Xin 冰心
bingfei suming, ershi kexue de biran 並非宿命, 而是科學的必然
"Biye ge" 畢業歌
"Bohui'er zhige" 伯惠爾之歌
"Bu fu lao" 不伏老
Bu Wancang 卜萬蒼
Bungei sensen 文芸戦線
*Buxiu zhi'ai*不朽之愛
changmian de ziyou 場面的自由
changqiang 唱腔
Changsha ribao 長沙日報
Changsha Shifan 長沙師範

chao ganjue de shijie 超感覺的世界
Chee Lai 起來
chenmo de dahai 沈默的大海
Chen San Wuniang (*Lijing ji*) 陳三五娘 (荔鏡記)
Chen Tianhua 陳天華
Cheng Fangwu 成仿吾
Chuangzao jikan 創造季刊
Chuangzao she 創造社
chuangzao xin nüxing 創造新女性
Chūgoku bunka 中国文化
Chūgokujin 中国人
Chūgoku no shingeki 中国の新劇
Chunliu she 春柳社
da houfang 大後方
Dai Bufan 戴不凡
daluren 大陸人
Danao tiangong 大鬧天宮
Dangfu xin 蕩婦心
Dao De Jing (*Tao Te Ching*) 道德經
Dao minjian qu 到民間去
"Daota" 倒塔
datong 大同
datongxue 大同學
daxi 大戲
dazhong de yundong 大眾的運動
dazhonghua 大眾化
dazhonghua zhuyizhe 大中華主義者
dazhong wenhua 大眾文化
dazhong xiaofei wenhua 大眾消費文化
Diantong huabao 電通畫報
Diantong yingye gongsi 電通影業公司
Dianying 電影
Dianying yishu 電影藝術
Di sishi yi 第四十一
Defen 德芬
Demokurashii デモクラシイ
Den'en no yūutsu/Tianyuan zhi youyu 田園の憂鬱/田園之憂鬱

"Disi jieji de furen yundong" 第四階級的婦人運動
Dōhō 同胞
Dou E yuan 竇娥冤
"Duanqiao" 斷橋
dubai 獨白
duibai 對白
duli pi 獨立癖
Engeki Kairyōkai 演劇改良会
Erbaiwu xiaozhuan 二百五小傳
er'huang 二黃
Ernü yingxiong zhuan 兒女英雄傳
Fa Hai 法海
fabu tongqing 髮不同青
Falanxi hao 法蘭西號
fali wubian 法力無邊
Fan'elin yu qiangwei 梵峨璘與薔薇
fan renxing 反人性
Fanxing 繁星
Fang Chengpei 方成培
fangjie 芳潔
Fangxia nǐ de bianzi 放下你的鞭子
fanpaiya 凡派亞
Fei Mu 費穆
fei xianshi de xingshi 非現實的形式
Feng Menglong 馮夢龍
Feng Zikai 豐子愷
"Fenghuang niepan" 鳳凰涅槃
fengjian de wanzhi 封建的頑執
Fengshen bang 封神榜
Fengyun ernü 風雲兒女
fenmu 分幕
Fu Yanchang 傅彥長
Fulian 婦聯
Fushide 浮士德
Gaimushō gaikō kiroku 外務省外交記録
geming qunzhong wenhua 革命群眾文化
"Gongyan zhiqian" 公演之前

Goshi undō zai Nihon 五四運動在日本
Guan Hanqing 關漢卿
guci 鼓詞
gudeng 孤燈
Guo Moruo 郭沫若
Guofeng bao 國風報
Guoge 國歌
Guoge licheng 國歌歷程
Guoju yundong 國劇運動
gushu 鼓書
guyue 孤月
han'er 漢兒
heimin/pingmin 平民
heimin shijin/pingmin shiren 平民詩人
He Lüting 賀綠汀
"Hebo" 合缽
Hei Tianshi 黑天使
Henhai 恨海
Hong Xiuquan 洪秀全
"Hongxian" 红线
Hongse niangzi jun 紅色娘子軍
Hu Shi 胡適
huaju 話劇
Huang Dasha 黃大傻
Huang Rikui 黃日葵
"Huanghe dahechang" 黃河大合唱
huanle zhidu 歡樂之都
Huanzhou 幻洲
Hubian chunmeng 湖邊春夢
Huguang huiguan 湖廣會館
Hunan gongheguo 湖南共和國
"Huohu zhiye" 獲虎之夜
"Hushang de beiju" 湖上的悲劇
ichioku isshin 一億一心
Jasei no in 蛇性の淫
Jian Bozan 翦伯贊
Jiang Guangci (chi) 蔣光慈（赤）

Jianghan yuge 江漢漁歌
jianghu laoda 江湖老大
Jiangnan 江南
jiazi 甲子
ji bugou name zuo, ye bugou name you 既不夠那麼左，也不夠那麼右
"Jieqin" 結親
jimo 寂寞
Jinbo ji 金缽記
jingju 京劇
Jingshi tongyan 警世通言
jinmin no naka e 人民の中へ
Jinwu yuekan 金屋月刊
"Jiubian" 酒變
jiuju zhong fan kexue de yimian 舊劇中反科學的一面
jiuxi 舊戲
jiyouli jiyouwei 極有力極有味
Jiyū Gekijō 自由劇場
jōmin 常民
Josei 女性
Juben 劇本
jueju 絕句
Jukan 劇刊
Junzi ruci chunxiao, zhennai kejing 君子如此純孝, 真乃可敬
Kafeidian zhi yiye 咖啡店之一夜
kagekiha 過激派
Kami to hito no aida/Shen yu ren zhijian 神と人の間/神與人之間
Kamiyama Sōjin 上山草人
Kanda Teikoku Gakushi Kaikan 神田帝国学士会館
kang 炕
Kang Jingzhao 康景昭
Kangzhan xiju 抗戰戲劇
Karashima Takeshi 辛島驍
Kawakami Hajime 河上肇
ke'ai de qingnian de xiongdi zimei 可愛的青年的兄弟姊妹
Kindaigeki kyōkai 近代劇協会
kokumin/guomin 国民
Kume Masao 久米正雄

Kumon no shōchō 苦悶の象徵
kuipo 窺破
kunqu 崑曲
Kuriyagawa Hakuson 厨川白村
laobaixing dou xiwen lejian 老百姓都喜聞樂見
laodong renmin 勞動人民
Laoxi de qianshi jinsheng 老戲的前世今生
Leifeng ta chuanqi 雷峰塔傳奇
Libao 立報
Li Baochen (Pao-ch'en Lee) 李抱忱
Li Bihua 李碧華
Li Chuli 李初梨
Li Dazhao 李大釗
Li Jieren 李劼人
Li Jinhui 黎錦暉
Li Zigui 李紫貴
Li Youcai banhua 李有才板話
Lianhua yingye gongsi 聯華影業公司
Liangu 蓮姑
Liang Qichao 梁啟超
Liaozhai zhiyi 聊齋志異
"Lin Chong" 林沖
Lin Weizhong 林維中
Lin Yutang 林語堂
ling de shijie 靈的世界
Lingguang 靈光
ling yu rou 靈與肉
Liren xing 麗人行
lishi 歷史
Liu Liangmo 劉良模
Liuxing de boximiya 流行的波希米亞
liuxing wenhua 流行文化
Lugou qiao 蘆溝橋
"Lun xin minzhu zhuyi xianzheng" 論新民主主義憲政
Ma Yuzao 馬玉藻
"Maibao ge" 賣報歌
Malu tianshi 馬路天使

Mao Zedong 毛澤東
Mato 魔都
Matsui Sumako 松井須磨子
Mei Lanfang 梅蘭芳
Meili 梅儷
"Meiyu" 梅雨
Mingmo yihen 明末遺恨
Mingxing dianying gongsi 明星電影公司
Mingyou zhisi 名優之死
Mingyue gewutuan 明月歌舞團
minjian shuochang 民間說唱
minzhong geyong hui 民眾歌詠會
minzu 民族
minzu baojian 民族保健
minzu gewuju 民族歌舞劇
Minzu shengcun 民族生存
Miyazaki Ryūsuke 宮崎隆介
mou dushi 某都市
Mudan ting 牡丹亭
Muqin 母親
Muramatsu Shōfū 村松梢風
museifu kyōsanshugisha 無政府共産主義者
Muxing zhiguang 母性之光
Nahan 吶喊
naihe gouqie tan zanhuan 奈何苟且貪暫歡
Nanfang zhoumo 南方周末
Nanguo 南國
Nanguo banyuekan 南國半月刊
Nanguo de xiju 南國的戲劇
Nanguo dianying jushe 南國電影劇社
Nanguo she 南國社
Nanguo yuekan 南國月刊
Nanshe 南社
Nanyang 南洋
nianbai 念白
Nie Er 聶耳
Nie Er jinian ji 聶耳紀念集

Nie Er riji 聶耳日記
"Nie Yinniang" 聶隱娘
nong chutou de xiaohuozi 弄鋤頭的小伙子
nü daxuesheng 女大學生
Nü fushide 女浮士德
Nüshen 女神
nü songhua baowen 女送花抱吻
Nü xun'an 女巡案
"Nü yu she" 女與蛇
Osanai Kaoru 小山内薫
Ouyang Yuqian 歐陽予倩
Pan Hannian 潘漢年
Pan Jinlian 潘金蓮
Piyaluo zhigui 辟亞羅之鬼
Qiangwei zhilu 薔薇之路
Qian Xuantong 錢玄同
qianwei 前衛
qiliang zhijing 淒涼之境
Qingshe quanxin ban 青蛇全新版
"Qinqiong fangyou" 秦瓊訪友
Qiusheng fu 秋聲賦
quanbu yousheng duibai gechang weizhuang reqing weiyi jupian 全部有聲對白歌唱偉壯熱情唯一巨片
qunzhong 群眾
rangwai bixian annei 攘外必先安內
Ren Guang 任光
renmin 人民
Renmin ribao 人民日報
"Rexue" 熱血
Ruan Lingyu 阮玲玉
sanbai 散白
Sanguo zhi 三国志
Sanye ji 三叶集
Sanyou 三友
Satō Haruo 佐藤春夫
Se, Jie 色，戒
Senku 先駆

setsumei 説明
Shagong 殺宮
shakaishugisha 社会主義者
shangguo jitian xue 上過幾天學
"Shanhai kenbunroku" 上海見聞録
"Shanhai kōyūki" 上海交遊記
Shaonian shijie 少年世界
Shaonian weite zhi fannao 少年维特之烦恼
Shaonian zhongguo 少年中國
"Shaonian zhongguo yu zongjiao wenti" 少年中國與宗教問題
Shaonian zhongguo zhi xin zongjiao 少年中國之新宗教
sharen bu zhayan de nümowang 殺人不眨眼的女魔王
Shen Jianshi 沈兼士
Shen Shiyuan 沈士遠
Shenbao 申報
shengbu tongchuang 生不同床
shenhou de renxing 深厚的人性
Shenzhou xuecong 神州學叢
Shenzhou xuehui 神州學會
Shenzhu zhinü 神主之女
Shi Zhecun 施蟄存
Shibao 時報
Shimamura Hōgetsu 島村抱月
shinajin 支那人
shimbei shugi 親米主義
shingeki/xinju 新劇
Shinjin/xinren 新人
Shinjinkai 新人会
"Shiren yu laodong wenti" 詩人與勞動問題
Shishi xinbao 时事新報
shitamachi 下町
shiying hui 試映會
Shōnen/shaonian 少年
"Shōnen to shinjin tono mondō" 少年と新人との問答
"Shuangfei die" 雙飛蝶
Shuzhi 蜀誌
"Siji ge" 四季歌

Situ Huimin 司徒慧敏
Sōjin 騒人
"Song yongshi chuzheng ge" 送勇士出征歌
Taiping yang 太平洋
Tang Huaiqiu 唐槐秋
Tanizaki Jun'ichirō 谷崎潤一郎
tanzhi 探知
Taoli jie 桃李劫
ta paoguoqu menglie baowen ta 她跑過去猛烈抱吻他
tenmin/tianmin 天民
Tian Han (Tian Shouchang/Chen Yu/Li Shuquan) 田漢 (田壽昌/陳瑜/李淑泉)
Tian Han quanji 田漢全集
Tian Han xiquji 田漢戲曲集
Tian Han zai riben 田漢在日本
Tian Han zhuan 田漢傳
Tian Qinxin 田沁鑫
"Tianya genü" 天涯歌女
"Tietixia de genü" 鐵蹄下的歌女
tiyan shenghuo 體驗生活
tokugi 德義
Tongmeng hui 同盟會
tongsu wenhua 通俗文化
tongxin 童心
tongxin shuo 童心說
toubi congrong 投筆從戎
T'oung Pao 通報
Tsubouchi Shōyō 坪内逍遥
Tsukiji Shōgekijō 築地小劇場
tuifei 頹廢
Tuqiao zhizhan 土橋之戰
Uchiyama Kanzō 内山完造
Ugetsu Monogatari 雨月物語
waiguo tangzi 外國堂子
Wang Guangqi 王光祈
wangu fenzi 頑固份子
Wang Renmei 王人美
Wanguo gongbao 萬國公報

wanzhong yixin 萬眾一心
Wei Minglun 魏明倫
"Wenhua yu xiaohuozi" 文化與小伙子
Wenhui bao 文匯報
Wenwei 文委
Wenxue yanjiuhui 文學研究會
Wenyi bao 文藝報
wenyi de dazhonghua 文藝的大眾化
wen yi zai dao 文以載道
wokou 倭寇
"Women de ziji pipan" 我們的自己批判
Wufan zhiqian 午飯之前
Wugui lieche 無軌列車
Wu Song 武松
Wuyou zhixiang 烏有之鄉
Wu zhi ge 五支歌
Wu Zuoren 吳作人
Xia Yan 夏衍
Xiao erhei jiehun 小二黑結婚
xiaosheng 小生
xiandairen de tiaowu 現代人的跳舞
xianfeng 先鋒
Xian Xinghai 冼星海
xiao zichan jieji 小資產階級
Xie Yaohuan 謝瑤環
Xihu yishu xueyuan 西湖藝術學院
"Xiju yu shehui" 戲劇與社會
Xin ernü yingxiong zhuan 新兒女英雄傳
Xinchao 新潮
Xingshi zhoubao 醒獅週報
xin guoju yundong 新國劇運動
Xinhua ribao 新華日報
"Xin jiaozi" 新教子
xinju yundong 新劇運動
"Xin Luoma" 新羅馬
Xinmin congbao 新民叢報
Xin nüxing 新女性

Xin qingnian 新青年
Xin shaonian dianying gongsi 新少年電影公司
"Xin Taohua shan" 新桃花扇
Xin wenyi 新文藝
xiqu 戲曲
xiqu dianying 戲曲電影
xiu qi zhi ping 修齊治平
Xixiang ji 西廂記
xixuegui 吸血鬼
Xu Beihong 徐悲鴻
Xu Dishan 許地山
Xu Teli 徐特立
Xu Xiacun 徐霞村
Xu Xian 許仙
Xu Xingzhi 許幸之
xuanchuan 宣傳
xuanchuan dui 宣傳隊
xuanchuan zhou 宣傳週
xuanlü de shijie 旋律的世界
xuanzhan shu 宣戰書
Xuedeng 學燈
xuerou changcheng 血肉長城
Xue yu xue 雪與血
"Ya de moyun" 雅的末運
Yamakawa Uraji 山川浦路
Yan'an wenyi zuotanhui 延安文藝座談會
Yangzijiang de baofengyu 揚子江的暴風雨
Yanzhao ernü 燕趙兒女
Ye Lingfeng 葉靈鳳
Yeban gesheng 夜半歌聲
Ye meigui 野玫瑰
Yi Junzuo 易君左
Yi Shuyu 易漱瑜
Yi Xiang 易象
Yi Jiangnan 憶江南
yingjiexi 应節戲
yingxiong huaihan 英雄懷漢

Yinse de meng 銀色的夢
Yinxing 銀星
Yiyao zhuan 義妖傳
"Yiyongjun jinxingqu" 義勇軍進行曲
yizhong yuzhou de yinyue 一種宇宙的音樂
Yoshino Sakuzō 吉野作造
"Youhu" 游湖
youli de zhanxian 有力的戰線
Yu Dafu 郁達夫
Yu Shan 俞珊
yuanben 院本
Yuan Muzhi 袁牧之
"Yuguang qu" 漁光曲
yunbai 韻白
Yūrakuza 有楽座
"Zairyū gaikokujin gaikyō" 在留外国人概況
Zaochun 早春
Zen'ei za 前衛座
Zeng Qi (Zeng Muhan) 曾琦（曾慕韓）
Zeng Xubai 曾虛白
Zhan jingtang 斬經堂
Zhang Difei 張滌非
Zhao Shuli 趙樹理
Zhao Yuanren (Chao Yüan-Jen) 赵元任
zhe junzi laocheng lingren xi 這君子老成令人喜
zhengdan 正旦
zhiguang 智光
Zhongguo dianying fazhan shi 中國電影發展史
Zhonghua ribao 中華日報
Zhonghua shuju 中華書局
zhongxi hebi 中西合璧
Zhou Enlai 周恩來
Zhou Fohai 周佛海
Zhou Xinfang 周信芳
Zhou Zuoren 周作人
Zhu Lianxiu 朱簾秀
zhuti ge 主題歌

zhuyao maodun 主要矛盾
Ziji de yuandi 自己的園地
ziranjie de aili 自然界的愛力
Ziye 子夜
Zōge no tō o dete 象牙の塔を出て
Zong Baihua 宗白華
zuihou de housheng 最後的吼聲
Zuo Shunsheng 左舜生

Bibliography

A Ying. *Wanqing wenyi baokan shulue* (A Brief Account of Late Qing Art Journals and Newspapers). Beijing: Gudian wenxue chubanshe, 1958.

A Ying. *Zhongguo xinwenxue yundongshi ziliao* (Research Materials on the Chinese New Literary Movement). Shanghai: Shanghai shudian, 1982.

Abbot Xinrong and Jiang Canteng. *Juzan fashi yanjiu* (Research on Abbot Juzan). Taipei: Xinwenfeng chuban gongsi, 2006.

Ai Wei Wei. "Louisiana Talks" series. See http://www.youtube.com/watch?v=xR6BcfmgVh0&feature=related, accessed March 8, 2013. Produced by Marie Friis Forchhammer and Martin Kogi and copyrighted by the Louisiana Museum of Modern Art, 2011.

Ai Wei Wei. "Shame on Me, Part 1: 'Shame on Me,'" interview in *Der Spiegel*, November 24, 2011, http://www.spiegel.de/international/world/ai-weiwei-shame-on-me-a-799302.html, accessed March 6, 2013.

Ai Wei Wei. "Shame on Me; Part 2: 'Do They Want Me to Leave?,'" interview in Der Spiegel, November 24, 2011, http://www.spiegel.de/international/world/ai-weiwei-shame-on-me-a-799302-2.html, accessed March 6, 2013.

Akiyama Aisaburō. *The Gion Festival*. Kyoto: Akiyama Aisaburō, 1924.

An E (Zhang Shiyuan). *An E wenji* (Collected Works of An E). Beijing: Zhongguo wenlian chuban gongsi, 2008.

An E (Zhang Shiyuan). *Wuyue liuhua zhao yanming: Peitong Shimotelai fangwen Li Xiannian zongdui* (Accompanying Smedley Visiting Li Xiannian's Army). Wuchang: Huazhong shifan daxue chubanshe, 1989.

An E (Zhang Shiyuan). *Yanzhao ernü* (Sons and Daughters of Northern China). Shanghai: Shenghuo shudian, 1938.

An Yu. "Zhanhuo zhong zouchu de hongse cainü: An E" (An E: A Red Female Talent Emerged from the Fire of War). *Dangshi bocai* (Records of Party History), no. 2 (2008), 44–46.

Anderson, Marston. *The Limits of Realism: Chinese Fiction in the Revolutionary Period*. Berkeley: University of California Press, 1990.

Andrews, Julia F. *Painters and Politics in the People's Republic of China, 1949–1979.* Berkeley: University of California Press, 1994.

Anon. "Yan'an minzhong kangzhan liuzhounian jinian dahui guanyu huyu tuanjie fandui neizhan tongdian" (A Public Telegram Issued By the People of Yan'an Calling for Unification against Civil War on the Occasion of the Sixth Anniversary of the Anti-Japanese War). *Jiefang ribao* (Liberation Daily, Yan'an), July 10, 1943.

Arner, G. B. L. Review of *Socialism: An Analysis,* by Rudolf Eucken, *American Economic Review,* vol. 12, no. 3 (September 1922).

Ashiwa Yoshiko, and David L. Wank, eds. *Making Religion, Making the State: The Politics of Religion in Modern China.* Stanford, CA: Stanford University Press, 2009.

Auden, W. H., and Christopher Isherwood. *Journey to a War.* New York: Octagon Books, 1972.

Austin, J. L. *How to Do Things with Words.* Cambridge, MA: Harvard University Press, 1962.

Avshalomov, Jacob, and Aaron Avshalomov. *Avshalomovs' Winding Way: Composers Out of China—a Chronicle.* Bloomington, IN: Xlibris, 2002.

Baishe zhuan (The White Snake). Beijing, 1996, Zhongguo changpian shanghai gongsi, VCD, with Li Bingshu as the White Snake.

Baishe zhuan (The White Snake). Tianjin, 2004, Tianjinshi wenhua yishu yinxiang chubanshe, VCD, with Zhao Yanxia as the White Snake.

Baishe zhuan (The White Snake). Beijing, 2005, Beijing wenhua yishu yinxiang chubanshe, DVD, with Diao Li as the White Snake.

Baishe zhuan (The White Snake). Beijing, 2007, Beijing wenhua yishu yinxiang chubanshe, DVD, with Zhang Huoding as the White Snake.

Bakker, Kees, ed. *Joris Ivens and the Documentary Context.* Amsterdam: Amsterdam University Press, 1999.

Bao Weihong. "Baptism by Fire: Spectatorship and Aesthetic Affect in Chinese Cinema from Shanghai to Chongqing." PhD diss., University of Chicago, 2005.

Barmé, Geremie R. *An Artistic Exile: A Life of Feng Zikai (1898–1975).* Berkeley: University of California Press, 2002.

Barnstone, Tony, and Chou Ping, eds. *The Anchor Book of Chinese Poetry* Web Companion. http://web.whittier.edu/academic/english/chinese/Ouyangxiu.htm. Accessed January 16, 2012.

Belden, Jack. *China Shakes the World.* New York: Harper, 1949.

Benjamin, Walter. "The Work of Art in the Age of Mechanical Reproduction." In *Illuminations: Essays and Reflections.* Edited with an introduction by Hannah Arendt, translated by Harry Zohn. New York: Harcourt, Brace & World, 1968.

Benjamin, Walter. "The Author as Producer." *New Left Review,* vol. 1, no. 62 (July-August 1970), 83-96.

Berman, Marshall. *All That Is Solid Melts into Air: The Experience of Modernity.* New York: Penguin Books, 1988.

Bernard, Elizabeth. "Tian Han's 'Reactionary Works': 1956–1962." In *The 30th International Congress of Human Sciences in Asia and North Africa, China 1,* edited by G. de la Lama. Mexico City: Colegio de Mexico, 1982.

Bernardi, Joanne R. "The Literary Link: Tanizaki and the Pure Film Movement." In *A Tanizaki Feast: The International Symposium in Venice,* edited by Adriana Boscaro and Anthony Hood Chambers. Ann Arbor: University of Michigan Press, 1998.

Bernardi, Joanne R. *Writing in Light: The Silent Scenario and the Japanese Pure Film Movement.* Detroit: Wayne State University Press, 2001.

Bernays, Leopold J., trans. *Goethe's Faust, Part II.* Translated from the German, partly in the meter of the original and partly in prose (with the original). London: S. Low, 1839.

Bernstein, Gail Lee. *Japanese Marxist: A Portrait of Kawakami Hajime, 1879–1946.* Cambridge, MA: Harvard University Press, 1976.

Bestor, Theodore C. *Neighborhood Tokyo.* Stanford, CA: Stanford University Press, 1989.

Bing Xin. *Fanxing* (Myriad Stars). Shanghai: Shangwu yinshuguan, 1933.

Birnbaum, Phyllis. *Modern Girls, Shining Stars, the Skies of Tokyo: Five Japanese Women.* New York: Columbia University Press, 1999.

Blake, William. *Songs of Experience.* London: The Author and Printer, W. Blake, 1794.

Bourdieu, Pierre. *The Logic of Practice.* Translated from the French by Richard Nice. Stanford, CA: Stanford University Press, 1990.

Bourdieu, Pierre. *The Field of Cultural Production: Essays on Art and Literature.* Edited and introduced by Randal Johnson. New York: Columbia University Press, 1993.

Bourdieu, Pierre. *The Rules of Art: Genesis and Structure of the Literary Field.* Translated by Susan Emanuel. Stanford, CA: Stanford University Press, 1996.

Burke, Peter. *Popular Culture in Early Modern Europe.* 3rd rev. ed. Farnham, England; Burlington, VT: Ashgate, 2009.

Bradley, Laura J. R. *Brecht and Political Theatre: The Mother on Stage.* New York: Oxford University Press, 2006.

Brady, Anne-Marie. *Marketing Dictatorship: Propaganda and Thought Work in Contemporary China.* Lanham, MD: Rowman & Littlefield, 2008.

Braester, Yomi. *Witness against History: Literature, Film, and Public Discourse in Twentieth-Century China.* Stanford, CA: Stanford University Press, 2003.

Braester, Yomi. *Painting the City Red: Chinese Cinema and the Urban Contract.* Durham, NC: Duke University Press, 2010.

Branigan, Tania. "Ai Weiwei: Everyday I think, this will be the day I get taken in again . . . ," *The Guardian*, Friday 25 November 2011, http://www.theguardian.com/artanddesign/2011/nov/26/ai-weiwei-china-situation-quite-bad, accessed March 6, 2013.

Brecht, Bertolt. *Brecht on Theatre: The Development of an Aesthetic.* Edited by John Willett. New York: Macmillan, 1964.

Brecht, Bertolt. "Die Maßnahme" (The Measures Taken) (1930). In *The Jewish Wife and Other Short Plays.* New York: Grove Press, 1965.

Brecht, Bertolt. "On the Formalistic Character of the Theory of Realism." In *Aesthetics and Politics,* with Theodor Adorno, Walter Benjamin, Ernst Bloch, and Georg Lukács, with an afterword by Fredric Jameson. London and New York: Verso, 1980.

Brecht, Bertolt. "Popularity and Realism." In *Aesthetics and Politics,* with Theodor Adorno, Walter Benjamin, Ernst Bloch, and Georg Lukács, with an afterword by Fredric Jameson. London and New York: Verso, 1980.

Brook, Timothy, and Andre Schmid. *Nation Work: Asian Elites and National Identities.* Ann Arbor: University of Michigan Press, 2000.

Brook, Timothy, Andre Schmid, and Bob Tadashi Wakabayashi, eds. *Opium Regimes: China, Britain, and Japan, 1839–1952.* Berkeley: Univeristy of California Press, 2000.

Brown, Carolyn T. "The Paradigm of the Iron House: Shouting and Silence in Lu Hsün's Stories." *Chinese Literature: Essays, Articles, Reviews,* vol. 6, nos. 1–2 (1984), 101–20.

Brown, Jeremy, and Paul G. Pickowicz, eds. *Dilemmas of Victory: The Early Years of the People's Republic of China.* Cambridge, MA: Harvard University Press, 2007.

Brown, Nicholas. *Utopian Generations: The Political Horizon of Twentieth-Century Literature.* Princeton, NJ: Princeton University Press, 2005.

Bru, Sascha, and Gunther Martens, eds. *The Invention of Politics in the European Avant-Garde (1906–1940).* Amsterdam and New York: Rodopi, 2006.

Bu Wancang, dir. *Hubian chunmeng* (Lakeshore Spring Dream). Conceived and with intertitles written by Tian Han. Shanghai, 1927, Mingxing dianying gongsi.

Budd, Michael. "Moments of Caligari." In *Cabinet of Dr. Caligari: Texts, Contexts, Histories.* New Brunswick, NJ: Rutgers University Press, 1990.

Bürger, Peter. *Theory of the Avant-Garde.* Translated from the German by Michael Shaw, foreword by Jochen Schulte-Sasse. Minneapolis: University of Minnesota Press, 1984.

Butler, Judith. *Gender Trouble: Feminism and the Subversion of Identity.* New York: Routledge, 1990.

Butler, Judith. *Undoing Gender.* New York: Routledge, 2004.

Button, Peter. *Configurations of the Real in Chinese Literary and Aesthetic Modernity.* Leiden: Brill, 2009.

Byrne, Peter. *Natural Religion and the Nature of Religion: The Legacy of Deism.* New York: Routledge, 1989.

Cai Chusheng, dir. *Xin nüxing* (New Woman). Shanghai, 1933, Lianhua yingye gongsi.

Cai Ye, and Wang Ling, adapters. *Baishe zhuan.* Guangzhou: Huanan renmin chubanshe, 1954. Chaozhou ballad.

Calhoun, Craig. *Nations Matter: Culture, History, and the Cosmopolitan Dream.* New York: Routledge, 2007.

Cao Jinghua, trans. *Di sishi yi* (The Forty-First). Beiping: Weiming she, 1929. Translation of Boris Lavrenyov's 1924 novel *Sorok pervyy.*

Carlson, Evans Fordyce. *Twin Stars of China: A Behind-the-Scenes Story of China's Valiant Struggle for Existence by a U.S. Marine Who Lived and Moved with the People.* New York: Dodd, Mead & Company, 1940.

Carter, Angela. *The Bloody Chamber.* New York: Harper & Row, 1979.

Cassel, Pär Kristoffer. *Grounds of Judgment: Extraterritoriality and Imperial Power in Nineteenth-Century China and Japan.* New York: Oxford University Press, 2012.

Chan, Sylvia. "Realism or Socialist Realism? The 'Proletarian' Episode of Modern Chinese Literature, 1927–1932." *Australian Journal of Chinese Affairs,* no. 9 (January 1983).

Chen Kaige, dir. *Huang tudi* (Yellow Earth). Nanning, 1984, Guangxi dianying zhipianchang.

Chen Liting, dir. *Liren xing* (Songs of Modern Women). Screenplay by Tian Han. Shanghai, 1949, Kunlun dianying gongsi.

Chen Qingsheng. *Chuangzao she jicheng* (Records of the Creation Society). Shanghai: Shanghai shehui kexue chubanshe, 1989.

Chen Sihe. "Lun Wusi xinwenxue yundong de xianfengxing" (On the Avant-Gardism of the May Fourth New Literary Movement). *Fudan xuebao* (Fudan Journal, social science edition), no. 6 (2005), 1–17.

Chen Sihe. "Xianfeng yu changtai: Xiandai wenxueshi de liangzhong jiben xingtai" (The Avant-Garde and the Norm: Two Basic Patterns in the History of Modern Chinese Literature). *Wenyi zhengming* (Literary and Artistic Debates), no. 3 (2007), 59–68.

Chen Tianhua. "Lun zhongguo yi gaichuang minzhu zhengti" (On the Democractic Governance of China). In *Chen Tianhua ji* (Works of Chen Tianhua). Shanghai: Minzhi shuju, 1928.

Chen Xiang. *Chensan Wuniang yanjiu* (Studies on Chensan Wuniang). Taipei: Taiwan Shangwu yinshuguan, 1985.

Chen Xiaomei. *Occidentalism: A Theory of Counter-discourse in Post-Mao China.* New York: Oxford University Press, 1995.

Chen Xiaomei. *Acting the Right Part: Political Theatre and Popular Drama in Contemporary China.* Honolulu: University of Hawai'i Press, 2002.

Chen Xiaomei. "Reflections on the Legacy of Tian Han: 'Proletarian Modernism' and Its Traditional Roots." *Modern Chinese Literature and Culture,* vol. 18, no. 1 (Spring 2006), 155–215.

Chen Xiaomei. "Tian Han and the *Nanguo* Phenomenon: Networking the Personal, Communal, and Cultural." In *Literary Societies of Republican China,* edited by Kirk A. Denton and Michel Hockx. Lanham, MD: Lexington Books, 2008.

Chen Xiaomei, ed. *The Columbia Anthology of Modern Chinese Drama.* New York: Columbia University Press, 2010.

Chen Xiaoming. *From the May Fourth Movement to Communist Revolution: Guo Moruo and the Chinese Path to Communism.* Albany: State University of New York Press, 2007.

Chen Youming, et al. *Baishe zhuan.* Guangzhou: Huanan renmin chubanshe, 1954. Cantonese Opera.

Chen Yueshan et al., eds. *Tang Huaiqiu yu zhongguo lüxing jutuan* (Tang Huaiqiu and the China Travel Drama Troupe). Beijing: Zhongguo xiju chubanshe, 2000.

Chen Yuqian, Chen Shiqi, and Yu Xiushan. *Yiyao zhuan* (Tale of a Righteous Spirit). 12 vols. Block print, double leaves, oriental style, in case, 1869.

Chen Zhengmao. *Lixiang yu xianshi de chongtu: "Shaonian zhongguo xuehui" shi* (Conflict between Ideal and Reality: A History of the Young China Association). Taipei: Xiuwei zixun keji gufen youxian gongsi, 2010.

Cheng Bugao. "Tian Han wei zhongguo jinbu dianying fendou." In *Yingtan yijiu* (Remembrances of the Film Circle). Beijing: Zhongguo dianying chubanshe, 1983.

Cheng, Eileen J. "Recycling the Scholar-Beauty Narrative: Lu Xun on Love in an Age of Mechanical Reproductions." *Modern Chinese Literature and Culture,* vol. 18, no. 2 (2006).

Cheng Jihua, et al., eds. *Zhongguo dianying fazhan shi* (A History of the Development of Chinese Film). Beijing: Zhongguo dianying chubanshe, 1980.

Cheng Rong, et al. *Baishe zhuan.* Beijing: Zuojia chubanshe, 1955. Yue Opera.

Chi, Robert. "'The March of the Volunteers': From Movie Theme Song to National Anthem." In *Re-envisioning the Chinese Revolution: The Politics and Poetics of Collective Memories in Reform China,* edited by Ching Kwan Lee and Guobin Yang. Stanford, CA: Stanford University Press, 2007.

Chiba Nobuo. "Jasei no in" (The Lust of the Serpent). In *Eiga to Tanizaki* (Film and Tanizaki). Tokyo: Seiabo, 1989.

Chou, Katherine Hui-ling. "Staging Revolution: Actresses, Realism, and the New Woman Movement in Chinese Spoken Drama and Film, 1919–1949." PhD diss., New York University, 1997.

Chow Kai-ming, ed. *Beyond the May Fourth Paradigm: In Search of Chinese Modernity.* Lanham, MD: Lexington Books, 2008.

Chow, Rey. *Women and Chinese Modernity: The Politics of Reading between West and East.* Minneapolis: University of Minnesota Press, 1991.

Chow, Rey. "A Souvenir of Love." In *Ethics after Idealism: Theory, Culture, Ethnicity, Reading.* Bloomington: Indiana University Press, 1998.

Chow, Rey. *Modern Chinese Literary and Cultural Studies in the Age of Theory: Reimagining a Field.* Durham, NC: Duke University Press, 2000.

Chow Tse-tsung. *The May Fourth Movement: Intellectual Revolution in Modern China.* Cambridge, MA: Harvard University Press, 1960.

Chukhrai, Grigori, dir. *Sorok pervyy* (The Forty-First). Soviet Union, 1956, Mosfilm.

Cohen, Paul A. *History in Three Keys: The Boxers as Event, Experience, and Myth.* New York: Columbia University Press, 1997.

"Commemoration of Huimin Situ's 100th Birthday." *Ivens Magazine* (European Foundation Joris Ivens), no. 16 (October 2010).

Dai Bufan. "Ping *Jinbo ji*" (Review of "Story of the Golden Bowl"). *Renmin ribao* (People's Daily), September 12, 1952.

Dai Bufan. "Shilun *Baishe zhuan* gushi" (A Tentative Discussion of the White Snake Story). *Wenyi bao* (Literature and Art Bimonthly), no. 13 (1953).

Daruvala, Susan F. *Zhou Zuoren and an Alternative Chinese Response to Modernity.* Cambridge, MA: Harvard University Asia Center, 2000.

"Datongxue" (Theory of Great Harmony). *Wanguo gongbao* (Review of the Times), nos. 121–24 (February–April 1899).

Dawley, Evan. "Changing Minds: American Missionaries, Chinese Intellectuals, and Cultural Internationalism, 1919–1921." *Journal of American-East Asian Relations,* vol. 12, nos. 1–2 (spring-summer 2003), 1–21.

Denton, Kirk A. *The Problematic of Self in Modern Chinese Literature: Hu Feng and Lu Ling.* Stanford, CA: Stanford University Press, 1998.

Deng Xingqi. "Tian Han xiju huodong yu chuangzuo nianpu" (A Chronology of Tian Han's Theatrical Activities and Writings). *Xiqu yanjiu* (Theater Studies), vol. 3 (1980); vol. 5 (1982).

Deng Xingqi. "Xianquzhe zhi lu" (The Road of a Pioneer). *Xiju luncong* (Theater Review), vol. 4 (1983).

Des Forges, Alexander. *Mediasphere Shanghai: The Aesthetics of Cultural Production.* Honolulu: University of Hawai'i Press, 2007.

Diamant, Neil Jeffery. *Revolutionizing the Family: Politics, Love, and Divorce in Urban and Rural China, 1949–1968.* Berkeley: University of California Press, 2000.

Dianying yishu (Film Art). Beijing: Zhongguo dianying chubanshe, 1988. Contains issues 1–12.

Dierkes-Thrun, Petra. *Salome's Modernity: Oscar Wilde and the Aesthetics of Transgression.* Ann Arbor: University of Michigan Press, 2011.

Dijkstra, Bram. *Idols of Perversity: Fantasies of Feminine Evil in Fin-de-Siècle Culture.* New York: Oxford University Press, 1986.

Dijkstra, Bram. "The Lords of Creation Battle the Vampires of Time." In *Evil Sisters: The Threat of Female Sexuality and the Cult of Manhood.* New York: Alfred A. Knopf, 1996.

Dirlik, Arif. *The Origins of Chinese Communism.* New York: Oxford University Press, 1989.

Doak, Kevin M. *Dreams of Difference: The Japan Romantic School and the Crisis of Modernity.* Berkeley: University of California Press, 1994.

Doane, Mary Anne. *Femmes Fatales: Feminism, Film Theory, and Psychoanalysis.* New York: Routledge, 1991.

Dolezelova-Velingerova, Milena, and Oldrich Kral, eds. *The Appropriation of Cultural Capital: China's May Fourth Project.* Cambrdge, MA: Harvard University Asia Center, 2001.

Dong Jian. *Tian Han zhuan* (A Biography of Tian Han). Beijing: Shiyue wenyi chubanshe, 1996.

Dong Jieyuan. *Dong Jieyuan Xixiang ji* (The Dong Jieyuan Version of the Western Chamber). 8 vols. Beijing: Renmin wenxue chubanshe, 1962.

Donohue, Joseph. "Distance, Death, and Desire in Salome." In *The Cambridge Companion to Oscar Wilde,* edited by Peter Raby. Cambridge: Cambridge University Press, 1997.

Drasner, David, ed. *Theatre in Theory, 1900–2000: An Anthology.* Malden, MA: Blackwell, 2008.

Duara, Prasenjit. "The Regime of Authenticity: Timelessness, Gender, and National History in Modern China." *History and Theory,* vol. 37, no. 3 (October 1998).

Duara, Prasenjit. *Sovereignty and Authenticity: Manchukuo and the East Asian Modern.* Lanham, MD: Rowman & Littlefield, 2003.

Duberman, Martin. *Paul Robeson: A Biography by Martin Duberman.* New York: New Press, 1989.

DuBois, Thomas David. *Religion and the Making of Modern East Asia.* Cambridge: Cambridge University Press, 2011.

Duus, Peter. "Yoshino Sakuzō: The Christian as Political Critic." *Journal of Japanese Studies,* vol. 4, no. 2 (Summer 1978), 301–26.

Dym, Jeffery A. *Benshi, Japanese Silent Film Narrators, and Their Forgotten Narrative Art of Setsumei: A History of Japanese Silent Film Narration.* Lewiston, NY: Edwin Mellen Press, 2003.

Eagleton, Mary. "Genre and Gender." In *Modern Genre Theory,* edited and introduced by David Duff. Singapore: Pearson Education Limited, 2000.

Eberstein, Bernd, ed. *A Selective Guide to Chinese Literature, 1900–1949*. Vol. 4: *The Drama*. Leiden: Brill, 1990.

Eisenstein, Sergei. "Montage of Attractions." Translated by Daniel Gerould. In *Re: Direction—a Theoretical and Practical Guide*, edited by Rebecca Schneider and Gabrielle H. Cody. New York: Routledge, 2002.

Epstein, Israel. *My China Eye: Memoirs of a Jew and a Journalist*. San Francisco: Long River Press, 2005.

Esterhammer, Angela. *The Romantic Performative: Language and Action in British and German Romanticism*. Stanford, CA: Stanford University Press, 2000.

Eucken, Rudolf. "Naturalism or Idealism?" In *Nobel Lectures: Literature, 1901–1967*, edited by Horst Frenz. Amsterdam: Elsevier, 1969. Nobel Lecture, March 27, 1909.

Fairbank, John K., and Albert Feuerwerker, eds. *The Cambridge History of China*. Vol. 13, pt. 2: *Republican China, 1912–1949*. Cambridge: Cambridge University Press; Taipei: Caves Books, 1986.

Fällman, Fredrik. *Salvation and Modernity: Intellectuals and Faith in Contemporary China*. Lanham, MD: University Press of America, 2008.

Fang Chengpei. *Leifeng ta chuanqi* (Legend of the Leifeng Pagoda). 4 vols. Shanghai: Shanghai guji chubanshe, 1995.

Farfan, Penny. *Women, Modernism, and Performance*. Cambridge: Cambridge University Press, 2004.

Feng Menglong. "Bai niangzi yongzhen Leifengta" (Lady White Forever Imprisoned under the Leifeng Pagoda). In *Jingshi tongyan* (Stories to Caution the World). Beijing: Renmin wenxue chubanshe, 1956.

Fengshen bang (Investiture of the Gods), Beijing: Renmin wenxue chubanshe, 1992.

Feuerwerker, Yi-tsi M. *Ideology, Power, Text: Self-Representation and the Peasant "Other" in Modern Chinese Literature*. Stanford, CA: Stanford University Press, 1998.

Finnane, Antonia. *Changing Clothes in China: Fashion, History, Nation*. New York: Columbia University Press, 2008.

Fitzgerald, John. "The Nationless State: The Search for a Nation in Modern Chinese Nationalism." *Australian Journal of Chinese Affairs*, no. 33 (January 1995).

Fogel, Joshua A. *The Literature of Travel in the Japanese Rediscovery of China, 1862–1945*. Stanford, CA: Stanford University Press, 1996.

Fogel, Joshua A. "'Shanghai-Japan': The Japanese Residents' Association of Shanghai." *Journal of Asian Studies*, vol. 59, no. 4 (November 2000).

Fogel, Joshua A. *Articulating the Sinosphere: Sino-Japanese Relations in Space and Time*. Cambridge, MA: Harvard University Press, 2009.

Fowler, Edward. *The Rhetoric of Confession: Shishōsetsu in Early Twentieth-Century Japanese Fiction*. Berkeley: University of California Press, 1992.

Freedman, Alisa. *Tokyo in Transit, Japanese Culture on the Rails and Road*. Stanford, CA: Stanford University Press, 2010.

Friedman, Geraldine. *The Insistence of History: Revolution in Burke, Wordsowrth, Keats, and Baudelaire*. Stanford, CA: Stanford University Press, 1996.

Fu Jin. *Laoxi de qianshi jinsheng* (The Past and Present of Old Theater). Beijing: Renmin chubanshe, 2007.

Fu, Poshek. *Passivity, Resistance, and Collaboration: Intellectual Choices in Occupied Shanghai, 1937–1945*. Stanford, CA: Stanford University Press, 1993.

Fu Yanchang, Zhu Yingpeng, and Zhang Ruogu. *Yishu sanjiayan* (Three Personal Views on Art). Shanghai: Liangyou tushu gongsi, 1927.

Fujii Shōzō. *Erosenko no toshi monogatari: 1920 nendai Tokyo, Shanhai, Pekin* (Erosenko's Urban Stories: Tokyo, Shanghai, and Beijing in the 1920s). Tokyo: Misuzu Shobō, 1989.

Fujitani Takashi. "Minshushi as Critique of Orientalist Knowledge." *positions: east asia cultures critique*, vol. 6, no. 2 (1998).

Gaimushō gaikō kiroku. *Ryūnichi Shina gakusei saikin ni okeru shisō oyobi dōsei ni kansuru ken* (On Recent Thoughts and Movements among Chinese Students in Japan), Japanese Foreign Ministry Office, Diplomatic Archives, document no. 20-1770, 1921.

Gaimushō gaikō kiroku. "Zairyū shinajin to honpō tokubetsu yō-shisatsunin no kankei" (The Relationship between Resident Chinese and Japanese under Close Surveillance). In *Zairyū gaikokujin gaikyō* (General Condition of Foreigners in Japan), marked as "top secret," Japanese Foreign Ministry Office, Diplomatic Archives, document no. 4-2-2, 1921.

Gaimushō gaikō kiroku. "Shinajin Shi Sontō tsuihō shobun ni taisuru zairyū Shinajin no kansō" (The Reaction of Tokyo Chinese to the Expulsion of Shi Cuntong), Japanese Foreign Ministry Office, Diplomatic Archives, document no. 4-2-6, 1921.

Gaimushō gaikō kiroku. "Shina kankei jimu gaiyō" (An Outline of China-Related Affairs), Japanese Foreign Ministry Office, Diplomatic Archives, document no. 3-10-5-17-2, 1922.

Gaines, Jane M., and Michael Renov, eds. *Collecting Visible Evidence*. Minenapolis: University of Minnesota Press, 1999.

Gao Minglu. *Total Modernity and the Avant-Garde in Twentieth-Century Chinese Art*. Cambridge, MA: MIT Press, 2011.

Glosser, Susan L., ed. and trans., *Li Fengjin: How the New Marriage Law Helped Chinese Women Stand Up*. Portland, OR: Opal Mogus Books, 2005.

Gluck, Mary. *Popular Bohemia: Modernism and Urban Culture in Nineteenth-Century Paris*. Cambridge, MA: Harvard University Press, 2005.

Gluck, Mary. *Liuxing de boshi miya: Shijiu shiji Bali de xiandai zhuyi yu dushi wen-*

hua. Translated with an introduction by Liang Luo. Hefei: Anhui jiaoyu chubanshe, 2009.

Goethe, Johann Wolfgang von. *Faust* (part 1). Translated by Peter Salm. New German-English ed. New York: Bantam, 1988.

Goethe, Johann Wolfgang von. *Italian Journey, 1786–1788*. Translated by W. H. Auden and Elizabeth Mayer. New York: Penguin Classics, 1992.

Goethe, Johann Wolfgang von. "Wilhelm Meister's Apprenticeship." In *Goethe: The Collected Works*, vol. 9. Princeton, NJ: Princeton University Press, 1995.

Goldstein, Joshua. *Drama Kings: Players and Publics in the Re-creation of Peking Opera, 1870–1937*. Berkeley: University of California Press, 2007.

Gong Ruofei, dir. *Guoge* (National Anthem). Twenty-episode TV series, 2010, produced by Hunan Sattelite TV, Changsha TV Station, and Yunnan TV Station.

Goodman, Emma. *The Social Significance of the Modern Drama*. Boston: Richard G. Badger, 1914.

Gordon, Andrew. "The Crowd and Politics in Imperial Japan: Tokyo, 1905–1918." *Past and Present*, vol. 121 (1988).

Gordon, Andrew. *A Modern History of Japan: From Tokugawa Times to the Present*. New York: Oxford University Press, 2003.

Graham, A. C. *Poems of the West Lake: Translations from the Chinese by A. C. Graham*. London: Wellsweep, 1990.

Graham, A. C., trans. "Rhapsody on the Sounds of Autumn" (1042) by Ouyang Xiu. In *The Anchor Book of Chinese Poetry*, edited by Tony Barnstone and Chou Ping. New York: Anchor Books, 2005.

Graves, Robert. *The White Goddess*. New York: Farrar, Straus & Giroux, 1948.

Grenier, Cynthia. "Joris Ivens: Social Realist versus Lyric Poet." *Sight and Sound*, vol. 27, no. 4 (Spring 1958).

Groys, Boris. *The Total Art of Stalinism: Avant-Garde, Aesthetic Dictatorship, and Beyond*. Translated by Charles Rougle. Princeton, NJ: Princeton University Press, 1992.

Guangdong sheng wenhua ju. *Kunqu "shiwu guan" lunwen xuanji* (Collected Essays on the Kun Opera *Shiwu guan*). Guangzhou: Guangdong sheng wenhua ju, 1956.

Guiley, Rosemary Ellen. *The Complete Vampire Companion: Legend and Lore of the Living Dead*. New York: Macmillan, 1994.

Gunn, Edward. *Unwelcome Muse: Chinese Literature in Shanghai and Peking, 1937–1945*. New York: Columbia University Press, 1980.

Gunn, Edward. *Twentieth Century Chinese Drama: An Anthology*. Bloomington: Indiana University Press, 1983.

Gunning, Tom. "Joris Ivens: Filmmaker of the Twentieth Century, of the Netherlands and the World." In *Cinema without Borders: The Films of Joris Ivens*. Nijmegen, the Netherlands: European Foundation Joris Ivens, 2002.

Guo Chao. *Guoge licheng* (The Journey of the National Anthem). Beijing: Zhongguo guoji guangbo diantai chubanshe, 2002.

Guo Moruo. *Nüshen* (The Goddess). Shanghai: Taidong tushuju, 1921.

Guo Moruo, trans. *Fushide* (Faust). Shanghai: Chuangzao she chubanbu, 1928.

Guo Moruo. "*Fenghuang niepan*" (The Nirvana of the Phoenix). In *Guo Moruo daibiaozuo* (Representative Works of Guo Moruo), vol. 1. Beijing: Huaxia chubanshe, 2009.

Guo Tao. "Baidai fuchen: Jindai Shanghai Baidai changpian gongsi shengshuaiji" (The Vicissitudes of the Pathé Gramophone Company in Modern Shanghai). *Shilin* (Historical Review), no. 5 (2008).

Guo Yanli. *Zhongguo jindai fanyi wenxue gailun* (An Outline of Translated Literature in Modern China). Wuhan: Hubei jiaoyu chubanshe, 1998.

Hagener, Malte. *Moving Forward, Looking Back: The European Avant-Garde and the Invention of Film Culture, 1919–1939*. Admserdam: Amsterdam University Press, 2007.

Han Sanzhou. "Yan'an 'guairen' Sai Ke de 'guaishi'" (The "Eccentric" Sai Ke's "Eccentric" Deeds in Yan'an). *Gejie* (All Circles), no. 3 (2011).

Hanyu dacidian (A Grand Dictionary of the Chinese Language). CD 2.0 version. Hong Kong: Shangwu yinshuguan, 2002.

Häringová, Jarmila. "The Development of Tian Han's Dramatic Writings during the Years 1920–1937." In *Studies in Modern Chinese Literature*, edited by Jaroslav Průšek. Berlin: Akademie-Verlag, 1964.

Harootunian, Harry D. "Figuring the Folk." In *Mirror of Modernity: Invented Traditions of Modern Japan*, edited by Stephen Vlastos. Berkeley: University of California Press, 1998.

Harootunian, Harry D. *History's Disquiet: Modernity, Cultural Practice, and the Question of Everyday Life*. New York: Columbia University Press, 2000.

Harootunian, Harry D. *Overcome by Modernity: History, Culture, and Community in Interwar Japan*. Princeton, NJ: Princeton University Press, 2000.

Harrell, Paula. *Sowing the Seeds of Change: Chinese Students, Japanese Teachers, 1895–1905*. Stanford, CA: Stanford University Press, 1992.

Harrison, Henrietta. *The Making of the Republican Citizen: Political Ceremonies and Symbols in China, 1911–1929*. New York: Oxford University Press, 1999.

Hashimoto Mitsuru. "Yanagita Kunio's Japan." In *Mirror of Modernity: Invented Traditions of Modern Japan*, edited by Stephen Vlastos. Berkeley: University of California Press, 1998.

Hauptmann, Gerhart. *The Sunken Bell; A Fairy Play in Five Acts*. Translated by Charles Henry Meltzer. In *Seven Contemporary Plays*, selected and edited by Charles H. Whitman. Boston: Houghton Mifflin, 1959.

Hayford, Charles W. *To the People: James Yen and Village China.* New York: Columbia University Press, 1990.

Hayot, Eric. *Chinese Dreams: Pound, Brecht, Tel Quel.* Ann Arbor: University of Michigan Press, 2004.

Hayot, Eric. *The Hypothetical Mandarin: Sympathy, Modernity, and Chinese Pain.* New York: Oxford University Press, 2009.

He Guimei. *"Xin qimeng" zhishi dang'an: 80 niandai Zhongguo wenhua yanjiu* (Knowledge Archives of the "New Enlightenment": On Chinese Culture of the 1980s). Beijing: Beijing daxue chubanshe, 2010.

He Lüting. *He Lüting yinyue lunwen xuanji* (Selected Essays on Music by He Lüting). Shanghai: Shanghai wenyi chubanshe, 1989.

He Yintai, and Li Dasan. *Tian Han pingzhuan* (A Critical Biography of Tian Han). Changsha: Hunan renmin chubanshe, 1984.

Helleberg, Victor E. Review of *Socialism: An Analysis* by Rudolf Eucken. *American Journal of Sociology,* vol. 28, no. 3 (November 1922).

Higashi Sumiko. *Virgins, Vamps, and Flappers: The American Silent Movie Heroine.* Montreal: Eden Press, 1978.

Higgins, John, ed. *The Raymond Williams Reader.* Malden, MA: Blackwell, 2001.

Hirai Shōichi, ed. *Migishi Kōtarō, Yoshihara Jirō, jojō no kosumorojī* (Migishi Kōtarō, Yoshihara Jirō, the Cosmology of Sentimentality). Tokyo: Hon no Tomosha, 2001.

Hitch, Marcus. *Goethe's Faust: A Fragment of Socialist Criticism.* Chicago: Charles H. Kerr, 1908.

Hockx, Michel. "Playing the Field: Aspects of Chinese Literary Life in the 1920s." In *The Literary Field of Twentieth-Century China,* edited by Michel Hockx. Honolulu: University of Hawai'i Press, 1999.

Hockx, Michel. *Questions of Style: Literary Societies and Literary Journals in Modern China, 1911–1937.* Leiden: Brill, 2003.

Hōsei Daigaku Ōhara Shakai Mondai Kenkyūjo, ed. *Shinjinkai kikanshi: Demokurashii, Senku, Dōhō, Narōdo* (Official Journals of the New Man Society: Democracy, Pioneer, Brothers, and Narod). Tokyo: Hōsei Daigaku Shuppankyoku, 1969.

Howard, Joshua H. "The Making of a National Icon: Commemorating Nie Er, 1935–1949." *Twentieth Century China,* vol. 37, no. 1 (2012), 5–29.

"Huajia Liu Xiaodong: Wo dui huahua yizhi you jikegan" (Painter Liu Xiaodong: I am Always Hungry about Painting), *Waitan huabao,* February 20, 2008.

Hsia, C. T. *C. T. Hsia on Chinese Literature.* New York: Columbia University Press, 2004.

Hsu, Rachel. *"Nuola" zai Zhongguo: Xin nüxing xingxiang de suzao jiqi yanbian,*

1900s–1930s (Nora in China: The Formation and Transformation of the New Woman Image, 1900–1930s). Taipei: National Chengchi University Press, 2003.

Hsu Wen-hung. "The Evolution of the Legend of the White Snake." *Tamkang Review*, vol. 4, no. 1 (1973).

Hu Jubin. *Projecting a Nation: Chinese National Cinema before 1949*. Hong Kong: Hong Kong University Press, 2003.

Hu Lili. "Hudong, jiaorong, he chongtu: Dushi wenhua yujing xia de liuxing gequ, dianying, yiji wenhua zhengzhi de guanxi" (Interactions, Convergences, and Conflicts: Urban Cultural Context and the Intersection of Popular Music, Film, and Cultural Politics). *Dianying pingjie* (Movie Review), no. 7 (2011), 93–95.

Hu Sha. *Pingju jianshi* (A Brief History of Ping Opera). Beijing: Zhongguo xiju chubanshe, 1982.

Hu Yingjian. "Lun Kangzhan shiqi jiuti shige de fuxing" (On the Resurgence of Classical-Style Poetry during the Anti-Japanese War). *Kangri zhanzheng yanjiu* (Journal of China's War of Resistance against Japan), no. 1 (2001).

Huang, Alexander C. Y. *Chinese Shakespeares: Two Centuries of Cultural Exchanges*. New York: Columbia University Press, 2009.

Huang Hu. *Zhongguo xinwen shiye fazhanshi* (History of the Development of Chinese Journalism). Shanghai: Fudan daxue chubanshe, 2007.

Huang Jishi. *Zhang Shu zhuan* (A Biography of Zhang Shu). Beijing: Tuanjie chubanshe, 1994.

Huang Rikui. *Huang Rikui wenji* (Collected Works of Huang Rikui). Guilin: Guangxi renmin chubanshe, 1989.

Huang Shang. *Xixiang ji yu Baishe zhuan* (The Western Chamber and the White Snake). Shanghai: Pingming chubanshe, 1953.

Hung, Chung-tai. *Going to the People: Chinese Intellectuals and Folk Literature, 1918–1937*. Cambridge, MA: Council on East Asian Studies, Harvard University, 1985.

Hung, Chung-tai. *War and Popular Culture: Resistance in Modern China, 1937–1945*. Berkeley: University of California Press, 1994.

Hung, Chung-tai. *Mao's New World: Political Culture in the Early People's Republic*. Ithaca, NY: Cornell University Press, 2010.

Huntington, Rania. *Alien Kind: Foxes and Late Imperial Chinese Narrative*. Cambridge, MA: Council on East Asian Studies, Harvard University, 2003.

Huters, Theodore. *Bringing the World Home: Appropriating the West in Late Qing and Early Republican China*. Honolulu: University of Hawai'i Press, 2005.

Huyssen, Andreas. "The Hidden Dialectic: Avantgarde-Technology-Mass Culture." In *After the Great Divide: Modernism, Mass Culture, Postmodernism*. Bloomington: Indiana University Press, 1986.

Ibsen, Henrik. *Et dukkehjem (A Doll's House)* (1879). Edited by Philip M. Parker. San Diego, CA: ICON Classics, 2005.

Idema, Wilt L. *Personal Salvation and Filial Piety: Two Precious Scroll Narratives of Guanyin and Her Acolytes.* Honolulu: Kuroda Institute and University of Hawai'i Press, 2008.

Idema, Wilt L. *Meng Jiangnü Brings Down the Great Wall: Ten Versions of a Chinese Legend.* Translated and introduced by Wilt L. Idema with an essay by Haiyan Lee. Seattle: University of Washington Press, 2008.

Idema, Wilt L. *The White Snake and Her Son: A Translation of the Precious Scroll of Thunder Peak with Related Texts.* Indianapolis: Hackett Publishing, 2009.

Idema, Wilt L., and Lloyd Haft. *A Guide to Chinese Literature.* Ann Arbor: Center for Chinese Studies, University of Michigan, 1997.

Idema, Wilt L., Wai-yee Li, and Ellen Widmer, eds. *Trauma and Transcendence in Early Qing Literature.* Cambridge, MA: Harvard University Asia Center, 2006.

Iida Kichirō. *Gendai Chūgoku bungaku kenkyū bunken mokuroku, 1908-1945* (Research Catalog of Modern Chinese Literature, 1908-1945). Rev. ed. Tokyo: Kyūko shoin, 1991.

Iriye, Akira. *China and Japan in the Global Setting.* Cambridge, MA: Harvard University Press, 1992.

Itō Toramaru. *Sōzōsha shiryō* (Materials on the Creation Society). Vol. 11: *Sōzōsha Kenkyū* (Research on the Creation Society). Tokyo: Ajia Shuppan, 1979.

Ivens, Joris, dir. *Études des mouvements* (Studies of Movements). The Netherlands, 1927, 4 min., 35 mm, black and white, silent.

Ivens, Joris, dir. *Regen* (Rain). The Netherlands, 1929, 12 min., 35 mm, black and white, silent.

Ivens, Joris. "Quelques réflections sur les documentaires d'avant-garde" (Some Reflections on the Avant-Garde Documentary). *La revue des vivants* (Journal of the Living), no. 10 (1931).

Ivens, Joris. "Zur Methode des dokumentarischen Films, in besondern des Films *Komsomol*" (On the Method of the Documentary Film, in Particular the Film *Komsomol*) (1932). Translated from the German by Kees Bakker. In Kees Bakker, "Inventory of the Joris Ivens Archives," European Foundation Joris Ivens, Nijmegen, the Netherlands, 1998, Inv. no. JIA 2.3.02.32.02-189 (JIA hereafter).

Ivens, Joris. "Notes on Hollywood" (1936). In *Joris Ivens and the Documentary Context,* edited by Kees Bakker. Amsterdam: Amsterdam University Press, 1999.

Ivens, Joris. Handwritten shooting notes and notes for sound effects for *The 400 Million,* shot on location in China during 1938. JIA 2.3.02.39.01-238.

Ivens, Joris, dir. *The 400 Million,* 1939, 53.51 min., 35 mm, black and white. New York: History Today Inc.

Ivens, Joris. "Documentary: Subjectivity and Montage." In *Joris Ivens and the Documentary Context,* edited by Kees Bakker. Amsterdam: Amsterdam University Press, 1999. Lecture at the Museum of Modern Art, New York, December 13, 1939.

Ivens, Joris, dir. *Das Lied der Ströme* (The Song of the Rivers). East Germany, 1954, DEFA, 90 min., 35 mm, black and white. Commissioned by World Federation of Trade Unions.

Ivens, Joris, artistic dir. *Die Windrose* (The Windrose). Dir. Alberto Cavalcanti et al., East Germany, 1957, DEFA, 104 min., 35 mm, black and white. Commissioned by the Women's International Democratic Federation.

Ivens, Joris. Handwritten draft essay "Five Countries: Five Songs," Peking (Beijing), March 8, 1958. JIA 2.3.02.56.02-311.

Ivens, Joris, dir. *Zaochun* (Early Spring). People's Republic of China, 1958, Central Newsreel and Documentary Film Studio, 38 min., 35 mm, color.

Ivens, Joris. "Jin sanshi nianlai jilu dianying fazhan gaikuang, wo de paishe jilu yingpian de fangfa" (A Brief Introduction to the Development of Documentary Film in the Past Thirty Years and My Creative Methods in Making Documentary Films). Lecture handout in Chinese, Beijing Film Academy short training session, August 1958. JIA 2.3.08-617.

Ivens, Joris. *The Camera and I.* New York: International Publishers, 1969.

Ivens, Joris. "How I Filmed *The 400 Million.*" In *Joris Ivens and China.* Beijing: New World Press, 1983.

Ivens, Joris, and Vladimir Pozner. *Das Lied der Ströme* (The Song of the Rivers). Berlin: Verlag Tribüne, 1957.

Jackson, Shannon. *Professing Performance: Theatre in the Academy from Philology to Performativity.* Cambridge: Cambridge University Press, 2004.

Jameson, Fredric. *Postmodernism; or, the Cultural Logic of Late Capitalism.* London and New York: Verso, 1991.

Jansen, Marius B. *The Japanese and Sun Yat Sen.* Cambridge, MA: Harvard University Press, 1954.

Jansen, Marius B. *The Making of Modern Japan.* Cambridge, MA: Harvard University Press, 2002.

Jervis, John. *Transgressing the Modern: Explorations in the Western Experience of Otherness.* Malden, MA: Blackwell, 1999.

Jiang Hui. "From Lu Xun to Zhao Shuli: The Politics of Recognition in Chinese Literary Modernity." PhD diss., New York University, 2007.

Jiang Jianlan. "Tianlao xie 'baishe zhuan' shimo" (The Circumstances Surrounding Tian Han's Writing of *White Snake*). *Zhongguo xiju* (Chinese Theater), no. 7 (1988).

Jiang Jin. *Women Playing Men: Yue Opera and Social Change in Twentieth-Century Shanghai.* Seattle: University of Washington Press, 2009.

Jinnai Hidenobu. *Tokyo: A Spatial Anthropology.* Translated by Kimiko Nishimura. Berkeley: University of California Press, 1995.

Johnson, David, Andrew J. Nathan, and Evelyn S. Rawski, eds. *Popular Culture in Late Imperial China.* Berkeley: University of California Press, 1985.

Jones, Andrew F. *Like a Knife: Ideology and Genre in Contemporary Chinese Popular Music.* Ithaca, NY: Cornell East Asia Institute, 1992.

Jones, Andrew F. *Yellow Music: Media Culture and Colonial Modernity in the Chinese Jazz Age.* Durham, NC: Duke University Press, 2001.

Jones, Andrew F. *Developmental Fairy Tales: Evolutionary Thinking and Modern Chinese Culture.* Cambridge, MA: Harvard University Press, 2011.

Jones, Andrew F. and Xu Lanjun, *Ertong de faxian—Xiandai zhongguo wenxue ji wenhua zhong de ertong wenti* (The Discovery of the Child: the Problem of the Child in Modern Chinese Literature and Culture). Beijing: Beijing daxue chubanshe, 2011.

Kaikkonen, Marja. *Laughable Propaganda: Modern Xiangsheng as Didactic Entertainment.* Stockholm: Institute of Oriental Languages, Stockholm University, 1990.

Kalyvas, Andreas. *Democracy and the Politics of the Extraordinary: Max Weber, Carl Schmitt, and Hannah Arendt.* Cambridge: Cambridge University Press, 2008.

Kamei Shunsuke. "Tanizaki Jun'ichirō's Modernism and His Relish for China." *Tamkang Review,* vol. 18, nos. 1–4, (1988).

Kamiyama Sōjin. *Sugao no Hariuddo* (Hollywood without Makeup). Tokyo: Jitsugyō no Nipponsha, 1930.

Kanagawa Bungaku Shinkōkai, ed. *Tanizaki Jun'ichirō ten* (The Tanizaki Jun'ichirō Exhibition). Yokohama: Kanagawa Kindai Bungakkan, 1998.

Kangzhan banian muke xuanji (Woodcuts of Wartime China) (1937–45). Shanghai: Kaiming shudian, 1946.

Kano, Ayako. "Visuality and Gender in Modern Japanese Theater: Looking at Salome." *Japan Forum,* vol. 11, no. 1 (1999).

Kano, Ayako. *Acting Like a Woman in Modern Japan: Theater, Gender, and Nationalism.* New York: Palgrave, 2001.

Kaplan, Randy Barbara. "The Pre-leftist One-Act Plays of Tian Han." PhD diss., Ohio State University, 1986.

Kaplan, Randy Barbara. "Planting the Seeds of Theatrical Realism in China: Tian Han's Contributions to Modern Chinese Drama, 1920–1929." *World Literature Today,* vol. 62, no. 1 (Winter 1988).

Kaplan, Randy Barbara. "Images of Subjugation and Defiance: Female Characters in the Early Dramas of Tian Han." In Tani E. Barlow, ed. *Gender Politics in Modern China: Writing and Feminism.* Durham, NC: Duke University Press, 1993.

Kaplan, Randy Barbara, trans. "The Night a Tiger Was Captured." *Asian Theatre Journal,* vol. 11, no. 1 (Spring 1994).

Karashima Takeshi. *Chūgoku no Shingeki.* Tokyo: Shōheidō, 1948.

Karashima Takeshi. *Chūgoku gendai bungaku no kenkyū: Kokkyō bunretsu kara Shanhai Jihen made* (Studies on Modern Chinese Literature: From the Separation of the KMT and the CCP to the Shanghai Incident). Tokyo: Kyūko Shoin, 1983.

Kasza, Gregory J. *The State and the Mass Media in Japan, 1918–1945.* Berkeley: University of California Press, 1988.

Katz, Ephraim. *The Film Encyclopedia.* 4th ed. New York: HarperCollins, 2001.

Kawashima, Ken. *The Proletarian Gamble: Korean Workers in Interwar Japan.* Durham, NC: Duke University Press, 2009.

Keaveney, Christopher T. *The Subversive Self in Modern Chinese Literature: The Creation Society's Reinvention of the Japanese Shishōsetsu.* New York: Palgrave Macmillan, 2006.

Keaveney, Christopher T. *Beyond Brushtalk: Sino-Japanese Literary Exchange in the Interwar Period.* Hong Kong: Hong Kong University Press, 2009.

Keene, Donald. *Dawn to the West: Japanese Literature of the Modern Era: Poetry, Drama, Criticism.* New York: Holt, Rinehart and Winston, 1984.

Kent, Stephen A. "Weber, Goethe, and the Nietzschean Allusion: Capturing the Source of the 'Iron Cage' Metaphor." *Sociological Analysis,* vol. 44, no. 4 (1983).

Kershaw, Alex. *Blood and Champagne: The Life and Times of Robert Capa.* New York: Thomas Dunne Books, St. Martin's Press, 2002.

Kinoshita Rigen, and Yamamura Bochō. "Kuriyagawa Hakuson." In *Kindai sakka tsuitōbun shūsei,* supervised by Inamura Tetsugen. Tokyo: Yumani Shobō, 1987.

Kishida Kunio. *Xiju gailun* (A Brief Theory of Drama). Translated from Japanese by Chen Yu (Tian Han). Shanghai: Zhonghua shuju, 1933.

Knight, Nick. *Marxist Philosophy in China: From Qu Qiubai to Mao Zedong, 1923–1945.* Dordrecht: Springer, 2005.

Kondō Haruo. *Gendai Chūgoku no sakka to sakuhin* (Modern Chinese Writers and Their Works). Tokyo: Shinsen Shobō, 1949.

Konishi, Sho. "Translation and Conversion beyond Western Modernity: Tolstoian Religion in Meiji Japan." In *Converting Cultures: Religion, Ideology, and Transformations of Modernity.* Leiden: Brill, 2007.

Kotani Ichirō. "Sōzōsha to Shōnen Chūgoku Gakkai, Shinjinkai: Den Kan no bungaku oyobi bungakukan o chūshin ni" (The Creation Society, the Young China Association, and the New Man Society: Centered on Tian Han's Literature and Literary Thoughts). in *Chūgoku bunka: Kenkyū to kyōiku* (Chinese Culture: Researches and Pedagogy), vol. 38. Ibaraki, Tsukuba: Otsuka Kanbun Gakkai, 1980.

Kotani Ichirō. "4.12 kūdetaa zengo ni okeru daisanki Sōzōsha dōjin no dōkō: Ryūnichi gakusei undō tono kakawarikara" (Activities of the Third Circle of

Members of the Creation Society after the 4.12 Incident: On the Segregation of the Chinese Student Movements in Japan). In *Chūgoku bunka: Kenkyū to kyōiku* (Chinese Culture: Researches and Pedagogy), vol 40. Ibaraki, Tsukuba: Otsuka Kanbun Gakkai, 1982.

Kotani Ichirō. "'Shanhai geidai' no koto domo: '1930 nendai bungei' no ichimen" ("Shanghai Art University" and Other Matters: One Aspect of the "Literature and Arts of the 1930s"). *Tōyō Bunka* (Oriental Culture) (Tokyo), no. 65 (April 1984).

Kotani Ichirō. "Sōzōsha to Nihon: wakaki hi no Den Kan to sono jidai" (The Creation Society and Japan: The Young Tian Han and His Times). In *Kindai bungaku ni okeru Chūgoku to Nihon: Kyōdō kenkyū Nitchū bungaku kōryūshi* (China and Japan in Modern Literature), edited by Itō Toramaru, Sofue Shōji, and Maruyama Noboru. Tokyo: Kyūko Shoin, 1986.

Kotani Ichirō. "Daiichiki Sōzōsha dōjin no deai to Sōzōsha no seiritsu: Sōzōsha to Nihon" (The Emergence of the First Circle of Members of the Creation Society and the Founding of the Society). In *Chūgoku bungaku no hikaku bungakuteki kenkyū* (Comparative Studies on Chinese Literature), edited by Furuta Keiichi. Tokyo: Kyūko Shoin, 1986.

Kotani Ichirō. "Muramatsu Shōfū to Chūgoku: Den Kan to Muramatsu, Muramatsu no Chūgoku ni taisuru shisei nado o chūshin ni" (Muramatsu Shōfū and China: Centered on Tian Han and Muramatsu, and Muramatsu's Attitude toward China). *Hitotsubashi Review* (Tokyo), vol. 101, no. 3 (March 1989).

Kotani Ichirō. "Nitchū kindai bungaku kōryūshi no naka ni okeru Den Kan: Den Kan to onaji jidai nihonjin sakka no ōrai" (Tian Han in the History of Modern Japanese and Chinese Literary Exchanges: On Tian Han's Association with His Contemporary, Japanese Writers). In *Chūgoku bunka: Kenkyū to kyōiku* (Chinese Culture: Researches and Pedagogy), vol. 55. Ibaraki, Tsukuba: Otsuka Kanbun Gakkai, 1997.

Kotani Ichirō, and Liu Ping, eds. *Tian Han zai Riben* (Tian Han in Japan), supervised by Itō Toramaru. Beijing: Renmin wenxue chubanshe, 1997.

Kracauer, Siegfried. *From Caligari to Hitler: A Psychological History of the German Film.* Princeton, NJ: Princeton University Press, 1966.

Kraus, Richard Curt. *Piano and Politics in China: Middle-Class Ambitions and the Struggle over Western Music.* New York: Oxford University Press, 1989.

Kume Masao: Hito to sakuhin (Kume Masao: The Writer and His Works). Kōriyama: Kōriyama Seinen Kaigisho, 1991.

Kuoshu, Harry H. "Visualizing Ah Q: An Allegory's Resistance to Representation." In *Lightness of Being in China: Adaptation and Discursive Figuration in Cinema and Theater.* New York: Peter Lang, 1999.

Kushner, Barak. *The Thought War: Japanese Imperial Propaganda.* Honolulu: University of Hawai'i Press, 2007.

Kwan, Stanley, dir. *Ruan Lingyu* (Center Stage). Hong Kong, 1992, Fortune Star, DVD.

Lai, Whalen. "From Folklore to Literate Theater: Unpacking *Madame White Snake.*" *Asian Folklore Studies,* vol. 51 (1992).

Laing, Ellen Johnston. *Selling Happiness: Calendar Posters and Visual Culture in Early-Twentieth-Century Shanghai.* Honolulu: University of Hawai'i Press, 2004.

Lam, Tong. *A Passion for Facts: Social Surveys and the Construction of the Chinese Nation-State, 1900–1949.* Berkeley: University of California Press, 2011.

Lane, Barbara Miller. *Architecture and Politics in Germany, 1918–1945.* Cambridge, MA: Harvard University Press, 1985.

Lang, Fritz, and Barry Keith Grant. *Fritz Lang: Interviews.* Jackson: University Press of Mississippi, 2003.

Larson, Wendy. *Women and Writing in Modern China.* Stanford, CA: Stanford University Press, 1998.

Larson, Wendy. *From Ah Q to Lei Feng: Freud and Revolutionary Spirit in 20th Century China.* Stanford, CA: Stanford University Press, 2009.

Le Bon, Gustave. *The Psychology of Socialism.* New York: Macmillan, 1899.

Lee, Ang, dir. *Se, Jie* (*Lust, Caution*), with Tony Leung Chiu Wai as Mr. Yee, Tang Wei as Wang Chia-chih, Joan Chen as Mrs. Yee, and Leehom Wang as K'uang Yu-min. United States, 2008, Universal Studios, DVD.

Lee, Haiyan. "Tears That Crumbled the Great Wall: The Archaeology of Feeling in the May Fourth Folklore Movement." *Journal of Asian Studies,* vol. 64, no. 1 (February 2005).

Lee, Haiyan. *Revolution of the Heart: A Geneology of Love in China, 1900–1950.* Stanford, CA: Stanford University Press, 2007.

Lee, Leo Ou-fan. *The Romantic Generation of Modern Chinese Writers.* Cambridge, MA: Harvard University Press, 1973.

Lee, Leo Ou-fan. "In Search of Modernity." In *Ideas across Cultures,* edited by P. Cohen and M. Goldman. Cambridge, MA: Council on East Asian Studies, Harvard University, 1990.

Lee, Leo Ou-fan. *Shanghai Modern: The Flowering of a New Urban Culture in China, 1930–1945.* Cambridge, MA: Harvard University Press, 1999.

Lee, Lily Hsiao Hung. "Local Color in Two of Ti'en Han's Early Works." *Journal of the Oriental Society of Australia* (Sydney), nos. 15–16 (1983–84).

Lee, Pao-ch'en, ed. *China's Patriots Sing.* Chungking: China Information Publishing Company, 1939.

Lee, Pao-ch'en, ed. "China's War Songs: Everybody Sings Them and Many Are Being Written and Distributed." *New York Times,* December 24, 1939.

Leith, James A. *Space and Revolution: Projects for Monuments, Squares, and Pub-*

lic Buildings in France, 1789–1799. Montreal: McGill-Queen's University Press, 1991.

Leutner, Mechthild, ed. *The Chinese Revolution in the 1920s: Between Triumph and Disaster*. New York: RoutledgeCurzon, 2002.

Levenson, Joseph R. *Revolution and Cosmopolitanism: The Western Stage and the Chinese Stages*, with a foreword by Frederic E. Wakeman. Berkeley: University of California Press, 1971.

Levine, Marilyn Avra. *The Found Generation: Chinese Communists in Europe during the Twenties*. Seattle: University of Washington Press, 1993.

Levine, Steven I. *Anvil of Victory: The Communist Revolution in Manchuria, 1945–1948*. New York: Columbia University Press, 1987.

Li Bihua. *Qingshe quanxin ban* (A New Version of Green Snake). Taipei: Huangguan wenxue, 1993.

Li Chuli. *Zenyang jianshe geming wenxue* (How to Create Revolutionary Literature). Shanghai: Jiangnan shudian, 1930.

Li Fang ed., *Li Huang*, in *Taiping guangji wubaijuan*. Shanghai: Saoye shanfang, 1924.

Li He. "Tian Han qianqi de huaju chuangzuo" (Tian Han's Early Dramatic Writings). In *Xiju luncong* (Review Series on Theater), no. 2 (1957).

Li Jianli. "'Zaizao' de qimeng yu jiuwang: Dui jietou ju 'Fangxia ni de bianzi' de kaocha" ("Re-created" Enlightenment and National Salvation: An Investigation of the Street Play "Lay Down Your Whip"). *Zhongshan daxue xuebao* (Journal of Zhongshan University, Social Science Edition), no. 4 (2007).

Li Jiannong. *The Political History of China*. Stanford, CA: Stanford University Press, 1956.

Li Suyuan. *Zhongguo xiandai dianying lilunshi* (The History of Modern Chinese Film Theory). Beijing: Wenhua yishu chubanshe, 2005.

Li, Wai-yee. *Enchantment and Disenchantment: Love and Illusion in Chinese Literature*. Princeton, NJ: Princeton University Press, 1993.

Li, Wai-yee. "Women as Emblems of Dynastic Fall in Qing Literature." In *Dynastic Crisis and Cultural Innovation: From the Late Ming to the Late Qing and Beyond*, edited by David Der-wei Wang and Shang Wei. Cambridge, MA: Harvard University Asia Center, 2005.

Li Wei. "Zailun jingju gaige de Tian Han moshi" (A Second Look at the Tian Han Model of Opera Reform). *Tongji daxue xuebao* (Journal of Tongji University, Social Science Edition), vol. 16, no. 6 (December 2005).

Li Wenbin. "Situ Huimin." In *Zhongguo dianyingjia liezhuan* (Biographies of Chinese Filmmakers), vol. 1. Beijing: Zhongguo dianying chubanshe, 1992.

Li Yi, and Cai Zhen, eds. *Guo Moruo pingshuo jiushinian* (Ninety Years of Studies on Guo Moruo). Beijng: Wenhua yishu chubanshe, 2010.

Li Yongchun. *"Shaonian zhongguo" yu wusi shiqi shehui sichao* ("Young China" and the Social Currents of the May Fourth Era). Changsha: Hunan renmin chubanshe, 2005.

Li Yu. *Changsha de jindaihua qidong* (The Beginning of Modernization in Changsha). Changsha: Hunan jiaoyu chubanshe, 2000.

Li Yuejin. "Hunan xiandai liuri zuojiaqun jiqi tedian" (Japan-Educated Modern Hunanese Writers and Their Characteristics). *Zhongguo wenxue yanjiu* (Studies on Chinese Literature), vol. 4 (2005).

Lieberthal, Kenneth G. *Revolution and Tradition in Tientsin, 1949–1952*. Stanford, CA: Stanford University Press, 1980.

Link, E. Perry. *Mandarin Ducks and Butterflies: Popular Fiction in Early Twentieth-Century Chinese Cities*. Berkeley: University of California Press, 1981.

Link, E. Perry, Richard Madsen, and Paul G. Pickowicz, eds. *The Winking Owl: Art in the People's Republic of China*. Berkeley: University of California Press, 1988.

Liu Fang. "Zai kunhuozhong xunqiu tupo: Tian Han houqi xiqu chuangzuo xinli tanmi" (Searching for a Breakthrough in a State of Confusion: An Investigation into the Psychology of Tian Han's Opera Writing in His Later Years). *Zhongguo xiqu xueyuan xuebao* (Journal of the National Academy of Chinese Theatre Arts), vol. 30, no. 3 (August 2009).

Liu Jianhui (Ryū Kenki). *Mato Shanhai: Nihon chishikijin no kindai taiken* (Demon Capital Shanghai: The Modern Experience for the Japanese Intellectuals). Tokyo: Kōdansha, 2000.

Liu, Jianmei. *Revolution Plus Love: Literary History, Women's Bodies, and the Thematic Repetition in Twentieth-Century Chinese Fiction*. Honolulu: University of Hawai'i Press, 2003.

Liu, Lydia H. *Translingual Practice: Literature, National Culture, and Translated Modernity: China, 1900–1937*. Stanford, CA: Stanford University Press, 1995.

Liu Na. *Chuangzao she yu Taidong tushuju*. Guilin: Guangxi jiaoyu chubanshe, 1999.

Liu Na'ou, Shi Zhecun, and Mu Shiying, eds. *Wugui lieche* (Trackless Train). Shanghai: Diyixian shudian, nos. 1–8 (Septebmer-December, 1928).

Liu Ping. *Xijuhun: Tian Han pingzhua* (Soul of Drama: A Critical Biography of Tian Han). Beijing: Zhongyang wenxian chubanshe, 1998.

Liu Ping. "Kangzhan paohuo zhong de xiju chuangzuo yu yanchu," http://www.china001.com/show_hdr.php?xname=PPDDMV0&dname=HLPO741&xpos=36. Accessed July 15, 2009.

Lovell, Julia. *The Politics of Cultural Capital: China's Quest for a Nobel Prize in Literature*. Honolulu: University of Hawai'i Press, 2006.

Löwy, Michael. "Marx, Weber, and the Critique of Capitalism." Translated from the French by Michael J. Thompson. *Logos: A Journal of Modern Society and Culture*, vol. 1, no. 3 (Summer 2002).

Lu Xun. "Kuangren riji" (Diary of a Madman) (1918). In *Lu Xun zhuyi biannian quanji* (A Complete Chronological Collection of Lu Xun's Writings and Translations), edited by Wang Shijia and Zhi An, vol. 3. Beijing: Renmin chubanshe, 2009.

Lu Xun. "Zixu" (Author's Preface). In *Nahan* (Call to Arms). Beijing: Xinchao she, 1923.

Lu Xun, trans. *Kumen de xiangzheng*. Shanghai: Beixin shuju, 1924. Chinese translation of *Kumon no shōchō* by Kuriyagawa Hakuson.

Lu Xun. "Biyacilai huaxuan xiaoyin" (Preface to Selected Paintings of Beardsley). *Yiyuan zhaohua* (Morning Sun of the Artistic Garden), vol. 1, no. 4 (May 1929).

Lu Xun. "Da Xu Maoyong bing guanyu kangri tongyi zhanxian wenti" (A Response to Xu Maoyong and on the Ani-Japanese United Front). *Zuojia* (Writer), vol. 1, no. 5 (August 1936).

Lu Xun and Zhou Zuoren, trans. *Yuwai xiaoshuo ji* (Stories from the Outside World) (1909), edited by Wu Guoqing, with a new translation by Ba Jin and Ru Long. Changsha: Yuelu shushe, 1981.

Lukács, Georg. *History and Class Consciousness: Studies in Marxist Dialectics.* Cambridge, MA: MIT Press, 1972.

Lukács, György. "Realism in the Balance." *The Norton Anthology of Theory and Criticism.* Edited by Vincent B. Leitch. New York: Norton, 2001.

Luo, Liang. "Reality Supplements Fantasy: Imagining Paris in a Shanghai Salon." Paper presented at the Seventeenth Congress of the International Comparative Literature Association, Hong Kong, August 10, 2004.

Luo, Liang. "The Theatrics of Revolution: Tian Han (1898–1968) and the Cultural Politics of Performance in Modern China." PhD diss., Harvard University, 2006.

Luo, Liang. "Modern Girl, Modern Men, and the Politics of Androgyny in Modern China." *Michigan Quarterly Review,* vol. 47, no. 2 (Spring 2008).

Luo Weihong. "Liu Liangmo and anti-Japanese mass singing activities," *Century* (Shiji), 2005, no. 5, 10–13.

Lutz, Jessie Gregory. *Chinese Politics and Christian Missions: The Anti-Christian Movements of 1920–1928.* Notre Dame, IN: Cross Cultural Publications and Cross Roads Books, 1988.

Ma Ke. *Xian Xianghai zhuan* (A Biography of Xian Xinghai). Beijing: Renmin wenxue chubanshe, 1980.

Mackie, Vera C. *Creating Socialist Women in Japan: Gender, Labour, and Activism, 1900–1937.* Cambridge: Cambridge University Press, 1997.

Mally, Lynn. *Culture of the Future: The Proletkult Movement in Revolutionary Russia.* Berkeley: University of California Press, 1990.

Manela, Erez. *The Wilsonian Moment: Self-Determination and the International Origins of Anticolonial Nationalism.* New York: Oxford University Press, 2007.

Mao Zedong. *Zai Yan'an wenyi zuotanhui shang de jianghua* (Talks at the Yan'an Forum on Literature and Arts). Yan'an: Jiefang she, 1943.

Mao Zedong. "Zhiwen Guomindang" (Questioning the Nationalists). *Jiefang ribao* (Liberation Daily, Yan'an), July 12, 1943.

Mao Zedong. *Mao Zedong xuanji* (Selected Works of Mao Zedong). Beijing: Renmin chubanshe, 1964.

Mao Zedong. Mao Zedong xuanji (Selected Works of Mao Zedong). Beijing: Renmin chubanshe, 1991, vol. 3.

Mao Zedong Zhuan (1886-1949) (A Biography of Mao Zedong, 1886-1949). Beijing: Zhonggong zhongyang wenxian yanjiushi, 1996.

Martin, James Alfred. *Beauty and Holiness: The Dialogue between Aesthetics and Religion.* Princeton, NJ: Princeton University Press, 1990.

Martin, Randy. *Performance as Political Act: The Embodied Self.* Foreword by Stanley Aronowitz. New York: Bergin & Garvey Publishers, 1990.

Maruyama Noboru. *Shanhai monogatari: kokusai toshi Shanhai to Nitchū bunkajin* (Shanghai Stories: International City Shanghai and Japanese/Chinese Intellectuals). Tokyo: Kōdansha, 2004.

Maruyama Noboru, Itō Toramaru, and Shinmura Tōru, eds. *Chūgoku gendai bungaku jiten* (Dictionary of Modern Chinese Literature). Tokyo: Tōkyōdō Shuppan, 1985.

Matsumura Masaie, ed. *Tanizaki Jun'ichirō to seikimatsu* (Tanizaki Jun'ichirō and the Fin-de-Siècle). Kyoto: Shibunkaku Shuppan, 2002.

McClary, Susan. "Structure of Identity and Difference in Bizet's *Carmen*." In *The Work of Opera: Genre, Nationhood, and Sexual Difference,* edited by Richard Dellamora and Daniel Fischlin. New York: Columbia University Press, 1997.

McDougall, Bonnie S. *The Introduction of Western Literary Theories into Modern China, 1919–1925.* Tokyo: Center for East Asian Cultural Studies, 1971.

McDougall, Bonnie S. "The Search for Synthesis: T'ien Han and Mao Tun in 1920." In *Search for Identity: Modern Literature and the Creative Arts in Asia,* edited by A. R. Davis. Sydney: Angus and Robertson, 1974.

McDougall, Bonnie S., trans. *Love-Letters and Privacy in Modern China: The Intimate Lives of Lu Xun and Xu Guangping.* Oxford: Oxford University Press, 2002.

McDougall, Bonnie S., and Mao Zedong. *Mao Zedong's "Talks at the Yan'an Conference on Literature and Art": A Translation of the 1943 Text with Commentary.* Ann Arbor: Center for Chinese Studies, University of Michigan, 1980.

Meisner, Maurice. *Mao Zedong: A Political and Intellectual Portrait.* New York: Polity Press, 2007.

Meltzer, Charles Henry, trans. *The Sunken Bell, a Fairy Play in Five Acts.* Garden City, NY: Doubleday, Page, 1911.

Meltzer, Françoise. *Salome and the Dance of Writing: Portraits of Mimesis in Literature.* Chicago: University of Chicago Press, 1987.

Meng, Yue. *Shanghai and the Edges of Empires.* Minneapolis: University of Minnesota Press, 2006.

Mitchell, John D., ed. *The Red Pear Garden: Three Great Dramas of Revolutionary China,* with an introduction by Richard E. Strassberg. Boston: David R. Godine, 1973.

Mitter, Rana. *The Manchurian Myth: Nationalism, Resistance, and Collaboration in Modern China.* Berkeley: University of California Press, 2000.

Mitter, Rana. "Modernity, Internationalization, and War in the History of Modern China." *Historical Journal,* vol. 48, no. 2 (2005).

Mittler, Barbara. *Dangerous Tunes: The Politics of Chinese Music in Hong Kong, Taiwan, and the People's Republic of China since 1949.* Wiesbaden: Harrassowitz, 1997.

Mittler, Barbara. *A Newspaper for China?: Power, Identity, and Change in Shanghai's News Media, 1872-1912.* Cambridge, MA: Harvard University Asia Center, 2004.

Mittler, Barbara. "Popular Propaganda? Art and Culture in Revolutionary China." *Proceedings of the American Philosophical Society,* vol. 152, no. 4 (December 2008).

Mittler, Barbara. *A Continous Revolution: Making Sense of Cultural Revolution Culture.* Cambridge, MA: Harvard University Asia Center, 2012.

Moses, Claire Goldberg, and Leslie Wahl Rabine. *Feminism, Socialism, and French Romanticism.* Bloomington: Indiana University Press, 1993.

Mullaney, Thomas S. *Coming to Terms with the Nation: Ethnic Classification in Modern China.* Berkeley: University of California Press, 2010.

Muramatsu Shōfū. *Mato.* Tokyo: Konishi Shoten, 1924.

Muramatsu Shōfū. *Sōjin.* Tokyo: Sōjinsha, 1927.

Murphy, Joseph. "Economies of Culture: The Taishō *bundan* Dallies with the Movies." *Japan Forum,* vol. 11, no. 1 (1999).

Najita, Tetsuo. "Some Reflections on Idealism in the Political Thought of Yoshino Sakuzō." In *Japan in Crisis: Essays on Taishō Democracy,* edited by Bernard S. Silberman and Harry D. Harootunian. Princeton, NJ: Princeton University Press, 1974.

Natsume Soseki. *Kokoro.* Tokyo: Iwanami Shoten, 1914.

Nedostup, Rebecca. "Civic Faith and Hybrid Ritual in Nationalist China." In *Converting Cultures: Religion, Ideology, and Transformations of Modernity,* edited by Dennis Washburn and A. Kevin Reinhart. Leiden: Brill, 2007.

Nedostup, Rebecca. *Superstitious Regimes: Religion and the Politics of Chinese Modernity.* Cambridge, MA: Harvard University Asia Center, 2009.

Nie Er (Hei Tianshi). "Zhongguo gewu duanlun" (A Short Discussion of Chinese Song and Dance). *Dianying yishu* (Film Art), no. 3 (1932).

Nie Er. *Nie Er riji* (Diary of Nie Er). Zhengzhou: Daxiang chubanshe, 2004.

Nishihara Daisuke. *Tanizaki Jun'ichirō to orientarizumu: Taishō Nihon no Chūgoku gensō* (Tanizaki Jun'ichirō and Orientalism: Taishō Japan's Fantasy about China). Tokyo: Chūō Kōron Shinsha, 2003.

Noble, Jonathan S., trans. "The Night the Tiger Was Caught (1922–1923)." In *The Columbia Anthology of Modern Chinese Drama*, edited with an introduction by Xiaomei Chen. New York: Columbia University Press, 2010.

Ōmi Komaki, and Satomura Kinzō. "Seiten hakujitsu no kuni e" (To the Country of Blue Sky and White Sun). In *Tian Han zai Riben* (Tian Han in Japan), edited by Kotani Ichirō and Liu Ping. Beijing: Renmin wenxue chubanshe, 1997. Originally published in *Bungei sensen* (Literary Front), June 1926.

Omori, Kyoko. "The *Benshi* Live Narrator as Modernist: Pyschological Films of the Early Twentieth Century in Japan," paper presented at the Modenist Media and the Pacific Rim stream, organized by Michael Coyle and Steven Yao, at the Twelfth Modernist Studies Association Conference, Victoria, British Columbia, November 11–14, 2010.

Ono Kazuko. *Chinese Women in a Century of Revolution, 1850–1950*. Edited by Joshua A. Fogel, translated by Kathryn Bernhardt et al. Stanford, CA: Stanford University Press, 1989.

Ono Shinji. *Goshi undō zai Nihon* (The May Fourth Movement in Japan). Tokyo: Kyūko Shoin, 2003.

Ottaviani, Gioia. "'Difference' and 'Reflexivity': Osanai Kaonu and the Shingeki Movement." *Asian Theater Journal*, vol. 11, no. 2 (Autumn 1994).

Ouyang Yuqian. *Pan Jinlian* (1927). In *Twentieth-Century Chinese Drama: An Anthology*, edited by Edward Gunn. Bloomington: Indiana University Press, 1983.

Ouyang Yuqian. *Dianying banlu chujiaji* (My Amateurish Film Career). Beijng: Zhongguo dianying chubanshe, 1984.

Ouyang Yuqian. *Ziwo yanxi yilai* (Since I Started Acting). Taipei: Longwen chubanshe, 1990.

Owen, Stephen. *Remembrances: The Experience of the Past in Classical Chinese Literature*. Cambridge, MA: Harvard University Press, 1986.

Owen, Stephen. "'I Don't Want to Act as Emperor Any More': Finding the Genuine in *Peach Blossom Fan*." In *Trauma and Trasendence in Early Qing Literature*, edited by Wilt L. Idema, Wai-yee Li, and Ellen Widmer. Cambridge, MA: Harvard University Asia Center, 2006.

Oxford English Dictionary. 3rd ed., December 2006, online version, December 2011. http://www.oed.com.ezproxy.uky.edu, accessed March 8, 2012.

Pang, Laikwan. *Building a New China in Cinema: The Chinese Left-Wing Cinema Movement, 1932–1937.* Lanham, MD: Rowman & Littlefield, 2002.

Pei Xing. "Nie Yinniang." In *Chuanqi* (Legends). Taipei: Shijie shuju, 1959.

Pfeiffer, Bruce Brooks. *Frank Lloyd Wright, 1867–1959: Building for Democracy.* Cologne: Taschen, 2004.

Pfister, Manfred. *The Theory and Analysis of Drama.* Translated from the German by John Halliday. Cambridge: Cambridge University Press, 1988.

Pickowicz, Paul G. *Marxist Literary Thought in China: The Influence of Ch'u Ch'iu-pai.* Berkeley: University of California Press, 1981.

Pickvance, Ronald. *Van Gogh in Arles.* New York: Metropolitan Museum of Art, 1984.

Pilnyak, Boris, and Vera T. Reck. *Chinese Story and Other Tales.* translated from the Russian by Michael Green. Norman: University of Oklahoma Press, 1988.

Pincus, Leslie. *Authenticating Culture in Imperial Japan: Kuki Shūzō and the Rise of National Aesthetics.* Berkeley: University of California Press, 1996.

Platt, Stephen R. *Provincial Patriots: The Hunanese and Modern China.* Cambridge, MA: Harvard University Press, 2007.

Plotkin, Ira L. *Anarchism in Japan: A Study of the Great Treason Affair, 1910–1911.* New York: Edwin Mellen Press, 1990.

Poggioli, Penato. *The Theory of the Avant-Garde.* Translated from the Italian by Gerald Fitzgerald. Cambridge, MA: Belknap Press of Harvard University Press, 1968.

Porter, David. "China Is Not a Foreign Country: The Promises and Perils of Cross-Cultural Comparion." in "China," special issue, *Michigan Quarterly Review,* vol. 47, no. 2 (Spring 2008).

Porter, David. *The Chinese Taste in Eighteenth-Century England.* Cambridge: Cambridge University Press, 2010.

Porter, David, ed. *Between Men and Feminism*. New York: Routledge, 1992.

Porter, Roy, and Mikuláš Teich, eds. *Romanticism in National Context.* Cambridge: Cambridge University Press, 1988.

Pozefsky, Peter C. *The Nihilist Imagination: Dmitrii Pisarev and the Cultural Origins of Russian Radicalism (1860–1868).* Middlebury Studies in Russian Language and Literature. New York: Peter Lang, 2003.

Průšek, Jaroslav. *The Lyrical and the Epic: Studies of Modern Chinese Literature.* Edited by Leo Ou-fan Lee. Bloomington: Indiana University Press, 1980.

Pu Songling. *Quanben xinzhu Liaozhai zhiyi* (A Complete Version of "Strange Tales from a Chinese Studio" with New Annotations). Edited and annotated by Zhu Qikai. Beijing: Renmin wenxue chubanshe, 1989.

Pu Songling. *Liaozhai zhiyi* (Strange Tales from a Chinese Studio). Shanghai: Shanghai guji chubanshe, 2005.

Qian Jiang. *Zhou Enlai yu Rineiwa huiyi* (Zhou Enlai and the Geneva Conference). Beijing: Zhonggong dangshi chubanshe, 2005.

Qian, Suoqiao. *Liberal Cosmopolitan: Lin Yutang and Middling Chinese Modernity.* Leiden: Brill, 2010.

Rachamimov, Alon. "The Disruptive Comforts of Drag: (Trans)Gender Performances among Prisoners of War in Russia, 1914–1920." *American Historical Review,* vol. 3, no. 2 (April 2006).

Ren Dong. "Xia Yan dui sanshi niandai zhongguo zuoyi dianying yundong de gongxian" (On Xia Yan's Contribution to Chinese Leftist Cinema of the 1930s). *Dianying wenxue* (Film Literature), no. 3 (2008).

Reynolds, Douglas. *China, 1898–1912: The Xinzheng Revolution and Japan.* Cambridge, MA: Council on East Asian Studies, Harvard University, 1993.

Richardson, Alan. *Literature, Education, and Romanticism: Reading as Social Practice.* Cambridge, MA: Cambridge University Press, 1994.

Richardson, LeeAnne M. *New Woman and Colonial Adventure Fiction in Victorian Britain: Gender, Genre, and Empire.* Gainesville: University Press of Florida, 2006.

Richie, Donald. *The Japanese Movie: An Illustrated History.* Tokyo: Kōdansha, 1966.

Richie, Donald. *Tokyo: A View of the City.* London: Reaktion Books, 1999.

Rigney, Ann. *Imperfect Histories: The Exclusive Past and the Legacy of Romantic Historicism.* Ithaca, NY: Cornell University Press, 2001.

Rimer, J. Thomas, ed. *Culture and Identity: Japanese Intellectuals during the Interwar Years.* Princeton, NJ: Princeton University Press, 1990. Sponsored by the Joint Committee on Japanese Studies of the American Council of Learned Societies and the Social Science Research Council.

"The Rise of State Capitalism: The Spread of a New Sort of Business in the Emerging World will Cause Increasing Problems." *Economist,* January 21, 2012.

Robeson, Paul. *Chee Lai.* Keynote, 1941, three 10-inch records.

Robeson, Paul, with Lloyd L. Brown. *Here I Stand.* Introduction by Sterling Stuckey. Boston: Beacon Press, 1988.

Robinson, David. "Return of the Phantom." *Film Quarterly,* vol. 53, no. 2 (Winter 1999–2000).

Ross, Steven J. *Working-Class Hollywood: Silent Film and the Shaping of Class in America.* Princeton, NJ: Princeton University Press, 1999.

Roth, Philip. *Portnoy's Complaint* (1969). In *Philip Roth, Novels, 1967–1972.* New York: Library of America, 2005.

Rudé, George. *Ideology and Popular Protest.* Foreword and updated bibliography by Harvey J. Kaye. Chapel Hill: University of North Carolina Press, 1995.

Russel, Charles. *Poets, Prophets, and Revolutionaries: The Literary Avant-Garde from Rimbaud to Postmodernism.* New York: Oxford University Press, 1985.

Russell, Archibald G. B. *The Engravings of William Blake.* London: G. Richards, 1912.

Ruttmann, Walter, dir. *Berlin: Die Sinfonie der Großstadt* (Berlin: Symphony of a Great City) (1927). Image Entertainment, 1999, DVD.

Said, Edward. *Orientalism.* New York: Pantheon, 1978.

Saji Toshihiko. "Chūgoku wageki undōshi tenbyō: wageki sōsōki no tenkai to akusenkutō" (A Sketch History of Modern Chinese Drama: Modern Chinese Drama in Its Initial Stage—the Development and the Desperate Fight). *Tōyō Bunka* (Oriental Culture) (Tokyo), no. 65 (April 1984).

Sakai, Naoki. *Translation and Subjectivity: On "Japan" and Cultural Nationalism.* Minneapolis: University of Minnesota Press, 1997.

Sakaki, Atsuko. *Recontextualizing Texts: Narrative Performance in Modern Japanese Fiction.* Cambridge, MA: Council on East Asian Studies, Harvard University, 1999.

Sakaki, Atsuko. "Japanese Perceptions of China: The Sinophilic Fiction of Tanizaki Jun'ichirō." *Harvard Journal of Asiatic Studies,* vol. 59, no. 1 (June 1999).

Sakaki, Atsuko. *Obsessions with the Sino-Japanese Polarity in Japanese Literature.* Honolulu: University of Hawai'i Press, 2005.

Sang, Tze-lan D. *The Emerging Lesbian: Female Same-Sex Desire in Modern China.* Chicago: University of Chicago Press, 2003.

Sangu, Makoto, ed. *Selected Poems of William Blake.* Tokyo: Kenkyusha, 1925. Kenkyusha English Classics.

Satō, B. H. "The Moga Sensation: Perceptions of the Modan Gāru in Japanese Intellectual Circles during the 1920s." *Gender and History,* vol. 5, no. 3 (1993).

Satō, B. H. "An Alternate Informant: Middle-Class Women and Mass Magazines in 1920s Japan." In *Being Modern in Japan: Culture and Society from the 1910s to the 1930s,* edited by Elise K. Tipton and John Clark. Honolulu: University of Hawai'i Press, 2000.

Satō Haruo. *Tianyuan zhi youyu* (*Den'en no yūutsu,* or "Rural Melancholy"). Translated by Li Shuquan (Tian Han). Shanghai: Zhonghua shuju, 1934.

Satō, Toshihiko. "Ibsen's *The Lady from the Sea,* Ti'en Han's *Return to the South,* and Satō Koroku's *The Disabled Horse:* A Comparative Study." In *Studies in Chinese-Western Comparative Drama,* edited by Yun-Tong Luk. Hong Kong: Chinese University Press, 1990.

Saussy, Haun. "Mei Lanfang in Moscow, 1935: Familiar, Unfamiliar, Defamiliar." *Modern Chinese Literature and Culture,* vol. 18, no. 1 (Spring 2006).

Schechner, Richard. *Performance Studies: An Introduction.* London: Routledge, 2002.

Schmid, Andre. *Korea between Empires, 1895–1919.* New York: Columbia University Press, 2002.

Schoenhals, Michael. *Doing Things with Words in Chinese Politics: Five Studies.* Berkeley: Institute of East Asian Studies, University of California, 1992.

Schoots, Hans. *Living Dangerously: A Biography of Joris Ivens.* Amsterdam: Amsterdam University Press, 2000.

Schorske, Carl. *Fin-de-Siècle Vienna: Politics and Culture.* New York: Vintage, 1981.

Schwarcz, Vera. *The Chinese Enlightenment: Intellectuals and the Legacy of the May Fourth Movement of 1919.* Berkeley: University of California Press, 1986.

Schwartz, Benjamin. *In Search of Wealth and Power: Yen Fu and the West.* Cambridge, MA: Harvard University Press, 1964.

Scott, Paul. "Uchiyama Kanzō: A Case Study in Sino-Japanese Interaction." *Sino-Japanese Studies,* vol. 2, no. 2 (May 1990).

Seidensticker, Edward. *Low City, High City: Tokyo from Edo to the Earthquake—How the Shogun's Ancient Capital Became a Great Modern City, 1867–1923.* New York: Alfred A. Knopf, 1983.

Shanghai geming wenhua dashiji, 1919.5-1937.7 (A Chronological Record of Revolutionary Cultural Events in Shanghai, May 1919–July 1937). Shanghai: Shanghai shudian, 1995.

Shen Congwen. "Xiaoxiao." In *Shen Congwen daibiaozuo* (Representative Works of Shen Congwen), edited by the Museum of Modern Chinese Literature, vol. 1. Beijing: Huaxia chubanshe, 2008.

Shen Hongxin, and He Guodong. *Zhou Xinfang zhuan* (A Biography of Zhou Xinfang). Shijiazhuang: Hebei jiaoyu chubanshe, 1996.

Shen, Shuang. *Cosmopolitan Publics: Anglophone Print Culture in Semi-colonial Shanghai.* New Brunswick, NJ: Rutgers University Press, 2009.

Shen, Vivien. *The Origins of Left-Wing Cinema in China, 1932–1937.* New York: Routledge, 2005.

Shi Nai'an, and Luo Guanzhong. *Shuihu zhuan* (The Water Margin). Beijing: Renmin wenxue chubanshe, 1975.

Shih, Shu-mei. *The Lure of the Modern: Writing Modernism in Semicolonial China, 1917–1937.* Berkeley: University of California Press, 2001.

Shih, Shu-mei. *Visuality and Identity: Sinophone Articulations across the Pacific.* Berkeley: University of California Press, 2007.

Shih, Shu-mei. "The Concept of the Sinophone." *PMLA,* vol. 126, no. 3 (May 2011).

Shimamura Hōgetsu. *Torawaretaru bungei* (Imprisoned Literature and Arts). Tokyo: Hokkō Shobō, 1948.

Shizuko, Koyama. "The 'Good Wife and Wise Mother' Ideology in Post–World War I Japan." *US-Japan Women's Journal,* no. 7 (1994).

Shoes. Dr. Lois Weber, performed by Mary MacLaren and Harry Griffith. United States, 1916, 60 min., 35 mm, silent.

Silverberg, Miriam. "Modern Girl as Militant." In *Recreating Japanese Women, 1600–1945,* edited by G. L. Bernstein. Berkeley: University of California Press, 1991.

Silverberg, Miriam. "Constructing a New Cultural History of Prewar Japan." In

Japan in the World, edited by M. Miyoshi and H. D. Harootunian. Durham, NC: Duke University Press, 1993.

Silverberg, Miriam. "The Café Waitress Serving Modern Japan." In *Mirror of Modernity: Invented Traditions of Modern Japan,* edited by Stephen Vlastos. Berkeley: University of California Press, 1998.

Situ Lian, and Guan Hui, eds. *Situ Huimin zhuanlue* (A Brief Biography of Situ Huimin). In *Guangdong wenshi ziliao,* vol. 60. (Guangdong Literary and Historical Materials). Guangzhou: Guangdong renmin chubanshe, 1989.

Smith, Arthur H. *Village Life in China: A Study in Sociology.* New York: Fleming H. Revell, 1899.

Smith, Henry DeWitt, II. *Japan's First Student Radicals.* Cambridge, MA: Harvard University Press, 1972.

Smith, Henry DeWitt, II. "Tokyo as an Idea: An Exploration of Japanese Urban Thought up to 1945." *Journal of Japanese Studies,* vol. 4, no. 1 (1978).

Smith, Karen. *Nine Lives: The Birth of Avant-Garde Art in New China.* Hong Kong: Timezone8, 2008.

Smith, Norman. *Resisting Manchukuo: Chinese Women Writers and the Japanese Occupation.* Vancouver: University of British Columbia Press, 2007.

Song Jiayang, and Jin Mingquan. "Zhou Enlai yu Zhou Fohai tongqi shixue Heshang zhao de chayi" (The Difference between Zhou Enlai and Zhou Fohai, Students of Kawakami Hajime at the Same Time). *Chongqing daxue xuebao* (Journal of Chongqing University), no. 2 (2006).

Stephens, John Richard. *Vampires, Wine, and Roses.* New York: Berkeley Books, 1997.

Stites, Richard. *Revolutionary Dreams: Utopian Vision and Experimental Life in the Russian Revolution.* New York: Oxford University Press, 1989.

Stites, Richard. *Russian Popular Culture: Entertainment and Society since 1900.* Cambridge: Cambridge University Press, 1992.

Strindberg, August. *Plays by August Strindberg.* Translated with an introduction by Edwin Bjorkman. London: Duckworth, 1913.

Strindberg, August. *Ett drömspel* (A Dream Play) (1901). Stockholm: Albert Bonniers Förlag, 1917.

Stuckey, G. Andrew. *Old Stories Retold: Narrative and Vanishing Pasts in Modern China.* Lanham, MD: Lexington Books, 2010.

Stufkens, André. "The Song of Movement: Joris Ivens's First Films and the Cycle of the Avant-Garde." In *Joris Ivens and the Documentary Context,* edited by Kees Bakker. Amsterdam: Amsterdam University Press, 1999.

Stufkens, André. "Lust for Life: An Introduction to Ivens and the 20th Century." In *Cinema without Borders.* Nijmegen: European Foundation Joris Ivens, 2002.

Su Guangwen. "Wenxue yu lishi: Zhongguo xiandai wenxue shiye li de '1.29 yundong'" (Literature and History: The December Ninth Movement from the Perspective of Modern Chinese Literature). *Guizhou shehui kexue* (Guizhou Social Sciences Magazine), no. 6 (2005).

Sullivan, Michael. *Art and Artists of Twentieth-Century China.* Berkeley: University of California Press, 1996.

Sun Ji'nan. *Zhongguo yinyue tongshi jianbian* (A Brief History of Chinese Music). Ji'nan: Shandong jiaoyu chubanshe, 1991.

Sun Kezhi. *Sanghae Hanin sahoesa, 1910–1945* (A Study of the Korean Community in Shanghai, 1910–1945). Seoul: Hanul Ak'ademi, 2001.

Sun Kezhi. *Shanghai Hanren shehuishi yanjiu* (A Study of the Social History of the Korean Community in Shanghai). Beijing: Xueyuan chubanshe, 2004.

Sun Shen, Li Yinghai, and Xiang Yansheng, eds. *Tian Han cizuo gequ ji* (Collection of Songs with Lyrics by Tian Han). Beijing: Renmin yinyue chubanshe, 2003.

Sun Yu, dir. *Ye meigui* (Wild Rose), starring Jin Yan and Wang Renmei. Shanghai, 1932, Lianhua yingye gongsi.

Symons, Arthur. *William Blake.* London: A. Constable, 1907.

Takayoshi Matsuo. "Kosumo kurabu shōshi" (A Brief History of the Cosmo Club). *Kyōto Nōtorudamu Joshi Daigaku kenkyū kiyō* (Bulletin of the Notre Dame Women's College of Kyoto), no. 26 (March, 2000).

Talmon, Joel. *Political Messianism: The Romantic Phase.* New York: Praeger, 1961.

Tam, Y. H. "An Intellectual's Response to Western Intrusion: Naito Konan's View of Republican China." In *The Chinese and the Japanese: Essays in Political and Cultural Interactions,* edited by Akira Iriye et al. Princeton, NJ: Princeton University Press, 1980.

Tamanoi, M. "The City and the Countryside: Competing Taishō Modernities on Gender." In *Japan's Competing Modernities: Issues in Culture and Democracy, 1900–1930,* edited by Sharon A. Minichiello. Honolulu: University of Hawai'i Press, 1998.

Tambling, Jeremy. "Ideology in the Cinema: Rewriting *Carmen.*" In *Opera, Ideology, and Film.* Manchester: Manchester University Press, 1987.

Tanaka Eizō. *Meiji Taishō shingekishi shiryō* (Materials for the History of New Drama in the Meiji and Taishō Eras). Tokyo: Engeki Shuppansha, 1964.

Tanaka, Stefan. *Japan's Orient: Rendering Pasts into History.* Berkeley: University of California Press, 1993.

Tang Shaohua. *Wentan wangshi jianzheng* (Eyewitness Accounts of Old Tales in Literary Circles). Taipei: Zhuanji wenxue chubanshe, 1996.

Tang, Xiaobing. *Global Space and the Nationalist Discourse of Modernity: The Historical Thinking of Liang Qichao.* Stanford, CA: Stanford University Press, 1996.

Tang, Xiaobing. "Echoes of Roar China! On Vision and Voice in Modern Chinese Art." *positions: east asia cultures critique,* vol. 14, no. 2 (2006).

Tang, Xiaobing. *The Origins of the Chinese Avant-Garde: The Modern Woodcut Movement.* Berkeley: University of California Press, 2007.

Tang Xiaobing. "Women zenyang xiangxiang lishi (dai daoyan)," *Zai jiedu: Dazhong wenyi yu yishi xingtai*, rev. ed. Beijing: Beijing daxue chubanshe, 2007.

Tang, Xiaobing, with Michel Hockx. "The Creation Society (1921–1930)." In *Literary Societies of Republican China,* edited by Kirk A. Denton and Michel Hockx. Lanham, MD: Lexington Books, 2008.

Tang Yonghua. *Zong Baihua yu "Zhongguo meixue" de kunjing: Yige fansixing de kaocha* (Zong Baihua and the Dilemma of "Chinese Aesthetics": A Reflective Study). Beijing: Beijing University Press, 2010.

Tanizaki Jun'ichirō. "Eiga no tekuniku" (Film Technique). *Bungei shunjū* (Annals of Literature and Art), October 1921.

Tanizaki Jun'ichirō. "Jasei no in" (The Lust of the Serpent). *Shufu no tomo* (Housewives' Companion), April 1922.

Tanizaki Jun'ichirō. *Shen yu ren zhijian* (*Kami to hito no aida,* or "Between God and Man"), translated by Li Shuquan (Tian Han). Shanghai: Zhonghua shuju, 1934.

Tanizaki Jun'ichirō. "Shanhai kenbunroku" (Records of Shanghai Travel). *Bungei shunjū* (Annals of Literature and Art), May 1926.

Tanizaki Jun'ichirō. "Shanhai kōyūki" (Shanghai Friends). Translated by Paul D. Scott. *Chinese Studies in History,* vol. 30, no. 4 (Summer 1997). Originally published in *Josei* (Women), May, June, August 1926.

Tanizaki Jun'ichirō, trans. *Uindamīya-fujin no ōgi.* Tokyo: Ten'yūsha, 1919. Japanese translation of *Lady Windermere's Fan* by Oscar Wilde.

Tao Dongfeng. "Liuxing wenhua huhuan xin de yanjiu fanshi" (Popular Culture Calls for New Research Paradigm). *Wenyi Yanjiu* (Literature and Art Studies), no. 5 (2001).

Tao Dongfeng. "Yanjiu dazhong wenhua yu xiaofei zhuyi de sanzhong fanshi jiqi xifang ziyuan" (Three Ways to Research Mass Culture and Commercial Culture and Their Western Sources). *Hebei Xuekan* (Hebei Academic Journal), vol. 24, no. 5 (Spring 2004).

Taubman, Howard. "Songs That Chinese People Are Singing These Days: Other Releases." *New York Times,* November 30, 1941.

Taubman, Howard. "'Firing Line' Songs Thrill Audience: Folk Ditties, Workers' Chants, War Songs Given under Negro Group's Auspices." *New York Times,* June 27, 1942.

Tertz, Abram. *On Socialist Realism.* Introduction by Czeslaw Milosz. New York: Pantheon, 1960.

Thomas, Calvin, ed. *Goethe's Faust.* Vol. 1: *The First Part.* Boston: D. C. Heath, 1892.

Thomas, Julia Adeney. "Naturalizing Nationhood: Ideology and Practice in Early Twentieth Century Japan." In *Japan's Competing Modernities: Issues in Culture and Democracy, 1900–1930*, edited by Sharon A. Minichiello. Honolunu: University of Hawai'i Press, 1998.

Thornbor, Karen Laura. *Empire of Texts in Motion: Chinese, Korean, and Taiwanese Transculturations of Japanese Literature.* Cambridge MA: Harvard University Asia Center, 2009.

Tian Benxiang, et al. *Tian Han pingzhuan* (An Analytical Biography of Tian Han). Chongqing: Chongqing chubanshe, 1998.

Tian Han. Tian Han quanji (The Complete Works of Tian Han). 20 vols. Shijiazhuang: Huashan wenyi chubanshe, 2000.

Tian Han, Guo Moruo, and Zong Baihua. *Sanye ji.* Shanghai: Taidong tushuju, 1920.

Tian Han et al. *Qianxian kangdi jiangling fangwenji* (Interviews with Officers Fighting the Japanese at the War Front). Shanghai: Qianjin chubanshe, 1937.

Tian Han (T'ien-Han) and Nieh Erh (Nie Er). "March of the Volunteers." *Music Educators Journal*, vol. 29, no. 2 (November–December 1942).

"Tian Han de 'Xie Yaohuan' shi yike da ducao" (Tian Han's "Xie Yaohuan" Is a Big Poisonous Weed). *Renmin ribao* (People's Daily), February 1, 1966.

Tian Han zhuanji (Studies on Tian Han). Shanghai: Shanghai xiju xueyuan xiju wenxuexi, 1980.

Tian Qinxin. *Tian Qinxin de xiju ben* (Tian Qinxin's Drama Script). Beijing: Beijing daxue chubanshe, 2010.

Tian, Xiaofei. "The Cultural Construction of the 'North' and 'South' in Medieval China." Talk given on May 8, 2006, Harvard University.

Tomlinson, John. *Cultural Imperialism: A Critical Introduction.* Baltimore: Johns Hopkins University Press, 1991.

Trotsky, Leon. "What Is Proletarian Culture, and Is It Possible?" (1923). In *Literature and Revolution.* Ann Arbor: University of Michigan Press, 1960. Ann Arbor Paperbacks for the Study of Communism and Marxism.

Tsurumi, E. Patricia. "Visions of Women and the New Society in Conflict: Yamakawa Kikue versus Takamure Itsue." In *Japan's Competing Modernities: Issues of Culture and Democracy, 1900–1930*, edited by Sharon A. Minichiello. Honolulu: University of Hawai'i Press, 1998.

Tung, Constantine. "T'ien Han and the Romantic Ibsen." *Modern Drama*, vol. 9, no. 4 (February 1967).

Tung, Constantine. "Lonely Search into the Unknown: T'ien Han's Early Plays, 1920–1930." *Comparative Drama*, vol. 2, no. 1 (Spring 1968).

Ueda Akirari. *Ugetsu Monogatari* (Tales of Moonlight and Rain) (1776). Translated into modern Japanese and annotated by Uzuki Hiroshi. Tokyo: Kadokawa Shoten, 1959.

Usandizaga, Aránzazu, and Andrew Monnickendam, eds. *Dressing Up for War: Transformations of Gender and Genre in the Discourse and Literature of War.* Amsterdam: Rodopi, 2001.

Ushihara Kiyohiko. *Kiyohiko eigafu 50-nen* (Fifty Years of Ushihara Kiyohiko's Film). Tokyo: Kagamiura Shobō, 1968.

Vlastos, Stephen, ed. *Mirror of Modernity: Invented Traditions of Modern Japan.* Berkeley: University of California Press, 1998.

Volland, Nicolai. "The Control of the Media in the People's Republic of China." PhD diss., University of Heidelberg, 2003.

Wagner, Rudolf G. "A Guide for the Perplexed and a Call to the Wavering: Tian Han's *Guan Hanqing* (1958) and the New Historical Drama." In *The Contemporary Chinese Historical Drama: Four Studies.* Berkeley: University of California Press, 1990.

Wagner, Rudolf G. "Tian Han's Peking Opera *Xie Yaohuan* (1961)." In *The Contemporary Chinese Historical Drama: Four Studies.* Berkeley: University of California Press, 1990.

Wagner, Rudolf G. "'In Guise of a Congratulation': Political Symbolism in Zhou Xinfang's Play *Hai Rui Submits His Memorial.*" in *Australian Journal of Chinese Affairs,* no. 26 (July 1991).

Wakeman, Frederic, Jr., and Wen-hsin Yeh, eds. *Shanghai Sojourners.* Berkeley: Institute of East Asian Studies, University of California, 1992.

Wan Laiming dir. *Da'nao tiangong* (Havoc in Heaven). Shanghai: Shanghai meishu dianying zhipianchang, 1961–64.

Wang, Ban. *The Sublime Figure of History: Aesthetics and Politics in Twentieth-Century China.* Stanford, CA: Stanford University Press, 1997.

Wang, Ban. *Illuminations from the Past: Trauma, Memory, and History in Modern China.* Stanford, CA: Stanford University Press, 2004.

Wang, Ban. "Discovering Enlightenment in Chinese History: *The Rise of Modern Chinese Thought,* by Wang Hui." *boundary 2,* vol. 34, no. 2 (2007).

Wang Benchao. *Ershi shiji zhongguo wenxue yu jidujiao wenhua* (Twentieth-Century Chinese Literature and Christian Culture). Hefei: Anhui jiaoyu chubanshe, 2000.

Wang, Chang-ling. "A Brief Comment on the Tien Han Case." *Issues and Studies,* vol. 2, no. 11 (August 1966).

Wang, David Der-wei. *Ficitional Realism in Twentieth Century China: Mao Dun, Lao She, Shen Congwen.* New York: Columbia University Press, 1992.

Wang, David Der-wei. *Fin-de-Siècle Splendor: Repressed Modernities of Late Qing Fiction, 1849–1911.* Stanford, CA: Stanford University Press, 1997.

Wang, David Der-wei. *The Monster That Is History: History, Violence, and Fictional Writing in Twentieth-Century China.* Berkeley: University of California Press, 2004.

Wang, David Der-wei. "Shishi shidai de shuqing shengyin: Jiang Wenye de yinyue yu shige" (The Lyrical in Epic Time: Jiang Wenye's Music and Poetry). *Hangzhou shifan daxue xuebao* (Journal of Hangzhou Normal University, Humanities and Social Sicences), vol. 33, no. 1 (Janurary 2011).

Wang, David Der-wei, and Shang Wei, eds. *Dynastic Crisis and Cultural Innovation: From the Late Ming to the Late Qing and Beyond.* Cambridge, MA: Harvard University Asia Center, 2005.

Wang, Eugene Y. "Tope and Topos: The Leifeng Pagoda and the Discourse of the Demonic." In *Writing and Materiality in China: Essays in Honor of Patrick Hanan,* edited by Judith T. Zeitlin and Lydia H. Liu, with Ellen Widmer. Cambridge, MA: Harvard University Asia Center, 2003.

Wang Fengye, et al., eds. *Hunan sheng Changsha Shifan Xuexiao xiaozhi, 1912–1992* (Historical Records of Changsha Normal School of Hunan Province, 1912–1992). Changsha: Hunan jiaoyu chubanshe, 1993.

Wang Hui. *Xiandai zhongguo sixiang de xingqi* (The Rise of Modern Chinese Thought), 2nd ed., 4 vols. Beijing: Sanlian shudian, 2008.

Wang Hui. *The Politics of Imagining Asia.* Edited by Theodore Huters. Cambridge, MA: Harvard University Press, 2011.

Wang Mingjian. "Yu Shan: Minguo caizi milian de jiaren" (Yu Shan: A Beauty Who Enchanted Republican Literati). *Wenshi bolan* (Literary and Historical Records), no. 5 (2009).

Wang Renmei, with Xie Bo. *Wo de chengming yu buxing: Wang Renmei huiyilu* (My Fortune and Misfortune: Memoirs of Wang Renmei). Shanghai: Shanghai wenyi chubanshe, 1985.

Wang Shifu. *Xixiang ji* (The Western Chamber). Shanghai: Shanghai guji chubanshe, 1978.

Wang Xufeng. "Zhongguo yousheng dianying chuqi de guochan dianying luyinji: Jinian Situ Huimin xiansheng danchen 100 zhounian" (The Domestically Made Recording Machine in the Early Years of Chinese Sound Film: Commemorating Mr. Situ Huimin's Centennial). *Xiandai dianying jishu* (Advanced Motion Picture Technology), no. 6 (2010).

Wang Zheng. *Women in the Chinese Enlightenment: Oral and Textual Histories.* Berkeley: University of California Press, 1999.

Wang Zheng. "'State Feminism'? Gender and Socialist State Formation in Maoist China." *Feminist Studies*, vol. 31, no. 3 (Fall 2005).

Wang Zhiyong, ed. *Dong Wang hekanben Xixiang ji yanjiu lunwenji* (Research on the Joint Dong Wang Version of *The Western Chamber*). Gaoxiong: Fuwen tushu chubanshe, 1991.

Weber, Betty Nancy. *Bertolt Brecht: Political Theory and Literary Practice.* Athens: University of Georgia Press, 2010.

Wei Minglun. *Pan Jinlian: Juben yu juping* (*Pan Jinlian:* The Play and Its Reviews). Beijing: Sanlian shudian, 1988.

Weiskel, Thomas. *The Romantic Sublime: Studies in the Structure and Psychology of Transendence.* Baltimore: Johns Hopkins University Press, 1986.

Weiss, Andrea. *Vampires and Violets: Lesbians in the Cinema.* London: Jonathan Cape, 1992.

Wen Kang. *Huitu ernü yingxiong zhuan* (Illustrated Edition of the Legend of Lovers and Heroes). Shanghai: Guangyi shuju, 1949.

Weston, Timothy B. *The Power of Position: Beijing University, Intellectuals, and Chinese Political Culture, 1898–1929.* Berkeley: University of California Press, 2004.

Wessing, Robert. *The Soul of Ambiguity: The Tiger in Southeast Asia.* Special Reports, no. 24. De Kalb: Center for Southeast Asian Studies, Northern Illinois University, 1986.

Wichmann-Walczak, Elizabeth, dir. *The White Snake.* Performed at the Kennedy Theatre, University of Hawai'i at Manoa, February 5–14, 2010. Peking Opera based on Tian Han's script.

Widmer, Ellen, and David Der-wei Wang . *From May Fourth to June Fourth: Fiction and Film in Twentieth-Century China.* Cambridge, MA: Harvard University Press, 1993.

Wilde, Oscar. *Salome: A Tragedy in One Act.* Translated from the French, illustrated by Aubrey Beardsley. London: Elkin Mathews & John Lane, 1894.

Wilde, Oscar. *The Picture of Dorian Gray.* Modern Library ed. New York: Random House, 1998.

Williams, Raymond. *Culture and Society.* London: Allen and Unwin, 1958.

Williams, Raymond. *The Country and the City.* New York, NY: Oxford University Press, 1973.

Williams, S. Wells, et al., eds. *A Syllabic Dictionary of the Chinese Language.* Tung chou [Tongzhou]: North China Union College, 1909.

Winkler, Elizabeth Hale. *The Function of Song in Contemporary British Drama.* Newark: University of Delaware Press, 1990.

Wolfe, Willard. *From Radicalism to Socialism: Men and Ideas in the Formation of Fabian Socialist Doctrines, 1881–1889.* New Haven, CT: Yale University Press, 1975.

Wong, Wang-chi. *Politics and Literature in Shanghai: The Chinese League of Left-Wing Writers, 1930–1936.* Manchester; New York: Manchester University Press, 1991.

"World-Famous photographer Ivens Returns from Tai'erzhuang to Wuhan. Wuhan Cultural Groups Welcome Him. The Anti-Japanese Documentary Will Be Spread to the World." *Wenhui bao* (Wenhui Daily, Shanghai), April 30, 1938.

Wu Sihong. "Diary of a Bohemian Girl." *Nanguo yuekan,* no. 2 (June 1929).

Wu Xiaolong. *Shaonian zhongguo xuehui yanjiu* (Research on the Young China Association). Shanghai: Sanlian shudian, 2006.

Wu Yigong, et al., eds. *Shanghai dianying zhi* (Records of Shanghai Cinema). Shanghai: Shehui kexue chubanshe, 1999.

Wu Yonggang, dir. *Shennü* (The Goddess), starring Ruan Lingyu. Shanghai, 1934, Lianhua yingye gongsi.

Wu Ziniu, dir. *Guoge* (National Anthem). Changsha, 1998, Xiaoxiang dianying zhipianchang.

Xia Jinlin, et al., trans. *The Civil Code of the Republic of China*. Shanghai: Kelly & Walsh, 1930.

Xia Yan. *Lanxun jiumeng lu* (Records of My Idle Search for Old Dreams). Beijing: Sanlian shudian, 1985.

Xia Yan. "Letter to Zhou Weishi." *Xin wenhua shiliao* (Sources on the New Culture Movement), no. 6 (1994).

Xia Yan, and Tian Han, trans. *Dibing zhenzhong riji* (Diaries of Enemy Soldiers on the Battlefield). Guangzhou: Lisao chubanshe, 1938.

Xian Xinghai. "Nie Er, zhongguo xinxing yinyue de chuangzao zhe" (Nie Er, the Creator of New Chinese Music) (1938). In *Xian Xinghai quanji* (Complete Works of Xian Xinghai), vol. 1. Guangzhou: Guangdong gaodeng jiaoyu chubanshe, 1989.

Xiao Hong. *The Field of Life and Death and Tales of Hulan River.* Bloomington: Indiana University Press, 1979.

Xiao Hong. *Xiao Hong quanji* (Complete Works of Xiao Hong). Harbin: Heilongjiang daxue chubanshe, 2011.

Xiao Xinqiao. *Xihu gudai baihua xiaoshuoxuan* (Selections of Traditional Vernacular Stories on the West Lake). Hangzhou: Zhejiang renmin chubanshe, 1982.

Xiao, Zhiwei. "The Political Ambiguities of Leftist Cinema in 1930s China." Paper presented at the Western Conference of the Association for Asian Studies, Denver, Colorado, September 29–October 1, 2005.

Xiaoxiao sheng and Mei Jie. *Jin ping mei cihua: Mengmeiguan jiaoben* (The Mengmeiguan Annotated Version of *Plume in a Golden Vase*). Taipei: Liren shuju, 2007.

Xie Jin, dir. *Hongse niangzi jun* (The Red Detachment of Women). Shanghai, 1960, Shanghai dianying zhipianchang.

Xiong Yuezhi, ed. *Shanghai tongshi* (A General History of Shanghai). Shanghai: Shanghai renmin chubanshe, 1995.

Xiong Yuezhi, Ma Xueqiang, and Yan Kejia, eds. *Shanghai de waiguoren, 1842–1949* (Foreigners in Shanghai, 1842–1949). Shanghai: Shanghai guji chubanshe, 2003.

Xu, Lanjun. "Affective Politics, Cold War, and Chinese Opera Film in the 1950s and 1960s Asia." Paper presented at the Cold War Cultures conference, University of Texas at Austin, Austin, September 30–October 3, 2010.

Xu Xiacun. "Modern Girl." *Xin wenyi* (New Literature and Art), vol. 3 (December 1929).

Xu Xingzhi, dir. *Fengyun ernü* (Lovers in Troubled Times), story by Tian Han, screenplay by Xia Yan, and starring Yuan Muzhi and Wang Renmei. Shanghai, 1935, Diantong yingye gongsi.

Yamaguchi Shin'ichi. "Wakaki no Den Kan no koto" (Things Regarding the Young Tian Han) (1959). In *Tian Han zai Riben* (Tian Han in Japan), edited by Kotani Ichirō and Liu Ping. Beijing: Renmin wenxue chubanshe, 1997.

Yamamoto Kikuo. *Nihon eiga ni okeru gaikoku eiga no eikyō: hikaku eigashi kenkyū* (Foreign Influences on Japanese Film: A Comparative Study of Film History). Tokyo: Waseda Daigaku Shuppanbu, 1983.

Yamamoto, Tatsuro, and Yamamoto Sumiko. "The Anti-Christian Movement in China, 1922–1927." *Far Eastern Quarterly*, vol. 12, no. 2 (February 1953).

Yan Pu, and Su Xue'an, et al. *Baishe zhuan* (The White Snake). Shanghai: Wenhua shenghuo chubanshe, 1955.

Yan Zhewu. *Nanguo de xiju* (Theater of the Southland). Shanghai: Mengya shudian, 1929.

Yanagita Kunio. *Tōno monogatari* (The Legends of Tōno). Tokyo: Yanagita Kunio, Meiji 43 (1910).

Yang Gang, Zhang Geng, and A Ying. "Guanyu *Baishe zhuan* de taolun" (Discussion of *The White Snake*). *Wenyi bao*, no. 23 (1952).

Yang Hansheng. "Huiyi wenhua gongzuo wenyuanhui" (Remembering the Cultural Work Committee). In *Chongqing kangzhan jishi* (Records of the Anti-Japanese War in Chongqing). Chongqing: Chongqing chubanshe, 1985.

Yang Li and the Museum of Modern Chinese Literature. *A Biographical Dictionary of Modern Chinese Writers*. Beijing: New World Press, 1994.

Ye Sishi, and Yang Yan. "Xin shiqi zhuliu wenhua qujie dazhong wenyi de lujing: Cong 'chaoji nüsheng,' 'hongge hui,' dao 'chang hong ge' huodong" (Mainstream Culture Takes the Route of Popular Culture in the New Era: From "Super Girls" and "Red Song Contest" to "Singing Red Songs"). *Xinwen zhishi* (Journalistic Knowledge), no. 7, (2011).

Yeh, Wen-hsin. *Provincial Passages: Culture, Space, and the Origins of Chinese Communism*. Berkeley: University of California Press, 1996.

Yin Qi. *Pan Hannian de qingbao shengya* (Pan Hannian's Spy Career). Beijing: Renmin chubanshe, 1996.

Ying Yunwei, dir. *Yi Jiangnan* (Memories of the South), screenplay by Tian Han, starring Zhou Xuan. Shanghai: Guotai yingye gongsi, 1947.

Yokomitsu Riichi. *Shanghai: A Novel by Yokomitsu Riichi*. Translated by Dennis C. Washburn. Ann Arbor: Center for Japanese Studies, University of Michigan, 2001.

Young, Helen Praeger. *Choosing Revolution: Chinese Women Soldiers on the Long March*. Urbana: University of Illinois Press, 2001.

Yuan Jiao. "Hongxian." In *Ganze yao* (Ballads of Timely Rainfall), edited by Tao Zongyi. Shanghai: Shangwu yinshuguan, 1927.

Zha Jianying. *Bashi niandai fangtanlu* (Interviews Regarding the 1980s). Hong Kong: Oxford University Press, 2006.

Zhang Henshui. *Baishe zhuan* (The White Snake). Beijing: Tongsu wenyi chubanshe, 1955.

Zhang Xianghua, ed. *Tian Han nianpu* (A Chronological History of Tian Han). Beijing: Zhongguo xiju chubanshe, 1992.

Zhang Yaojie. "Tian Han zhisi de rendao fansi" (A Humanist Reflection on the Death of Tian Han). *Changcheng* (Great Wall), no. 2 (2003).

Zhang Yaojie. *Yingju zhiwang Tian Han: Aiguo weimei de langman rensheng* (The King of Film and Drama, Tian Han: A Romantic Life of Patriotism and Aestheticism). Taiyuan: Shanxi jiaoyu chubanshe, 2003.

Zhang, Yingjin. *Cinema and Urban Culture in Shanghai, 1922–1943*. Stanford, CA: Stanford University Press, 1999.

Zhang, Yingjin. *Cinema, Space, and Polilocality in a Globalizing China.* Honolulu: University of Hawai'i Press, 2010.

Zhao Qin. *Li Baochen.* Taiwan yinyueguan zishen yinyuejia congshu, no. 23. Taipei: Shibao wenhua, 2003.

Zhao Qingge. *Baishe zhuan* (The White Snake). Translated by Paul White, bilingual ed. Beijing: New World Press, 2000.

Zhao Shuli. "Wenhua yu xiao huozi" (Culture and the Young Fellows). *Zhongguo wenhua jianshe xiehui Shanxi fenhui yuekan* (Association for Chinese Cultural Construction Shanxi Branch Monthly), vol. 2, no. 2 (February 16, 1936). Published under the pseudonym Chang Zhai.

Zhao Shuli. "'Ya' de moyun" (The End of "Elegance"). *Zhongguo wenhua jianshe xiehui Shanxi fenhui yuekan* (Association for Chinese Cultural Construction Shanxi Branch Monthly), vol. 2, no. 2 (February 16, 1936). Published under the pseudonym Chang Zhai. Included in *Zhao Shuli zuopin xinbian,* edited by Dai Guangzhong. Beijing: Renmin wenxue chubanshe, 2011.

Zhao Shuli. *Li Youcai banhua: Tongsu gushi* (Rhymes of Li Youcai: Popular Story). Dalian: Dazhong shudian, 1946.

Zhao Shuli. *Xiao erhei jiehun: Chatu ben* (The Marriage of Young Blacky, Illustrated Edition). Ha'erbin: Dongbei huabao she, 1948.

Zhao Shuli. "Yesuan jingyan" (In Place of Experience). In *Zhao Shuli quanji* (Complete Works of Zhao Shuli), vol. 4. Taiyuan: Beiyue wenyi chubanshe, 2000.

Zhao Shuli. "Huiyi lishi, renshi ziji" (Reflecting on History, Understanding Myself) (1966). In *Zhao Shuli zuopin xinbian,* edited by Dai Guangzhong. Beijng: Renmin wenxue chubanshe, 2011.

Zheng, Yangwen. "Women's Liberation in China during the Cold War." In *The Cold War in Asia: The Battle for Hearts and Minds,* edited by Yangwen Zheng, Hong Liu, and Michael Szonyi. Leiden: Brill, 2010.

Zhong, Xueping. *Masculinity Besieged? Issues of Modernity and Male Subjectivity in Chinese Literature of the Late Twentieth Century.* Durham, NC: Duke University Press, 2000.

Zhong, Xueping. *Mainstream Culture Refocused: Television Drama, Society, and the Production of Meaning in Reform-Era China.* Honolulu: University of Hawai'i Press, 2010.

Zhong, Xueping, Wang Zheng, and Bai Di, eds. *Some of Us: Chinese Women Growing Up in the Mao Era.* New Brunswick, NJ: Rutgers University Press, 2001.

Zhongguo gudai sida minjian chuanshuo (Four Traditional Chinese Folk Legends). Changchun: Jilin wenshi chubanshe, 2010.

Zhonghua renmin gongheguo xianfa (Constitution of the People's Republic of China), chap. 4, item 136. Beijing: Quanguo renmin daibiao dahui, 2004.

Zhou Dunyi. *Zhouzi tongshu* (eleventh century), with guided reading by Xu Hongxing. Shanghai: Shanghai guji chubanshe, 2000.

Zhou Xinfang. *Zhou Xinfang wutai yishu* (The Stage Art of Zhou Xinfang). Interview by Wei Ming and Lu Zhong. Beijing: Zhongguo xiju chubanshe, 1961.

Zhou Zhaokuan, ed. *Yiwei rensheng: Wu Zuoren de yisheng* (Art as Life: The Life of Wu Zuoren). Xi'an: Shanxi renmin meishu chubanshe, 1998.

Zhou Zuoren. "Riben de xincun" (The New Village in Japan). *Xin qingnian* (New Youth), vol. 6, no. 3 (1919).

Zhou Zuoren. "Fang riben xincun ji" (On My Visit to a Japanese New Village). *Xinchao* (New Tide), vol. 2, no. 1 (1919).

Zhou Zuoren. "Ziji de yuandi" (One's Own Garden). In *Ziji de yuandi.* Shanghai: Beixin shuju, 1927.

Zhu Boxiong, and Chen Ruilin, eds. *Zhongguo xihua wushinian, 1898–1949* (Fifty Years of Western Painting in China, 1898–1949). Beijing: Renmin meishu chubanshe, 1989.

Ziolkowski, Theodore. *German Romanticism and Its Institutions.* Princeton, NJ: Princeton University Press, 1990.

Zou Ping. *Tian Han: Zhongguo huaju de dianjiren* (Tian Han: The Founding Father of Chinese Drama). Shanghai: Shanghai jiaoyu chubanshe, 1999.

Zuo Shunsheng. "Tantan wo suo renshi de jige gongchan danren: Zhang Wentian, Tian Han, Li Da, ji qita" (On a Few Communists I Knew: Zhang Wentian, Tian Han, Li Da, and Others). *Zhengxin xinwenbao* (Taipei), July 23, 1966.

Index